Proceedings of the American Catholic Phi

Social Justice: Its Theory an

Volume 79, 2005

Edited by:
Michael Baur
Fordham University

Papers for the regular sessions were selected by the program committee:
Thomas Jeannot
David Kaplan
Anne Pomeroy

Issued by the National Office of the American Catholic Philosophical Association
Fordham University
Bronx, NY 10458

The *Proceedings of the American Catholic Philosophical Association* are published as an annual supplement to the *American Catholic Philosophical Quarterly* and distributed to members of the ACPA as a benefit of membership. The *Proceedings* are also available for purchase to libraries, departments, institutions, and individuals. For information regarding subscriptions and/or back issues, please contact:

Philosophy Documentation Center
P.O. Box 7147
Charlottesville, VA 22906-7147
Phone: 800-444-2419 (U.S. and Canada); 434-220-3300
Fax: 434-220-3301
E-mail: order@pdcnet.org
Web: www.pdcnet.org

The *Proceedings of the American Catholic Philosophical Association* are indexed in *Academic Search Premier, American Humanities Index, Catholic Periodical and Literature Index, Current Abstracts, Expanded Academic ASAP, Index Philosophicus, Index to Social Science & Humanities Proceedings, InfoTrac OneFile, International Bibliography of Periodical Literature (IBZ), International Philosophical Bibliography, ISI Alerting Services, Periodicals Index Online, Philosopher's Index, Reference and Research Book News,* and *Religious & Theological Abstracts.*
The *Proceedings of the American Catholic Philosophical Association* are also available in POIESIS: Philosophy Online Serials, and the full text of over thirty volumes is available online to libraries that subscribe both to the *Proceedings* and to POIESIS. For more information, contact the Philosophy Documentation Center at order@pdcnet.org.

ISSN 0065-7638
ISBN 1-889680-52-4

Published by the Philosophy Documentation Center, Charlottesville, Virginia.

Proceedings of the American Catholic Philosophical Association

Social Justice: Its Theory and Practice

Volume 79, 2005

TABLE OF CONTENTS

Self-Appropriation and Liberation: Philosophizing in the Light of Catonsville

James L. Marsh

Abstract: Considering the play written by Daniel Berrigan about his own civil disobedience (burning hundreds of draft files in Catonsville, Maryland), the author asks whether Catholics have adopted the American dream at the expense of Christianity. How should we live and philosophize in an age of American empire? Philosophy must be both practical and transformative. We need to question our political situation since 2001, and arrive at a liberatory philosophy and social theory "from below" so as to meet Berrigan's liberatory, prophetic theology "from above," resulting in a philosophy and theology of liberation of and from the seductive imperialist center. The author further stresses individual self-appropriation and the critique of imperialism through a Marxist understanding of surplus value (as arising from labor time for which workers are not paid). There is a link between capitalistic imperialism and militarism, and President Bush has made illegitimate use of religion in the attempt to legitimate empire. Liberation is the good and the happiness that together result from doing the work of justice, free from capitalist corruption. In challenging capitalist empire, we ought to aim for the "downward mobility" of a simpler lifestyle, where self-appropriation leads to moral, religious, and practical conversion. An inhumane, capitalist society is fundamentally at odds with us as human beings, as philosophers, and as Christians.

Our apologies,   good friends, for the fracture
of good order   the burning of paper
instead of children   the angering of the orderlies
in the front parlor of the charnel house
We could not   so help us God   do otherwise
For we are sick at heart   our hearts
give us no rest for thinking of the Land of Burning Children
and for thinking of that other Child of whom
the poet Luke speaks.[1]

These words, of course, are from *The Trial of the Catonsville Nine*, written by Daniel Berrigan, S.J. The words are uttered by the character Daniel Berrigan in the trial of himself and eight others, who entered the draft board in Catonsville, Maryland, removed hundreds of draft files, poured blood on them, and burned them with home-made napalm. It was an act of non-violent, civil disobedience that called into question not only the Vietnam war but also the growing identification of the Catholic, Christian religious consciousness with the secular, war-making state and economy. The Catholic Church in the 1960s moved from being a marginalized, ghetto church to being mainstream, American, fully part of the secular city. And there was much joy and celebration and self-congratulation among American Catholics about this phenomenon. Is it not great to be part of and to participate in the The American Dream in the greatest, most powerful nation in the world? And Catholic universities followed suit in the great celebration.

For many thousands of Catholics, Christians, and other religious people, and I include myself here, Catonsville made all of this problematic. A big question mark emerged about the celebration. What if The American Dream is in fact, to a significant extent, a nightmare? What if the price of human affluence is more and more men and women coming home in body bags? What kind of unhappiness lurks behind the superficial happiness promised by Madison Avenue, and what kind of ugliness lurks behind the pleasing, commodified images of Hollywood? Is there a danger of Catholics and Christians, even those who are liberal, being too uncritically pro-American in a way that implicitly or explicitly violates their moral and religious consciences? Summing up all of these questions into one, the main question that emerges from the play for me is this: "How do we live as human beings, citizens, philosophers, and Christians of conscience in the midst of the most virulent empire in history?" And to add a few evidential indicators on that point, we might note the more than twenty million people a year who die in the Third World due to structurally induced starvation, the three billion out of six billion on the planet who are forced to live on less than two dollars a day, the 1.2 billion who live on less than 1 dollar a day, and the virtually worldwide extent of the American empire under President Bush.[2] What previous imperialists like Alexander, Caesar, Napolean, or Hitler could only dream about is within our reach. Many in the U.S. celebrate this state of affairs enthusiastically, but we as philosophers by our very calling should keep our distance and be more critical. Is this situation something to be celebrated or mourned, praised or condemned, supported or resisted? Is this global domination compatible with our philosophical, Christian consciences, or incompatible?

Berrigan, from a prophetic, religious, biblical perspective, argues incompatibility, and that is his challenge to us. His play is prophetic in a couple of ways, first, about the injustice of the Vietnam war, and second, about the kind of country the U.S. was more and more turning into, more militaristic, more consumeristic, exploitative, and imperialistic. And how can we deny that, almost forty years later, we have become, or are several further steps along the way to becoming, precisely the kind of nation he was warning us against? Two wars in the Gulf, the self-contradictory terroristic war against terrorism in Afghanistan, and the problematic intervention in Kosovo are indications of this point. The U.S. and the U.S.-led empire have within their grasp worldwide domination, hegemony, and exploitation.

Berrigan's play from above, from a prophetic religious viewpoint, challenges us as human beings, philosophers, and Christians to philosophize in its light. What would it be like to philosophize in the light of Catonsville? If, as he says, Christianity in its full prophetic reach is incompatible with capitalism and imperialism, then what would a consistent Catholic philosophy look like? And by "Catholic" I mean, first and minimally, what is done in Catholic universities and colleges, and second and more specifically, a tradition of *philosophia perennis* that has developed from Plato to Aristotle to Augustine to Aquinas to Maritain and Lonergan. My recommendation in my 2002 Plenary Session Address, "Justice, Difference, and the Possibility of Metaphysics: Toward a North American Philosophy of Liberation," was that a new step has to be taken to respond to the destructiveness of The New World Disorder.[3] Philosophical reason has to become formally practical and transformative as well as contemplative and speculative, and the most adequate content for such a practical reason is radical, not liberal or conservative. This rationality linked to radicalism is threefold: a self-appropriation leading horizontally to an ethical-social critique of capitalism, and vertically to a metaphysics, philosophy of religion, and liberation theology grounding a critique and overcoming of neo-imperialism. A triple rationality and radicalism based on and flowing from self-appropriation. As I say in one of my earlier books, *Radical Fragments*, "To think and to think radically—the phrase is redundant."[4]

Already some indications are emerging for you of how I think philosophy needs to respond to the Berriganian challenge. As I began to work out my own perspective, especially in the trilogy *Post-Cartesian Meditations, Critique, Action, and Liberation*, and *Process, Praxis, and Transcendence* when I came to Fordham in 1985 and began to meet and get to know Berrigan, the man, and his students, disciples, and colleagues, I experienced a strange shock of recognition as I began to sense that Berrigan and his witness were at least part of what my work was leading up to and pointing to philosophically, social theoretically, metaphysically, and religiously. Even though my own work is in my own voice, if I were to describe it in terms of persons and thinkers who have deeply influenced me, the trajectory would be from Lonergan as the father of self-appropriation to Berrigan as the author of *The Trial of the Catonsville Nine*. And perhaps, in between the two, Marx as the father of critical social theory. From Lonergan through Marx to Berrigan—two Jesuits and an atheist.

At Fordham when I arrived there in 1985, I felt that I needed to confront the great speculative, contemplative Jesuits there like Gerald McCool and Norris Clarke, giants all, learning from them but also challenging them and myself to come up with a more adequate conception of philosophy linking theory to praxis, contemplation to action, celebratory wondering articulation of the world to relentless critique of the world. One of these great Jesuits, John Courtney Murray, who had passed away by the time I arrived, already practiced and embodied this unity of theory and praxis in works like *The Problem of God* and *We Hold These Truths*. But my sense was and is that now we need something like *We Hold These Radical Truths* and that the "we" is not and should not be liberal-conservative Catholics happily at one with the secular city but a radical community on the way to liberation. And the mediating links between theory and praxis need to be worked out more than Murray has done. Perhaps, I thought, what troubles Catholic universities in the theory and practice of justice is a one-sided contemplative conception at the heart of the academic enterprise itself, such that the theory and praxis of justice seemed relatively external to and marginal to serious academic work. And maybe as a philosopher I could do something about that.

As I also said in 2002, this triple rationality and its link with radicalism does not deny the legitimacy of any sub-discipline in philosophy, and all or most are present in my three volumes. But a necessary, legitimate, contemplative element in philosophy has to be complemented by a practical, critical, transformative element. This link between contemplation and action is also affirmed by Berrigan on a religious prophetic level.[5] I argue, for example, for a legitimate, necessary, contemplative openness to the mystery of the natural, human, marginalized, ontological, and religious other, but also argue that that contemplative articulation has to be complemented by a critique of the socio-economic system that tends to do in that otherness, exploit it, marginalize it, deny it, kill it. And do we reflect practically upon the fate of the natural, poor, dispossessed, and marginalized other in the First World and in the Third World? We can do so only if we are open to the other contemplatively and practically and commit ourselves to a theoretical-practical praxis of liberation from capitalism and empire and militarism, the major enemies of otherness in our time.

What I am going to do in this essay is to respond to Berrigan's challenge from above by formulating a philosophical, social-theoretical response from below attempting to do justice to his questions and his insights. This effort will have three aspects. First, I will undertake a Socratic, existential questioning of our particular national and international situation since 2001, moving from the war and occupation of Iraq to the legal and moral reasons for the wrongness of that effort and finally to the structure of empire that underlies it and that has been with us for many decades. This effort contrasts with my more abstract account of 2002 and presumes that as premise and context. Second, along the way, as the essay proceeds, my thought will interact with Berrigan's in a way that, I hope, is mutually fructifying and beneficial. Finally, at the very end of my paper, my thought joins his and comes together with it. A liberatory philosophy and social theory from below meets a liberatory, prophetic theology from above, and what emerges is a philosophy and theology of liberation of and from the *imperial center*, not the periphery, like Dussel's.

Just as such a philosophy-theology includes but goes beyond previous spiritual and speculative theologies as a more adequate response to our present situation, so my effort criticizes a liberal and conservative ethical-political stance and goes beyond them. While liberalism and conservatism have valid aspects to them, they are judged inadequate because they do not move to a critique of capitalist, militaristic imperialism in principle and thus end up supporting it and tolerating it; and they, liberalism and conservativism, are deficient as social theory because they do not theorize empire in all of its complex rationality and irrationality. By liberalism and conservativism, I mean simply thinkers who support an interventionist welfare state versus those who do not—think Rawls and Nozick. An example of a liberal social theorist, enormously insightful but also deficient in the above sense, is Jürgen Habermas, and an example of a conservative social theorist is Milton Friedman.

I find it important at the beginning of this paper to stress the singular, the individual, and the existential. My attention is on the role of "the philosopher" rather than "philosophy" or "philosophy as such." Where do I, Jim Marsh, as this unique philosopher situated in this time and place, stand? Do I stand somewhere, do I pay up for my beliefs, do I speak out, to use a few phrases from Daniel Berrigan, or do I remain quiet, apolitical, aloof, getting on with professional business as usual? "Don't rock the boat." There is a link in his thought between the existential individual and social critique and action that parallels and inspires my own. In my work, this individual aspect is linked always to universal aspects. Self-appropriation is not an act performed by any anonymous subject, by any Tom, Dick, or Harry, but by me, Jim Marsh, as I discover and affirm and choose to know, choose, and be faithful to the exigencies of the pure desire to know. And transcendental method is the explicit experiencing, understanding, judging and choosing of myself as an experiencing, understanding, judging, and choosing subject in relation to being.[6]

A merely speculative, contemplative philosophy is incomplete even as philosophy. When crisis takes the form of war, as it does now, then, because truth is the first casualty of war, speaking the truth in my own voice becomes an especially important task. And, as we will see, correlated to the fallibilistically self-appropriated, self-knowing individual is the dispossessed, marginalized, alienated, exploited other, especially the Third World other. Self-appropriation leads to solidarity with this other and to non-solidarity with the capitalistic, imperialistic system that exploits and marginalizes this other. Within contemporary *academe*, the former point is more readily and easily acknowledged than the latter.

Drawing on Lonergan's four transcendental precepts, be attentive, be intelligent, be reasonable, and be responsible, corresponding to the fundamental levels of experience, understanding, judgment, and decision, we could specify and amplify the fourth precept by saying, "speak up," "stand somewhere," "speak truth to and about power," or, more colloquially, "raise hell." And part of that speaking up is questioning false claims and equations such as the equation of the terror directed against us on 9–11 with terror as such. This, as Chomsky points out, is mere retail terror directed by the oppressed against the oppressor, the pirate against the emperor. The more destructive kind of terror is wholesale terror, the terror of the emperor, the oppressor, against the Third World. And one crucial task of the philosopher at all times, but especially in times of crisis, is to make such distinctions.[7] Speaking the truth, then, should be our own task as philosophers in all times, but especially in bad times, because truth is a scarce commodity in such times. Is it any surprise that this speaking of truth is also the task of Christians as Berrigan conceives them: "Unsealing, unmasking, revealing, these are affairs of the truth, of God. Need one add, of ourselves? . . . The unmasking of the Big Lie is a characteristic of Christian activity in bad times: or ought to be."[8] And if such unmasking is necessarily prophetic, is not that claim true of philosophers also, especially of Christian, Catholic philosophers? To our work of contemplatively and theoretically disclosing the truth *positively*, do we not all need to denounce critically and prophetically violations of that truth *negatively*? And if we are passionate lovers of the truth, if our hearts have not grown cold, should not such violations make us angry, make us mourn, make us weep? Berrigan's religious, prophetic critique, then, reminds us of and recalls us philosophers to our own proper work, the rigorous, relentless, no holds barred critique of everything that exists.

That we are a nation and world in crisis is little in doubt. The U.S., the most powerful state in history, has proclaimed loud and clear that it intends to rule the world by force, a dimension in which it reigns supreme. This kind of behavior puts us in very uncomfortable moral and political territory, that shared with the great tyrants and dictators of history such as Alexander or Caesar or Napoleon or Hitler. Unlike these past leaders, we have world imperial domination within our grasp. What they could only dream about we are in the process of realizing. For my part, I am struck by the horror of what the U.S. has been doing to itself and the world the last four years. Just think of these names, places, and dates: Abu Graib, Guantanamo, Falluja, Baghdad, "Shock and Awe," The Patriot Act, The Homeland Security Act, Karl Rove and what he did to Valerie Plame, November and December in Florida in 2000, the Downing Street Memo. Berrigan's works express a prophetic outrage over what was being done in our name and voice in the 1960s. What would it take for us as philosophers to feel a similar prophetic outrage over what is being done now? "If you are not angry, you are not paying attention."

Such a situation is readily applauded by many who glory in such expansion, but we as philosophers need to think about this issue ethically and politically. If such expansion is unjust for many different reasons, as I will show, then critique is appropriate, not approval; mourning, not celebration; and resistance, not collaboration and support. And it is the task of the radical philosopher, as I have defined that for myself, who goes all the way with reason in that he allows reason to be fully radical, to question and remove his own blinders and those of others and to be publicly critical of such injustice, relentlessly, in season and out of season.

Has the U.S., I ask myself, ever been at a lower point morally and ethically and politically? Empire, of course, is not a new reality in our nation since we have been pursuing empire for a few hundred years, but it has never been pursued with such brazen arrogance, with such open contempt for national and international law, with such disregard for the opinion of allies, with such manifest aggressiveness, and with so little justification for anything resembling a just, defensive war.

The war in Iraq was, first of all, an illegal war, in violation of our own constitution, because Congress did not declare war; and in violation of the U.N. Charter, which forbids wars of aggression and requires the Security Council to approve any intervention. This is just the most recent instance of the U.S. functioning as a "rogue state" outside the limits of law, much more than states like Iraq that we have condemned in the past and present for functioning that way. Consider our mining of the harbor in Nicaragua in the 1980s, which was condemned by the World Court and which we ignored, and the wars in Afghanistan and Yugoslavia undertaken without U.N. approval.

In a way that should displease liberals, the war and occupation are, second, unjust in many different ways. And while I am sympathetic to the pacifist point that a war cannot be just because of the destructiveness of modern weapons, it is instructive to consider the ways in which this war in unjust. The real purpose of the war, that of aggressive, imperial expansion and control of oil, into which I will go later, is an unjust purpose and thus violates the just end principle. As Germany and France insisted, violence was not being used here as a last resort; inspections were working. Why not give them more time? There was no proportionality between legitimate positive effects and negative effects such as damage to environment through use of depleted uranium, civilian infrastructure, water systems, electrical systems, and so on. Reports indicate there was no serious attempt to respect the distinction between combatants and non-combatants, no declaration by legitimate authority, and no morally legitimate means, because the weapons are so destructive. Because the end of the war was unjust, all of its intended effects were unjust, and the first innocent civilian killed made the war illegitimately disproportional. In my opinion, then, the war violates all of the criteria of just war theory. It does not even come close. And because the war was unjust, the occupation is also.

The most comprehensive account of the irrationality and wrongness of the war is that is was an imperial war. Its illegality and its injustice were aspects and effects of the imperial intent of the war. As one person said about the 1990–1991 Gulf War, the real story about the war is how our oil came to be under their ground. Such imperial expansion violates a prima facie moral intuition that the raw material, labor, resources, and economic, social, and political institutions of a country should be under the control of the people of that country and redound to their benefit. When some "unreasonable" people like Castro of Cuba or Allende of Chile or Ortega of Nicaragua begin to insist on the legitimacy of that intuition, then they have to be demonized. Political, economic, and social pressure is brought to bear on the government, and when all else fails, we send in the marines. That scenario has been enacted literally hundreds of times by the U.S. in the last two-hundred years.[9] When the Third World Other ceases to function as a means to First World well-being and begins to question and resist such a state of affairs, then that other has to be put down, demonized, attacked, and, if necessary, murdered.

What is imperialism? Imperialism or neo-imperialism is simply capitalism transplanted abroad in search of markets, raw materials, cheap or cheaper labor, indulgent, supportive governments, and lower taxes. The New World Order (NWO) is a neo-imperial system with linked, internally related aspects: multinational corporations, U.S. military might as an enforcer of last resort to insure that what we say goes, international organizations like the International Monetary Fund (IMF) and World Bank functioning to keep the Third World in thrall to First World capital, corrupt local monarchies and oligarchies like those currently running Guatemala and Colombia kept in power by the U.S and supportive of U.S. aims against the interests of their own people, rich, landowning capitalist classes in the Third World that exploit and oppress the poor, and police and military officers trained by the U.S. in the latest technologies of repression, terror and torture in places like Fort Benning, Georgia's School of the Americas, nicknamed by its victims in Central and Latin America "the School of Assassins." Many of the officers participating in the 1991 Haiti coup and subsequent repressive rule, the assassination of Romero in El Salvador, and the El Mezote massacre in El Salvador are star pupils and graduates of this school.

The basic point or goal of this imperial structure, we could say, using and drawing on Chomsky, is the Fifth Freedom: the right of U.S., Japanese, and European corporations to rob, kill, repress, and exploit indigenous peoples with impunity. Other freedoms, as our sponsoring of intervention after intervention against democratic governments in Guatemala (1954), the Dominican Republic (1966), Chile (1973), Nicaragua (1980s), and Haiti (1991) indicates, we are quite ready to jettison when they do not serve or when they endanger the Fifth Freedom. Indeed Chomsky and Herman in another work have shown an empirical correlation between increasing terror and denial of democracy in Third World countries and increasing U.S. aid. As terror in Colombia rapidly increased in the last few years, U.S. aid shot up dramatically.[10]

Dussel, using Marx, states that the goal of the NWO is the international transfer from South to North of surplus value, labor time for which labor is not paid. The goal of capitalism in general as private ownership and control of the means of production is to produce and extract such surplus value. Hundreds of billions of dollars per year are transferred from Third World to First World countries, while the poor majorities in those countries starve. Such transfers occur through such mechanisms as debt payments to U.S. banks, the World Bank, and the IMF.[11]

Surplus value is labor time for which the worker is not paid, and it is the basis of capitalist profit. Value is the average, socially necessary amount of labor time required to produce a product, and is the basis for exchange of equivalents in circulation. Surplus value cannot arise in circulation because there, as a rule, equivalents are exchanged. Therefore, surplus value can only arise in the productive sphere either from means of production or labor. But means of production, which includes instruments and materials of production, can only transfer to the product value what they already contain and cannot be the source of surplus value. Consequently surplus value can only arise from labor working more time than the time for which it is actually paid. Because surplus value as the basis for capitalist profit is inherent in capitalism itself, capitalism is inherently exploitative, unjust. Liberal or conservative reformism can mitigate the amount or degree of this exploitativeness, but cannot remove it entirely.[12] And while capitalism has achieved some good things such as increased productivity and, as linked to political and social institutions, increased awareness of the dignity of the individual, human rights, and democracy, these are always in tension with and overwhelmed by the bad things such as alienation, domination, and exploitation. And even the good things are so badly distributed that most people do not adequately benefit. Thus the "rich, many-sided individual" that Marx sees capitalism as creating the conditions for is prevented from emerging, for the most part, by the social structure of capitalism itself.

What about, someone might ask in objection, the supposed "economic miracles" that have occurred in Central and Latin America in the last fifteen to twenty years? Do not the people in those countries benefit? The general answer to this objection is that the top one or two percent of the wealthy in these countries benefit, but that the fortunes of the poor majorities in those countries have not only not been helped but have worsened. During the 1980s U.S. investments in Latin America were heavy; the result was 230 billion transferred to the U.S. through debt service, dividends, and profits. The results for most Latin Americans have been disastrous. Over half the population, 222 million people, now live in poverty, 70 million more than in 1980.[13]

My own account argues for an internal link between capitalistic imperialism and militarism. Such a link is also asserted by Berrigan.

> If everything has a price, and everyone, it follows that the price is—everyone and everything. The market subsumes creation, seizes on all reality: values, religion, fruit of the earth, humans themselves.
> And to protect, secure, and enlarge this empery, this mad Croesus, war is necessary, inevitable.
> At this point, property possesses its possessors; it has become simply idolatrous. And by the same token the human is devalued to the point of absolute contempt. Property and war: Those who wage war in defense of property also dispose of great numbers of non-combatants, the aged, women, children. These have become expendable. They are known to the sycophants of Mars as nothing more than 'collateral damage.'[14]

These words of Berrigan express and confirm and develop much of what I have been trying to say here and in my 2002 essay: the internal link between capitalism and war, empire and war, the tendency on the part of empire to subordinate and sacrifice everything to the pursuit of wealth and profit, the tendency of capitalistic empire to fetishize itself, becoming an object of worship, on which altar millions of victims are sacrificed every year, the tendency of property to alienate us from our own humanity and to possess its possessor, tempting us to confuse being with having; the inevitable tendency of capitalist empire to marginalize unjustly the poor, colored people, women, working people, and the destitute. To take these words seriously is to see how inadequate liberal or conservative efforts are to reform such an inhumane system. It makes as much sense to talk about reforming slavery—a kinder, gentler slavery—or reforming fascism or reforming apartheid.

In a way similar to Marx, Berrigan asks us to think about the "universal prostitution" of everything human under the reign of capital, commodity fetishism in which a relationship between human beings takes the form of a relationship between things. "I am what I make." But in a way very different from Marx, Berrigan invites us to think religiously and biblically about other non-economic realities as similarly fetishized and divinised, for example, "Lord Nuke."

> I sought the name of the genius who ran the press and composed its message. I came up with the name: Lord Nuke. And in naming him, I came on a biblical secret. Naming the beast, breaking the code, was also the prelude to any turnabout, any hope: to whatever good news one could create.
> Once the beast was named, one noted with relief how the mind was cleansed of false names, those by which the beast deceived all. The masks came down: normalcy, security, national interest, family values, legitimate defense, just war, flag, mother, democracy, leadership, religion. The beast stood there. He was naked and known. More: once named, he was also in chains.[15]

What, then, are the real reasons for this war and occupation? We should note here that capitalist empires, like all empires, lie, especially in times of war. We can generally assume that the reasons given for the war are not the real reasons but are ideological and propagandistic, expressed for public consumption and legitimation to a population still decent enough not to buy the real imperialistic reasons. Consequently we can easily dismiss the justification of removing weapons of mass destruction, because none were found; the link between Saddam Hussein and al-Queda–Osama bin Laden was not shown; and that Saddam Hussein was an evil dictator is true but such a claim overlooks the fact that we supported him in the 1980s against Iran and that we currently support regimes that are as bad or worse such as Turkey or Colombia.

What are the real reasons? These are imperial and as such unjustified and unjust, and number, by my accounting, at least eight. The first and most important reason is oil, not only because the control and profits from oil fall into the hands of the U.S., but such control puts the U.S. government in a position to effect the price of oil by determining how much of it is put on the market at any one time and enables us to secure the role of the dollar as the currency of choice in purchase of oil by other countries.

2) Secure the water supplies with which Iraq is very much blessed and upon which all other countries are dependent.

3) Establish American military and political power in the heart of a major Arab country for an indefinite period to help insure the existence of friendly governments and market economies throughout the region, and to use as leverage against Europe, Russia, and China.

4) We have a reason to expand the military budget, and with it the profits of the arms industry, which also includes and relates to the oil industry.

5) Help Americans to forget that we failed to achieve our objectives in Afghanistan, which was not to remove the Taliban, but to destroy al-Queda and capture Osama bin Laden.

6) Upstage the media attention given to failures of the government's economic policies (unemployment up 35%, stock market down 34%, and so on, since President Bush took office).

7) President Bush's policies created an atmosphere of permanent crisis with effects of fear and patriotism helping the GOP to push through the rest of the ultra-conservative political agenda and win the 2004 election.

8) The war and occupation contribute to securing Israel's national interests in several ways: providing Israel with some relief from a growing sentiment among the American public that the U.S. should cut off or reduce significantly military and economic aid to Israel until it vacates all Arab lands, giving some cover to Sharon for dealing as he wishes with the Palestinians, perhaps expelling them into surrounding countries; destroying what is left of Iraq's military power neutralizes Israel's most important rival in the region, establishing a permanent American presence in the area in such a way as to allow U.S. troops to police the whole area for Israel if that is necessary, and controlling Iraqi oil and water resources in such a way as to allow Israel, our best friend in the Middle East, to have a significant share of both.

We have here a multi-causal, multi-level account, stressing economic, cultural, and political factors. Our support for Israel, for example, puts us in the position of favoring it over against Muslim, Arab religious and ethnic groups when they conflict with Israel's policies. Thus there is some basis for seeing a religious motive for 9–11, rooted in a fanatical, one-sided form of nationalism and one-sided interpretation of the Muslim religion, but this factor has to be seen in relation to political-economic factors, because, if I am correct, the U.S. and Israel are enforcing an unjust form of domination and exploitation over the whole region.

Berrigan also challenges us to think about the relationship between religion and empire. One distinction that emerges from all of his works is that between an authentic religious belief, that refuses to align itself with empire and criticizes it prophetically, and an inauthentic religious belief that tolerates, supports, and legitimizes imperial violence and exploitation. Reflecting on these last four years, who can hesitate to condemn President Bush's right-wing use of Christianity to legitimate empire? Such a use of Christianity betrays Christianity.

The problem, of course, is not just President Bush; he is too easy a target. The U.S. Catholic Bishops met in the fall of 2001, after 9–11, in Washington, D.C. They presided over a mass for peace, during which an admiral from the Pentagon was invited to read from the Scriptures. The then outgoing president of the Bishops Conference read from the Sermon on the Mount—an urgent plea from Jesus that His disciples love their enemies and react with hatred toward no one. After the admiral's reading, the bishops made clear their support for the war in Afghanistan, and the next day the newly elected president also made his approval of the war clear. Berrigan's response to this sorry state of affairs deserves to be quoted in full.

> If the American Catholic bishops were consistent and honorable, they
> would publicly burn the Gospels. Then they would contrive a liturgy of
> a different sort, forming a procession, entering a church, holding aloft
> the Marine Handbook of War. The Antigospel would be placed on the
> high alter and incensed.[16]

And again, a little earlier in the same text:

> Church and State, it shortly became clear, stood foursquare, in close col-
> lusion. A Crusade: The bishops, demoralized by scandal, evangelically
> illiterate, walked *peri passu* with the warmaking state.
> A warmaking Church, an oxymoron.
> The twin towers fell to rubble. The twin powers turned to war.[17]

We cannot but admire the honesty and truth and truthfulness of these sentences, which challenge us, challenge me to live up to our vocation as philosophers to speak the truth. But how often do we do that, and how often do we temporize and compromise on that task, saying, "Well, on the one hand," and "then, on the other hand"? How much and how often do we speak the truth to and about unjust imperial power and how often do we rule that kind of question out as "not being real philosophy"? Thus empire rolls on scorching the earth and devastating the people of the earth with our implicit or explicit cooperation, all quite professionally expressed, of course.

It is not just right-wing religion that is the problem, but people inside and outside the Church, in Christian, Catholic institutions of higher learning, for instance, who should know better. In any event, by Berrigan's criteria and my own, any religious belief that does not resist or that tolerates or supports empire betrays itself, sells itself short as religious belief, as does all so-called Catholic philosophy that plays the same game. The religious alternative to this is the "law of the Cross," Lonergan's name for the non-violent, suffering love of Jesus and his disciples as the answer to the problem of personal and social imperial evil by returning good for evil, love for hate, in a process of mercy and forgiveness and non-violent resistance to our violent, unjust policies and structures. And Berrigan's commitment to this kind of non-violent, suffering love in discipleship with Jesus is also well-known and is exemplified by Catonsville.[18]

Such non-violent, suffering love brings into question our system of imperial militarism and violence and links up to and completes the non-violent communicative praxis and self-appropriated knowers and lovers in community that I defend in my work. Such violence may be as American as apple pie, as the old bromide goes, but, if so, America is profoundly anti-Christian in any full, profound, and complete sense of Christianity. Imperial violence and militarism are both anti-philosophical and anti-Christian.

One objection that can be made and has been made is that such non-violence is merely symbolic and not determinate enough and programmatic enough to lead to or achieve real change. This objection misses the point that sometimes such action is quite determinate and programmatic, for example, in trying to end the Vietnam war, close down the School of the Americas, or ending the occupation of Iraq. Second, such an objection misses the morally and contemplatively rooted nature of right action, done to achieve results at least in the long run, but also because it is the right thing to do and valid, therefore, independently of results. Third, such an objection misses that such protest and action represents a religious contribution to discussions in the so-called public sphere endorsed by Habermas and others, in which the immediate point is to change and raise consciousness and not directly to change social structures. Berrigan's life and work thus challenges us to expand our notions of what legitimate protest and action are, including not just action oriented to determinate results but also symbolic action oriented to raising consciousness.

Finally, at the end of the essay we come to the theme of liberation. Liberation as I understand it is the good that corresponds to the right of justice, the happiness, personal and collective, that corresponds to the duty of striving for justice. Aristotle and Kant come together, which I articulated more fully in my 2002 address and in other works, as I articulated a threefold ethic moving from right to morality to justice. Liberation, then, is the good and happiness of being free negatively from capitalist, imperialist injustice, in its different aspects of racism, sexism, heterosexism, classism, environmental devastation, exploitatitiveness, marginalization of the poor, militarism, and so on; and positively liberation is full individual and social self-realization. Elsewhere I have laid out seventeen or eighteen aspects of imperial injustice, but its roots lie in the exploitative process and structure oriented to extracting surplus value from labor.[19]

Liberation, then, is simply the good and happiness that results from doing the work of justice on all levels of collective life, local, national, and international. Negatively it is overcoming capitalist imperialism in all of its aspects. Positively, it is the self-appropriated community claiming for itself the means of economic, cultural, and political self-development and flourishing hitherto cut off from and separated from it in alienating capitalist control and ownership of these means. I have argued elsewhere that the content of such liberation is full economic, political, and social democracy, a minimal welfare state, local, regional, and national planning commissions to give economic and political aid based on need and merit, and a market socialism allowing free exchange of goods and commodities but forbidding exchange between capital and labor, because that distinction is abolished in principle. The structure of empire abroad is to be abolished, as we bring home all our troops from hundreds of bases around the world and dismantle our multinational corporations. We steer a middle ground between a one-sidedly individualistic liberal capitalism and an one-sidedly collectivistic state socialism.[20]

Berrigan's challenge to us, however, is to go further and to come closer to home. For he motivates us to think about a theory and praxis in the imperial center as linked to and in solidarity with liberation in the imperial periphery in the Third World, such as is articulated in the work of Dussel. Center is to periphery as rich is to poor, powerful to weak, dominator to dominated, exploiter to exploited, First World to

Third World. Although such a theory and praxis of liberation in the center is linked to and in solidarity with liberation in the periphery and has the same enemy and same goal, each project is also distinct and has different challenges and opportunities. In the center the ideology mills grind long and hard, twenty-four hours a day, and so much affluence obtains that the temptation to be bought off, distracted, or narcotized is pretty high. On the other hand, there is still in most countries in the imperial center a large space for speaking out, acting out, and demonstrating non-violently, such that Berrigan's recommended praxis of non-violence is not only ethically preferable but politically feasible. In the periphery, on the other hand, the oppression, poverty, and exploitation is much more visible and its cause more easy to see, but the political space for dissent is much less. Putting the matter differently, we might say alienation and exploitation in the center come bearing gifts, whereas injustice in the periphery stalks its victims with a gun.[21]

Because of these differences between center and periphery, secular and religious activists in the center have begun a practice of "downward mobility" that opposes the upward mobility of those who wish to serve the empire and benefit from such service. Drawing on disciplines of prayer, contemplation, literacy, and reading to supplement more secular forms of analysis, critique, and motivation, people have begun to free themselves from the narcotizing addiction of consumerism and advertising. Motivated by a "preferential option for the poor," people have begun a "downward mobility," identified with Christ in his downward mobility, opting out of the reckless pursuit of money, pleasure, power, and success, and opting for justice, happiness, community, and genuine social liberation. Juliet Schor in a book written several years ago, *The Overspent American*, has identified in rigorous empirical research a growing community of "downshifters," 20 percent of all adult Americans, who have opted for a simpler lifestyle, more leisure, more time for family and children, more meaningful but perhaps less remunerative work. Put simply, such a lifestyle is more rewarding and enriching, in our words, more liberating.[22] Such people and others in their way of living, their simple lifestyles, their economic sharing, their decisions to live in poor or poorer neighborhoods and to work with and to serve people in those neighborhoods, and their regular practice and support of non-violent activism and civil disobedience begin to foreshadow and anticipate and create a more just, liberated society, as well as to work for institutional, structural social change. The non-violent love of God and Christ is translated into a non-violent love of the neighbor and praxis of liberation.[23]

Conclusion

At the end of our discussion, we need to draw together some of the main points. The basic starting point is radical self-knowledge and self-affirmation leading to radical self-choice, radical political conversion, speaking out and acting out against injustice and for justice on behalf of the marginalized and oppressed racial, sexual, heterosexual, and poor others, in the matter before us, the poor majorities of Iraq, Palestine, and the Middle East. If I began the search for truth rooted in the desire to know, then that leads to a choice and love of and speaking up for the truth, and this witness occurs in season and out of season, independently of results. I may hope for and aim for results, but my basic motivation is the rightness of what the situation calls for. What is historically dominant is, as Kierkegaard warns us, a poor guide to what is philosophically or ethically or politically or religiously right, and this is especially true today as we see the dominance of "The New Barbarism" and "The Bush Reich."

Paradoxically, full self-knowledge and self-appropriation does not lead to an ignoring or a being closed off to the marginalized, dispossessed other, but to a response to that other, what we might even call a conversion to that other. But such a conversion is mediated by a transcendental-existential account of the self, a normative ethic, and a meta-narratival, hermeneutical account of capitalism and empire. Being faithful to the desire to know truth leads me to a radical choice of myself as human being and philosopher in solidarity with the poor and oppressed of the world. There is a preferential option for the poor that can be argued for philosophically as well as religiously, and this option puts me into theoretical and lived opposition to the socio-economic system that oppresses and exploits and marginalizes the poor, a theoretical and practical "either-or" if you like. Here is another aspect of that link between rationality and radicalism that I described earlier. And this link is different from, and in my opinion, superior to, post-modern accounts, in that the dichotomy between self and other is overcome, an account is given of what oppresses the other, and an account is given of why that oppression is wrong.

A phrase of my own that indicates the philosophical link with Berrigan's perspective is that "intellectual, moral, and religious conversion lead to radical political conversion." Intellectual conversion is the movement out of the capitalist and state socialist cave into the sunlight of intelligibility, the world mediated by meaning. Moral conversion is my coming alive to the sphere of moral values on the fourth level of freedom, and religious conversion is simply falling in love with God. Intellectual conversion is an aspect of self-appropriation as I conceive it, and moral and religious conversion flow from it as fruit and gift. Thus the movement of my essay is from self-appropriation articulated philosophically through intellectual, moral, and religious conversion, to radical political conversion, in which the philosophical and prophetic, rational and religious, and philosophical and theological are linked together and flow into one another.[24]

At the end of this fairly long paper, I am tempted to put matters in more simple terms. Basically the issue is a fundamentally indecent, inhumane society at odds with us as human beings, philosophers, and Christians. And what philosophy and theology counsel is fundamental change in all the basic institutions of society, including the groves of *academe*. A fundamental either-or emerges that is at once existential and cognitive, to do that work of criticism and theorizing about fundamental change, or to cop out on that, to temporize, to say like Prufrock, "That is not what I meant, not what I meant at all."

To make these points, however, is not to say or imply that we will do what is required. Philosophers, even Catholic philosophers, are not immune from human weakness and temptation; like everyone else, we can be bought off or intimidated or coerced or bribed to go along in order to get along and thus to betray our calling as human, philosophical, and religious. We can go along in a great communal celebration of empire, setting off rockets on the fourth of July, as Bush tightens the neo-fascist noose around our necks and we sing "America the Beautiful" at baseball games and the like. Or we can begin, tentatively at first and then more forcefully and confidently, to loosen the noose. We can, to change the metaphor, cheerfully and smugly go down in the self-destructive imperial Titanic, singing the Star-Spangled Banner as the waves wash over our heads, or we can save ourselves from the Titanic by getting off the ship. *Non Serviam.* In fact, that might not be a bad description of liberating philosophy, social theory, and theology in these bad times, to save ourselves and others and as much of the world as possible from the imperial Titanic. We save ourselves and students and colleagues from "America" in this destructive sense; we cease being lost in America.

I end with another quotation from *The Trial of the Catonsville Nine* that is more hopeful in looking forward to a liberated future.

Redeem the times
The times are inexplicably evil
Christians pay conscious   indeed religious tribute
to Caesar and Mars
by the approval of overkill tactics   by brinkmanship
by nuclear liturgies   by racism   by support of genocide

They embrace their society with all their heart
and abandon the cross
They pay lip service to Christ
and military service to the powers of death
And yet   and yet   the times are inexhaustibly good
solaced by the courage and hope of many
The truth rules   Christ is not forsaken
In a time of death some
the resisters   those who work hardily for social change
those who preach and embrace the truth
such overcome death
their lives are bathed in the light of the resurrection
the truth has set them free
In the jaws of death
they proclaim their love of brothers and sisters
We think of such men and women
in the world   in our nation   in the churches
and the stone in our breast is dissolved
we take heart once more.[25]

All of us, students, faculty, and administrators, can be or become such men and women. What would happen, I ask myself, if the thousands of those graduating from our colleges and universities every year learned not to live with late capitalism and love it in a kind of personal and professional upward mobility but to become agents of resistance and social transformation? What would happen if we and our students ceased to be happy campers in the great American Dreamland and wasteland, and became creatively unhappy, happy enough with our own humanity to end up challenging a fundamentally inhumane, unjust system that regularly, day in and day out, violates that humanity? What would happen if we and our students in our personal, social, and professional lives became, each in our own way, "bathed in the light of the resurrection"? Now that would truly be a fate devoutly to be wished. That would be to be truly, fully rational and radical, prophetic and liberatory, human and Christian. That would truly be the faith that does justice.

Fordham University

Notes

1. Daniel Berrigan, *The Trial of the Catonsville Nine* (New York: Fordham University Press, 2004).

2. Jack Nelson Pallmeyer, *Brave New World Order* (Maryknoll, N.Y.: Orbis Books, 1992), 4–5. Doug Henwood, *After the New Economy* (New York: The New Press, 2003), 129.

3. James L. Marsh, "Justice, Difference, and the Possibility of Metaphysics: Toward a North American Philosophy of Liberation," *Proceedings of the American Catholic Philosophical Association* Volume 76, 2002 (Bronx, N.Y.: National Office of the American Catholic Philosophical Association, Fordham University), 57–76.

4. James L. Marsh, *Radical Fragments* (New York: Peter Lang, 1992), 13.

5. See Daniel Berrigan, *The Nightmare of God* (Portland: Sunburst Press, 1983), 49–50.

6. James L. Marsh, *Post-Cartesian Meditations* (New York: Fordham University Press, 1988), 106–114.

7. *Pirates and Emperors, Old and New: International Terrorism in the Real World* (Cambridge: South End Press, 2002), vii.

8. Berrigan, *The Nightmare of God*, 48–49.

9. William Appelman Williams, *Empire as Way of Life* (New York: Oxford University Press, 1980).

10. Noam Chomsky, *Turning the Tide* (Boston: South End Press, 1985), 47.

11. Enrique Dussel, *Ethics and Community*, trans. Robert Barr (Maryknoll, N.Y.: Orbis Books, 1988), 139.

12. James L. Marsh, *Critique, Action, and Liberation* (Albany, N.Y.: SUNY Press, 1995), 267.

13. Larry Everest, "The Selling of Peru," *Z Magazine*, Volume 7 (September 1994): 35–36.

14. Daniel Berrigan, *Minor Prophets, Major Themes* (Marion, S.D.: Fortkamp Books, 1985), 49–50.

15. Daniel Berrigan, *To Dwell in Peace: An Autobiography* (New York: Harper & Row, 1987), p. 334. For Marx on "universal prostitution," see *The Grundrisse*, trans. Martin Nicolaus (New York: Vintage, 1973), 163.

16. Daniel Berrigan, *Lamentations: From New York to Kabul and Beyond* (Lanham, Md.: Sheed and Ward, 2002), 13.

17. Ibid., 313–330.

18. Bernard Lonergan, *Insight: A Study of Human Understanding*, ed. Frederick Crowe and Bob Doran (Toronto: The University of Toronto Press, 1992), pp. 721–22. Daniel Berrigan, *Jesus Christ* (Garden City, N.Y.: Doubleday and Company, 1973). Bob Doran, *Theology and the Dialectics of History* (Toronto: The University of Toronto Press, 1989), 113–115, 198–206.

19. Marsh, *Critique, Action, and Liberation*, 113–124.

20. Ibid., 313–330.

21. James L. Marsh, *Process, Praxis, and Transcendence* (Albany, N.Y.: SUNY Press, 1999), 298–320.

22. Juliet Schor, *The Overspent American: Upscaling, Downshifting, and the New Consumer* (New York: Basic Books, 1998), 111–142.

23. Marsh, *Process, Praxis, and Transcendence*, 318.

24. Ibid., 21–29.

25. Berrigan, *The Trial of the Catonsville Nine*, 95.

Presentation of the Aquinas Medal

Anthony Lisska

This evening it gives me indeed great pleasure to introduce Brian Davies as the recipient of the 2005 Aquinas Medal, which is bestowed annually on a significant philosopher by The American Catholic Philosophical Association. Brian Davies in one sense needs no introduction to many of us in this room. Brian's work on Thomas Aquinas has not only been substantive and noteworthy, but also his prolific writings and lectures have been influential in terms of assisting late twentieth century philosophers outside of classical neo-Thomism understand so much better the significance and the philosophical insights of Thomas Aquinas.

Brian is an old friend. I first met Brian when he was a young Dominican Friar serving as Lecturer in theology as well as the librarian of the Dominican priory on St. Giles in Oxford—Blackfriars—when I lived in Oxford while on sabbatical from my home institution. Brian introduced me to his Dominican colleagues and generously gave me free rein to use the library holdings on Aquinas at Blackfriars. He and I became fast friends, and I have profited so very much from our intellectual interchanges over the past two decades.

My first awareness of Brian intellectually was from a magnificent set of lectures that he gave during Michelmas Term on the Philosophy of Religion as a member of the Oxford faculty. These lectures at Blackfriars had a very large audience, and Brian demonstrated in his own lively and inimitable way the seriousness of purpose with which he took the analytic method for doing philosophy. Brian adeptly applied that method to more than several significant issues in classical philosophy of religion. Those lectures complemented nicely an early book of his, which was the first edition of his very popular Oxford paperback, *The Philosophy of Religion*. Brian himself has been deeply devoted to the work and memory of his late Dominican confrere, Herbert McCabe. Through his fine work editing the unpublished writings of Father McCabe, Brian has almost single handedly kept the writings of Herbert alive and well.

This evening Brian will share with us several of his insights into the philosophy of religion as taken from the works of Thomas Aquinas. Like many analytic philosophers in the last half of the twentieth century, Brian came to Aquinas after having drunk deeply from the well of philosophical analysis. Brian is part of an important emerging analytic tradition in doing work with medieval philosophers in general and, of course, Thomas Aquinas in particular. His extended study of Thomas has been in print by Oxford University Press for well over a decade. In addition, Brian has written a second book on Thomas, has edited recently a new series of readings on Thomas and a series of readings in the philosophy of religion, and has served as the general editor of a series on great philosophers edited by Oxford University Press. Moreover, Brian has lectured all across the United States and has held lectureships in both Oxford and Rome.

This evening Brian will unpack for us what he takes to be two significant claims in Aquinas' philosophy of religion and how both claims make theological sense and hang together coherently.

It is with great personal pleasure and deep affection that I introduce Father Brian Davies, a member of the English Province of the Dominicans and associated now with the Department of Philosophy at Fordham University, as the well-deserved recipient for the 2005 Aquinas Medal. Please welcome Brian to our meeting this fine autumn evening.

Denison University

Aquinas Medalist's Address

Thoughts about God

Brian Davies

Abstract: The author recounts his own journey from inductive arguments for God's existence and the Free Will Defense, to the Thomistic claim that we do not know God's essence (which implies, among other things, that God cannot be classified among things in the world). Propositions can be truly affirmed of God, if we distinguish knowing that a proposition is true and understanding what makes the proposition true. We can say "God exists" without knowing what God is. If God is the Unknown that makes all other things to be, are all our choices positively caused, not just permitted, by God? Since God is not an agent among other agents in the world, he does not coerce us from outside. We are free not in spite of God, but rather because of Him. This does not mean that all our actions are pre-determined; it means, rather, that God creatively makes people who act as they do, *to be*. The reasons for supposing that we do not know what God is, are the same as the reasons for thinking that He (as the creative source of everything) is more present to us than any creature is.

I should start by saying how very honored I am to have been awarded the Association's Aquinas medal. A few years ago this was conferred on Peter Geach. He was not able to accept it in person, so I was deputed to read his medalist's address (to pretend to be Peter Geach, as it were). It was a privilege to do so. But it is now even more of a privilege to speak to you on my own behalf (to pretend to be myself, so to speak). I have been told that I am not to talk for more than twenty minutes. So I shall try to be brief in what I have to say.

Since it's an Aquinas Medal that I've been given, it seems only right that I should talk about Aquinas. To begin with, however, perhaps I can bore you with some autobiography.

I worked for my Ph.D. dissertation at King's College, London, and had the fortune to do so under the direction of the late Professor H. D. Lewis (of whom I was scared to death when I first met him since by that time he had published up a storm, had delivered a series of Gifford Lectures, had founded the journal *Religious*

Studies, and had been President of the Mind Association and the Aristotelian Society.) My dissertation title was 'Reasons and Belief: The Case for Natural Theology.' Happily never published, this work proceeded on the assumption that one author not to be taken seriously was Aquinas, whom I then knew only from the text of the famous Five Ways. In less than one page I dismissed these as being philosophically misguided, and I proceeded to insist that all truth lay with theistic philosophers of religion writing in the analytical tradition. When I was working for my Ph.D the two stars in the heaven when it came to analytical philosophy of religion were Richard Swinburne and Alvin Plantinga. So, following Swinburne, I defended an inductive argument for God's existence, one drawing heavily on thoughts about what a God would be likely to do. Following Plantinga, and with an eye on the topic of God and evil, I vigorously maintained that theists should strongly support the so-called 'Free Will Defense'—according to which my free actions should be thought of as permitted by God though not directly caused by him.

Having got my Ph.D and having, to my satisfaction, inductively shown that God exists, I had, of course, no option but to conclude that I was graced with a religious vocation. So, for reasons that I shall spare you, I decided to join the Dominicans. Even now I can vividly remember a conversation I had with one of them when I was what they call a 'sniffer'—i.e., someone inquiring into the Order while spending time in one of its houses. This particular Dominican was delighted to learn that I had a Ph.D in philosophy. He said 'So it is obviously Saint Thomas who brings you to us.' Thinking of my attempted refutation of the Five Ways, I, of course, said 'Certainly not.'

A few years later I was studying at Blackfriars in Oxford (the Studium of the English Dominicans). At that time, as is still the case, Aquinas was very much in the air there. But I managed to avoid reading him for a long time. To my mind, much more appealing than Aquinas was the weekly conventual recreation at which wine was provided for the brethren. During one of these events I was chatting with the late Fr. Herbert McCabe, who liked nothing better than to argue philosophy (especially over wine). At one point in the discussion I told him what you can expect a God to produce, and I lectured him on the virtues of the Free Will Defense. He asked me 'What basis do you have for second-guessing God?' 'Do you really think that you know what God is?' He then went on to say that if I thought along the lines of the Free Will Defense, then I really had no reason to believe in God at all.

That discussion left me thoroughly confused, but I came to learn that McCabe's response to me only expressed what you might look for from someone well versed in, and sympathetic to, the writings of Aquinas. Herbert was criticizing me with an eye on two major Thomistic claims: that God's essence is unknown to us (that we do not know what God is, that, when it comes to God, we cannot answer the question 'Quid est?), and that God is always actively present to everything other than himself as making it to exist. Lots of people who say that they believe in God do not subscribe to either of these claims. Yet Herbert did. And I have, over time, come to agree with him. These claims of Aquinas seem to me true, important, and of particular relevance today given ways in which people now often talk about God.

Aquinas's assertion that we do not know God's essence does not, of course, commit him to the conclusion that we cannot make many true statements about God, ones which we can defend philosophically as well as by appeal to divine revelation. It does, however, warn us against thinking of God as something classifiable, as a member of the world, as something essentially creaturely. Aquinas, to be sure, is, like the authors of the Bible, happy to speak of God by naming him from creatures. So he has no problem when saying that God is, for example, a shepherd, a king, an eagle, a woman, a betrayed husband, or even a case of dry rot. It is obvious that God can be literally none of these things. Yet Aquinas thinks that there are reasons which sometimes make it appropriate to pretend that this is not so. On the other hand, however, he also thinks that we should be very clear that *pretending* is what we are doing here. We should, he insists, never think of God as literally being one of a kind, something we can really get our minds around, something with respect to which we can even *begin* to develop anything that we would normally think of as a scientific account. Such accounts come from people who can get their hands on things in the world, distinguish them from other such things, and note ways in which they resemble and differ from each other. Yet if God is indeed the Creator, the Maker of all things in heaven and earth, the cause of the existence at any time of everything other than himself, then, says Aquinas, there can be no science of God (no knowledge of what God is).

That conclusion seems right to me. It rests on Aquinas's conviction that we need to think of God as accounting for the existence of everything other than himself. For Aquinas, God (though not essentially so) is the mysterious answer to the question 'How come something rather than nothing?' Now you may, of course, wish, as many do, to resist that question or take issue with it for one reason or another. If you do not, though, as I do not, then you are going to have to end up saying something like what Aquinas ends up concluding. You shall need to agree that God cannot be something material and, therefore, identifiable and classifiable as things in the world are. You shall also need to concede that God can be in no way derived, that there can be nothing about him which results from the causal activity of what is not divine. In short, you are going to have to end up agreeing that we are seriously in the dark when it comes to the question 'What is God?'

How much in the dark? Enough, I think, to warrant us in strongly fighting shy of ways of talking about God that even remotely seem to suppose that we have a concept of divinity. For various philosophical and theological reasons, perhaps we may say that God is X, Y, or Z. Truly affirming something of a subject, however, does not necessarily amount to understanding what the subject is or what it is for the subject to be as one says that it is. One might truly assert that John's brain tumor caused his death without understanding what a brain tumor really is. By the same token (though analogously speaking), your having reason to say that God is X, Y, or Z does not mean that you understand what it is for God to be X, Y, or Z. We can readily distinguish between (a) knowing (or having reasons for supposing) that a proposition is true and (b) understanding what it is that makes the proposition true (the reality onto which the proposition is latching). I can know or have reason to believe that I have a brain tumor without understanding what is actually going on in my head. Or, as Aquinas puts it, we can know that the proposition 'God exists' is true without knowing what God is.

One way of making this point is to say that we should do well to remember that God is not a god and that when speaking of him we always dress him up verbally in second-hand clothes—in 'words that have been quite scandalously ripped from their proper context and stretched and bent and distorted to suit our purposes.'[1] Yet many of our contemporaries seem to me not to have latched onto this point as much they should. Anthropomorphic approaches to God are now more common than not. Unsurprisingly, perhaps, they abound in day to day discourse and in what we find said by Christians, Jews and Muslims who would not recognize a philosophical argument even if it bit them. More worrying, however, they also seem to prevail in the writings of professional philosophers and theologians. An indication of this is the alacrity with which some of them tell us that the first and most important thing to say about God is that he is a person.

From my reading of the literature, those who make this claim normally depend heavily on a view of people roughly corresponding to what Descartes offers when seeking to say what he essentially is. 'What then am I?' he asks. While agreeing that he is something connected to a body, his final view is that he is first and foremost an incorporeal thinking substance, a non-material conscious mind, existing through time, with beliefs as well as knowledge, while willing some things but not others.[2] I cannot now embark on a discussion of Descartes's view of himself. But I think it worth noting that the currently common insistence that God is a person strongly appears to make God a magnified or enlarged version of what Descartes took himself essentially to be.

We are often, for example, told that the person God is observes and takes risks. We are equally often told that he reacts, changes, learns, and has moral obligations or duties. I do not understand how the Creator of the Universe, the cause of their being anything other than himself, can sensibly be said to do or have any of these things. Yet there are platoons of philosophers and theologians who seem to assume that God is up to the job. Some of them have even told us that, by introspection, we can actually *imagine* what it is like to be God. Confronted by such thinkers, it seems to me that Aquinas is a very useful antidote and I commend him to you accordingly. You might resist my commendation by saying that God is one among the many persons that there are. Notice, though, that, even should this assertion prove to be somehow defensible, it is not to be found in the Bible. We have no biblical text stating that God is a person. Nor do we find patristic and medieval authors asking us to believe that this is what God is. I believe that the first occurrence in English of the formula 'God is a person' comes in the report of a trial of someone called John Biddle. In 1644 Biddle was brought before the magistrates of Gloucester, England, on a charge of heresy. His 'heresy' was claiming that God is a person. Biddle, it turns out, was explicitly defending Unitarian beliefs about God previously taught by people well beyond the range of the Gloucester magistrates before whom he appeared. Like Socinians in Europe, he was denying the doctrine of the Trinity (which, of course, does not claim that God is three persons in *one* person).

So it helps, I think, to deny that God is a person (even if we wish to say that God is somehow 'personal'—thinking, say, that the ground of all cannot be less than all or inferior in any regard). Indeed, it helps to deny that God is anything at all—meaning that he is no inhabitant of the universe, not something among other things, no extra item alongside everything else, no individual (in the sense of 'individual' according to which to call something an individual is to imply that there could be more of the same kind). Or, as Aquinas suggests in his commentary on Aristotle's *Peri Hermeneias*, we might reasonably claim that if God is the Creator of all things (making them to be whenever they are), then God is 'extra ordinem entium existens, velut causa quaedam profundens totum ens et omnes eius differentias' ('existing outside the realm of existents, as a cause from which pours forth everything that exists in all its variant forms').[3] If Aquinas is right here, then we are seriously ignorant when it comes to divinity. And if Aquinas really means what he says here, he is, in a sense, an agnostic—not, of course, because, like Thomas Huxley, he says 'We do not know, and the universe is a mysterious riddle,' but because he says 'We do not know what the answer is, but we do know that there is a mystery behind it all which we do not know, and if there were not, there would not even be a riddle. This Unknown we call *God*. If there were no God, there would be no universe to be mysterious, and nobody to be mystified.'[4]

That line of thinking pervades Aquinas's writings.[5] Is it original to him? I think he would have (rightly) denied that it was. He would, I am sure, have taken it to be part and parcel of what Jews, Muslims, and Christians have always officially believed. But he emphasizes it in an unusually clear-sighted way and, for that reason, seems especially worth commending in a climate in which both philosophers and theologians frequently talk about God as though he actually lived in the next street. And, it seems to me, Aquinas also draws on what I have just reported in a way that ought to leave us seeing why Herbert McCabe attacked me so strongly with respect to the Free Will Defense.

McCabe's basic point was that if God is indeed the Creator, the reason why there is something as opposed to nothing, then there can be no such thing as a human free choice which is not caused by God. McCabe was thinking that if God is the source of the existence (the continued and total existence) of everything other than himself, then my making a choice has to be something that God is *making to be*. And Aquinas takes exactly the same line (so much so that he is even prepared to say that the human action of sinning comes from God).[6] 'Insofar as a thing can be called an action,' he says, 'God is its cause.'[7] And, so I have come to think, it is extremely difficult to resist this conclusion given that one takes God to be that which makes everything other than himself to be at any time. We are frequently told that our free choices are *allowed* or *permitted* by God and that it is good that this should be so. Yet the language of allowance and permission seems to me jarring where the notion of God the Creator is in question. If everything other than God owes all that it is to God, then he must be positively the source of my free choices. For these are there instead of not being. Whatever my freedom means, it cannot mean not depending (in the creative sense) on God.[8] If there is indeed a Creator God, then my free choices must be as *made* as anything else. Or as Antony Flew pointedly asks: 'Just how is the idea of God as the sustaining cause of all creation to be reconciled with the insistence that this creation included uncaused causes?'[9]

Some, of course, will say that if we agree with Aquinas here, then there is no human freedom and Aquinas is a theological determinist. And Flew is someone who takes this line. Having correctly drawn attention to Aquinas's insistence that God operates in every operation, including human acts of will, he describes the resulting picture as 'monstrous' since it depicts us as 'puppets or automata' whom God has no business punishing.[10] What Flew hasn't noted here, however, is the way in which Aquinas wishes to distinguish between God and the world.

Indeed, he thinks, my freedom would be undermined by a created agent acting on me from outside so as to compel me in what I do. But God, he adds, is no such agent since he is 'extra ordinem entium existens, velut causa quaedam profundens totum ens et omnes eius differentias.' For Aquinas, as the creative cause of my actions God does not *interfere* with me or *coerce* me from *outside*—as a top person sharing the world with me as potters share the world with the clay they mold. For Aquinas, God makes me to be *me*—an agent to which human freedom can, for various reasons, be intelligibly ascribed, someone who is free not *in spite of* God but *because of* him.

An implication of this view, of course, is that with human freedom we have the *direct* causal activity of God, not God as bringing something about by means of other created causes, not God as causing other things to cause. One may be tempted to say that such a conclusion has to be understood as stating that all that we do is pre-determined by God. As Aquinas develops it, however, that is not at all how it should be construed. His point is not that God makes people act thus and so. His idea is that God makes people who act as they do *to be*. And, to my mind, he rightly views this line of thinking as posing no threat to human freedom.

If we take God creatively to account for the existence at any time of all that is not divine (a fairly traditional position), then we have to suppose that he creatively accounts for there being whatever human free choices there are. If we think there are no free human choices, that can only be a conclusion to be defended with reference to our account of what there actually is in the world, not with reference to the fact that God is what the world depends on from moment to moment. God, we might say, makes no *difference* to anything since, as Creator, he makes things to be whatever they are and is not something alongside them tinkering or modifying them. Or as James Ross once observed: 'The fact that God's causing is necessary for whatever happens cannot impede liberty; it is a condition for it. . . . Nothing possible can be impeded by its necessary conditions. . . . It is the whole being, doing as it does, whether a free being or not, that is entirely produced and sustained for its time by God.'[11]

This is certainly not a common view among contemporary philosophers, including philosophers of religion. And it is certainly one that needs to be developed and defended at some length. However, since I have been told not to speak to you at length, perhaps I may now be allowed simply to assert that I think that this view is right and that McCabe, those years ago, was correct to chide me for not taking it seriously. As I have tried to indicate, I think that he was also right to insist on our ignorance when it comes to what God is.

Notice, though, that to say all that is not at all to imply (as some suppose) that God is distant or remote. For Aquinas, the very reasons that ought to leave us concluding that we do not know what God is are reasons for supposing that God is more present to us than any creature can be to any other. We do not, he thinks, know what God is since God is the creative source of everything we can identify and classify. Correspondingly, he holds that God acts in our choices just because he is that: the creative source of everything we can identify and classify. Many would denigrate such a conclusion. For now, though, I commend it to you, while also hoping that God might soon bring it about that someone freely chooses to offer me another glass of wine.

Fordham University

NOTES

1. Herbert McCabe, *God Still Matters* (Continuum: London and New York, 2002), 3.

2. Cf. *The Philosophical Writings of Descartes*, Volume II, translated by John Cottingham, Robert Stoothoff and Dugald Murdoch (Cambridge University Press: Cambridge, 1984), 19ff.

3. Aquinas, *In Aristotelis Librum Peri Hermeneias*, 1:14.

4. Here I am quoting from Victor White, one of McCabe's own teachers, who also taught at Blackfriars, Oxford. See Victor White, *God the Unknown* (The Harvill Press: London, 1956), 18f.

5. For a distinguished study of Aquinas on how we fail to know God, see Gregory P. Rocca, *Speaking the Incomprehensible God* (The Catholic University of America Press: Washington D.C., 2004).

6. Cf. *Summa Theologiae*, 1a2ae, 79,2.

7. *Summa Theologiae*, 1a2ae, 79,2. See also *De Malo*, III,2.

8. Cf. Herbert McCabe, *God Matters* (Geoffrey Chapman: London, 1987), 11.

9. Antony Flew, *The Presumption of Atheism and Other Essays* (Elek/Pemberton: London, 1976), 88.

10. Flew, op.cit., 94.

11. James F. Ross, 'Creation II,' in Alfred J. Freddoso (ed.), *The Existence and Nature of God* (University of Notre Dame Press: Notre Dame and London, 1983), 131 and 134.

Redemption in the Midst of Phantasmagoria
(Dispelling the Fate of Socialism)

Drucilla Cornell

Abstract: Socialism has been dismissed as a dream in the reality of the world of 9/11. But a mythical narrative that erases the possibility of moral agency does not honor the dead. In Walter Benjamin's language, photographs of the actual dead can supply the "dialectical jolt" that illuminates a possible beyond. Myth is dangerous when it teaches that things will always be as they are now, but myth can also point to a different form of knowledge of the world, beyond the despair that says only violence can save the world. Socialism, through mutual respect and responsibility, calls us to be people in whose actions the present promises the future, shaping the world and becoming ourselves something different. Benjamin and Derrida agree that any attempt to describe experience fails because it points beyond itself to its own limit and how that limit opens space beyond it. Derrida's "impossible" should not be read as knowledge of what cannot be done, but as a recognition that every experience points to its limit, and we are left with our own responsibility for justice in any given context. Beyond despairing meta-narratives, freedom comes in forming character through effort.

I am, today, still a socialist. I write today "still" because we have all encountered many commentaries on the supposed death of socialism. Over and over again throughout the 1990s we hear that the dream of a redeemed humanity, one that finally realizes the truth of its freedom in democratic control over the means of life and of death, has itself died. There is an obvious irony here in what does it mean to condemn a dream to death. After all, isn't a dream exactly what can not be killed off because it does not have actual existence? The death of the dream, at least on the part of those determined to put it to death, clearly has an implicit, if not explicit, agenda to marginalize those who still identify themselves as socialists as dreamers.

Particularly after 9/11 dreamers and idealists were condemned as being hopelessly out of touch with reality. The supposed reality of the post 9/11 world is one in which "we" were pitted against "them" and had to take all the steps "we" needed to make sure that "we" contained "them" before "they" obliterated "us." But is this reality, or itself just a myth? Have we not heard over and over again about this reality from the cold war until the present? Indeed, it is precisely the simple outlines of this reoccurring claim cementing our reality as the end of history that Walter Benjamin would have called myth in the negative sense: to denote the fate of an eternal recurrence that wipes out the possibility of any meaningful moral agency where we have no choice but to go after "them" because this is the way the world must be. But, Benjamin teaches us there is also, in even the most brutal reality, a dialectical opening that can illuminate another way of being in the world that allows us at least to have a glimpse of what a redeemed world might be like and, perhaps more importantly, what we have as a responsibility to those who have lived and died for it. As Benjamin reminds us:

> Fate is the guilt context of the living. It corresponds to the natural condition of the living, that illusion not yet wholly dispelled from which man is so far removed that, under its rule, he was never wholly immersed in it, but only invisible in his best part. It is not, therefore, really man who has a fate; rather, the subject of fate is indeterminable. . . . For fateful moments only exist in bad novels.[1]

Of course, the story of how we are fated to live in a post 9/11 world in which violence and war are inevitable counterparts of each other, does not deny the terrible suffering of those who encounter the wrath of these two antagonisms. So many people have died in the wake of this needless suffering: thousands after the collapse of the World Trade Center and even more on both sides in the ongoing War on Iraq. But, what is particularly shameful, and perhaps dialectically startling, are the moments when people feel that there is seemingly no way out of the nightmare of advanced capitalism and its apartheids against race, class, and gender. Even faith is not outside of the reach of this nightmare, such as when we saw several young people become suicide bombers last summer in England—something that perhaps only could be understood as the flip side to a bad novel.[2]

Expanding on this idea of living in a world that phantasmagorically seems to swallow up our deepest dreams of freedom in various capitalist nightmares of despair we can look to South Africa for further harrowing images of suffering that confront us with the brutal reality of their lived and living apartheid. Many of those images have been kept alive in museums that have been built alongside the new South Africa. I am going to speak of only two such images, which in the language of Walter Benjamin I hope will give us the sort of dialectical jolt that might move us further into awakening and out of the nightmare-like slumber at hand.

First, there is a famous photograph taken during the Soweto uprising in which thousands upon thousands of children rebelled against being taught in what they saw as the language of the oppressor: Afrikaans. They were indeed children. Famously, the police gave no heed to that reality and shot into the crowd leaving hundreds dead, more injured, and many who were never seen again after that tragic day. In a famous photo a young woman, perhaps in her early teens, is carrying the dead, or dying, body of Hector Petersen. By her side is a young man who is running along her side. On both faces is a look of absolute horror. To this day, we do not know where that young woman is, nor do we know where the young man by her side is. What we have of these two children is this moment into which they have been forever frozen: a moment in which a child, rather than simply flee to save herself, picks up her dead and dying friend with the hope of saving him, or at least salvaging his then dead body from further brutalization by the police.

This image undoubtedly represents an act of salvation, of the young girl salvaging what she could of what remained of Hector Petersen. Her companion is with her—grief and terror stricken—but with her still. This photograph can help us understand what Walter Benjamin means by a dialectical image. In the background we can see the township and the children who are rebelling against their oppressors. But, she is running toward us. Who is this "us"? It is a generation that is beyond temporalization: a constellation of past, present, and future generations that are all being called to in equal force. As Walter Benjamin explains in thesis five on the *Theses on the Philosophy of History*:

> The true picture of the past flits by. The past can be seized only as an image which flashes up at the instant when it can be recognized and is never seen again. "The truth will not run away from us": in the historical outlook of historicism these words of Gottfried Keller mark the exact point where historical materialism cuts through historicism. For every image of the past that is not recognized by the present, as one of its own concerns threatens to disappear irretrievably. (The good tidings which the historian of the past brings with throbbing heart may be lost in a void the very moment he opens his mouth).[3]

If Benjamin teaches us anything, then we should always remember that it is not a coincidence that "history" is best told in images. From the standpoint of those who had to endure apartheid such a lived brutality could be nothing other than senseless suffering. To give it meaning as a significant form of human social organization would already be a betrayal of those who had to live under its brutal disregard of their humanity.

As Benjamin also writes "a dialectical image flashes up at a moment of danger"[4] but it also illuminates a possible beyond. In that "possible beyond" we hear the call to justice that those children with the daring and courage to shout out at their oppressors what their humanity demanded, "Justice! Noting more or nothing less." But we do not see a "risk manager" in this photograph. We see a young girl, even in her terror, cherishing the body of her fallen comrade, and yet she is but a child herself. But we know that she saw something that not only took her out to the streets that day—perhaps a hope for a redeemed world beyond apartheid—but that she showed in her act of salvation of Hector Petersen the depths of a humanity that would not bow down before the bullets and simply flee. She will never be gone to history, in Benjamin's sense, *if we* remember her. But, we can only remember her if we allow ourselves to see her. It is up to us to do it.

This is Benjamin's fundamental point when he calls us to animistic solidarity. As Benjamin writes:

> The past carries with it a temporal index by which it is referred to re-demption. There is a secret agreement between past generations and the present one. Our coming was expected on earth. Like every generation that has preceded us, we have been endowed with a *weak* Messianic power, a power to which that past has a claim. That claim can not be settled cheaply. Historical materialists are aware of that.[5]

What does it mean to "fan the spark of hope"[6] in the past if at the same time it demands that we look and force ourselves to see the terrible suffering inscribed forever on those children's faces as they confront the unbearable reality that another child has died, and that no matter what she does she will not be able to save him? For Benjamin, in this "call" we are made to face the figure of the one who refuses to stand still before the dialectical image. It is this call that, despite all odds, demands that we live up to such an image, one archetype of many, giving us a glimpse of the animistic solidarity with the dead we must bring into our own lives.

The dialectical image blows apart messages of good cheer and at the same time keeps open forms of experience in Benjamin's unique use of the word *erfahrung*, which makes accessible the possibility of self reflective passage through myth and with it the moral agency that insists such an experience is impossible. In German the title of *Arcades Project* is *Passagen-Werk*, which we can at least understand as working through the passages of both history and myth. Thus, although Benjamin is critical of myth when it temporalizes the self as inevitability teaching a lesson that things will always be as they are now, this rebellion against historical compulsion still seeks to keep alive a horizon that does not relinquish the potential of myth to point to a different form of knowledge of the world around us. This *passage way*, and the rights of passage, between dreamful sleep and awakening is a phatasmagoric zone for Benjamin that in a deep sense breaks apart myth by its own means and thus salvages from it the possibility of a redeemed world of humanity despite our nightmarish surroundings. This fidelity before the threshold of another world that "might yet be" shows us that this *passage way* is open before us if we allow ourselves to move through mythical constraints so as to find the future under the ultimate myth of advanced capitalism claiming that there is no true different future but only the forever new that displaces one commodity only for another commodity that is new only in so far as it is the same: a commodity.

Against what Benjamin thinks of as tired and fated truth he takes us through a *passage way* in which we can still be exposed to the *wahr-traum*. Literally translated this word means "true dream," or to dream of what is true in the promise of the dialectical image itself: a humanity worthy of its own name. What is the trueness of the dream? How can a dream be true? It is true to what humanity "might yet be" when it is salvaged from the sameness of advanced capitalism. But, we do not have to wait for that truth because as we saw in the image the young woman who runs away with the dead body of Hector Petersen we have already glimpsed what it means to be a true human being (true here in the sense that it is true to an ideal that refuses to give in to the world weariness of inaction).

In his endless effort to show us the reworking of symbols and allegory, we can still find a *passage way* that lights up the "tireless leap of action" Benjamin forever held onto as the truth of revolutionary courage. We find that courage in the act of the young woman. Yes, it is true that Benjamin tells us that the messiah might enter time at any minute. But, we are not fated to remain and wait. As Benjamin tells us, "The Messiah comes not only as the redeemer, he comes as the subduer of antichrist. Only that historian will have the gift of fanning the spark of hope in the past who is firmly convinced that *even the dead* will not be safe from the enemy if he wins. And this enemy has not ceased to be victorious."[7] There is a sense in which we, the next generation with the weak messianic power, can subdue the antichrist. And it is only we who can do it. Benjamin never ceased calling us to action in the name of justice. As he tells us "the past carries with it a temporal index by which it referred to redemption."[8] Perhaps, the antichrist is our stillness before the dialectical image.[9] For those of us in the United States that we must subdue the antichrist should ring true indeed. For this antichrist comes very close to what Kant would have called the absolutely morally unfettered will, the *willkur*, which can come to us in the endless longing of the consumer for the false promises of empire that suggest we, and only we, are the ones, the chosen ones, who can drive the SUVs.

But Benjamin's animistic solidarity itself keeps open the *passage way* between the living and the dead, but not in the historicist sense that we in any way belie the suffering of those who died by giving it a meaning as it were itself part of a context that already fated people to do what they did. We know that young woman as one who broke with apartheid and all of its claims upon her in that moment for which she is captured forever; we must heed her demand on us that we remain faithful to our own messianic power as the next generation is called to the struggle for a just world. Seeing that woman gives us an image, heeding her call makes it dialectical.

In another photograph from South Africa, one of many that haunt me, a mother is speaking to the charred remains of her son. She is waving her hands gently over the body, coming as close as she can to stroking those ashen remains. She can not touch these remains otherwise the body will dissolve. And she seeks to take her child home to the ancestors: the one place where this young man can finally rest in peace. Khulumani, an organization in South Africa, dedicates itself to those who continue to seek out the dead and the missing, and who by so doing keep open what Benjamin would call a *passage way* between the dead and the living. It is an ongoing work that is itself a remembrance of the horror under which so many died and a constant reminder of the ever pressing danger which we are called to guard against. In a deep sense, the dead are allowed to speak to us.

Alongside the charred remains of the lost son is an AK-47 which for so many young people of my generation, and still in the world today, remains a symbol of empowerment even if it can only deliver vengeance. Again, we see the dialectical image before us in the sense Benjamin suggests to us. It is a deep ambiguity, this gun, because it represented, or became a kind of symbol loaded with the myth of liberation precisely in Benjamin's sense of the negative aspect of myth. In this figure, liberation is reduced to a tragic necessity of violence—a tragic necessity that Benjamin believed in some circumstances "we might be called to" but may itself turn would be liberators into shadows. In the recent movie Lord of War, a film in the "present," we also see young children proudly holding that same gun which is now a popular item often sold by local gun runners. Benjamin teaches us how to unpack this simple thing, this gun, that promises what it itself can not deliver, but only if we allegorize it through the lens of the despair that inheres in the belief that only in violence can we hope to save the dream of the better world.

Indeed, the very figure of the suicide bomber can be read as the figure who no longer believes that there can be meaningful action that could actually change the world. And, yet, still the call to act is necessary. In a deep sense, suicide bombing carries within it the recognition that any kind of killing must exact its retribution. But we are far here from the dream of armed struggle that could deliver us from the nightmare world of colonialism and, of course, advanced capitalism. The suicide bomber, in a profound sense, figures the moral basis for action as part of how we shape who we are as freedom fighters in the world (to use an old fashioned phrase). The suicide bomber figures the moral basis for action precisely in the implicit acceptance of retribution as the result of killing. Suicide bombing is in a sense a last act, a last gasp that seeks to break out of the enclosure of a suffocating reality that buries the messianic power within by turning us toward death. Such a last gasp is the acceptance that to die is better to live cut off from what is most meaningful in a human life: to transform ourselves together into who we might be in a better world which would not silence the heed to the call of justice. It is the call to justice that echoes in the shattering blast of the suicide bomber that reminds us what was sought after was really a better world and not the obliteration of oneself in the fate turned character of killing.

This ethical basis for action was often lost in some of the Marxist-Leninist groups and parties, turning it into either a strategic necessity or the scientifically mandated end of capitalism. I was in many of those Marxist-Leninist groups in the late 1960s and early 1970s, and tried my best to defend then what I am defending here: the idea that socialism, is a better way of living together because it insists on mutual respect and responsibility for the world we make together, is always with each one of us now as a call to make ourselves the kind of person who in day-to-day actions in the present already promises the future. I know that may sound abstract. But, in my days as a union organizer—and a feminist union organizer at that—we did of course fight to bring an actual union into the work place. But we also did so by working together *in union* now. This being together *in union* was to be an experience in Benjamin's sense of the world *ehrfaungl*.

Benjamin in his first published essay on experience writes against the so-called common sense notion of experience. He writes:

We, however, know something different, which experience can neither give to us or take away: that truth exists, even if all previous thought has been an error. Or: that fidelity shall be maintained, even if no one has done so yet. Such will cannot be taken from us by experience. Yet—are our elders, with their tired gestures and their superior hopelessness, right about *one* thing—namely, that what we experience will be sorrowful and that only in the inexperienceable can courage, hope, and meaning be given foundation? Then the spirit would be free. But again and again life would drag it down because life, the sum of experience, would be without solace.[10]

Benjamin is ironically commenting on how experience that points to hopelessness can never ground itself in the very idea of itself because experience is something we are always bringing into being. To return to my example about being *in union*, we were bringing into our day-to-day lives the experience of what, in Benjamin's sense, had been inexperienceable in the brutal work places where I organized: solidarity, comfort, solace, and support for each other in all of the actions we undertook together. It is not just that Lenin had it exactly wrong when he said the end justifies the means—although of course I believe he did—it is that the struggle for a better world is constantly brining into our experience not only how we might shape that world, or what that world would look like, but how we ourselves become different as we try to actualize ethical relationships amongst ourselves. Sadly, it is only through bringing that experience into existence together, as so many of us did in the 60s and 70s, that we can retain a memory of different forms of solidarity and support: a memory that points us toward the future that many young people who do not have that "experience" refuse to struggle with today and see as beyond their reach. Ironically, it is the young now who before their time are world-weary, telling us that the fate of the world is such that the longing for socialism can not be but utopian.

In his book *Specters of Marx*, Jacques Derrida argues that all of the meta-narratives of "the end" run afoul of the mistake that inheres in Hegelian philosophical history. We read back the institutional structure of European modernity into all previous stages of history as if they were just incomplete precursors of it. Clearly, this kind of argumentation is circular at best and a self-congratulatory myth, in Benjamin's sense, at worst. For Benjamin, myth inheres in the sedimentation of what is our actual and ever-changing history in which all of the small challenges and resistances go unnoticed with the story of the victor claiming itself as truth. Derrida stands with Benjamin in that there is a an undeconstructable experience of what he calls an "experience of the impossible" which marks the limits of history to finalize itself in the self-proclaimed inevitability of advanced capitalism as the only meaningful form of social organization. Derrida and Benjamin are using the word experience in a similar, if not identical, manner. But what both definitions of experience share is that any attempt to fully describe experience fails because it always points beyond itself to its own limit and how that limit opens up the space of the beyond.

In my book *Philosophy of the Limit*, I renamed deconstruction the philosophy of the limit to bring out this integral connection between Benjamin's early writing on experience and Derrida's experience of the impossible. To quote Derrida:

> Well, what remains irreducible to any deconstruction, what remains undeconstructable as the possibility itself of deconstruction is, perhaps, a certain experience of the emancipatory promise; it is perhaps even the formality of a structural messianism, a messianism without religion, even a messianic without messianism, an idea of justice—which we distinguish from law or right and even from human rights—and an idea of democracy—which we distinguish from its current concept and from its determined predicates today [permit me to refer here to "force of Law" and *The Other Heading*].[11]

For Derrida, it is only in this experience of the impossible limit that keeps the beyond as the beyond and the other as the other so that we can ethically respect, and indeed heed, the coming of the other and the other's demand on us. For Derrida, this "coming of the other" as the event, as the one who demands our hospitality, is a messianism without the messiah. If we are open to it then it can always pull us out of the supposed world of day-to-day experiences. An event for Derrida is only possible if it is indeed impossible in the common sense notion of experience that Benjamin speaks of in his early essay. That world-weary experience predicts that everything will have to continue as it is now, but an event that could be described and predicted in all of its outlines would not be an event.

In 1992, I was writing against deconstructionists who interpreted Derrida's experience of the impossible as leaving us with another version of waiting for God to save us, or for a passivity before what might call us if we were to wait in silence. This reading of Derrida relies on his supposed alliance with Heideggerian pessimism where we are fated to wait for God to save us; I have always read Derrida against this pessimism. Derrida tells us again and again that ultimately we have a promise to the other and that as a promise we must seek its fulfillment. Towards the end of his life Derrida argued that this promise actually calls us to institutional action now, or what he calls "the demand of negotiation." This demand for negotiation and institutionalization can not, then, remain content with the "yes yes" of a Nietzschian abstract affirmation. So, one must be patient but also organized. To quote Derrida:

> That is to say that in its self institutionalization in its very success threatens the movement of unconditional affirmation. And yet this needs to happen, for if the affirmation were content—how shall I say it—to wash its hands of the institution in order to remain at a distance, in order to say "I affirm, and then the rest is of no interest to me, the institution does not interest me . . . let the others take care of that," then the affirmation would deny itself.[12]

In a deep sense, then, the ethical call of this other demands that we risk "dirtying our hands." We risk knowing that any attempt to act *in union* might turn against itself precisely because we are struggling to move experience beyond itself as we shape a different way of being together. Although I can not repeat that argument here, Derrida's experience of the impossible should never be read as knowledge of what is impossible, including the big dreams of socialism and justice. Indeed, the opposite is the case. Precisely because we can not know what is impossible, precisely because every experience points beyond itself to its limit—which both defines the experience and yet marks it as limited—we are left with our own responsibility in whatever context we are in to struggle for justice. Derrida tried to make more and more explicit in his later writings that in the call for infinite responsibility to the other that is beyond, we are never "off the hook" just because we can say it is no longer possible for us to live differently or for us to live well.

To return to Benjamin's essay on "Fate and Character," Benjamin reminds us that we can by definition not be fated to have a particular character, nor can any previously ordained character be found to be the basis of our suffering. In the quotation I read earlier from Benjamin, he writes that "fate is the guilt context of the living" and he also reminds us that in notions of our fate what is best in us—our capacity for moral and ethical action—remains invisible. For Benjamin, our character is ultimately ethical, and in this of course he follows Immanuel Kant. But for our purposes Benjamin points to the ethical interests of those who are amongst the oppressors—all who live with all of the privileges of empire and the spoils of racism—in finding in themselves a source of responsibility that is not self-punishing but unfolds from an aspiration to be worthy of happiness.

To take us back to the example of Africa, Wole Soyinka argues that the beneficiaries of colonialism have a reason for accepting, and indeed demanding, of themselves reparations to all of the enslaved in Africa and of course those who were brought to the "new world." In broad brush strokes, Soyinka's argument was directed at a Truth and Reconciliation process, such as the one that was realized in South Africa, demanding it hold on to an idea of justice. Simply put, there can be no reconciliation without justice. But, I am in agreement with Soyinka that the challenge of South Africa is to be found in this struggle for justice, and that what justice demands—if it is not to be vengeance—has yet to be adequately addressed. But I want to return to the Benjaminian point here which I want to argue helps us to understand the profundity for each one of us as an individual of what it might mean to free ourselves from our so-called fated position as the beneficiaries of colonialism.

Instead, for Derrida the call for mourning and respect for what has gone before and therefore constitutes us from within a relationality of debt is ultimately inseparable from our mourning for actual ghosts: the ones who have gone before us, the ones who have suffered and died so that we may be. To quote Derrida again:

> And all the grave stakes we have just named in a few words would come down to the question of what one understands, with Marx and after Marx, by effectivity, effect, operativity, work, labor [*Wirklichkeit*,

Wirkung, work, operation], living work in their supposed opposition to the spectral logic that also governs the effects of virtuality, of simulacrum, of 'mourning work,' of ghost, *revenant,* and so forth. And of the justice that is their due. . . . Inscribing the possibility of the reference to the other, and thus of radical alterity and heterogeneity, of differance, of technicity, and of ideality in the very event of presence, in the presence of the present that it dis-joins a priori in order to make it possible [thus impossible in its identity or its contemporaneity with itself], it does not deprive itself of the means with which to take into account, or to render an account of, the effects of ghosts, of simulacra, of "synthetic images," or even, to put it in terms of the Marxist code, of ideologems, even if these take the novel forms to which modern technology will have given rise.[13]

There is a certain sense in which this openness to the other can keep us from bowing down to our fate as a colonizer: the privileged class who has joined the so-called victors of history. There is no apology for suffering except the action of redemption. As we have seen in Derrida, we must negotiate and pay back what can never be paid. Soyinka invites us all, as a hypothetical experiment in the imagination, to ask ourselves why there should not be a general levy imposed for such reconciliation, and defended in terms of reparations on the population of South Africa as part of their own struggle to free themselves from the imposed fate of the inevitable oppressor of the black population. To quote Soyinka:

If, however, this attribution of self-redeeming possibilities within the psychology of guilt remains within the utopian imagination, and some external prodding proved necessary, the initiative could be taken up by someone of the non-establishment stature of Archbishop Desmond Tutu. The respected cleric and mediator mounts his pulpit one day and addresses his compatriots on that very theme: "White brothers and sisters in the Lord, you have sinned, but we are willing to forgive. The scripture warns us that the wages of sin are death but, in your case, they seem to be wealth. If therefore you choose to shed a little of that sinful wealth as a first step to atonement . . . etc. etc."[14]

Benjamin would argue against the use of religious language of sin and atonement here and insist instead on the self-redeeming possibilities inherent in the unknow-ability of character, as we might yet become men and women of justice and begin to carve out a new pathway—one which would include the freedom that inheres not only in our acceptance but in our call for reparations for African slaves more generally. Soyinka is actually a part of a movement calling for reparations to Africa, but I am not speaking here about the programmatic efforts to make such a demand a reality. I want to stay with Benjamin's point about the self-redeeming possibilities of a character that does not submit to its fate to live out its life unjustly. I believe it is the Benjaminian insight that led Derrida to begin his book with the question: what does it finally mean to learn to live (and I would add "well")? If Benjamin teaches us anything, then it is that we can not learn what it means to learn well once and for all but we can seek to live up to its call and, indeed, do so in the name of our own freedom as well as that of others.

Benjamin's essay writes against the kind of discursive fate that gets frozen into bad idealizations of human nature. We all know of these static representations. For example, some say we are all utility maximizers and we can be no other way in this world. Or, we are all risk managers, and therefore incapable of something like true courage. But, these assumptions should be seen for what they are: myths propping up what we are fated to be in unjust world. And, yet, we know that millions upon millions of people in the twentieth century alone showed the falsity of such characterizations of fated nature by giving their lives for the fight for socialism. South Africa has become both a symbol and an allegory for many in the world today because the victorious struggle against apartheid ultimately took place in negotiations rather than through armed revolution that would have led to some system of government and law capitulating to the other in annihilation. In a certain sense the victory over apartheid is one of the most notable institutional state victories of a party that was once firmly committed to socialism. But the negotiations of course were only made feasible by wave after wave of rebellion and resistance as each next generation took on its own struggle against apartheid long after the leaders of the ANC were in jail and the party in exile. Certainly, the ANC has wavered in its commitment, and some critics would argue capitulated to the demands of advanced capitalism. But, Benjamin and Derrida are suggesting to us that there is no end to what South Africa can become because of some meta-narrative that dooms it in advance: to be eaten up by the machinery of capitalism.

Ironically, there is an ethical warning in Derrida about what it means to ascribe to such meta-narratives because they allow us to get ourselves off the hook and ultimately fail to see that we are submitting to a fate as if it were necessary when our very submission was part of what it makes it seem as if it were inevitable. We may not be able to tell grand stories that will guarantee the ultimate success of socialism, but it is precisely because we can not tell such grand stories that doom it to failure that leaves it up to us to make the "truth" of the ideal of socialism something that can not be beaten out of this world. It is indeed up to us, and Benjamin gives us a complex answer as to why we might want to take up the challenge to live our lives in accordance with the call of justice rather than to submit to the fate of our utility maximizing self interest. For, it is in this struggle that we find our freedom, precisely because freedom is never something that is just there but in the slow work of forming a character that knows itself only in its endless effort to be other then its so-called fate. In this struggle we find our dignity; it is what we owe to ourselves and the dead.

Rutgers University

Notes

1. Walter Benjamin, "Fate and Character," in *Walter Benjamin Reflections: Essays, Aphorisms, Autographical Writings*, Peter Demetz, ed. (New York: Schocken Books, 1978), 308.

2. For these insights, I am grateful to the careful reading and thoughtful contribution of my student, Kenneth Michael Panfilio.

3. Walter Benjamin, "Theses on the Philosophy of History," in *Walter Benjamin Illuminations: Essays and Reflections*, Hannah Arednt, ed. (New York: Schocken Books, 1968), 255.

4. Benjamin, *Walter Benjamin Illuminations*, 255

5. Ibid., 254

6. Ibid., 255

7. Ibid.

8. Ibid., 254

9. For this insight, I am grateful to the careful reading and thoughtful contribution of my student Kenneth Michael Panfilio.

10. Walter Benjamin, *Walter Benjamin: Selected Writings, Volume 1, 1913–1926*, Marcus Bullock, ed. (Cambridge, Mass.: Belknap Press, 2004), 1–5.

11. Jacques Derrida, *Specters of Marx: The State of Debt, The Work of Mourning, and the New International*, Peggy Kamuf, trans. (New York: Routledge, 1994), 59.

12. Jacques Derrida, *Negotiations: Interventions and Interviews, 1971–2001 (Cultural Memory in the Present)*, Elizabeth Rottenberg, ed. and trans. (Palo Alto, Calif.: Stanford University Press, 2002), 25.

13. Derrida, *Specters of Marx*, 75.

14. Wole Soyinka, *The Burden of Memory, The Muse of Forgiveness* (New York: Oxford University Press, 1999), 25–26.

Doing Justice and the Practice of Philosophy

William Desmond

Abstract: There is a sense of doing justice prior to the juxtaposition of theory and practice, accounting for an ontological vulnerability prior to both social power and social vulnerability. Justice in the sense of "being true" involves fidelity to truth that we neither possess nor construct, preceding all efforts to enact justice. The charge to be just precedes any just act. There is a "patience of being," or a receiving of being before acting, which we must then actively take up. All this has implications for the practices of philosophy, including transcending the will to power by not clinging to one's own place in History. The philosopher stands back and enters the void space of the human soul which is vulnerable, both terrorized and capable of terrorizing. This void is a "porosity of the soul" rather than pure nothingness. Though it is no particular project or activity, it allows all openness, receiving, and self-transcendence, and out of it comes the practical energy that feeds activity. The poverty of philosophy means relinquishing meaningless activity of construction in a purposeless universe by a willingness to be nothing, understanding the patience of being before servility and sovereignty, and the justice beyond them.

I want to thank Professor James Marsh for the honor of being asked to speak here. I admire what he is trying to do in his work. I admire his efforts to unite political and social concerns with metaphysical and religious considerations. His twinning, shall we say, of Marx and metaphysics might seem quixotic to some, but I have been surprised by it and found many arresting things in it. I too would like to bring metaphysics into closer accord with ethical and political considerations, but perhaps I have spent too much time studying Hegel and his descendents to be sanguine in vesting much hope in them. When I look around at my illustrious co-presenters, Professors Enrique Dussel and Drucilla Cornell, I wonder if I am a mistake—a kind of Burkean reactionary dropped by some inscrutable hand among admirers of the left-Hegelian inheritance. I hope I am not a reactionary, though I do value Burke's prudence, albeit sometimes frenzied into prophecy with regard to the intoxications of revolutionary praxis.

My focus is not directly on social justice in terms of more usual discussion, for instance, in terms of this or that organization of social power, or the relation of freedom and equality, understood in more liberal terms. It is about reserved considerations concerning our habitation of the ethos of being, wherein determinate efforts to realize social justice in this way and that might be enacted. In that sense, it is at an angle to such discussion, trying to name some matters more or less recessed in the intricacies of foreground social and political discussion. In the effort to bring into closer accord metaphysics and issues of justice, I want to attend to the first side as entailing a "doing justice" not always noted in the second, but of consequence for it.

My concerns, one might say, are archeological rather than just teleological, relative to a sense of *archē* which makes possible diverse practices of justice but which entail a call to do justice that is not exhausted by any of these determinate practices. We must consider an originating "doing justice" rather than simply justice defined as the telos of an ethical and political practice.

I focus on the following considerations. First, I offer some remarks on a prior sense of doing justice in relation to the more traditional juxtaposition of theory and practice, and its criticism. Second, I look at a sense of doing justice that does not quite conform or fit into the terms of such a juxtaposition. Third, I connect this sense of doing justice with a certain understanding of "being true," and hence with a fidelity to something prior to our efforts to enact justice. Fourth, I consider the intermediate nature of our efforts to be truthful. Fifth, I reflect on the significance of what I call the patience of being. Sixth, I return to the issue of theory and practice in the light of this being true and this fidelity, and offer some remarks on its implication for the practices of philosophy. Finally, I offer some reflections of doing justice in connection with the philosophical transcendence of will to power, and the philosophical importance of, as I put it, "being nothing."

A Prior "Doing Justice"?

It is fair to say that philosophy has always been concerned with justice. One sometimes comes across the view that philosophy from its inception displays a certain bias against praxis. I think of Arendt, for instance, in her stylization of Platonic philosophy as tilted towards the primacy of theory and hence towards a certain contemplative ideal. Moreover, this contemplative bias is sometimes associated with putative claims to a kind of absolute knowledge. Platonic *theōria* is said to be determinative for the entire tradition wherein theory in the end dictates to praxis, and justice becomes a top down superimposition on the raw, formless mass of humanity, as the aristocrat or monarch imposes power on the many who otherwise all but count for nothing. Arendt herself calls for a revaluation of praxis, but this I think is continuous with a longer tendency in modern thought which is perhaps encapsulated in Marx's eleventh thesis on Feuerbach: the philosophers till now have understood the world, the point is to change it. What percolates in Marx's dictum circulates through many forms of modern discourse. It is true that the relation of theory and practice is at issue, but the terms of its formulation are said no longer to reflect the old contemplative bias of the tradition—suitable for a top down hierarchical society, whether of humans or knowers—but not appropriate for a democratic, egalitarian autonomous ethos where no one is to dictate to another what is true or to be true, whether in knowing or in deed.

It is true notwithstanding that philosophy has always been concerned with justice. I do not particularly want here to enter into the contested interpretation of Plato, but justice is surely one of the central concerns of his whole work. This is certainly true of the *Republic* whose question: What is justice? is not just theoretical, since it has an explicit bearing on the nature and practice of philosophy itself. A charge is laid on the philosopher by a true understanding of justice which entails that the philosopher comes under the demand and solicitation of doing justice. It is hard to accept the view of Plato as, so to say, a hyper-theorist. To be sure, there is something "hyper" in the vision offered: there is a glimpse of the good that is above (*huper*) us whose measure we are not and that rather subjects us and our measures to true measure. Nevertheless, the doing justice of the philosopher is crucial. He or she is a servant of justice, not a dictator of it. Instead of being top-down dictatorial "theory," the *return to the cave* is a sign that we must develop a kind of *night vision* to discern differences amidst fluctuating forms. We must go down, as Socrates says, into the common dwelling places and become accustomed to see the things that are dark (*ta skoteina: Republic*, 520b5–c3). Discerning differences is a form of doing justice to what is happening. Nor is it a matter of an escape beyond—even though there is a beyond.

Premodern as much as modern philosophy, and now postmodern thought are concerned with justice, but the terms of their engagements differ. One thinks of Aristotle: the human being is not the highest in the universe. Aristotle also remarks that if man were the highest being, politics would be the highest science. But there is a measure beyond human measure, difficult as it may be exactly to determine what this measure is. I cannot see how this necessarily must be assimilated to some invidious tyrannical top-down superimposition of hyper-theory. Much depends on how that measure is conceived. But granting it, and granting that we are not the absolute measure, changes our relation to ourselves and nature, as well as the divine. We are not the makers of justice even when in our deeds we must do justice. Our doing of justice calls for a discernment that cannot be simply called practical, since the practical is itself in question relative to its claim to be true to justice. Without its permeation by something like this discernment, practice itself looks more like lurching in the dark.

This does not mean that it is a matter of just having the right theory either—certainly not if we mean by theory some neutral, disembodied hypothesis or ensemble of concepts that claim to comprehend what is at stake in practice, and that dictates what is to be done there. If there is a kind of theory, it must be of a different sort—its intimate relation to praxis entails a practice not identical with praxis, and without which praxis becomes the bluster of blind power. A simple contrast of theory and praxis will not do, either in terms of giving some disengaged priority to theory, or some ultimacy to a reformulated praxis. There is something more.

Doing Justice and Being True

In ordinary language there are reserves to the notion of "doing justice" that are helpful for our reflection. A teacher, for instance, will speak of trying to do justice to his or her subject, or to the examinations of his or her students. A parent will encourage a promising child to do justice to themselves, say, in the forthcoming talent contest. An honest, representative political leader will worry that he is doing justice to the often divergent demands of his constituency. A performer may be concerned whether he or she has done justice to the great score of Mozart. A gifted athlete will torment himself or herself with having finished second, wondering if the placing did justice to his or her talents. Of course, there are some perhaps less somber instances of doing justice. My mother places a fine meal before me, and I do justice to it. I eat it up with relish. What is doing justice here? It is not merely in the consumption, but in the gusto of the appreciation. My pleasure in the meal does justice to it, and communicates my being pleased with its maker. Doing justice communicates my thanks. The meal is not a bad example, for doing justice in connection with the sharing of a meal recalls us to something elemental of what I would call the agapeics of being.

There are many more examples I might cite but I think at the core of all of them is a certain notion of "being true." Doing justice entails no abstract plan of perfection imposed from the outside—though in certain instances, the need of a plan may be necessary. It entails the solicitation of a certain being true that is discerned to be immanent in the practice or the practitioner—and that asks something of the practice or practitioner that is both intimate and transcendent at the same time. Intimate: for this requirement is felt in the immanence of the practice; transcendent in that it may call for something more that might be difficult to account for in terms of immanence alone. Philosophy is itself a practice, and there are different practices of philosophy,[1] but none of them can escape from the demands of "doing justice" in this sense of "being true."

I would say that doing justice in the sense here intended is not a determinate activity, not a particular passivity but refers us to *a more primal patience of being*. I will come to this. Of course, doing is obviously a word of act and action. We often feel at home with action, and nowhere more than in relation to justice. We are called to do something; and our sometime frustration with an unjust situation is alleviated by doing something. Philosophers traditionally have been criticized for their diffidence when it comes to acting. They demur and excuse themselves as thinkers not doers. I have already referred to Marx's rejoinder in his thesis on Feuerbach: till now the philosophers have interpreted the world, now they must change it. If there is a prior patience, we risk being seduced by the sloganesque character to this thesis. I know it has been immensely influential in defining the comportment of many thinkers. We have a bad conscience about being "mere" thinkers—say, armchair metaphysicians. We are eager to prove we are happy campers in the real world. We are often exaggerated in own announcement of our engagement. I think of Sartre—anxious lest history with a big H should pass him by. One can prove the point of engagement to the extreme of becoming a groupie of some currently ascendant ideology. In such a situation, one might say that such a philosopher doth protest too much.

One becomes what one might call *an agenda philosopher*. There is nothing wrong with agendas: an agenda is literally "what is to be done," "what must be done." The fundamental conditions of life make human beings agenda creatures. What we are is defined by the question (made (in)famous by Lenin): What is to be done?—and how we respond to it. I grant that: but an agenda philosophy, one suspects, is as constraining of thought, perhaps more constraining, than the allegedly "top-down" dictatorial theorist. For there is a determination in advance of what is to be thought in terms of an anticipated response to the question "What is to be done?" The agenda determines what is to be thought, as well as what is to be done. Agendas can be immensely helpful in confused practical circumstances; they can also be dictatorial. They can especially be dictatorial when they define how we relate to reality as a whole, dictating in advance the kind of mindfulness and praxis that is deemed appropriate—not about this situation or that, but in a more pervasive and encompassing sense. What being is, or reality is to be, is determined in terms of the agenda we bring to bear on it. To be at all means to be on the agenda. Thus viewed, the agenda can induce a kind of *policing* of our thinking.

There is a doing justice that is not, or seeks not to be, agenda driven. There is a doing justice that, just as a being true, is not either a matter of the hyper-theory of "absolute knowledge" or the projects of agenda driven humans. Such doing justice is something intermediate for humans. This means that before all agendas there is something received. As well as something given, this intermediate nature also means we have to reckon with human fallibility, failure, ignorance, and malice—be we as well-intentioned as we can. We betray the promise of what we have received. We mess things up.

Doing justice, being true is in between. I think one must reject terms which imply that the whole tradition is guilty of overstated claims of absolute knowing qua theory to the devaluation of praxis (such as we find with Arendt). There is a practice of philosophy that goes with this "being true," this "doing justice." The simple contrast of theory and practice does not do justice to our ontological situation. Philosophy, as I understand it, is a practice of life asking us to do justice to the most opposed requirements, and with all the tension of this: remoteness and engagement, distance and intimacy. If it were a matter of mere remoteness, the result would be the loss of life. If it were a matter of mere engagement, the result might be the loss of lucidity. Mere distance can breed a kind of arrogance, even when it touches nothing. Mere intimacy can beguile us with an apparent relevance. But to be intimate and to know distance, to be engaged and to respect range—this is not easy.

In one sense, the view I would want to defend is the easiest and the hardest. Easiest, because we all know our ontological vulnerability. Hardest, because we find it least easy to grant this and what follows from it. What we intimately know, we expressly refuse to grant. There is an ontological vulnerability prior to definition by social status. Social status and all the issues of social justice that go with the good governance of power in a human community are themselves responses to this prior vulnerability. We make ourselves secure only because we live out of an intimate ontological vulnerability. Taking an extreme instance: To be on top, to be number one, to be boss, to be sovereign—understood socially—are themselves derivative configurations of our social life—derivative from responses of power that want to recess even more the recessed patience of being. It is not only the socially vulnerable who are vulnerable. The issue of this prior doing justice does not take place on the level of derivative configurations of this more primal ontological condition—this more primal poverty. The view is again hardest to defend because we do not want to acknowledge this about ourselves, about our very being. In accession to power(s), we are tempted, again and again, with the apotheosis of invulnerability. Again and again we succumb.

If the contrast of theory and practice is often too crudely drawn, the matter is not one of simply reactively reasserting the virtues of the contemplative life—though I would certainly stress the perennial importance of the contemplative. I want to say that doing justice must be understood in relation to a more primordial patience—and this relative to the character of being true with respect to human beings, and their good governance of power in a just social accord. There is a sense of doing justice which I think is connected to, and can become the fruit of, a deeper metaphysical patience. Let me explain this in relation to truth, or better put, being true.

Being True and Our Intermediate Being

There is a strong tendency in modernity to give a certain privilege to praxis in line with the dictum of Vico: the true is the made. Marx cites this with approval, and there is a widespread view that there is no truth for itself, the true is the constructed. I want to argue that this does not do justice to a sense of truth prior to construction, and that enables construction. The true here is not the made, and to do justice to it, we need an understanding of doing justice as inseparable from a fidelity to this prior "being true."

This sense of "being true" and of "doing justice" prior to the normal contrast of the theoretical and the practical, has something to do with our *intermediate* nature. It may be true that we do not possess absolute truth; perhaps only God can and does. That we do not possess the absolute truth is not a postmodern view—it is as old as the despised Plato. Human beings are not God, hence we do not, in a sense, cannot possess absolute truth. But this does mean we are licensed to construct "truth" such as we consider relevant or interesting for ourselves. Not possessing absolute truth, we seek the true, but we could not seek at all were there no relation between us, our desire, and the truth sought. To know we do not know the absolute truth is already to be in relation to truth. Otherwise we could not know our ignorance, nor seek what we lack and obscurely anticipate. We are intermediate beings: neither in absolute possession of truth, nor in absolute destitution: somewhere between.

We do not construct this "somewhere between."[2] It is the space, indeed ethos of being, within which we might seek to construct this or that, but it is presupposed by all our constructing power. This being in the *metaxu* (Greek for "between") defines our participation in the milieu of being within which our own middle being intermediates with what is, and itself, seeking to do justice to itself and what it is to be, as well as to what is other. We are endowed before we construct.

Taking seriously this intermediacy, implications follow for doing justice. There emerges in our very searching a call to fidelity to truth we neither possess nor construct, and yet which endows us with the power to do justice, not only in this practical endeavor or that, but in a being true that keeps faith. The point does not have to be put negatively. It is not a matter just of showing certain deep instabilities in denying a sense of truth that is not our own construction—though this is important. It is rather a matter of attending to the fact that in the search for all truth, even in the denial that we possess the truth, we are called upon to "be truthful." Being truthful and doing justice are inseparably connected. Moreover, one can be truthful, even in searching for the truth, and even in knowing that one does not possess the truth. Our being truthful, our doing justice to this, is testament to that intermediate condition: the human seeker as between the fullness of truth of the divine and the ignorance of the beast: beyond the second, though the first be beyond us, and yet in intimate relation to what is so beyond us, by virtue of the call to be truthful. Twinned with this call to be truthful is the call to "do justice" that is prior to the truth or justice of this or that determinate theory or form of praxis. The justice or truth of the latter comes to manifestation out of this prior "being true" and "doing justice."

The charge to be truthful is an exigence that makes a call on us before we endeavor to construct any system of science or philosophy that might claim to be true, and before we seek to put into practice any agenda we deem needful for the just governance of human affairs. It may call us actively to construct or act; but the call itself shows us to be open to something other than our own self-determination, something that endows us with a destiny to be truthful and just to the utmost extent of our human powers. In that regard, once again there is no way of separating the theoretical and the practical, the metaphysical and the ethical. For this being truthful is also called to a fidelity that solicits a way of life appropriate to it, that issues in a way of being mindful in which we are to live truthfully, and to live truly. Doing justice to this unavoidable call to be truthful is needed if we are to remain true to doing justice in this or that practical endeavor.

This being truthful is not a univocal, objective truth fixed "out there" but has a bearing more on the *immanent porosity* of the human being to being as it is, and to what is good and worthy in itself to be affirmed. If it is not simply objective, it is not simply subjective either. We know the call to be truthful intimately in our own selves, but there is something trans-subjective about this. Something here comes to us, something here endows us with a promise of being we could not produce through ourselves alone. The spirit of truthfulness in us points to something trans-subjective in our own selves or subjectivity. As trans-subjective, it is also "objective" in the sense of communicating something other to us, even while being in intimate relation to us. This is not objective in terms of this object or that; rather the spirit of truthfulness witnesses in what is objective to something that is trans-objective. Without it we would have no participation in objective truth, but it itself is not this or that objective truth. It endows us with the ability to do justice to this or that objective truth.

I find Pascal's distinction between *l'esprit de géométrie* and *l'esprit de finesse* helpful here. Such truths as we pursue in the hard sciences and mathematics call upon *l'esprit de géométrie*. But we need especially *l'esprit de finesse* when we try to do justice to the human being, in the deep ambiguity of its being. The spirit of truthfulness, our being truthful, calls first upon powers of mindfulness that flower in *l'esprit de finesse* rather than *l'esprit de géométrie*, which is not to say the latter does not participate in it. In a sense, this spirit of truthfulness transcends the difference of the two, if we are tempted to see these as dualistically opposed. But it is itself intimate to the finesse of the human being.

Finesse is very important in a time such as ours in which *l'esprit de géométrie*, floating high with powerful theoretical knowledge, is often in the ascendant. Finesse is rather a readiness for a more intimate knowing, bearing on what is prior to and beyond geometry. It bears on a mindfulness that can read the signs of the equivocity of human existence, and not simply by the conversion of these signs into a univocal science or a philosophical system. By its nature finesse is an excellence of mindfulness that is singularly embodied. It cannot be rendered without remainder in terms of neutral and general characteristics. One might say that ethical and political finesse find their practical embodiment in the excellences of *phronēsis*. For finesse concerns the concrete suppleness of living intelligence that is open, attentive, mindful, attuned to the occasion in all its elusiveness, subtlety and unrepeatable singularity. Singularity here is not a kind of autism of being. It communicates of what is rich with a promise, perhaps initially not fully communicated, and yet available for, making itself available for, communicability. Communicability itself cannot be confined to articulation in neutral generality, or homogeneous universality. Finesse is in attendance on what is elusive in the intimacy of being, but that intimacy is at the heart of living communicability.

The need of finesse is very important in a time of postmodern pluralism which often claims to celebrate ambiguity, equivocity, and so on. Finesse has to do with a discernment that does justice to what is worthy to be affirmed in the ambiguity. It is not the indiscriminate glorification of ambiguity. It is the excellence of mindfulness that does not deny the ambiguity, is not false to it, but seeks to be true to what is worthy to be affirmed in it—and not everything is worthy to be affirmed. If nothing else, finesse is not just a matter of construction or an agenda. It is a matter of doing justice. The gifts it fosters are receptivity, attentive mindfulness of singular occasions, happenings, and person, openness to the singularity of things, a readiness for the surprising and the genuine other—a feeling for the intimacy of being itself, and intimate nourishment of the spirit of truthfulness in our own selves. In the past, religion and art have been the great mistresses of finesse. In circumstances of ethical ambiguity, without finesse there is no discerning ethical judgment. Without finesse, there is no serious and profound philosophy also. Without finesse in politics, the huckster, or worse, usurps the place of the statesman.

Doing Justice and the Patience of Being

I now want more explicitly to connect these remarks on doing justice as being true with the patience of being. Agenda philosophers generally think that our being is to do, to act: in the beginning, the middle and the end is the act, the constructive act. My point is not to deny the act but to relativize, in more senses than one, the tendency to absolutize the claims of the constructivist. With us the constructive act is not the first or the last, or the middle either. The spirit of being true indicates first on our part a certain patience to the truth before we ourselves are called to be truthful in a more active sense. There is a doing justice to what is not made, or not "made up."

There is a patience of being before there is an endeavor to be, a receiving of being before an acting of being, in accord with our singular characters as humans. The patience and receiving make the endeavor and the acting possible; and when acknowledged with finesse, the latter are understood differently than within a philosophy that wants the self-absolutizing of our activist character or our endeavor to be. I put it thus: More primal than the *conatus essendi* is the *passio essendi*. Spinoza describes the *essence* of a being as its *conatus*—and this is defined by its power to affirm itself and its range. This range for Spinoza is potentially unlimited, in the absence of external countervailing beings who express their power of being in opposition or in limitation of the power of other beings. For Spinoza the *conatus essendi* is the being of a being. It is also the being of the human being. Without an external limitation, the endeavor to be is potentially infinite. An external other always hence presents itself as potentially hostile to my self-affirming. The other, so seen, is alien to my self-affirmation. On this view, our relation to the other always harbors implicit hostility. The continuation of the *conatus essendi* must disarm the threat of the other, or arm itself against it from the outset. On such a view passivity is to be avoided or overcome. For being patient to something places us in a position of subordination. To receive from the other is a sign of weakness. To receive is to be servile, while to endeavor and to act is to be sovereign. This attitude fits in with the ethos of modernity in which the autonomus subject as self-law (*auto-nomos*) and self-affirming is implicitly in ambiguous, potentially hostile relation to what is other, or *heteros*.

By contrast, the view offered here of the *passio essendi* suggests something different. We are first given to be, before anything else. (One might say that at a theological level this bears on our being creations: creatures of an absolute source that gives us to be and gives us to be as good: the good of the "to be" in which we participate but which we do not construct—that allows us to construct.) The *passio essendi* calls on the recognition of an otherness more original than our own self-definition. We are only self-defining because we have originally given to be as selves; only creative because created; only loving because already loved and shown to be worthy of love; only become good to the degree that we are grateful for a good we do not ourselves produce; only become truthful because there is a truth more original than ourselves which endows us with the power to seek truth and the confidence that should we search truly we will find that truth, in so far as this can be understood by the finite human being.

Being patient, or being in the patience of being, is not here a defect. It is only a defect from the point of view of a *conatus* given over to the temptation to affirm itself alone, and hence closed off from the acknowledgment that it is at all because it is first given to be before it can give itself to itself. The point is not at all the denial of the *conatus* but a changed vision of it as deriving from something other to itself. Think of *the healthy body*, for example. We immediately see in it something of the *conatus* in the will to self-perpetuation and self-affirmation that marks it. This is our being—to affirm itself—and indeed to affirm itself as good—it is good to be. I do not deny this at all, but the question is its meaning and whether there is something more that relativizes self-affirmation—gives it to be at all, and makes it porous relative to something other than itself, and not just as a servile passivity. I would say this: we *find ourselves* in this self-affirmation; we do not first construct it. Spontaneously we live this affirmation of the "to be" as good—we do not first have a choice—it is what we are. Since we find ourselves as thus self-afffirming, there is a patience to this primal self-affirmation. There is something received in our being given to be, something not constructed through our own powers alone.

One might say that we are an original "yes" to being, but we find ourselves as already given to be in an original "yes" to being that is received and not produced through ourselves alone. Our incarnate being communicates this original "yes." But of course, we have to say "yes" to this original "yes" to being, and in doing so we can develop our powers diversely. The endeavor to be in a more self-chosen way here emerges, and necessarily so. If we decide to live in a healthy way, this decision is along the lines of following on the first "yes." It is the living of a second "yes" which tries to respect, for instance, the integrity of the body, to live with finesse for its subtle rhythms, to embody a kind of reverence, even for a sort of sanctity that is intimate to the human body. But none of this expression of our further endeavor to be tells against the more primal patience. The agenda driven projects of constructivist philosophies too often tend towards an amnesia of this patience. At an extreme they may even give rise to a hatred of this patience, for it is the incontrovertible reminder of our status as finite creatures, a constitutive sign of the fact that we are not the masters of being, not even of our own being. Paradoxically, when we turn away from our porosity to the more primal patience, our self-affirmation can turn into a kind of self-hatred. The givenness that makes possible our being at all is refused as such. This refusal, just in self-affirmation, is self-refusal. In thus affirming ourselves, we have not done justice to what we are.

Doing Justice and the Practice of Philosophy

Can the above reflections throw any light on the relation of doing justice and the practices of philosophy? While philosophers have always been overtly concerned with justice, and with many approaches, justice has much to do with power, its circulation and governance. One recalls the identification of might and right we find, for instance, in Thrasymachus. Here we witness what one might call the hypertrophy of the *conatus essendi*—the overriding of the *passio essendi* in the sense of primal reception or receptivity, and instead all passion and endeavor is poured into will to power, blunt or devious as circumstances dictate. Yet justice does have to do with the good governance of power, the distribution and balance of powers, the correction of overweening powers. We are talking about the measure of power, the moderation of power, and the fulfillment of power(s). There is also the betrayal of the promise of power. The power of the "to be," at bottom, is the power of the good, or the "to be" as good.[3] Injustice has no power in itself. The patience of being suggests that justice is a condition of being more primal than the exercise of power, and the doing of justice has to do with our condition of being as being more than will to power. There are modern theories of justice that tend to take more account of the will to power of the protagonists, and in a minor key, the *passio* of those lacking power. The standard of reference is the possession of power—and hence the justice of the patient is not always done justice to. Nor is justice done to the power of the good of the "to be." If my reflections to this point are not entirely wrong, we need to consider this patience at a deeper level than the usual duality of activity and passivity that often defines our understanding of the endeavor to be.

When we think of social justice we tend to think of issue connected with those less well off in society. We think of the poor and ways of alleviating their poverty; or of those in other lands and continents less well off, and to whose distress we ourselves both contribute, and sometimes help to diminish. There is no doubt but that philosophy cannot turn a deaf ear to these concerns, though it is not immediately clear what it distinctively can contribute to their consideration. One does not have to be a philosopher to offer one's services to the many agencies dealing with issues of social justice; or to dedicate oneself to the study of the economic aspects of social justice; or to give one's life to the political processes necessary to protect and enhance ways of life hospitable to social justice. We can contribute to various reflective debates about what all of such things amount to; can reflect on issues like individualism and communitarianism, the conservative and the progressive, the reformist and the revolutionary. All these issues are extremely important in their own way.

It is not that philosophers should not be involved in such issues but there are other questions no less important—perhaps more important—and that often are recessed when our thoughts are too absorbed in the foreground of immediate happening. There is excitement and intoxication in being engaged in the forefront. There is nothing lonelier than standing back and trying to take the longer look. History with a big H (sigh . . .) might be passing one by. I think again of the fretting Sartre.

There are absolutely crucial considerations that can very easily become *recessed* rather than expressed. It is the very nature of practical life to bring about that recess. Human beings as finite must engage life under determinate conditions. Reflection on those conditions is not always the first condition for those engagements. Quite the opposite: too much thinking on those conditions can be eviscerating of a practice of life, or paralyzing to the sources of engagement. The passion of engagement is relativized by this posture of standing back, and hence the purpose turns awry and we lose the name of action. The patience involved in doing justice is not quite this standing back. One sometimes has no time to weigh options, one has to act. But even in extreme circumstances of urgency the doing justice of the primal patience can still inform the acting itself. Admittedly, to live with poise in the midst of urgency, to do justice to the patience of being in the stresses of immediately requisitioned action, is an excellence of rare wisdom. But it is not impossible.

For instance, when Hamlet praises Horatio it is something of this poise to which he is drawn. Hamlet initially cannot act, but is not patient either. He has not found access to the doing of justice that is beyond retributive justice, and that may be cryptically hinted in the providence of the fall of a sparrow. As not able to act, Hamlet is often taken as emblematic of something of the condition of modernity initially paralyzed by its hyper self-reflexivity. But one might wonder if one way of seeking release from this condition of paralyzing self-reflection is a turn towards hyper-activity which does not so much overcome the paralysis as fly from it. But hyper-activity brings this paralysis with its flight: not being true to the patience of being, it really suffers from a secret lassitude of being which it alleviates by ceaselessly throwing itself into this project and that. But it still is itself and nothing but itself—in lassitude or in hyper-activity. The practice of philosophy can quickly become an agenda driven ideology when it is too seduced by foreground circumstances to the oblivion of the recessed conditions that enable the practices of different forms of life. Philosophers offer something more true to practical life when they nurture mindfulness of these enabling recesses. Thinkers who love the forefront keep themselves to the forefront. They do not impress one with poise. Willingness to be nothing—this is part of philosophy—the willingness to count for nothing—the willingness to be a nobody—in order to open to everybody and everything.

There is a sense in which the patience of being and the endeavor to be can be doubled equivocally in theory and practice in the form of hyper-theory and hyper-activity. Interestingly, hyper-theory and hyper-activity can often go together—perhaps not so much in the same person, as in a community, or even an entire epoch. Am I wrong to detect in modernity a passage from activity to hyper-activity—with less and less of the patience of being, less and less of the ultimate porosity which is to the divine? It is said that in pre-modernity, there was hyper-theory such as the putative God's-eye view of the Platonic philosopher. Given our intermediacy, very much granted by Plato, this is too simple. The finitude of the philosopher, of the human being seems incontrovertible: between beasts and gods, we remain intermediate, hence finite, even were we to become like God—for we never are, nor ever will be God. Modern philosophy strikes one often as much more hyper-theoretical. Our more elemental participation in being, communicated in the primal patience, suffered as wonder, is overtaken by an ontological distrust, when doubt, distanced from a more celebrant astonishment, becomes hyperbolic. Suspicion of being as other overtakes love. "Theory" will construct for us the intelligibility of the world, but it is sucked more into the space of being an instrumental hypothesis, which in sometimes remote, sometimes proximate manners, serves a particular purpose of practical humanity. As we move from activity to hyper-activity, at a certain point we pass a threshold and a lack of measure follows, or a defect of patience. This hyper-activity becomes defective in the "doing justice" that is also our "being true." In all of this, paradoxically there is nothing truly "hyper"—nothing above—hence no basis of a reverence for the divine on our part, for we claim to be the measure of ourselves and what is other.

Doing Justice and Being Nothing

Doing justice points to a fidelity to good already given, not just a good actively constructed or done—but making possible all active constructions and doing. In some ways, the relation of philosophy and social justice is analogous to the relation of religion and the practice of justice. There is never a necessary guarantee that practice will faithfully conform to theory or what one holds to be true. In life there are always failures to hold true to what one holds to be true, to what holds one to the true. We do not enact what being true promises and solicits of us. We are dealing with freedom. There is the equivocity of the human condition. There are uses of both philosophy and religion which are ideological in the worst sense: they serve merely as means to an end. Again they are too agenda driven. Instead of agapeic service, their service is one of serviceable disposability.[4]

Consider, for instance, what follows if Spinoza is right in his way of speaking of religion: religious piety is salutary with respect to social order, salutary in serving obedience to the political sovereign. By contrast, philosophy, it is said, serves truth, not piety. In being religious is there nothing more ultimate to which we are to be true, or to do justice, than such obedience to the sovereign? If there is nothing more, is this not to subject religion to the requirements of serviceable disposality—serviceable to the political sovereigns, but disposable with respect to claims of ultimate truth? I ask: Does philosophy itself escape the temptation to serviceable disposability in a similar sense? Or escape committing sins similar to a religion that bows before Caesar and none other? Philosophy too has served obedience to the sovereign. Clearly this happened with Marxism, but there were well-paid excusers within the space of consumer capitalism. So too, just as there are theologians there are philosophers like Job's comforters who can come up with a theory of unimpeachable logic to mollify our discomforts or even to shrug off every horror.

There is a deeper level—and it is not just the transition from theory to practice. This is the more primordial level of the patience of being, patience in being true. A true practice of religion in a society fosters this patience and fidelity. I think the true philosopher is also servant of this patience—keeping open the porosity of the human being to the most ultimate and important—not letting this porosity get clogged with dubious theories, and with practices that are not faithful to the good of human desire. Doing justice at this level of the patience of being is the most difficult. It is the most important in the long run. Its immediate importance is not always evident. Quite to the contrary, it can seem prevaricating and unhelpful, indeed cowardly in not willingly committing itself to now needed action. It seems to make cowards of us. In fact, we require courage in a different dimension—courage to take the long view, the wider view, the more ontologically intimate view. Such would be the courage of the love of wisdom.

Take, for example, the issue of terror. Granted, in certain circumstances immediate steps must be undertaken, and done in order to do justice. But there is an equally important, sometimes in the longer run more important matter of doing justice. This entails trying to truly understand the sources of terror. Among other things, now not foregrounded, one recalls not a few decades ago the ideological intoxication on the left with political terror. One recalls further back in the nine-teenth century the historical appearance of the political terrorist as such. One recalls the connection of terror and theory in the left-Hegelian line of thinking, summed up by Bruno Bauer's call for the "terrorism of pure theory."[5] One recalls the French Revolution as the mother of all modern political terrors, a terror and revolution which Hegel both judged and exculpated for being sourced in "abstract" freedom. One recalls the ambiguous Burke, prescient of the ominous horror stirring with modern political terror.

But more recessed than these considerations, one must philosophically enter what appears to be the void space of the human soul which is both susceptible to being terrorized as well as capable of terrorizing. Terror before an enemy, perhaps even need of an enemy,[6] take form in these voids—on both the side of the terrorizing and the terrorized. One endeavors to be oneself over against the other; the *conatus* overrides the *passio essendi*, both one's own and that of the others; all patience is a void to be overcome, lest one sink back into oneself as one's own void. I, as active *conatus*, endeavor to be over every other as patient to me, as the conquered *passio essendi*. But all of us, whether sovereign or servile, whether ascendant or dejected, are what we are simply as a porosity of being, and hence in our ontological roots vulnerable to terror and tempted to terrorize. This is where we can appreciate some of the redeeming power of tragedy: coming to know our patience to the terrible (*to deinon*), we are brought to an acknowledging of our finitude, in a knowing marked with the sacred patience of compassion (*eleos*). I will return to this.

The deeper sources of terror are not simply in proximate grievances. I would prefer to speak of the *porosity of the soul* than just the void—though this porosity opens up a kind of *fecund void*. Out of this void of the soul, there can come to be an entire nihilistic outlook—be it religious or secular. This must be addressed. In the end, it can only be addressed in terms of metaphysics—and in a more communal sense with religious communications that keep open the porosity. There have been philosophies that have gloried in the language of terror. There are languages overtly religious which are closures of this porosity—to God, to one's neighbor. Be it in religious or secular form, the *conatus* that arrogates truth for itself can overtake the *passio* that endows us with the promise of being true. Once again to address this matter, to do justice to it, requires we face the nothing—and the porosity of our being and its vulnerability. Understanding this does not mean one will have a panacea for dealing with terror. It does not mean the exculpation of evil acts. It need not mean the evasion of social responsibilities, in inciting terror and responding to it. But it will mean that recessed dimensions of the issue are granted, and the deepest not ignored.

There is a fundamental porosity to the human soul that, by contrast with this particular project or that, seems to look like a void. But it is a nothing that allows all openness, all receiving, all self-transcendence. Out of it comes all the practical energy that feeds this project and that. That there is such a porosity, or fecund void to the soul also means the nothing can be looked at otherwise than a justification for nihilism, theoretical or practical. This is an important point—for there is a nihila-tion whose reduction is, so to say, a desacralization of the human being. (Trotsky:

"We must get rid of, once and for all, this Quaker-Papist babble about the sanctity of human life.") Not too far behind desacralization comes along the desecration. By contrast, I am talking about a sacred nothing, if one could say that—a nothing that marks the human being's porosity to the divine, and that constitutes something of the trace of the divine in the human being.

If there is something like a patience to the true in doing justice, there is also a kind of porosity and destitution in what we are. There is a justice for the vulnerable—there is justice as a vulnerability. There is justice as a kind of *poverty*: poverty in opening a space for not only one's own good but the good of the other. I would say that the *practice of philosophy* also calls for its own kind of poverty: the poverty of philosophy.[7] Once again this situates philosophy in the same family as the religious. In a sense, there is to be an abdication of power for power's sake: the practice of philosophy doing justice is not at all will to power, not even self-determining reason. It is reasonable mindfulness, indeed agapeic mindfulness, in the services of the true: thought thinking the other to thought. It means a willingness to be as nothing. There is a poverty which is a "being nothing" to make a way for what is true to communicate itself; to make way for those who have lost their way, or have no way, or are seeking a way. This poverty is being a way along no way: even in the desert. There is a return to zero which interfaces newly with creation as given. Doing justice asks a pilgrim philosophy from the wayfarer, *homo viator*.

Relative to such a poverty, the first point for the practice of philosophy would not be quite the more normal task of a practical fight, say, against poverty. This last is not inconsiderable, and not at all to be slighted, but we are moving in a different space, one that seeds the promise of struggles against debilitating poverties (again in the more usual sense). Not granting this other space, there can come to be a certain activism that is worrying. Here one often wonders if many of us in the west still suffer from what has been a recurrent and sapping debility of spirit in modernity: horror at the emptiness of life. To buffer ourselves against meaninglessness, we throw ourselves into hyperbolic activity, thus alleviating the lassitude that squats at the bottom of our souls. This lassitude is not the patience of being. I sometimes wonder about what follows if it were true that we do live in hyper-active times. Hyper-activity, as we know, is connected with what we call "attention deficit disorder." What if an epoch suffers from hyper-activity? Is that epoch then not also marked by attention deficit disorder? Where is the medicine, is there a Ritulin enough, is there Ritulin at all, to cure such an attention deficit on an epochal scale?

Horror at the emptiness of life: We cannot stand the silence. We cannot wait and let the silence communicate. We speak into the silence. We shout into the silence. We insist on telling the silence what its meaning is. We tell our story to the silence. There is nothing there to hear this story. We hear nothing but our own echo. We tell this story to ourselves. It is our song of ourselves, and it can be sung in the notes of agony or smugness, but it is sung to protect ourselves against being nothing. It is a dictation to nothing. The human being cannot sit still. Something has to be done. There is something untrue about all of this. The hyperbolic dimension of the soul has tried to exhaust itself in activism: exhaust itself with its own activity. One thinks of those individuals who exercise and exercise not to attain the maximum of physical well-being, but in order to run from themselves. Perhaps in the past there were certain ascetic practices in religion which offered a similar therapy for self, but now no religious justification can be offered for these secular therapies—beyond fear of having to face oneself, fear of the silence—fear of being nothing, fear of the porosity that we are, act up as we will.

The historical narratives of secular modernity are often these songs of self—be the self the more solitary individual, or the privileged nation, or the party, or one's race or class. They can serve as huge diversions from the nakedness at the core of the human being. They are fables of justification we tell ourselves as we sit around the campfire and keep at bay the night that circles on the outside. Of course, the night is in us all, and so we are singing to drown the silence that is there in the deeper porosity of our being.

These historical philosophies have exerted bewitching effects on many of the major ideologies of modernity. One thinks of Marxism, of course, but there are other bewitchments in the glorification of technological progress, or the deification of market economics. Humans are intent to construct purpose in what appears to them as a purposeless universe. But if the universe is purposeless, we as participants in the universe also finally are purposeless. We do not want to face this, and the consequences that follow from it, and hence we sing around the camp fire. But of course, the camp fire is almost everything now, since we have let the blaze burn over every non-human other in nature—nature the fuel by which we keep the incessant lights burning through the night. We suffer from light pollution. More often than we grant, we are the light that pollutes the night.

There are so many carapaces of protection against nothing. Doing justice re-quires something more than the construction of these carapaces. It is true we have to construct protections for the naked human being—much justice asks to be done in this mode. But if this mode is made the absolute, and makes us forget the naked-ness, then it is built upon a lie. The point is something evident in the fact that this *just* activism, constructivism can serve to do justice to those who are nothing: those who are naked, those destitute. The nakedness we flee in ourselves comes back to haunt us in the nakedness of the destitute other.

This nakedness is something social. Most of the time we can cover ourselves before human others. We can be in cover up even before ourselves. I speak in homage to Job: there is an other before whom we all stand naked—God. For some activisms no true space is allowed for any such an other. It is the idolization of our own autonomy that fuels the constructivism. There are religious practices infected by the idolatry of certain activisms: do something, we are told, to make the world a better place. But more often than one would think, it is the foreground distraction that we seek. We are almost incapable of silence and attending on what it can communicate.

Defection from the patience of being is sometimes evident in the way we have divorced ourselves from the play of nature: for instance, in our unwillingness to generate new life beyond ourselves—in our reduction of the mystery of eros to recreational sex, morally preaching about its own rights of self-determination—resisting being given over to anything greater than its own selfish satisfaction. Nature can be a great teacher, but we reck it not, unless it can be made to serve us. Animals sometimes now are more universal than we are. They live beyond themselves, are lived beyond themselves in the erotic rhythms of nature—except of course where our interventions have polluted and hindered the spontaneous unfolding of these dances of begetting.

We have said we are historical not natural beings, but in the stories we have constructed the core *intimacy* of our being comes back. There is nowhere more evident than in the play of eros—it saturates everything. It is as if in our denial of the dance of nature, the music and its rhythms come back, and we still find ourselves going through the motions but we neither attend to what we are doing nor wonder why at all. There is the subjection of eros to the dictates of serviceable disposability: making it a means to an end—and we are the end—for after all, is not every historical story just the song of ourselves. We make history we say, even if we are made by history: it is the only self-begetting power. It is we who have made ourselves the *causa sui*. The catch cry will not be *deus sive natura* but *deus sive historia sive humanitas*. All of this, of course, can be claimed in the name of doing justice. If so, it is extremely doubtful if this is at all doing justice to the patience at the heart of doing justice.

So we sometimes act as if we were nature's (or God's) most important gift to existence. We pride ourselves with the power to improve the world. We say: we make the world a better place. But it all goes askew, when we act as if we could *outdo God*, as if we could *best God*. The old saying had something truer: There but for the grace of God go I. This is in, fact, only a half truth. For by the grace of God we all go there. There is the astonishing beatitude: "Blessed are the poor." One will be scorned for repeating this as escapism from the practical call of social justice. I beg to differ. Being poor: By the gift of the divine we are all naked. We are all like Job. Naked we come hither, naked we go hence, in between we cover up. In the between, though, we are all offered the patience of being: patience to a more ultimate good we do not construct ourselves; patience to a justice more ultimate than our own construction. We are given to be as constituted by a fundamental porosity of being: itself the opening in us that allows our every act of self-transcending but that itself in not any act of self-transcending. It allows, it creatively possibilizes self-transcending; allows doing justice to ourselves, to the others. For there is a promise in the porosity that asks to be redeemed, though it can be betrayed. It is betrayed if we act as if it did not exist.

We owe a debt of gratitude to the destitute and the sick and the dying for they remind us of the givenness of our being, and the graced porosity that allows us to be at all. We think doing justice is doing them a favor but there is a sense in which it is quite the opposite. We hate what they remind us of, for we are happy when we cover ourselves. When we take mind of them, we step back from becoming monstrous. Our cover up is blown away.

I conclude by citing the poem of W. B. Yeats called "The Great Day":

Hurrah for revolution and more cannon-shot!
A beggar on horseback lashes a beggar on foot.
Hurrah for revolution and cannon come again!
The beggars have changed places, but the lash goes on.

One of the important implication of what I have tried to say is that if there is a patience of being, then there is a doing justice that is *beyond servility and sovereignty*.[8] It is beyond the passive and the active and calling for a new poise—a poise that is a readiness defined in a freedom beyond the servility of the slave and the sovereignty of the master. What this calls for is some of the nakedness of Yeats's beggar but without the soul of will to power that finds its outlet in the lash—whether on horseback or on the ground. There is a nakedness—a "being nothing" to which the practices of philosophy must be open in a new poverty of mindfulness, beyond science and system and beyond agendas.

There is a tragic element to this in one way. I mentioned above the redeeming power of tragedy: exposure to the terrible which endows us with a sacred compassion. We spend a life, expend the endeavor to be, in covering ourselves—and sometimes are relatively successful—though always relatively. One thinks of King Lear—here was the sovereign—he was the regal self—and then he gave away his kingdom, gave away his power. He did not first know it but he was being unclothed, being stripped, in giving his power away. Regal Lear becomes un-selved—becomes a nothing. The Fool: "I can tell why a snail has a house." Lear : "Why?" The Fool: "Why, to put 's head in; not to give it away to his daughters, and leave his horns without a case" (*King Lear*, I, v, 28–32). Lear becomes like the Tom O' Bedlam—even less—like Edgar who says of himself: "Edgar I nothing am" (II, iii, 21). But there is an idiot wisdom to this nothing. Edgar is as wise in his compassion, as Lear's Fool, a "bitter fool" (I, iv, 140) is wise in his worldly savvy. The king and the beggar are no selves, become nothings, but in becoming nothing, they also begin to come to see. And not least begin to see things from the bare stripped outlook of the nothings who have nothing. "Nothing almost sees miracles but misery" (II, ii, 167–168). There is a certain "democracy" of suffering—it is a kind of catholicism of patience—in our being ultimately patient in the intimate condition of being. Doing justice begins anew in being nothing. Being nothing Lear becomes able to make way for the Fool: "In, boy, go first . . . you houseless poverty—Nay, get thee in. I'll pray, and then I'll sleep. . . . O, I have ta'en too little care of this! Take physic, pomp; Expose thyself to feel what wretches feel" (III, iv, 26ff.).

There is much on patience in Shakespeare's *King Lear* but it is not a matter of romantic sentimentality about poverty.[9] Nor is it a matter of being nothings, understood as Marx understood the proletariat—the nothings who, owning nothing, will become everything through revolutionary praxis and war against the sovereigns, the exploiting capitalists. Hegel's self-relating negativity becomes historically incarnate in the weaponed nothings, through whom the revolutionary violence of the endeavor to be overtakes the *passio essendi*, and the deeper meaning of the patience of being is mutilated in this overriding. It should not surprise anyone who thinks on it that the outcome cannot but be disastrous, if this understanding is projected and enacted as a project on a world historical scale. The lash becomes king of all.

I am not asleep to the lash hidden in the seemingly gentler caresses of consumer capitalism.

It is true: The sovereigns who refuse justice as masters construct the servile, by deconstructing them, as food for their wrath. In the name of the injustice they call justice, they do not do justice.

It is equally true: The servile who revolt against the old sovereigns construct themselves, in wrath, as new sovereigns. In the name of justice, they do no justice.

Being nothing can begin to reveal something other to both. We can come to know intimately that there is a patience of being before servility and sovereignty and beyond them; that there is a justice before servility and sovereignty, calling us to the doing of justice beyond them. The call comes from before servility and sovereignty, and solicits us into an agapeic service beyond the master lashing and for the slave lashed.

Katholieke Universiteit Leuven

Notes

1. On this see my "Between System and Poetics: On the Practices of Philosophy," in *Between System and Poetics: William Desmond and Philosophy after Dialectics*, ed. Thomas Kelly (Aldershot: Ashgate Publishers, 2006), chap. 1.

2. See *Being and the Between* (Albany: SUNY, 1995) for an attempt to articulate the metaphysics of the between, and *Ethics and the Between* (Albany: SUNY, 2001), for the ethics. Chapter 12 of *Being and the Between* deals with different senses of being true.

3. On this see *Being and the Between*, chap. 13, and *Ethics and the Between*, passim.

4. On the meaning of serviceable disposability, see *Ethics and the Between*, chap. 14.

5. On the connection with critique, see "Is there Metaphysics after Critique?" *International Philosophical Quarterly*, vol. 45, no. 2, June 2005, 221–241

6. See my "Enemies," in *Is There a Sabbath for Thought? Between Religion and Philosophy* (New York: Fordham University Press, 2005), chap. 9.

7. See my "Religion and the Poverty of Philosophy," in *Is There a Sabbath for Thought?*, chap. 3.

8. See my "Neither Servility nor Sovereignty: Between Politics and Metaphysics," *Theology and the Political: The New Debate*, ed. Creston Davis, John Milbank, and Slovoj Žižek (Durham and London: Duke University Press, 2005), 153–182.

9. See *King Lear*, II, iv, 218ff. "I prithee, daughter, do not make me mad. . . . I can be patient." II, iv, 269–270: "You heavens, give me patience, patience I need." III, ii, 37–38: "No, I will be the pattern of all patience, I will say nothing." There is much on the nothing, on being nothing in I, iv, especially after lines 186.

Crime and Catholic Tradition: Restoration or Retribution?

Elizabeth A. Linehan

Abstract: The U.S. Catholic Bishops (2000) have endorsed a model of criminal justice that is *restorative* rather than *retributive*. Some interpreters of Catholic tradition defend retribution as a necessary feature of responding to crime (e.g., John Finnis). I argue in this paper that this difference is substantive, not merely linguistic. The essential question is what elements of past Catholic thinking about criminal justice are normative for today. I argue that there are strong moral reasons, consistent with both Catholic tradition and larger principles of social justice, to endorse the bishops' statement on criminal justice reform, and with it a restorative approach to crime.

I t is difficult to imagine a social justice issue more in need of serious examination today than our (U.S.) society's response to crime—or, I venture to say, one that receives less. Most crimes are unjust to someone, wrongdoing that we must try to prevent or to correct. The operating assumption in the contemporary United States is that we have "corrected" a crime if we have inflicted a measured amount of suffering (or deprivation, as of freedom) on the offender that is somehow proportionate to the offense. This is what we call 'retributive justice.' The injustices perpetrated under that banner are enormous, and they encompass all parties to crime: offenders, direct victims, indirect victims, society as a whole.

In a letter issued in November, 2000, the National Conference of Catholic Bishops find much to criticize in the U.S. criminal justice system. As it operates at present, measured by fundamental principles of Catholic social teaching, it is an abysmal failure.[1] Its failures include: violation of the human dignity of both victims and offenders; corrections policies that undermine family ties; discrimination against the poorest and most vulnerable; violations of subsidiarity; inadequate conceptions of the 'common good'; lack of support for actual communities.

The stated aims of the system include deterrence, protection of society (incapacitation), reform, and retribution. These goals conflict with and impede each other. In practice, I believe that the central purpose that dictates penal policy today is retribution or "just deserts."[2] In fact I think what we have today amounts almost to a *reductio ad absurdum* of retributive approaches to criminal justice. In the name

© 2006, American Catholic Philosophical Association, *Proceedings of the ACPA*, Vol. 79

of being "tough on crime" the U.S. criminal justice system has six million people under its jurisdiction at any given time, including more than two million confined in jails and prisons. As a percentage of the U.S. population, we have far more persons in custody than in any nation with which we would wish to compare ourselves.[3] The recidivism rate is high, as high as two-thirds rearrested within three years after serving time in prison, with more than 50 percent reincarcerated. Prisons tend to be overcrowded, violent places, in which inmates face daily threat of assault, including sexual assault. We also inflict a number of unofficial and hidden punishments, including the loss of many opportunities after release from prison.[4] In effect, we stigmatize convicted criminals for life.

The bishops summarize "the paradoxical Catholic teaching on crime and punishment" in this way:

> We will not tolerate the crime and violence that threatens the lives and dignity of our sisters and brothers, and we will not give up on those who have lost their way. We seek both justice and mercy. Working together, we believe our faith calls us to protect public safety, promote the common good, and restore community. We believe a Catholic ethic of responsibility, rehabilitation, and restoration can become the foundation for the necessary reform of our broken criminal justice system. (55)

"Responsibility" in context of the letter refers both to the offender being held accountable, and ideally accepting accountability, and the larger community owning its failures. "Rehabilitation" has its standard sense of bringing about positive change in offenders. "Restoration" refers to making things as right as possible for crime victims and for the community. Primary responsibility for restoration belongs to the offender, but the larger social context of crime is also recognized. It is important to note that "retribution" is not part of their foundation for reforming the system. In fact the conjunction of responsibility of offender, restoration of victims, and rehabilitation describes a model that contrasts with the present retributive one. The letter thus calls for significant change.

Essentially, the change is to a system that is *restorative*. The bishops' bottom line: "A Catholic approach leads us to encourage models of restorative justice that seek to address crime in terms of the harm done to victims and communities, not simply as a violation of law" (17). I believe this letter constitutes a genuine advance in Catholic social teaching, but that it is an advance the best of the tradition supports.

On the other hand, John Finnis has recently defended a view of Catholic tradition regarding criminal punishment with which I believe the bishops' position is incompatible. Finnis's reference points include, centrally, Thomas Aquinas's discussions of the debt of punishment, and the morality of vengeance in the *Summa*.[5] In this paper I will respond to Finnis's implicit critique of the paradigm shift involved in restorative justice. I will argue that the restorative justice model is compatible with the traditions of Catholicism, and further, that a restorative response to crime is morally preferable to a retributive response.

This project will require me to argue in support of three interrelated theses:

1. Finnis and the bishops really are in substantial disagreement; this is not simply a linguistic difference;

2. There is good reason to dispute Finnis's claim that the tradition as he describes it is normative for today;

3. There are strong moral reasons, consistent with Catholic tradition, to endorse the bishops' statement on criminal justice reform.

The contrast between the NCCB letter and Finnis's discussion of criminal punishment begins with the sources of their respective arguments. Finnis particularly relies on Aquinas's reasoning. The bishops' arguments, in contrast, do not primarily come from Aquinas or from natural law, but from scripture, sacramental practice, the experience of participants in the criminal justice system (particularly Catholics) whom the bishops consulted, and Catholic social teaching as the bishops summarize it. Reference is also made to the *Catechism of the Catholic Church*, but with two important additions. Their summary:

> [P]unishment by civil authorities for criminal activity should serve three principal purposes: (1) the preservation and protection of the common good of society, (2) the restoration of public order, and (3) the restoration or conversion of the offender. (24)

They go on to note that "repair of the harm done to the victims and to society by criminal activity, is also important to restoring the common good" (24). The common good is "undermined" both by criminal behavior that "threatens the lives and dignity of others" and by "policies that seem to give up on those who have broken the law" (1). Among the present policies they criticize are the rates of incarceration in the U.S., mandatory minimum sentences, treating juveniles as if they were adults, the use of isolation, and the death penalty. "All those whom we consulted seem to agree on one thing: the status quo is not really working—victims are often ignored, offenders are often not rehabilitated, and many communities have lost their sense of security" (6).

The scriptural arguments are easy to imagine. The bishops cite both Old and New Testament texts about God's justice tempered with mercy, Jesus' call to care for the victims of crime (Good Samaritan), to welcome and celebrate the return of the sinner (Prodigal Son), and to remember that we are all sinners and no one is beyond God's love.

What I think is especially important here, and what has characterized most of the letters of the NCCB, is that the scriptures are an integral part of the Catholic tradition on social justice. So are liturgical and sacramental practice.

The argument from sacramental practice concerns Penance and the Eucharist: the Eucharist as a sign of reintegration of sinners into the community, and Penance as a model of restorative justice practice. The model includes: true contrition, acknowledgment of responsibility in confession, "satisfaction" in the form of prayers or good deeds, seen as a form of restitution, and absolution. In giving absolution, the priest representing Jesus and the Church, welcomes the sinner back to full communion with the community.

There are two key structural differences between retributive and restorative justice. First, in retributive justice crime is conceived as an offense against the state. Restorative approaches, in contrast, see a crime first of all as an offense against a concrete person who is the direct victim; secondarily as against all others affected, and as against the particular community in which the crime took place; effects on society as a whole would be distant considerations, if relevant at all. This difference dictates the participants and the procedures for responding to crime.

A retributive system looks to determine guilt ("beyond a reasonable doubt") and to punish individuals who are found guilty. 'Punishment' involves a deliberately inflicted deprivation or suffering, imposed by someone in authority, as the consequence of a person's wrongdoing. In this way it differs from other responses (e.g., treatment, rehabilitation, protection of society).[6] Restorative justice, on the other hand, does not aim at punishment but at offender accountability and constructive action to make things "as right as possible." This is the second major difference. Facing the victim and doing what is in her power to make things right may be painful, and may involve deprivation of some kind, but *these are not the point, and they are not necessary to achieving the point.* If it turns out, for example, that the offender has already suffered remorse for her crime and is eager to have a chance to apologize to the victim, all the better. If the actions she agrees to as atonement give her satisfaction and relief of painful guilt feelings, also fine. If one result of the restorative process is a more secure relationship between the offender and the community, that counts as a success. The aim is that everyone benefit from a restorative process, rather than engaging in a zero-sum game in which the victim's gain is the offender's loss, and vice versa.

John Finnis claims that Catholic tradition would insist on the two distinguishing features of retributive justice that I have just summarized. Following Aquinas, he distinguishes between civil and criminal law in terms of "the difference between one's duty to compensate and one's liability to punishment." Both branches aim at restoring an equality that has been upset, or eliminating an unjustified inequality between persons. "But the one branch [civil law] looks to the losses incurred by specific persons, the other to a kind of advantage gained over all the other members of a community."[7]

The advantage criminal wrongdoers have gained is in preferring their own will to the society's specified requirements for the common good—that is, claiming a freedom they have no right to. "Balancing" involves doing something to them against their will. Hence it is not pain which is essential to punishment, but the subjection of their wills in proportion to the unlawful freedom they have claimed.[8] The scale of punishment is based on the severity of the offense, which is not based on how much harm was done but on "the extent of the offender's manifested self-preference in disregard of the path marked out by law which others constrain themselves to follow."[9]

The wrong of crime is in relation to all other members of society, in that the offense is against the law of the society and therefore the common good. Thus Finnis maintains that punishment cannot rightly be imposed by the victim, or on behalf of the victim, but "only on behalf of the community of citizens willing to abide by the law." This seems to imply that in principle, the direct victim is no more wronged than every other (law-abiding) member of the community. In light of that implication, any practice of giving victims a role in criminal proceedings (other than as witnesses) would be inappropriate.[10]

Negating the advantage gained by the offender restores equality between him and all the law-abiding, but it does nothing to restore to the victim what has been specifically taken by the offense. This reflects the present system, in which actual crime victims have no role and no voice. Finnis's focus is on the community as a whole (I would maintain "community in the abstract") as represented by state authority, and on the offender who needs correction and reform. It is not difficult to show that his interpretation of Catholic tradition is not compatible with the U.S. bishops' interpretation. The bishops differ with Finnis on precisely the two key points in which restorative justice contrasts with retributive justice: the importance of addressing the harm done to concrete victims of crime [primary aim vs. illegitimate],[11] and the necessity of inflicting a deprivation on the offender.

I contend that Catholic tradition not only accommodates restorative justice, but that it gives reasons for preferring it, at least in the contemporary U.S. context. I will support this claim in three ways: First, by indicating that there is room for a restorative justice approach even in Aquinas, particularly in his discussion of the Sacrament of Penance; second, by sketching the historical relationship between theories of Jesus' atonement for our sins and thinking about criminal justice; and third, by making a substantive argument that restorative justice preserves more of the values the Catholic tradition aims at than our present retributive system.

Although it is possible in Aquinas's context to distinguish between a *sin* and a *crime*, they are generally intimately related in practice. Natural Law is the source of moral obligation, and human laws must be in conformity with Natural Law in order to be morally binding. I will restrict myself here to human (criminal) law violations which are also against the Natural Law.

The human will is subject to three orders: a person's own reason, legitimate spiritual or temporal authority, and the universal order of the divine government. Thus a transgression deserves a three-fold punishment: remorse of conscience, humanly-inflicted punishment, and punishment inflicted by God (ST, I–II, q. 87, art. 1). Divine and human punishment are parallel. In both cases, the offender must pay some sort of "penal compensation" to restore "the equality of justice." "[A]ccording to the order of Divine justice, he who has been too indulgent to his will, by transgressing God's commandments, suffers, either willingly or unwillingly, something contrary to what he would wish. This restoration of the equality of justice by penal compensation is also to be observed in injuries done to one's fellow men" (ST I–II, q. 87, art 6).

For punishment to "avail for satisfaction" (pay the debt, remove the stain), the sinner must either willingly take on the punishment of past sin or bear patiently the punishment God inflicts. "Now when punishment is satisfactory, it loses somewhat of the nature of punishment; for the nature of punishment is to be against the will; and although satisfactory punishment, absolutely speaking, is against the will, nevertheless in this particular case and for this particular purpose, it is voluntary."[12]

The distinction between punishment being against the will (coercively imposed) and punishment being voluntarily assumed comes to the fore in the contrast between what Aquinas calls "vindictive justice" and the atonement aspect of the sacrament of Penance. In vindictive justice a judge decides how atonement is made, and not the offender or the persons offended (victims); in the sacrament of Penance the offender chooses to atone. "[T]he offense is atoned according to the will of the sinner, and the judgment of God against Whom the sin was committed, because in the latter case we seek not only the restoration of the equality of justice, as in vindictive justice, but also and still more the reconciliation of friendship, which is accomplished by the offender making atonement according to the will of the person offended" (III, q. 90, art. 2).[13] I suggest that *this is a restorative process which parallels victim-offender mediation, with the willing participation of both parties.*

Thus we see that for Aquinas commutative justice has two parts: compensation (offender making some kind of satisfaction) and retribution (punishment on the part of the one offended against) (III, q. 85, art. 3). Commutation occurs "when, on account of an offense committed against another, a man is either punished against his will, which pertains to vindictive justice, or makes amends of his own accord, which belongs to penance, which regards the person of the sinner, just as vindictive justice regards the person of the judge" (Reply.obj. 3).

It should be noted that even if a sin or a crime is forgiven, there are amends to be made. However, it may be the case that the sinner/offender is not able to compensate the one offended adequately, or to completely restore that order that has been violated. The paradigm example, of course, is the debt of our sins (against God), which we of ourselves cannot ever pay. Aquinas puts the question of whether one man can make satisfaction for another, and he gives a qualified answer: Satisfactory punishment has a twofold purpose, both paying the debt and preventing future sin. One person can pay the debt for the other but cannot accomplish the second purpose, "for the flesh of one man is not tamed by another's fast" (III, Supplement q. 13, art. 2). Christ's Passion is sufficient "to remove all debt of punishment" (III, q. 86, art. 4, reply obj. 3).

I believe we can draw these implications from Aquinas's discussions of sin, punishment, penance and satisfaction:

1. Because the sinner/criminal assumed a freedom s/he was not entitled to, the will she expressed in the sin must be corrected in order to restore a proper balance. Correction can come in one of two principal ways: by imposing something on the sinner against her will, or by a change from within, so that she herself wills to correct what she has done and make amends. The second is preferable, because it makes possible a reconciliation between

the sinner and the one sinned against; even the restoration of friendship between them.

2. Restoring of justice by penal compensation—willing or unwilling—applies when the one offended against is human, as well as when the sinner is dealing with God.

3. Willing penal compensation can be distinguished from punishment, which is by definition against the will of the one punished.

4. If atonement is made "according to the will of the person offended," on a human level this suggests a role for crime victims.

5. Thus there is space in Aquinas for key aspects of restorative justice: a direct relationship between offender and victim, in which the offender has the opportunity to accept responsibility, express remorse, and make amends, and in which the victim has the right to propose what is required to make satisfactory amends. The victim also has the opportunity to forgive the offender, but is not required to do so (as God forgives us freely, out of love).

But now, a wild card: satisfaction can be made for a guilty person by an innocent person. In the one paradigm case, it *must* be made for us by Another, because adequate satisfaction is beyond human capacity. This seems to fit best with a retributive model of justice: God requires expiation from *somebody* for sins against him.

The theory of Jesus atoning for our sins through his passion and death that I grew up with said, roughly, that since our sins offended an infinite Being, no amount of penitential suffering on our parts could atone for them. Atonement required the suffering and death of God's Son, who was equal to the one offended, but also one with us in sharing human nature. Hence the innocent suffered for the guilty, and we should be deeply grateful. Jesus, the sinless One, died for our sins!

This atonement theory, Timothy Goringe argues plausibly, began with Anselm.[14] In *Cur Deus Homo* Anselm speaks of sin as the frustration of God's purpose in creating human beings, or "failure to render God his due."[15] This view of sin, and of the consequences Anselm draws from it, make a kind of sense in the hierarchical social order of Anselm's time that they do not make today. In that society, social status determined the gravity of a crime as much as the substance of the crime itself.

> A blow exchanged between two peasants might call for nothing but a mutual pardon, but if directed by a peasant against the king would threaten the integrity of the whole social order and demand the death sentence. (Gorringe, 93)

By the same token, "even the most trivial offense against God demands an infinite satisfaction" (93). This satisfaction can be rendered only by someone who shares our human nature but who is also God, an infinite Being.

According to Anselm, in relation to both God and other humans, it is a necessary requirement of justice that either adequate punishment or adequate satisfaction follow all sin. Thus the only alternative to eternal punishment for all of us is Christ's sacrificial death. It is of central importance to note that the "punishment or satisfaction" alternative, and the scale of guilt based on the status of the one offended, were assumptions built into the criminal law of Anselm's time. Gorringe's thesis in *God's Just Vengeance* is that the theological account of how it is that Jesus' death was redemptive for us, and the theory of satisfaction for crime reflected in the criminal law, have been linked throughout the history of modern criminal law. They have exercised mutual influence, but perhaps the strongest direction of influence has been the law influencing theology. The retributive theory drawn from a society in which order depends on appropriate honor for each based on his (or her) place in the social hierarchy influenced and parallels a satisfaction theory of redemption as order-restoring.

Many contemporary retributivists also appeal to the need to restore order, but they assume as a starting point essentially equal persons. "Balance" and "unfair advantage" don't work very well here. For one thing, it is strange to think of some crimes as "taking unfair advantage" or not exercising the restraint that everyone else is exercising. There are some crimes that most people are not tempted to commit. Another problem is determining "proportion" between crime and its punishment, if it is not based on a hierarchy of persons offended against. Still it is the case, as Gorringe suggests, that Anselm's theology of the atonement has many adherents, and continues to support the penal theory that proportional retribution is necessary for a just response to crime. The balance in the society, damaged by the crime, must be restored by punishment. If God himself required the death of his Son in satisfaction for sin, then surely human justice cannot ask less of us mortals than our own atoning sacrifices.

We have seen that Aquinas follows Anselm in the vision that sin is essentially the disturbance of order, which order has to be restored. They differ, significantly, on the question of whether God can simply forgive sin without demanding satisfaction. For Anselm, this would not be fitting; for Aquinas, God *and* human victims are free to exercise mercy.[16] This allows for a higher way of responding to sin/crime than retributive punishment.

There have been competing interpretations of Jesus' atonement for a thousand years of the Church's history. Abelard's is a notable early one. In his *Commentary on Romans* he questions the necessity of Christ's sacrifice for atonement. His first objection is to the claim that shedding innocent blood could be necessary for *anything*:

> How cruel and wicked it seems that anyone should demand the blood of an innocent person as the price for anything, or that it should in any way please him that an innocent man should be slain—still less that God should consider the death of his Son so agreeable that by it he should be reconciled to the whole world![17]

Is it so obvious that God even demands the shedding of *guilty* blood? Or that God defines "guilt" the same way human societies do? Some contemporary discussions of the atonement give reason to question the sharp distinction we make between criminals and non-criminals, so sharp that we brand criminals and cast them out of our midst. Gorringe, following Rene Girard, suggests that this scapegoating of those who commit crime is a clear example of the violence with which humans define themselves by creating an enemy to oppose. The "enemy" may be innocent by all standards, like Jesus, or at least no more guilty in a real sense than the rest of us. James Alison is another theologian who finds Girard's theory of scapegoating persuasive.[18]

In this final section of the paper, I consider the conflict between our retributive practice and Catholic social justice teaching. Unfortunately, time limitations force me to be brief here.

At the outset I must concede that in theory, retributive justifications of punishing offenders support important social justice values. They take seriously the obligation to correct evils, so far as we can, within the limits set by the dignity of all persons, including the wrongdoers. The good of society is served by insisting on fundamental fairness. Most of us have accepted certain restraints on our behavior, for the good of all, and it is unfair for some to take advantage of our compliance by rejecting those restraints. If we cannot prevent this ahead of time (deterrence—a separate justification of punishment), we at least can correct it after the fact and restore the balance that has been violated.

Our response to the wrongdoer takes her seriously as a person (treats her with respect) if and only if it is directed to what she has freely decided to do, knowing that it is wrong and knowing the consequences. In other words, criminal wrongdoing has a responsibility component; crime-deserving-punishment is not just a matter of harm done.[19] Further, we respond to another person's choice only if our response is *proportional* to the crime. To sentence a person to twenty years in prison for the possession of one marijuana cigarette is seriously disproportionate and seriously disrespectful of that person's dignity and rights.[20]

John Finnis (and of course many others) would accept criminal punishment as authorized by Catholic tradition if it were addressed to the offender as a person with inherent dignity, responded in a proportionate and respectful way to her responsible choice to commit the crime, and served the common good. Much in our actual practice fails to meet these requirements. Mandatory minimum sentencing does not allow for respectful response to an individual offender and her degree of desert. Neither does treating juveniles as adults, or ignoring mental illness or mental retardation as relevant to desert. If offenders are to be treated justly, sentencing must be individualized to a significant degree. Judges must have discretion.

Statutory penalties may be proportionate in the sense that the worst crimes get the most severe penalties. That begs the question of what the upper and the lower limits of the punishment scale should be—what we might call "absolute desert" rather than relative desert. This is what Goringe calls "the surd in all retributive thinking: . . . the idea of commensurability between retributory sufferings and the evil for which the offender is held responsible" (99). Finnis's formulation does not seem to provide any help here: the severity of the offense, which is supposed to be the basis for the scale of punishment, is "the extent of the offender's manifested self-preference in disregard of the path marked out by law which others constrain themselves to follow" (*Aquinas*, 214). It may be in recognition of this difficulty that

Finnis says in the "Retribution" article: "There is no 'natural' measure of punishment, that is to say, no rationally determinable and uniquely appropriate penalty to fit the crime" (12).

Even if the theoretical problem of a just scale of penalties could be solved, an empirical issue would remain, based on all of the sufferings and deprivations following from a criminal conviction. The legislature could never morally approve physical abuse and rape of prisoners; abandoning psychotic individuals to be tortured by their demons; denial of care for diseases that are expensive to treat,[21] confining prisoners hundreds or even thousands of miles from their families, discrimination in sentencing based on race or economic class. However, these unintended consequences are well known. Along with other effects that legislatures *have* approved, such as denial of educational benefits and food stamps, permanent loss of voting privileges, the permanent stigma of a criminal record which amounts practically to banishment from society, these additional penalties for crimes are disproportionate (wildly so, in some cases).[22]

What we are doing today is attempting to collect an abstract "debt" owed to "society" (also an abstraction), and neglecting actual victims and their needs. The offender pays a price, but no one really benefits. In the meantime, we have created a large class of permanently stigmatized and alienated people, whose humanity and possibilities of constructive change we refuse to recognize.

And then there are two very desirable goals which our retributive system does not even *aim* to accomplish: inducing offenders to take responsibility for what they have done (not just have responsibility assigned to them), and giving the victim of the crime a voice. After all, the offender has not just taken unfair advantage of society in the abstract. She has wronged and harmed *someone in particular*, and that is what she should become accountable for. For genuine and full restoration to be possible, the immediate parties to the crime must have an opportunity to engage each other as persons and to arrive at ways of making things as right as possible between them. Such an encounter can be transforming for both parties, and indeed for the entire community.

I believe, then, that our increasingly punitive system of criminal justice cannot be squared with Catholic principles of social justice. It fails to meet the requirements of respecting the dignity of criminal offenders; it approaches a strict liability system, in which the subjective moral requirements for responsibility (intention, knowledge, freedom) play no role; it fails to proportion punishment to offense. It also fails to meet the legitimate needs of crime victims. I believe that the excesses I have described are not accidental, but are the predictable outcomes of the practical logic of retribution. Theoretically, a retributive justification for punishment respects limits, but in practice it does not.

The rights and dignity of all humans, offenders and victims included, is at the heart of the bishops' plea for a restorative approach. We need to take them seriously, not because of their authority but because we have examined their reasons.

Saint Joseph's University

Notes

1. U.S. Catholic Conference, "Responsibility, Rehabilitation and Restoration: a Catholic Perspective on Crime and Criminal Justice," November 15, 2000. The social justice principles they discuss concern: Human dignity (all persons); Human rights/responsibilities; Family, community and participation; Common good; Option for the poor and vulnerable; Subsidiarity and solidarity (21–25). I believe the bishops are right in their criticisms of the present system, but to develop and ground these criticisms would require another—longer—paper.

2. As Gerald Bradley maintains, "Sentencing patterns in America outside the juvenile system are no longer much influenced by a rehabilitative theory of punishment. The federal sentencing guidelines reject rehabilitation as an end or goal of punishment. Being 'tough on crime,' which is to say, being very tough in sentencing convicted criminals, is now the common aim of both major political parties. This seismic swing in moral aspirations and in policy decisions is reflected in the staggering number of inmates in our prisons." "Retribution and the Secondary Aims of Punishment," *The American Journal of Jurisprudence* 44 (1999).

3. The bishops cite the imprisonment rate in 1998 as 668 per 100,000 population, six to twelve times higher than in other western countries (8). The rate has risen since then. The most recent statistics show that it was 726 per 100,000 in mid-2004. "Briefing Sheet: New Incarceration Figures," The Sentencing Project, 2005. sentencingproject.org.

4. These are discussed in detail in *Invisible Punishment*, ed. Marc Mauer and Meda Chesney-Lind (New York: the New Press, 2002).

5. *Aquinas*, (New York: Oxford University Press, 1998), especially 210–215. See also Finnis, "Retribution: Punishment's Formative Aim," *American Journal of Jurisprudence* 44 (1999).

6. For a useful discussion of the essentials of punishment, see Lode Wolgrave, "Has Restorative Justice Appropriately Responded to Retribution Theory and Impulses?" in *Critical Issues in Restorative Justice,* ed. Howard Zehr and Barbara Toews (Monsey, N.Y.: Criminal Justice Press, 2004). He maintains that an essential element in punishment is the intention to inflict deprivation (48).

7. *Aquinas*, 210.

8. *Aquinas*, 212. Cf. *Summa Theologiae* II–II q. 108, art.4, "by means of punishment the equality of justice is restored, insofar as he who by sinning has exceeded in following his own will suffers something that is contrary to his will."

9. *Aquinas*, 214.

10. "Retribution: Punishment's Formative Aim," 11.

11. How crime is defined—offense against the state through lawbreaking vs. offense against particular victims through inflicting unjustified harm—is included here implicitly.

12. See also ST III, Suppl. q. 15, art. 2.

13. Further gloss on voluntary atonement comes with a remark on "satisfaction." Satisfaction requires a "penal" work—i.e., some kind of deprivation of the sinner. In general, the more difficult, the more satisfying. However, if the work becomes easier because of the charity with which it is done, that "does not lessen the efficacy of satisfaction, but increases it" (III, Suppl. q. 15, art. 1, reply obj. 2).

14. *God's Just Vengeance* (Cambridge University Press, 1996).

15. I.I, cited by Gorringe, 92.

16. "The man who waives satisfaction and forgives an offence done to himself acts mercifully, not unjustly." "Done to himself" is key here; a judge is not free to dismiss a crime without punishment. Aquinas, ST, cited by Gorringe, 119.

17. Cited by Gorringe, 109. The second objection, apparently, is that Anselm's notion of satisfaction compromises God's freedom.

18. See especially Alison's *The Joy of Being Wrong: Original Sin Through Easter Eyes* (New York: Crossroad, 1998), and *Raising Abel* (New York: Crossroad, 1996).

19. In Jeffrie Murphy's words, we have a "choosing system" rather than a strict liability system. Jeffrie Murphy and Jules Coleman, *The Philosophy of Law: an Introduction to Jurisprudence* (Totowa, N.J.: Rowman and Allanheld, 1984).

20. California's "Three Strikes" laws have resulted in a man who stole several videotapes to give his children receiving a sentence of life without parole. His first two "strikes," also nonviolent crimes, occurred years earlier. The U.S. Supreme Court upheld a state's right to deter crime with such laws in *Lockyer v. Andrade* (2003).

21. There was a recent scandal in New Jersey about the failure to treat, or even to test for, hepatitis, which was rampant in the system. Mark Fazlollah and Jennifer Lin, "N.J. Prisons Fail to Treat an Epidemic," *Philadelphia Inquirer* (July 21, 2002), A-1ff.

22. The fact that it takes 100 times as much powder cocaine as crack cocaine to trigger the same mandatory penalties is an infamous example—much criticized but still operative.

Strict Just War Theory and Conditional Pacifism

Emily Crookston

Abstract: With regard to the morality of war, political philosophers have defended one of two basic positions, just war theory or absolute pacifism, but between these two opposing views are various moderate positions. Throughout its long history, the Catholic Church has taken various stances, some strong and others more moderate, on the question of war. Unfortunately, the most recent formulation of the Church's position is a moderate position without clear guidelines. In this paper I argue that if one wishes to maintain that war is permissible in certain circumstances, it is important to have a position which rules out certain other types of wars as wrong in principle. Neither conditional pacifism nor the modern formulation of just war theory provides such a principled position; instead, the most plausible attempt to place the appropriate limits on war ought to begin from traditional just war theory. This view, which I refer to as strict just war theory, emphasizes particular aspects of traditional just war theory.

Introduction

J ust war theory and pacifism are often understood as two irreconcilable positions concerning the morality of war, but in fact closer analysis of the principles motivating both shows that these positions are remarkably similar in at least one important respect. Perhaps the best place to begin examining these two antithetical positions and other moderate positions between the two is with the Catholic Church's stance on war. Throughout its long history, the Church has occupied various positions on the question of war but the underlying assumption has remained consistent: war is an evil consequence of the sinful state of mankind; and as such, warfare is an evil to be avoided whenever possible.[1] Nevertheless, the Church's official stance has been that war is justified or even obligatory when certain conditions have been met. The specification of such conditions constitutes just war theory. However, within the past few decades, the Church has moved away from a hardline just war theory toward a more central position. In recent years, the Church has accepted pacifism as a legitimate response to modern warfare; however, its pretended pacifism has most often taken a moderate form that attempts to temper the absolute pacifist position. Given that many Christian pacifists wish to avoid the dangers and impracticalities of denouncing violence entirely, they are often tempted to evaluate particular wars on a case-by-case basis. As a result, they risk creating arbitrary exceptions without appealing to solid principles. I argue that this case-by-case analysis is unnecessary and problematic making the so-called conditional pacifist position untenable. Just war theory offers a viable alternative to conditional pacifism. By appealing to the reasonableness of the just war approach in its classical form, first discussed by St. Augustine and more fully articulated by St. Thomas Aquinas, the pacifist may find principles upon which to argue for the permissibility of violence in cases of self-defense and for the defense of other innocents.

I have divided this paper into the following four sections. In section one I provide some brief historical background before presenting the traditional formulation of just war theory as articulated by Aquinas and point to general problems with the theory. In the second section I discuss pacifism concentrating especially upon the position known as Christian pacifism. In section three I argue that Aquinas's version of just war theory, which includes a presumption against war, offers a principled basis upon which to restrict the pacifist's fundamental prohibition against war. In the fourth section I conclude with a few remarks on the relevance of just war theory today.

I. Traditional Just War Theory

First, it is important to understand just war theory in the context of its original formulation. St. Augustine was the first to formulate a concept of justified war in his political writings and evaluation of Cicero's history of Greek and Roman wars.[2] Augustine gives two criteria for judging the justice of a war: war must only be fought for a just cause and by the proper authority.[3] Later, Aquinas elaborates upon Augustine's concept of just war adding a third condition: right intention. I focus upon these three criteria as the original form of the just war doctrine.[4] In the *Summa Theologiae* II–II, question forty, Aquinas addresses an important question debated by Christians at the time: Is it always a sin to wage war?[5] Understanding this question requires some brief historical background.

Many Christians prior to the rule of Constantine (306–337 A.D.) had been absolute pacifists. They were committed to nonviolence and were prepared to become martyrs for their faith. Augustine struggled to reconcile this commitment with the reality of the threat posed by the Vandals during the fifth century.[6] This group of barbarians had already attacked Rome and were preparing to invade Africa. There is little doubt that these violent circumstances influenced Augustine's writings on just war; still, I think it is fair to say that there is a clear presumption against war evident in the traces of the earlier pacifistic thinking that can also be seen in Augustine.

With Augustine's writings and the pacifism of earlier Christians in mind, Aquinas addresses the tension between the Christian ethic of love and the sinfulness of violence in war. Having presented arguments for the proposition that all war is sinful, Aquinas refutes the proposition by specifying three famous criteria for waging a just war. The first criterion of traditional just war theory is that a just war may only be waged by the proper authority. Referencing Augustine, Aquinas says that the natural law commands that the power to wage war should rest in the hands of those who have supreme authority.[7] Because Aquinas was especially concerned with "a fear of the injustice of chaos [and] the free rein [that] absence of political order gives to individuals to pursue their private selfish ends to the detriment of others,"[8] he emphasizes the obligation of the sovereign, as opposed to the individual, to maintain order and promote the common good. Appealing to an analogy to domestic affairs, Aquinas says that the ruler must protect his people from external attack and this grants him the right to use military force if necessary. Just as the sovereign may use violence in punishing criminals in order to provide for the safety of society and the common good, he may also use violence in defending the people against foreign attacks.[9] When the sovereign takes up the sword for the sake of justice he acts as an agent of divine justice and as such he is free from blame.

The second criterion for waging war is just cause. Aquinas states this condition rather simply; in fact, he offers only two sentences on the subject. A just cause requires that:

> those who are attacked are attacked because they deserve it on account of some wrong they have done. So Augustine, 'we usually describe a just war as one that avenges wrongs, that is, when a nation or state has to be punished either for refusing to make amends for outrages done by its subjects, or to restore what it has seized injuriously.[10]

Now a critic of traditional just war theory could argue that this statement implies that Augustine and Aquinas would support a state's going to war over something as trivial as territory or property in order to restore what has been "seized injuriously."[11] This would violate a supposed presumption against war. However, just war theorists have interpreted the presumption against war in two different ways: the American Catholic Bishops assert that just war theory contains a strong presumption against *the use of force* which may be violated only in extraordinary circumstances; by contrast, authors such as James Turner Johnson argue that moral reasoning about war ought to loosen the restriction upon violence slightly and begin from a broader presumption against *injustice*.[12] Taking the above quote out of context, it seems clear that Aquinas's notion of just cause cannot support the stronger presumption against violence, but upon closer examination we see that the presumption against force is consistent with the use of force in cases of rectifying injustice. Acts of violence considered in themselves, that is separate from their ends, are wrong. In this sense there is a general presumption against the use of force, but this is completely consistent with the use of violence in the service of just ends. Though the act of harm is wrong *per se*, that wrong is outweighed by the good that results from that act. Even so, it is clear that both Augustine and Aquinas do accept punitive wars as necessitated by the common good or even the good of the enemies themselves and this also challenges a purported presumption against war. Thus, we must examine whether punishment could ever be a just end of warfare.

The permission to wage war to punish wrongdoing is problematic. In purely defensive wars, the cause remains just and the means remain limited because defensive wars take the presumption against war seriously.[13] But when the discussion turns to punitive wars, questions concerning just cause become more grave. It is difficult, for example, to see how one polity gains the authority to punish another. Returning to Aquinas's analogy to domestic affairs, the sovereign has the authority to punish criminals as a means of defending the common good. Defense, in this context, involves not only taking the guilty criminals off the street, but also deterring potential criminals. This obligation extends to the international realm granting the leader the right to use violence as a means to national self-defense because defense from outside attack is a responsibility of leaders entrusted with the protection of the common good. However, the analogy breaks down when speaking about one state punishing another beyond merely preventive attack. The citizens of the offending nation do not become subjects of the defending state in virtue of their attack and so are not liable to the authority of that state in any way that would make them subject to something like the punishment of a criminal. Thus, I reject Aquinas's allowance of punitive war because the analogy to the right of the authority to punish criminals in order to protect the good of the community does not hold. Just war theory ought to focus upon defense rather than punishment.

In addition to proper authority and just cause which are common to the accounts of both Aquinas and Augustine, Aquinas adds a third criterion: right intention. Right intention, simply stated, is the requirement that those waging war "intend to promote the good and to avoid evil."[14] The intention to avoid evil is crucial to distinguishing right intention from just cause. Although a war may be waged by the proper authority for a just cause, the means by which that cause is achieved may reveal unjust intentions. According to Aquinas's criterion of just intention, just cause does not give the sovereign the unconditional authority to attain, by any means necessary, even the most justified objective. In fact, a just cause that is achieved by a perverse intention is invalid.[15] The criterion of right intention reinforces this point. Right intention requires that promotion of the common good steer every stage of planning, and steps be taken to avoid the death of innocents whenever possible. The Church fathers believed that 'war for the sake of peace' required rulers to accept the dictates of practical reason and prudence. Peace, as the proper objective, would then limit actions to defense of the common good. And once the objective has been achieved, the ruler must put an end to all war activity because continuing violent action beyond the achievement of peace will likely include the intentional killing of innocents. Aquinas clearly maintains that innocents must never be intentionally killed; this is an exceptionless constraint.[16] Any war being waged for the sake of peace must then exclude cruelty precisely because such a war is waged for the repression of evil.

Although just war theorists cite Aquinas as the authority on questions of warfare, his actual treatment of the issue is quite brief. He dedicates only one question to war in the *Summa Theologiae* and scarcely mentions warfare in his other works. Though Aquinas devotes just a few pages to the morality of war, the just war tradition based upon his texts is voluminous. That tradition extends over seven centuries; within the past fifty years, however, discussions of the morality of war have shifted away from traditional just war theory. Despite the modification of the Church's teachings about the morality of waging war, Church leaders have remained reluctant to condemn modern wars from either a just war perspective or that of unconditional pacifism. As a result of the ambiguity of the Church's recent teachings on war and the general indifference among Church leaders, many lay Christians adopt a moderate pacifist position. Let us turn now to this opposing view.

II. Pacifism

Pacifism takes several different forms. In what follows, I will first discuss the absolute pacifist position because it illustrates most clearly the contrast between pacifism and just war theory. I will later discuss Christian pacifism and its relationship to just war theory. Unlike just war theory and conditional pacifism, unconditional pacifism is based upon the premise that the use of deadly force, indeed the resort to violence in any form, is *ipso facto* wrong.

First, absolute pacifists react to the just war requirement for proper authority saying that the authority, rather than encouraging or using violent means, ought to encourage or use nonviolent means to achieve the same protective goals. Simply stated, the pacifist position is that "human beings, whether as private individuals or as agents of the public, are never justified in the use of killing force against other human beings."[17] Absolute pacifists reject just war theory because, they argue, it assumes the necessity of war and such acceptance of violence contributes to its increase in the world.

Along the same lines, absolute pacifists also condemn the just cause condition as opening the door for abuse. They argue that it is the focus upon just cause as the most important condition for the resort to war that has led to the most egregious harms. In recent history, the just cause criterion has been used (contrary to Aquinas's intention, I must add) to justify any means to attain one's strategic goal. For example, the United States used the just cause criterion to justify the dropping of atomic bombs upon Hiroshima and Nagasaki in order to bring an end to World War II. Thus, pacifists conclude that just cause is indistinguishable from the consequentialist notion that the ends justify the means. Pacifists deny consequentialism contending that no cause is sufficient to justify any form of violence, whether it be lethal or non-lethal.

In addition, absolute pacifists find Aquinas's acceptance of punitive wars especially tough to swallow. First, the sovereign authority of a particular nation does not have the authority to punish foreign attackers because he lacks the necessary impartiality needed to adjudicate disputes. Just as the private citizen lacks the authority to punish his attacker, a single nation lacks the authority to punish an aggressive nation. The pacifist's objection points to a genuine inconsistency in Aquinas's just war theory: vengeance in the case of individuals is always wrong, but nothing in the theory prevents vigilanteism in interactions between states. So pacifists reject Aquinas's notion of just cause.

Finally, absolute pacifists reject Aquinas's third contention: the notion that good intentions may excuse an action that is wrong *per se*. They argue that there is no way to kill someone lovingly. There is an inherent quality in the act of killing another human being that prevents that act from being good in any way.[18] This argument challenges Aquinas's assertion that wars may be fought for the sake of peace and that killing may be done with the proper intention in just wars. Indeed, it is difficult to understand the intent to kill as anything but the intent to harm another human being; at the most, one might say that the right intention, if it truly is peace, excuses the wrong intention, killing, but that does not nullify the wrong intention itself.

Now, let us turn to the specifically Christian pacifist position. Christian pacifists assert that war is "understood as rooted most deeply in our 'natural' (since the fall) sinful human impulses."[19] Notice that this notion does not significantly diverge from the just war theorist's position. On the just war theorist's view, "it is the value of a victim's life that justifies the use of killing force against a wrongdoer."[20] While the Christian pacifist focuses upon maintaining peace, the just war theorist focuses upon working for justice, but peace and justice are certainly not incompatible. In short, both Christian pacifists and just war theorists teach that peace is a gift from God and an important part of the natural order.[21] For instance, just war theorists argue that while it is clear that Jesus taught nonviolence and nonresistance whenever practical, these rules were taught as an ideal rather than a strict moral obligation. Thus, while Jesus encourages nonviolence whenever possible, in cases of extreme evil and especially when the sovereign is under the obligation to protect his people, resistance is permissible. The only requirement is to limit such violent resistance to ending the harmful action.

Others who take the early Christians to be offering more of a presumption against injustice than a presumption against war have interpreted the command to "turn the other cheek" as an act of defiance. Walter Wink suggests that the passage refers to a slap which is meant to insult the enemy, not necessarily to injure him. By turning one's cheek, the opponent is actually inviting the attacker to strike the first blow in an outright fist fight.[22] Therefore, by encouraging his disciples to "turn the other cheek" Jesus is encouraging true resistance but only after patiently accepting insult and finding oneself in a "final resort" situation. Wink's interpretation here is unusual, but he does find some support in the teachings of Augustine concerning Christ's preaching on the compatibility of Christianity and politics. In *Letter 138*, to Marcellinus, Augustine says that if we take seriously Christ's motivation in the *Sermon on the Mount* that good must overcome evil, then those who maintain patience and benevolence in their hearts still must resist evil for the common good. Christ's teachings, then, are not contrary to the virtues of a strong republic, but resistance must maintain its proper place in society. "Jesus, in short, abhors both passivity and violence. He articulates, out of the history of his own people's struggles, a way by which evil can be opposed without being mirrored," not by returning evil for evil but by opposing evil when it is appropriate. [23]

III. Strict Just War Theory

When viewing the two opposing positions comprehensively it becomes clear that the just war tradition excludes pacifism defined as absolute opposition to violence. So if one wishes to hold any moderate position, arguing that war is justified in certain situations, then one needs a position which rules out certain types of war as wrong in principle. Neither conditional pacifism, nor the modern formulation of just war theory provides such a principled position; instead, the most plausible attempt to place appropriate limits on the conduct of war ought to begin from traditional just war theory. Strict adherence to the principles of just war theory: proper authority, just cause, and right intention, avoid the pitfalls of conditional pacifism. Strict just war theory, emphasizes particular aspects of the traditional just war theory of Aquinas and Augustine: the presumption against war, the permissibility of violence in cases of self-defense, and the permissibility of violence in cases of the defense of other innocents.

Recognizing that both the just war theorist and the pacifist share significant moral principles, the strict just war theorist accepts these principles as the starting point for his position. First, both the pacifist and the just war theorist recognize the value of human life and the worthiness of peace. Thus, the disagreement between just war theorists and pacifists is not on a fundamental moral level but on a practical or empirical level.[24] The real difference between the two contrary positions is that whereas the absolute pacifist believes that in order to overcome sinful impulses all must strive to avoid violence, the just war theorist argues that it is precisely this sinful nature that necessitates the use of war as a means to bring about true peace. The strict just war theorist seeks to resolve this practical disagreement by reaffirming the presumption against war and taking the commitment to peace seriously. Strict just war theory, then, seeks the mean between absolute pacifism and the abuse of just war theory.

The first criterion of strict just war theory is the presumption against war. The commitment to this principle is central to the traditional theory insofar as Aquinas and Augustine upheld the doctrine of war for the sake of peace. Aquinas affirms his presumption against war in encountering the third objection to just warfare. The objection is that it seems that war is contrary to peace, but Aquinas replies that those who wage war intend peace.[25] Strict just war theory maintains that peace is an active notion, "which is realized most fully in the active neighborliness of willing cooperation in purposes which are both good in themselves and harmonious with the good purposes and enterprises of others."[26] Peace then requires an active commitment and continual striving for the betterment of the world. The just war tradition teaches that the suspension of peace is only justified if one's end includes the enhancement of peace.[27] The strict just war theorist is committed to this requirement as an unconditional specification. War, if it is to be just, must be fought in the service of peace, for the purpose of correcting the sinful nature of the enemy, and for the general good that is being threatened by evil. One cannot gain peace by evil and corruption, or if peace is gained through such means, then it is not a legitimate peace.

In addition to the presumption against war demonstrated by the commitment to peace, strict just war theory is also committed to the notion that limited violence is sometimes necessary as a means to defend one's own nation and other innocents. According to Augustine, God's divine law of love commands that one not kill or harm others for his own personal defense, but it also necessitates that Christians help those who are being attacked by malefactors.[28] Thus, according to the tradition, the commandment entails a duty to use force to aid others and this duty is especially binding for those holding supreme authority.[29] This is the main justification for defensive wars. Yet, just as with the "turn the other cheek" passage, insult is not enough to justify violence. The strict just war theorist understands the need for evaluation of the situation with the hope that war may be averted, but also with the commitment to defend the innocent by violent means if necessary.

With the above considerations in mind, let us turn to a more specific exposition of strict just war theory following Aquinas's three criteria for just war. First, on the issue of proper authority strict just war theory requires that those preparing to wage war have at least *solid probable cause* to believe that they are the proper authority.[30] This in turn will grant them the right to exercise power if the other two criteria are met. In situations of self-defense, the question of proper authority is easily answered. Whenever one nation is directly attacked by another nation, and the attack has not been provoked, the leader of the victimized nation presumably has the right to defend his people using the necessary force. The right to life is a fundamental natural right and because the sovereign has a duty to protect the rights of his people, he must defend his nation against aggression. Thus, Aquinas says, "if we are to hold to the course of reasonable living, we require, not only political prudence to promote the common good, but also military prudence, to repel the assaults of enemies."[31] Also, we can understand the right to national defense by appealing to an analogy to personal self-defense. An individual has the right to defend himself when he faces a direct attack because this is a circumstance where the state cannot protect that individual; in this case, self-defense is an act that maintains peace. Likewise, an individual state has the right to defend itself as a means to maintain peace in the international realm. This analogy also extends to the defense of other innocent lives. In the domestic realm, Good Samaritan laws exist in order to engender others to help victims overcome those who harm them unjustly; again such laws maintain peace. The same laws ought to hold in the international realm in order to preserve peace. Because there is no higher law among nations, it is especially important that stronger nations be obliged to help innocent, victimized nations or peoples.

In addition to proper authority, right reason dictates that the cause be just and that the war objectives aim at this cause and not other benefits that may result.[32] Nonetheless, the conditions for just war are difficult to apply to concrete situations. Consequently, the just cause criterion has been the most widely abused by leaders seeking to justify their decisions to enter into war. As a result of the distrust of leaders' ability to judge a war time situation objectively, recent just war theorists seek simply to limit such authority.[33] Aquinas was not blind to the problem of bias on moral issues. However, he did have a different solution than that advocated by most contemporary theorists. Aquinas insisted upon the well-ordering of one's passions in order to make true judgments, this is the virtue of prudence.[34] The ability to control one's passions in order to deliberate well in specifically political situations Aquinas calls political prudence. It is this virtue which ought to rule the soul of the leader and those who demonstrate this virtue are granted greater responsibility. By contrast, there has been an effort to reduce the responsibility granted to leaders by contemporary just war theory. Although the power to wage war ought to be regulated, current just war theory actually fosters an apathetic attitude about war rather than encouraging leaders to critically examine and justify their reasons for entering war. Instead, the response to worries about abuse has too often been the expansion of a list of criteria, which only fosters the search for new loopholes. Also, the enlargement of just war theory in such a way does little to clarify the theory and, in fact, threatens its underlying coherence. The addition of these further criteria address only one symptom of a greater problem facing just war theorists today; the real problem, an unwillingness on the part of leaders to adhere to the principles of just war theory, cannot be solved by amending the original just war theory. Thus, it is also important that just war theory emphasize that no single criterion trumps any other. All three criteria must be met before a war may be judged as just. If the end toward which a war aims is unjust, all actions committed in the service of this end are also unjust.

The third criterion, right intention, is equally important according to strict just war theory. Right intention means that those waging war are acting in accordance with the "objective criteria of just war."[35] Statesmen must always act with the genuine intention of attaining a greater peace. Pacifists deny that such a requirement can ever be met in states of war. They argue that it is not possible to kill another human being peacefully, but just war theory focuses upon the broader intentions of the proper authority as an instrument of justice. The killing of innocents is a consequence of war, but war itself is a consequence of the threat of a still greater evil. It is the responsibility of the authority to protect his people from this greater harm. However, the tendency toward abuse of power leads the pacifist to be most skeptical about right intention. If it is possible, say the pacifists, to wage war with the intention of attaining peace, then how could any vengeful war be justified? This is a valid criticism and punitive wars are more likely to be vengeful. Therefore, it is important that punitive wars never be acceptable for strict just war theory. Defensive wars must be limited to ending the harm by achieving certain war objectives. Hence, one may consistently hold true opposition to war while still maintaining that war is justified as a means of defense because aggression is a real possibility. By understanding war as an evil to be avoided but necessitated by uncontrollable circumstances, the just war tradition acts as an excellent restraint upon the evils of war.

IV. Conclusion

Justice with regard to war is the mean between the extremes of cowardice and rashness. Even in times of war one must remember that the natural state of mankind is a state of active peace. To that end, the just war tradition was never meant to be an apology or defense of war; rather, it teaches that wars are *"certainly unjustified" unless* certain conditions are met.[36] Thus, explaining such criteria and urging dialogue around the issue are the important tasks for just war theorists today. The just war theorist and the pacifist must meet on grounds of moral constraint in war situations. By emphasizing the presumption against war and accepting only defense as a legitimate use of force, the strict just war theorist appeals to the conditional pacifist's preference for nonviolence.

Strict just war theory neither falls to the negligence of inaction nor to the zealous vengeance of returning evil for evil. Discovering the justice of war depends upon a vigorous search for reasonable action; it is not a standard appeal to consequentialism nor to an absolute moral rule. Rather it is a healthy recognition that such serious matters deserve serious consideration and respect for the necessity of reason.

Washington University in St. Louis

Notes

1. St. Augustine, for example, often speaks of the evils of war; see, *City of God*, XIX, chap. 7.

2. Augustine's political writings include: *The City of God, Contra Faustum, On Free Choice*, and various letters and sermons.

3. *Contra Faustum* XXII, 75.

4. It is important to mention that more recent formulations of just war theory separated justifications for entering into war, *jus ad bellum* from limitations on conduct in the midst of combat, *jus in bello*. Aquinas himself did not make such a distinction. Also, development of Aquinas's theory by prominent Thomistic scholars has included more specific criteria (the current formulation contains somewhere between five and nine conditions), such as proportionality and last resort. But acceptance of such additional criteria as developing from the original three is somewhat controversial.

5. Aquinas, *Summa Theologiae* II–II, q. 40, art. 1.

6. Bernard Adeney, *Just War, Political Realism, and Faith*, 27–28.

7. Aquinas, *Summa Theologiae* II–II, q. 40, art. 1 (citing Augustine, *Contra Faustum* XXII, 75).

8. James T. Johnson, "Aquinas and Luther on War and Peace: Sovereign Authority and the Use of Armed Force."

9. Joseph Boyle, "Just War Doctrine and the Military Response to Terrorism." 158–159.

10. Aquinas, *Summa Theologiae* II–II. reply 2 to q. 40, art. 1.

11. It is precisely this worry that has caused modern just war theorists to reject the permissibility of punitive wars, but I shall say more about this later.

12. Gregory M. Reichberg, "Is There a 'Presumption Against War' in Aquinas's Ethics?" 337–338. Also, note that it is possible to reconcile these two positions by simply defining injustice as an "extraordinary circumstance" that allows rulers to override the presumption against the use of force, but it does seem problematic to include injustices such as petty disputes over property rights as extraordinary circumstances that justify the loss of innocent lives.

13. There will always be disputes about an authority's *true* motivations in going to war to defend another sovereign nation or people, but for purposes of this discussion let us assume that a purely defensive war is possible.

14. Aquinas, *Summa Theologiae* II–II. reply 3 to q. 40, art. 1.

15. Ibid.

16. Aquinas, *Summa Theologiae* II–II. q. 64, art. 6.

17. Richard Regan, : *Principles and Cases*, 4.

18. Theodore Koontz, "Christian Nonviolence: An Interpretation," 187.

19. Ibid., 180.

20. Regan, *Just War*, 6.

21. John Finnis, "The Ethics of War and Peace in the Catholic Natural Law Tradition." 34.

22. Wink, 104. Wink also writes that the Greek word used in the passage, *antistenai*, literally meaning to stand against, is a technical term for war used throughout the Old Testament. Anyone hearing this term in Jesus' time would have understood him to be talking about war.

23. Wink, 109.

24. Joseph Boyle, "Just War Thinking in Catholic Natural Law," 43.

25. Aquinas, *Summa Theologiae* II–II. q. 40, art. 1.

26. Finnis, 16.

27. Finnis, 17.

28. *Contra Faustum* XXII, 73–79.

29. Regan, 17.

30. Regan, 85.

31. Aquinas, *Summa Theologiae* II–II. q. 50, art. 4.

32. Regan, 85.

33. For example, the official declaration of modern just war theory articulated by the Catholic Bishops in 1983 specifies three additional criteria designed to clarify the issue of just cause: last resort, probability of success, and proportionality.

34. Gregory M. Reichberg, "Is There a 'Presumption Against War' in Aquinas's Ethics?" 361–362.

35. Regan, 84.

36. Finnis, 33.

Bibliography

Adeney, Bernard T. 1988. *Just War, Political Realism, and Faith*. Metuchen, N.J.: The American Theological Library Association and the Scarecrow Press, Inc.

Aquinas, St. Thomas. 1975. *Summa Contra Gentiles*. Vernon J. Bourke, trans. South Bend, Ind.: Notre Dame Press.

————. 1972. *Summa Theologiae*. Thomas R. Heath O.P., trans. Great Britain: Black Friars Publishing Co.

Augustine. 1958. *The City of God*. Trans. Gerald Walsh, S.J. et al. New York: Doubleday Publishing Group, Inc.

————. 1994. *Political Writings*. Michael Tkacz and Douglas Kries, trans. Ernest Fortin and Douglas Kries, eds. Indianapolis/Cambridge: Hackett Publishing Company, Inc.

Boyle, Joseph. 1996. "Just War Thinking in Catholic Natural Law" in *The Ethics of War and Peace: Religious and Secular Perspectives*, ed. Terry Nardin. Princeton: Princeton University Press.

————. "Just War Doctrine and the Military Response to Terrorism." 2003. *The Journal of Political Philosophy*. Vol. 11. No. 2. 153–170.

The Catechism of the Catholic Church. 1994. Rome: Libreria Editrice Vaticana.

Finnis, John. 1996. "The Ethics of War and Peace in the Catholic Natural Law Tradition," in *The Ethics of War and Peace: Religious and Secular Perspectives*, ed. Terry Nardin. Princeton: Princeton University Press.

Holmes, Robert. 1992. "Can War Be Morally Justified?: The Just War Theory," in *Just War Theory*, ed. Jean Bethke Elshtain. Washington Square, N.Y.: New York University Press.

Johnson, James Turner. 2003. "Aquinas and Luther on War and Peace: Sovereign Authority and the Use of Armed Force." *Journal of Religious Ethics, Inc*. Vol. 31. No. 1. 3–20.

Koontz, Theodore. 1996. "Christian Nonviolence: An Interpretation." *The Ethics of War and Peace: Religious and Secular Perspectives*, ed. Terry Nardin. Princeton: Princeton University Press.

Regan, Richard. 1996. *Just War: Principles and Cases*. Washington, D.C.: The Catholic University of America Press.

Reichberg, Gregory M. 2002. "Is There a Presumption Against War in Aquinas's Ethics?" *The Thomist*. Vol. 66. No. 3. 337–367.

Teichman, Jenny. 1986. *Pacifism and the Just War: A Study in Applied Philosophy*. Oxford: Basil Blackwell, Ltd.

U.S. Catholic Bishops' Pastoral Letter. 1992. "The Challenge of Peace: God's Promise and Our Response." *Just War Theory*, ec. Jean Bethke Elshtain. Washington Square, N.Y.: New York University Press.

Wink, Walter. 1996. "Beyond Just War and Pacifism," in *War and Its Discontents: Pacifism and Quietism in the Abrahamic Traditions*, ed. J. Patout Burns. Washington, D.C.: Georgetown University Press,

Aquinas's Naturalized Epistemology

Richard C. Taylor and Max Herrera

Abstract: Recently much interest has been shown in the notion of intelligible species in the thought of Thomas Aquinas. Intelligible species supposedly explain human knowing of the world and universals. However, in some cases, the historical context and the philosophical sources employed by Aquinas have been sorely neglected. As a result, new interpretations have been set forth which needlessly obscure an already controversial and perhaps even philosophically tenuous doctrine. Using a recent article by Houston Smit as an example of a novel and anachronistic modern interpretation of Aquinas's abstractionism, this paper shows that Aquinas follows the *intentional transference* of Averroes who proposes a genuine doctrine of abstraction of intelligibles from experienced sensible particulars. The paper also shows that Aquinas uses the doctrine of primary and secondary causality from the *Liber de causis* when he asserts that human abstractive powers function only insofar as they are a participation in Divine illumination.

A great deal of interest has been shown in recent years in the notion of intelligible species as the key element in the explanation of human knowing of the world and universals in the thought of Thomas Aquinas. However, in some cases the historical context and the philosophical sources employed by Aquinas have been neglected with the consequence that novel and anachronistic interpretations have been set forth needlessly obscuring a clear albeit controversial and even perhaps philosophically tenuous doctrine. Such neglect has been particularly evident in the case regarding remarks made concerning Aquinas's asserting that the human power of abstraction called agent intellect is a 'light' which carries out its function only thanks to participation in Divine illumination from God in Whom the perfect exemplars of all things properly exist. Using a recent article by Houston Smit as an example of a problematic modern interpretation of Aquinas, this paper shows that Aquinas follows Averroes in proposing a genuine doctrine of abstraction of intelligibles from experienced particulars of the world and also shows that Aquinas follows the doctrine of primary and secondary causality in the *Liber de causis* when he asserts that our abstractive powers function only insofar as they are a participation in Divine illumination.

In section one, we sketch Smit's position. In section two, we sketch Avicenna's position and Aquinas's rejection of it. In section three, we sketch Averroes's notion of *intentional transference* and Aquinas's acceptance of it. In section four, we highlight the Neoplatonic basis for primary and secondary causality in the *Liber de Causis* and Aquinas's acceptance of it. Section five concludes the paper.

I

In an article entitled "Aquinas's Abstractionism," Houston Smit presents a new reading of Aquinas's notion of abstraction.[1] According to Smit, Aquinas combines an Augustinian theory of internal illumination with an Aristotelian conceptual empiricism.[2] Smit contends that no formal likeness of a thing's nature is communicated via sense or imagination, and the reason is three-fold. First, sensation only receives sensible forms of the proper sensibles. That is to say, *species*, which are intentional forms, only communicate color, sound, flavor, odor, temperature, and moisture to the sense organs. Consequently, the sense organs are only informed by the external accidents of a thing; the sense organs are not informed concerning the nature of a thing. Second, the common sense generates the forms of the common sensibles by comparing the intentions of proper sensibles. In other words, the common sense generates the forms for the common sensibles: motion, rest, quantity, shape and size. Third, because neither the sense organs nor the internal senses can generate a formal likeness of substances, the formal likeness of a thing's substance is not present in the phantasm. Having established that the formal likeness of a thing's nature is not propagated from sensation to the phantasm, Smit concludes that Aquinas's notion of abstraction is "not one in which it [the agent intellect] separates an intelligible form received directly in sense cognition from the material conditions with which it is mixed."[3]

According to Smit, "the agent intellect illumines the phantasms insofar as it produces an ordering of phantasms which captures the proper accidents of a material thing."[4] Abstraction from a phantasm provides the intellect with the formality about what a thing has, a thing's accidents, but does not provide the formality of what a thing is. On Smit's reading, "Aquinas holds that to cognize a thing's nature is to form an intention which is a determinate likeness of that nature. . . . Cognizing the nature of a created thing consists in having spiritual light insofar as this light constitutes an intention, which is a likeness of the way in which that thing is an imperfect participating likeness in the divine being."[5] In other words, the agent intellect, which is the spiritual light, produces or generates the formal likeness of material things. Furthermore, the agent intellect is able to do so because "the agent intellect can make sensible forms actually intelligible only in virtue of its containing virtually, as a participating likeness in the divine light, cognition of the divine being which . . . itself eminently contains the natures of possible created things."[6] That is to say, the ability to produce these formal likensses is due the agent's participation in the Divine Intellect, which contains unabstracted intelligibles in act, the exemplars of all things. Specifically, the agent intellect has innate concepts of unity and truth.[7] "Only through the agent intellect's supplying of this general cognition of being and unity do we come to form intentions of material things which are formal likenesses of the natures of things."[8] However, applying the notion of unity and being to the *rationes* abstracted from accidents does not account for what a thing is, for there may be many things with those accidents. For example, a white shirt and a white skirt have many accidents in common, yet a skirt is not a shirt. What is lacking is a means for the agent intellect to constitute one formal likeness versus another formal likeness. Smit handles this problem by introducing the particular reason.

Particular reason, an internal sense organ in the brain, "makes it possible for the agent intellect to produce intelligible species by producing an ordering of phantasms. . . . The intentions in which the phantasms are ordered is . . . what the particular reason's sensing of a particular thing 'as existing in its common nature' consists in."[9] In other words, particular reason orders the phantasms as if the phantasms belonged to some common nature. However, as Smit contends, the common nature is not produced by the internal sense organs, nor does it come from sensation, so how does the particular reason order phantasms under a common nature? The agent intellect uses the particular reason to order the phantasms so that the agent intellect can produce the universal *rationes* "under which the particulars it compares are to be subsumed in understanding those particulars."[10] Yet this argument seems incoherent, for, if the universal *rationes* need to be produced from the ordering of the phantasms, how is it that the phantasms are being ordered unless the particular reason already has the universal *rationes* to order the phantasms? Consequently, the universal *rationes* must be held to pre-exist in general in the light of the agent intellect, in partial active potency. Thus, with these universal *rationes* existing in some sense in the agent intellect, Smit draws the conclusion that "a created intellect cognizes a thing's nature by participating, however faintly and imperfectly, in God's grasp of the way in which that thing participates in divine being."[11]

In this account the denial of the ability of the external senses and internal sense powers to apprehend the *rationes* of things in the world for a genuine intellectual abstraction in the formation of the intelligibles understood by intellect results ultimately in the positing of a transcendent source for intelligibles. Here Divine Intellect is participated by human intellect both for the activity and for the content of understood intelligibles. Such a view seems to be supported by many texts from Aquinas in which human intellect is said explicitly to have its efficacy only insofar as it participates in the Divine Intellect or the Divine Light.[12] In fact, however, the interpretation provided by Smit bears greater similarity to views of Avicenna rejected by Aquinas.

II

Like al-Farabi before him and Averroes after him, Avicenna held to the existence of the active power of human intellect as the transcendent and separately existing Agent Intellect shared by all human beings. According to the traditional account of the thought of Avicenna,[13] an account accepted by Aquinas,[14] the Agent Intel-lect is responsible for the emanation of the forms of all sublunar substances and also responsible for the emanation of the intelligible forms by which human beings know. On this understanding, Avicenna denies that external senses and internal sense powers, including the active power of imagination, provide the intelligible content for the activity of abstraction. Rather, in some fashion the activities of sense powers prepare the individual human intellect for the reception of intelligibles from the Agent Intellect where all intelligibles in act, which are the bases of things in the world, are ontologically located. Human apprehension of intelligibles here is not an abstraction of intelligible content from the intentions formed consequent upon the apprehension of sensible things. Rather, it involves a linking with the separate Agent Intellect. The reasons for this view are not found solely in the influence of the Plotinian doctrine of one transcendent and shared Intellect or Nous in the Arabic philosophical tradition. For Avicenna the very nature of intelligibles in act requires this sort of account.

In his *De Anima* Avicenna makes three key assertions concerning the onto-logical status of intelligibles.[15] First, the intelligibles, which are intelligible forms, exist *per se* and not through another as do accidents. Second, each intelligible form is unique both because it must be immaterial and because it must function as the foundation for the intersubjective discourse which universals make possible. Third, the ontological status of the intelligible forms requires that they be extrinsic to the individual human soul and intellect. Thus, individual human beings, who are sometimes understanding intelligibles and sometimes not, must turn to and link with the separate Agent Intellect to establish the connection termed 'emanation' consisting in human intellectual apprehension. According to Avicenna, nothing from the sensible world nor anything in the internal sense powers derived from the sensible world can be an object of intellection.[16] Thus, the objects of human intel-lection, universals, are the intelligibles in act: immaterial intelligible forms existing *per se* in a separated immaterial agent intellect.

It follows, according to Avicenna, that the human soul first knows in potency then in actuality.[17] However, going from a state of potentially knowing to actually knowing requires a cause that is actually knowing.[18] Here the agent intellect is eternally and actually knowing the intelligibles in act and, in order for the human intellect actually to know intelligibles in act, the agent intellect must communicate an emanation to our intellects in order to move us from potentially knowing to actually knowing. Study of intentions in the inner senses merely "prepares the soul for the emanation (*abstractio, mujarrad*) which pours forth (*emanet, yafīdu*) into [the soul] from the Agent Intellect."[19] This emanation is an intentional form that comes into the human soul and disposes it to conjoin with the Agent Intellect. When the human soul turns away from the agent intellect, the emanated inten-tional form ceases and so does the connection with the agent intellect needed for human understanding.[20]

In sum, for Avicenna the objects of intellection are the intelligibles in act, which subsist in the separate Agent Intellect, and abstraction is the pouring forth of an intentional form from a separate substance into the human material intellect. Via the form that is presented into the human intellect, the human intellect participates in the intellectual activity of the Agent Intellect, which is eternally apprehending the intelligibles in act in itself. Aquinas understood Avicenna's notion of abstraction as outlined above and rejected it.[21] His rejection of the Avicennian account also entails a rejection of the account of Smit, as will be seen in what follows.

For Aquinas, Avicenna's epistemology is problematic for a number of reasons. First, because there is no causal connection between the formal likeness of the natures of sensible things and the intellect's apprehension of those natures, one ends up with a form of epistemological occasionalism. That is to say, on the occasion that one has a phantasm, the agent intellect informs the human intellect so that a formal likeness of the intelligible in act—not derived directly from the phantasm—is present to the human intellect. Second, the objects of intellection for Avicenna, then, are not things in the world; rather, the objects of intellection are the intelligibles in act in the separate Agent Intellect. Third, the formal causes of knowing, consisting of both the power of the Agent Intellect and the intelligibles in act in it, are outside of the individual human knower.

By parity of reason, it would follow that, apart from Divine revelation, Aquinas rejects Divine illumination, for if one were to obtain the formal likenesses of natures by means of participation in the Divine Intellect, then the object of intellection would be an imperfect grasp of the ideas in the Divine Intellect. Moreover, there would be no causal connection between the sensible world and our knowledge of the sensible world. Thus, some of form of epistemological occasionalism would be required: on the occasion of a phantasm, God would need to inform us with the formal natures of things. Furthermore, if the formal likeness of natures exist in God and we are participating in God's knowing of the Divine Ideas, then the formal cause of intellection resides outside of the individual. Thus, for the very same reasons that Aquinas rejects Avicenna's epistemology, he must reject any similar understanding of Divine illumination, including Smit's. This is evident when Aquinas writes,

> If the agent intellect is a certain separate substance, it is evident that it is beyond the nature of human beings. However, the operation which human beings exercise solely by virtue of some supernatural substance, is a supernatural operation, as is performing miracles, prophesying and other things of this kind, which human beings carry out by Divine gift. Therefore, since man is able to understand intellectually only by the power of the agent intellect, if the agent intellect is some separate substance, it follows that intellectual understanding is not a natural operation of human beings. Thus, human beings would not have been able to be defined as intellectual or rational. In addition, nothing carries out an activity except through some power which is formally in itself. . . . Therefore, it is necessary that the principles in virtue of which these actions are attributed [to human beings], namely the possible intellect and the agent intellect, be certain powers existing formally in us.[22]

If the source of our knowledge is a separate substance (e.g., God or the agent intellect), then all knowing would be supernatural with the consequence that it would be a misnomer to call man a rational animal. Yet, man is a rational animal. Thus, it cannot be the case that the formal likenesses of natures come from God, nor is it the case that we can participate in God's act of knowing. Thus, apart from Divine revelation, Aquinas denies that knowing is due to Divine illumination properly so called.

Not only does Aquinas reject the notion of Divine illumination, he also rejects the notion that the agent intellect contains the formal likeness of natures. When the objection is made that the agent intellect cannot be in us because then the agent intellect would account for our ultimate perfection (and the beatific vision of God would not be our ultimate perfection),[23] Aquinas states that the agent intellect in and of itself cannot move the possible intellect from potentiality to actuality because the formal likenesses of the natures of things do not exist in the agent intellect.[24]

Only in a disembodied state is it appropriate that something other than the phantasm provide the formal likeness of natures because phantasms reside in a body, and so are not present to provide any formality to the agent intellect. As a matter of fact, Aquinas's statement is consonant with what he states in *Summa Theologiae*:

> Therefore the mode of understanding through turning to phantasms of bodies which are in corporeal organs befits the soul according to that mode of being by which it is united to the body. However, when it is separate from the body, there befits it another mode of understanding through turning to things which are simply intelligible, as [is the case] for other separate substances. Hence, the mode of understanding by turning to phantasms is natural to the soul, as is being united to the body; but to be separate from body is beyond the character of its nature and, likewise, to understand without turning to phantasms is beyond its nature.[25]

The human intellect is made to abstract formalities from phantasms in order for it to understand. Thus, if there is going to be understanding in a disembodied state, the formalities must come from an actually intelligible source because phantasms, which reside in a material organ, are not available in a disembodied state. Hence, in a disembodied stated, the formalities for understanding are provided by God who is actually intelligible.[26]

In sum, according to Smit's reading of Aquinas, the formal likenesses of the natures of things do not come from sensible things in the world. Yet for Aquinas, as indicated, in natural knowing the formal likenesses of natures do not come from separate substances (e.g., a separate Agent Intellect or God), nor do the formal likenesses of natures exist in the individual person's agent intellect. What have been overlooked in the formation of Smit's incongruent interpretation are two central historical sources for the two philosophical considerations required for the coherence of the doctrine of Aquinas. Those sources are the philosophical psychology of Averroes with its account of abstraction from sense experience and the metaphysics of the *Liber de causis* with its account of primary and secondary causality.

III

In his *Long Commentary on the De Anima of Aristotle* Averroes rejected the Avicennian account of a transcendent agent intellect as the sole source of knowledge of intelligibles. For Averroes, abstraction or conceptualization (*tasawwur bi-l-ʿaql, formare per intellectum*) is genuinely based on human perceptual experience for its content and does not rely on illuminative pouring forth or emanation of intelligible content from a transcendent entity. From the external senses and its own apprehension, the common sense forms images which are deposited in imagination. These images, causally grounded in the world, are said by Averroes to be the subject which is the basis for the truth of the intelligible which is formed by abstraction. The needed formation of an intention suitable for presentation to the separate Agent and Material Intellects for abstraction takes place when the particular image or intention formed in the internal sense powers is denuded of non-essential characteristics through the activity of the cogitative power and deposited in memory. This intention, still the intentional form of a particular existing in the human brain, is then presented before the separate Intellects for abstraction.[27] For Averroes, this involves the *intentional transference* of an apprehended image or intention from one mode of being into another, from being an individual intention which is intelligible in potency into being an intention intelligible in act received in the separate Material Intellect shared by all human beings.[28] In this way, the subject by which the intelligible in act is true consists of the image in the internal sense powers of the individual human knower who has derived the content from sensory experience of the world.[29] The subject in which the intelligible in act has its existence is the receptive Material Intellect. The role of the Agent Intellect in this account is solely to explain the way that intentions which are intelligible in potency come to be intelligible in act by its intentional light, making possible an intentional transfer. With its light it makes actual what was presented to it as potential, namely the intentions, and then it impresses these on the Material Intellect in the same act since these intentions now intelligible in act require a subject for their existence.[30]

For Averroes the intelligibles thus attained are understood as the intelligibles in act (*intelligibiles in actu, maʿqûlât bi-l-fiʿl*) which make human intersubjective discourse possible by being the common referents of language and thought. In this way the attainment of intellectual understanding of things of the world by way of their forms apprehended and abstracted takes place only when the Agent Intellect is joined to the dispositional intellect (*intellectus . . . in habitu*)[31] in us as "the final form belonging to us by means of which we extract and make intelligibles."[32] Since this abstraction takes place by our will and we display evidence of understanding, Averroes concludes that the Agent Intellect and the Material Intellect, although separate in substance and existence, must nevertheless be powers in our souls. Abstraction, then, takes place only by a conjoining with Agent Intellect; our knowing takes place only by a link to the Material Intellect by way of the individual person's providing experienced intentions for the process of abstraction. The Agent Intellect, then, must be understood to be "form for us" and "our final form" simply because that in virtue of which something carries out its proper activity is its form.[33]

This principle, that a thing's form is that in virtue of which it carries out its proper activity, is accepted by Aquinas who reverses the order and argues not that a separate Agent Intellect must somehow be in us as our form, but rather argues that this requires that the formal principles by which we are knowing, the agent and possible intellects, be existing *individually* in each human being.[34] The agent and possible intellects are not separately existing substances as Averroes held but rather two powers existing in the individual human soul making all our understanding possible.[35] Aquinas also accepts in principle Averroes' account of abstraction of intelligibles from particulars of experience from the beginning of his career in his *Commentary on the Sentences of Peter Lombard*:

> Similarly, when the intellect understands some quiddity, it is necessary that the likeness of its *ratio* in species come to be in it, although perhaps the mode of being for each is not the same. For the form existing in intellect or in sense is not the principle of knowing according to the mode of being it has in each, but according to the *ratio* in which it shares with the exterior thing.[36]

In the same work at Book 2, d.17, q.2, a.1, resp., Aquinas also asserts that, while sensible things have their own distinct natures and are potentially intelligible, the sensible species or images in the soul become intelligibles in act (*intelligibiles actu*) thanks to the abstractive intellectual light of the power of agent intellect and thanks to the receptive power of the possible intellect.[37] However, these intelligibles in act in the thought of Aquinas are not the ontologically separate intelligibles in act which come to exist in the separate Material Intellect on the account of Averroes or the intelligibles in act in the Agent Intellect on the account of Avicenna. Rather, intelligible species are multiplied in the plurality of individual human intellects for Aquinas. Thus, while the proper objects of intellectual understanding for Averroes as well as Avicenna are the ontologically separate intelligibles in act, for Aquinas the proper objects of knowing are the natures of things apprehended by individual knowers by means of representative intelligible species bearing the same *ratio* or intention in another mode of being.[38] This is what we have called *intentional transference* in Averroes above.

Still, on the issue of the power for abstraction, the invocation of the metaphors of participation and illumination by Aquinas to describe the relationship of the human agent intellect to the Divine Intellect requires careful explication consonant with his metaphysical teaching. He writes that human intellect is a participation in the perfect Divine intellectual power and that human 'light' of intellect, the agent intellect, is itself illuminated by the Divine so that it may perform its activity of abstraction.[39] However, this does not mean that the Divine Light must become form for us or must be ontologically the very actuality we employ in our activity of abstraction, for in that case there would be no natural principle of knowing in us and we would not be *per se* rational.[40] Yet, it cannot be denied that Aquinas repeatedly states that human knowing requires a participation in the Divine Light and yet holds that the formal power by which we know must be ontologically and naturally present in human beings. The proper explication of this doctrine lies in the notion of primary and secondary causality.

IV

The opening proposition of the *Liber de causis* provides a succinct statement of the principle of primary causality for Aquinas: "Every primary cause has greater influence on its effect than does a universal secondary cause."[41] According to Aquinas's understanding of primary and secondary causality, an understanding rooted in the doctrine expressed in this opening proposition of the Neoplatonic *Liber de causis*,[42] God is the primary cause of all beings and all their activities. As he puts it in his *De potentia*, "In any given thing, God acts insofar as any given thing requires his power in order to act."[43] For Aquinas, however, this does not rob things of their own natures, for if natural things were not able to act in their own right, then it would be teleologically worthless for them to have natural forms and natural powers.[44]

It is in light of this understanding of primary and secondary causality that Aquinas's "natural light" metaphors need to be conceived. God is the cause of the natural power of agent intellect in the individual, yet it is the agent intellect in the individual that acts, that is, that converts that which is potentially intelligible, the phantasm, to that which is actually intelligible, the intelligible species. Here the agent intellect is a secondary efficient cause of intellection acting by its own nature, while, nevertheless, God also is necessarily acting as the primary efficient cause of intellection. Thus, as with all other activities of created substances, God is present in every action of intellection. What is more, this consideration of primary and secondary efficient causality makes possible the explanation why Aquinas distinguishes between "natural light" and the "new light." Natural light refers to the abstractive power existing in human begins by secondary and primary causality, while "new light" refers to the notion of supernatural Divine illumination as is the case of prophesy in which God provides the formal content of intellection.[45]

V

Without sufficient consideration of the historical and philosophical context of the remarks of Aquinas, the meaning of the phraseology of participation and illumination as used by him can easily lead to the generation of novel problems and issues not found in his texts. When his discussions of abstraction and the role of Divine illumination are read in light of the doctrines and arguments of his sources translated from Arabic, in particular the accounts of Avicenna and Averroes and that found in the *Liber de causis*, it becomes evident that two notions, naturalistic abstraction and Divine illumination, are only seemingly contradictory in the account of Aquinas. Following Averroes, Aquinas held for intellectual understanding of the natures of things in the world to take place by the abstractive light of the agent intellect acting upon the phantasms or intentions in the inner senses causally grounded in experience of the world. Following the *Liber de causis*, he asserted the necessary dependence upon separately existing Divine light in the natural operations of abstraction in an application of the doctrine of primary and secondary causality. These historical sources help to highlight the proper meaning of the teaching of Aquinas. However, they do not solve the many problems implicit in his epistemology, not the least of which is just how the *rationes* or intentions represent, or are of, the natures of things in the world.[46]

Marquette University

Notes

This paper is one of the initial fruits of the "Aquinas and the Arabs" Project at Marquette University.

1. Smit, 2001.

2. Ibid., 102.

3. Ibid., 97 Those who hold to a form propagation theory would agree with Smit's assertion because as long as a formal likeness of a nature is contained in a bodily organ, the imagination, the form in the phantasm is sensible, not intelligible. Intelligible forms are of a higher ontological order because they do not have matter nor the concrete conditions of matter. Thus, one would never *draw* an intelligible form from a phantasm because the form in the phantasm is potentially intelligible, not actually intelligible.

4. Ibid., 105.

5. Ibid., 103.

6. Ibid., 105.

7. Ibid., 108.

8. Ibid., 112.

9. Ibid., 116.

10. Ibid., 117.

11. Ibid., 103.

12. The conclusion to Smit's article spells out his view: "According to St. Thomas, the intelligible forms that come to inform our intellects are not propagated to our souls through our senses. Indeed, they are not present in any sensible cognition. They are, rather, forms produced through our share in the divine spiritual light. This connatural light of our souls produces these forms, in and through particular reasoning, in a process which aims for the perfection, in *scientia*, of our natural potency to cognize. Moreover, it is capable of doing so only because all *scientia* preexists in it virtually and universally, in partial active potency. But, in order for our intellect thus to reduce itself from potency to act, this light, being dim, requires the phantasms provided by our sensible cognition. It requires phantasms, not because they already contain what we represent abstractly in concepts, but because, in supplying images of material things, phantasms provide enough information to permit the agent intellect to render distinct the content which pre-exists in its light in a 'general and confused way.' In

this way, Aquinas maintains that we derive our intelligible species from our sense cognition without holding that these species 'come in' from outside us in this cognition." Ibid. 118. The view of Aquinas is clear in the following sampling of texts: *Et sic necesse est dicere quod anima humana omnia cognoscat in rationibus aeternis, per quarum participationem omnia cognoscimus. Ipsum enim lumen intellectuale quod est in nobis, nihil est aliud quam quaedam participata similitudo luminis increati, in quo continentur rationes aeternae. ST* Ia q. 84 a.5, resp. *Dictum est enim supra quod illuminatio proprie est manifestatio veritatis, secundum quod habet ordinem ad deum, qui illuminat omnem intellectum. ST* Ia q. 109 a.3 resp. *Ad quartum dicendum, quod ipsum lumen intellectus agentis est quaedam irradiatio primae lucis; secundum quod dionysius dicit, quod omnes bonitates in creaturis participatae, sunt quidam radii divinae bonitatis; et ideo non oportet quod huic irradiationi aliud lumen superaddatur in his quae naturali rationi sunt subdita. In 2 Sent.,* d. 28 a. 5 ad 4.

13. The traditional view found, for example, in Davidson 1992, is criticized by both Dimitri Gutas and Dag Hasse who argue in favor of a form of abstraction in Avicenna. See Gutas 2001 and Hasse 2001.

14. *Similiter etiam ponunt, quod scientia in nobis non efficitur nisi ab agente separato; unde Avicenna ponit in VI de naturalibus, quod formae intelligibiles effluunt in mentem nostram ab intelligentia agente. De Veritate* q. 11. a.1 resp.

15. Avicenna, *Liber de Anima,* 5. 5, 146–147 *Aut dicemus quod ipsae formae intelligibles sunt res per se existentes, quarum unaquaeque est species et res per se existens, sed intellectus aliquando aspicit illas et aliquando avertitur ab illis, et postea convertitur ad illas, et est anima quasi speculum ipsae vero quasi res extrinsecae quae aliquando apparent in ea et aliquando non apparent. Et hoc fiat secundum comparationes quae sunt inter eas et animam; aut ex principo agente emanet in animam forma post formam secundum petitionem animae, a quo principio postea cum avertitur, cesset emanatio.* . . . *Avicenna's De Anima (Arabic Text),* 245–246. Our concern here is primarily with the Latin text read by Aquinas. There is no significant doctrinal differences between the Latin and Arabic in the passages cited in this paper, although there are textual differences and some omissions. For the latter differences, see the notes of Van Riet to the Latin text.

16. Avicenna, *Liber de Anima,* 5. 6, 146; *Avicenna's De Anima (Arabic Text),* 245.

17. Avicenna, *Liber de Anima,* 5. 5, 126–27; *Avicenna's De Anima (Arabic Text),* 234–235.

18. Ibid.

19. *[E]x consideratione eorum aptatur anima ut emanet in eam ab intelligentia agente abstractio.* Avicenna, *Liber de Anima,* 127; Avicenna, *Avicenna's De Anima (Arabic Text),* 235. The same notion is found in the Latin at 147 where *emanatio* correctly renders the Arabic *al-faid; Avicenna's De Anima (Arabic Text),* 246.

20. Avicenna, *Liber de Anima,* 5. 6, 147; *Avicenna's De Anima (Arabic Text),* 245–246.

21. ST. Ia q. 79. a.6. resp; Ia q. 84. a.4. resp.

22. *Adhuc. Si intellectus agens est quaedam substantia separata, manifestum est quod est supra naturam hominis. Operatio autem quam homo exercet sola virtute alicuius supernaturalis substantiae, est operatio supernaturalis: ut miracula facere et prophetare, et alia huiusmodi quae divino munere homines operantur. Cum igitur homo non possit intelligere nisi virtute intellectus agentis, si intellectus agens est quaedam substantia separata, sequetur quod intelligere non sit operatio naturalis homini. Et sic homo non poterit definiri per hoc quod est intellectivus aut rationalis.*

Praeterea. Nihil operatur nisi per aliquam virtutem quae formaliter in ipso est: unde Aristoteles, in II de anima, ostendit quod quo vivimus et sentimus, est forma et actus. Sed utraque actio, scilicet intellectus possibilis et intellectus agentis, convenit homini: homo enim abstrahit a phantasmatibus, et recipit mente intelligibilia in actu; non enim aliter in notitiam harum actionum venissemus nisi eas in nobis experiremur. Oportet igitur quod principia quibus attribuuntur hae actiones, scilicet intellectus possibilis et agens, sint virtutes quaedam in nobis formaliter existentes (Summa Contra Gentiles, 2, 76 nn.17–18).

23. Thomas Aquinas, *Quaestiones disputatae De anima* Q.1. a.5 obj. 9.

24. Ibid., Q.1, a.5 ad 9. *Ad nonum dicendum quod intellectus agens non sufficit per se ad reducendum intellectum possibilem perfecte in actum, cum non sint in eo determinatae rationes omnium rerum, ut dictum est. Et ideo requiritur ad ultimam perfectionem intellectus possibilis quod uniatur aliqualiter illi agenti in quo sunt rationes omnium rerum, scilicet deo.* Ultimate perfection of human intellect in the post mortem beatific vision does involve a joining with God Who does not recreate human intellect but rather enhances natural intellectual powers to make it possible for the blessed to see Him 'face to face.' See *In 2 Sent*, d.17, q.1, a.1, resp.

25. *ST* 1a, q.89, a.1, resp.

26. Like Averroes whose teachings are dicussed below, Aquinas affirms that the formality for understanding comes via the phantasm. Averroes does not have to give an account as to what provides the formality to the intellect when one is in a disembodied state because for Averroes, the soul is not immortal. However, for Aquinas, the soul is immortal; thus, Aquinas must come up with some other manner for providing the formality to the intellect.

27. For an account of this process, see Taylor 2000.

28. *Et fuit necesse attribuere has duas actiones anime in nobis, scilicet recipere intellectum et facere eum, quamvis agens et recipiens sint substantie eterne, propter hoc quia hee due actions reducte sunt ad nostram voluntatem, scilicet abstrahere intellecta et intelligere ea. Abstrahere enim nichil est aliud quam facere intentiones ymaginatas intellectas in actu postquam erant in potentia; intelligere autem nichil aliud est quam recipere has intentiones. Cum enim invenimus idem transferri in suo esse de ordine in ordinem, scilicet intentiones ymaginatas, diximus quod necesse est ut hoc sit a causa agenti et recipienti. Recipiens igitur est materialis, et agens est efficiens* (Averroes, 439). "It was necessary to ascribe these two activities to the soul in us, namely, to receive the intelligible and to make it, although the agent and the recipient are eternal substances, on account of the fact that these two activities are reduced to our will, namely, to abstract intelligibles and to understand them. For to abstract is nothing other than to make imagined intentions intelligible in act after they were [intelligible] in potency. But to understand is nothing other than to receive these intentions. For when we found the same thing, namely, the imagined intentions, is *transferred in its being from one order into another*, we said that this must be from an agent cause and a recipient cause. The recipient, however, is the material [intellect] and the agent is [the intellect] which brings [this] about." All translations are ours unless otherwise indicated. Emphasis added. We call this doctrine of abstraction *intentional transference*. Averroes surely is drawing on al-Fârâbî's *Letter on the Intellect*: "But when they become intelligibles in actuality, then their existence, insofar as they are intelligibles in actuality, is not the same as their existence insofar as they are forms in matters. And their existence in themselves [as forms in matters] is not the same as their existence insofar are they are intelligibles in actuality" (Al-Farabi 1983, 16; English by Hyman, 216).

29. "Conceptualizing, as Aristotle says, is just as apprehending by sense. But apprehending by sense is something which is actualized through two subjects, one the subject in virtue of which the sense is true (this is the thing sensed outside the soul) and the other the subject in virtue of which the sense is an existing form (this is the first actuality of the sense organ). Hence, the intelligibles in act must also have two subjects, one the subject in virtue of which they are true, namely, the forms which are true images, and the other that in virtue of which the intelligibles are among the beings in the world, and this latter is the material intellect" (Averroes, 400). Cf. Taylor 2000.

30. [E]t respectus formarum materialium ipsum est respectus coloris ad diaffonum. Quemadmodum enim lux est perfectio diaffoni, sic intellectus agens est perfectio materialis. Et quemadmodum diaffonum non movetur a colore neque recipit eum nisi quando lucet, ita iste intellectus non recipit intellecta que sunt hic nisi secundum quod perficitur per illum intellectum et illuminatur per ipsum. Et quemadmodum lux facit colorem in potentia esse in actu ita quod possit movere diaffonum, ita intellectus agens facit intentiones in potentia intellectas in actu ita quod recipit eas intellectus materialis. Secundum hoc igitur est intelligendum de intellectu materiali et agenti (Averroes 410–411). "[T]he relation of the material forms [411] to [the material intellect] is [the same as] the relation of color to the transparent [medium]. For just as light is the actuality of the transparent [medium], so the agent intellect is the actuality of the material [intellect]. Just as the transparent [medium] is not moved by color and does not receive it except when there is light, so too that intellect does not receive the intelligibles which are here except insofar as it is actualized through that [agent] intellect and illuminated by it. Just as light makes color in potency to be in act in such a way that it can move the transparent [medium], so the agent intellect makes the intentions in potency to be intelligible in act in such a way that the material intellect receives them. This, then, is how the material intellect and the agent [intellect] should be understood."

31. The dispositional intellect (intellectus in habitu / al-`aql bi-l-malakah) is the disposition in the individual soul consequent upon an intelligible having been understood. After understanding, the soul of the individual is now positively disposed with the intelligible in someway so as to enable rethinking of it and also use of it in further production of knowledge.

32. Averroes, 490.

33. "[I]t is necessary that a human being understand all the intelligibles through the intellect proper to him and that he carry out the activity proper to him in regard to all beings, just as he understands by his proper intellection all the beings through the dispositional intellect (intellectus in habitu), when it has been conjoined with forms of the imagination" (Averroes, 500).

34. Thomas Aquinas, Quaestiones disputatae De anima, Q.5 response: Oportet autem in unoquoque operante esse aliquod formale principium quo formaliter operetur. Non enim potest aliquid formaliter operari per id quod est secundum esse separatum ab ipso, set etsi id quod est separatum sit principium motiuum ad operandum, nichilominus oportet esse aliquod intrinsecum quo formaliter operetur, siue illud sit forma siue qualiscumque impressio. Oportet igitur esse in nobis aliquod principium formale quo recipiamus intelligibilia et aliud quo abstrahamus ea. "However, in any given thing acting, there must be some formal principle by which it formally acts. For something cannot formally act in virtue of what is separate in being from it. Even if what is separate is a moving principle for acting, still there must be something intrinsic by which it formally acts, whether that [principle] be a form or some sort of impression. Therefore there must be in us some formal principle by which we receive intelligibles and another by

which we abstract them." For a valuable account of the role of the work of Averroes in the development of thought of Aquinas on intellect, see Wéber 1978 and Wéber 1995.

35. *Similiter dico quod se habet res sensibilis ad animam intellectivam: res enim sensibilis est potentia intelligibilis, et actu naturam distinctam habens: in anima vero est actu lumen intellectuale; sed determinatio cognitionis respectu hujus vel illius naturae est in potentia; sicut pupilla est in potentia respectu hujus vel illius coloris; et ideo anima virtutem habet per quam facit species sensibiles esse intelligibiles actu, quae est intellectus agens; et habet virtutem per quam est in potentia, ut efficiatur in actu determinatae cognitionis a specie rei sensibilis, factae intelligibilis actu: et haec virtus vel potentia dicitur intellectus possibilis: et harum duarum virtutum operationes sequitur omne nostrum intelligere, tam principiorum, quam conclusionum; unde apparet falsum esse quod quidam dicunt, habitum principiorum esse intellectum agentem. In 2 Sent,* d. 17, q. 2, a. 1, resp.

36. [E]*t similiter ad hoc quod intellectus intelligat aliquam quidditatem, oportet quod in eo fiat similitudo ejusdem rationis secundum speciem, quamvis forte non sit idem modus essendi utrobique. Non enim forma existens in intellectu vel sensu, est principium cognitionis secundum modum essendi quem habet utrobique, sed secundum rationem in qua communicat cum re exteriori. In 4 Sent,* d.49, q.2, a.1, Resp. *http://www.corpusthomisticum.org/snp40492. html* (Textum Parmae 1858 editum ac automato translatum a Roberto Busa SJ in taenias magneticas denuo recognovit Enrique Alarcón atque instruxit.) Aquinas surely has in mind the text of Averroes cited in note 28 above.

37. *Similiter dico quod se habet res sensibilis ad animam intellectivam: res enim sensibilis est potentia intelligibilis, et actu naturam distinctam habens: in anima vero est actu lumen intellectuale; sed determinatio cognitionis respectu hujus vel illius naturae est in potentia; sicut pupilla est in potentia respectu hujus vel illius coloris; et ideo anima virtutem habet per quam facit species sensibiles esse intelligibiles actu, quae est intellectus agens; et habet virtutem per quam est in potentia, ut efficiatur in actu determinatae cognitionis a specie rei sensibilis, factae intelligibilis actu: et haec virtus vel potentia dicitur intellectus possibilis: et harum duarum virtutum operationes sequitur omne nostrum intelligere, tam principiorum, quam conclusionum; unde apparet falsum esse quod quidam dicunt, habitum principiorum esse intellectum agentem. In 2 Sent,* d.17, q.2, a.1, resp., p.428.

38. Thomas Aquinas, *Quaestiones disputatae De anima,* Q.5, A.3, ad 7: *Ad septimum dicendum quod licet species intelligibilis qua intellectus formaliter intelligit sit in intellectu possibili istius uel illius hominis, ex quo intellectus possibiles sunt plures, id tamen quod intelligitur per huiusmodi species est unum, si consideremus habito respectu ad rem intellectam, quia uniuersale quod intelligitur ab utroque est idem in omnibus. Et quod per species multiplicatas in diuersis id quod est unum in omnibus possit intelligi, contingit ex immaterialitate specierum, que representant rem absque materialibus conditionibus indiuiduantibus, ex quibus una natura secundum speciem multiplicatur numero in diuersis.* "To the 7th objection it should be said that, although the intelligible species, by which the intellect formally understands, is in the possible intellect of this or that man, from which it follows that the possible intellects are many, nevertheless what is understood through species of this sort is one, if we consider it with respect to the thing understood, because the universal which is understood by each person is the same in all [human beings]. And that what is in all [human beings] can be understood through species multiplied in different [human beings], occurs because of the immateriality of the species which represent the thing without individuating material conditions on the basis of which a nature one in species is multiplied in number in different [human beings]."

39. *Aliorum vero opinio est, quod intellectus agens sit quaedam potentia animae rationalis; et hanc sustinendo, non potest rationabiliter poni, quod oporteat ad cognitionem veri, talis de quo loquimur, aliquod aliud lumen superinfundi: quia ad hoc verum intelligendum sufficit recipiens speciem intelligibilem, et faciens speciem esse intelligibilem in actu: et utrumque est per virtutem naturalem ipsius animae rationalis; nisi forte dicatur, quod intellectus agens insufficiens est ad hoc; et ita natura humana aliis imperfectior esset, quae non sibi sufficeret in naturalibus operationibus. Et ideo dicendum est, quod haec vera, sine omni lumine gratiae superaddito, per lumen naturale intellectus agentis cognosci possunt.* In 2 Sent d. 28 a. 5 resp.

40. [*N*]*on enim videtur probabile quod in anima rationali non sit principium aliquod quo naturalem operationem explere possit; quod sequitur, si ponatur unus intellectus agens, sive dicatur Deus, vel intelligentia.* In 4 Sent d. 17, q. 2, a.1, resp.

41. *Omnis causa primaria plus est influens super suum casuatum quam causa secunda universalis* (Pattin, 46). This is an adequate rendering of the Arabic version. For the Arabic, see Bardenhewer 1882, 58. Cf. Aquinas, *Super Librum de causis expositio*, 5–10.

42. This work, based on the thought of Proclus and Plotinus, was translated from Arabic into Latin in the twelfth century, probably by Gerard of Cremona. Aquinas was familiar with it throughout his entire career and wrote a detailed commentary on it toward the end of his life. See D'Ancona and Taylor 2003. The doctrine of primary and secondary causality in the *Liber de causis* is quite similar to that of al-Kindi in his short treatise, "Al-Kindi's Treatise on the One True Perfect Agent." See al-Kindî 1998.

43. *Deus in qualibet re operatur in quantum eius virtute quaelibet res indiget ad agendum.* . . . *De potentia* q.3, a.7, resp.

44. *De potentia* q.3, a.7, resp.

45. In his *Expositio super librum Boethii De Trinitate*, q. 1 a. 1, resp. Aquinas argues that no new addition of a new light is required for intellectual cognition by natural reason, although Divine activity is required. He makes his view particularly clear in his response to the seventh objection where he writes that the human "intellect cannot know any truth whatsoever without Divine motion, but it is able to do so without an infusion of new light, although [such is] not [the case for] things which exceed natural cognition." In his response to objection six, he writes that "God always causes the natural light in the soul, not differently for different people, but in the same way. For He is not only the cause of [the mind's] coming to be but also of the being of that [activity]. Therefore, in this way God continuously operates in the mind because He causes the natural light in it and He directs it; in this way the mind does not carry out its own activity without the activity of the first cause." Supernatural light involved in prophetic vision is mentioned at *In 3 Sent*, d.24. q.1, a.2, resp. Wéber (1998) credits Averroes for making evident the formal and efficient causality of the intelligible for Aquinas (256) and credits ps.Dionysius and the author of the *Liber de causis* for highlighting the issue of formal exemplar causality for Aquinas. (254). As we understand it, the *intentional transference* of the formality in the internal senses consequent upon sense perception is the cause of the formal content of the intelligible in act which comes to exist in the separate Material Intellect for Averroes. That formality in the internal senses (the subject and cause of truth) is that by which the intelligible in act exists in the Material Intellect (subject and cause of existence of the intelligible in act). For Averroes what is known is the intelligible in act in the Material Intellect. For Aquinas, to put it in Averroes's language, the cause of the truth of the *species intelligibilis* in the individual intellect is the formality in the internal senses, while the cause of the existence of the *species intelligibilis* is the respectively active and receptive intellectual powers called agent

intellect and possible intellect in each knowing human individual. What is known as object of knowledge for Averroes is the intelligible in act existing in the separate Material Intellect; what is known as object of knowledge for Aquinas is the nature existing in the thing in the world. The issue of the ontological status of the intelligible in act for Averroes is clear and Aquinas rightly labels this view a form of Platonism. See *De unitate intellectus* 5.165–170, 312. However, Aquinas has his own difficulties accounting for the ontological status of the intelligible in the particular as the object of knowledge. But that is a topic beyond the limits of this paper. Regarding the influence of the thought of ps.Dionysius and that of the *Liber de causis*, we do not understand Aquinas himself to accept that the formality understood is given to the human intellect from a transcendent source, though these works may certainly have called his attention to the importance of the doctrine of *intentional transference* in Averroes.

46. We want to thank Lloyd Newton for his helpful comments. Unfortunately, due to page constraints we were unable to adequately elaborate on primary and secondary causality in this paper. We have, however, covered the issue in much detail in a paper that we presented May 2005 at Cornell University. The Cornell paper is now under revision for publication.

We also want to thank John W. Carlson for chairing the session and for calling to our attention that the term "intentional transferrence" may be misconstrued as a physical movement from one place to another. As we had previously stated, Aquinas obviates any misunderstanding by stating the following:

> Sed virtute intellectus agentis resultat quaedam similitudo in intellectu possibili ex conversione intellectus agentis supra phantasmata, quae quidem est repraesentativa eorum quorum sunt phantasmata, solum quantum ad naturam speciei. Et per hunc modum dicitur abstrahi species intelligibilis a phantasmatibus, *non quod aliqua eadem numero forma, quae prius fuit in phantasmatibus, postmodum fiat in intellectu possibili, ad modum quo corpus accipitur ab uno loco et transfertur ad alterum. Summa Theologiae* Ia q. 85 a.1 ad. 3. (Emphasis added)

We also want to thank Douglas Flippen for calling attention to a key text in Aquinas's account of primary and secondary causality. This is a text we had included in our Cornell paper:

> Quia actio eius quod movetur ab altero, est duplex, una quidem quam habet secundum propriam formam; alia autem quam habet secundum quod movetur ab alio. Sicut securis operatio secundum propriam formam est incisio, secundum autem quod movetur ab artifice, operatio eius est facere scamnum. Operatio igitur quae est alicuius rei secundum suam formam, est propria eius; nec pertinet ad moventem, nisi secundum quod utitur huiusmodi re ad suam operationem, sicut calefacere est propria operatio ignis; non autem fabri, nisi quatenus utitur igne ad calefaciendum ferrum. Sed illa operatio quae est rei solum secundum quod movetur ab alio, non est alia praeter operationem moventis ipsum, sicut facere scamnum non est seorsum operatio securis ab operatione artificis. Et ideo, ubicumque movens et motum habent diversas formas seu virtutes operativas, ibi oportet quod sit alia propria operatio moventis, et alia propria operatio moti, licet motum participet operationem moventis, et movens utatur operatione moti, et sic utrumque agit cum communione alterius. *Summa Theologiae* III q. 19 a.1 resp

Last but not least, we want to thank Stephen Dumont for his reminder that primary and secondary causality has to do with God giving existence to the creature. That is to say, God communicates the first act of existence, by which the creature exist, and a second act of existence, by which the creature operates.

Bibliography

al-Fârâbî, Abu Nasr. 1973. *Alfarabi. Risalah fi al-`aql*, ed. Maurice Bouyges, S.J. (Beyrouth: Dar el-Machreq Sarl, 19832). Partial English trans. Arthur Hyman in *Philosophy in the Middle Ages*, ed. Arthur Hyman and James J. Walsh. Indianapolis: Hackett Publishing Co., 215–221.

al-Kindî, Abu Ya`qub. 1958. *Rasâ'il al-Kindî fi al-fâ`il al-haqq al-awwal al-tamm.* . . . "Al-Kindî's Treatise on the One, True, Perfect Agent," *in Oeuvres Philosophiques et Scientifiques d'al-Kindî, v.2 Métaphysique et Cosmologie*, 167–171. Roshdi Rashed and Jean Jolivet, eds. Leiden: Brill, 1998. A French translation accompanies the Arabic text. An English translation can be found in Alexander Altmann and S. M. Stern, *Isaac Israeli. A Neoplatonic Philosopher of the Early Tenth Century*. Oxford: Oxford University Press. See pp.68–69.

Averroes. 1953. *Averrois Cordubensis Commentarium Magnum in Aristotelis De Anima Libros*, F. Stuart Crawford, ed. Cambridge: Mediaeval Academy of America.

Avicenna. 1959. *Avicenna's De Anima (Arabic Text)*, F. Rahman, ed. London: Oxford University Press.

———. 1968. *Liber de Anima seu Sextus de Naturalibus*, 2 v., ed. S. Van Riet. IV–V Louvain: Éditions orientalistes, Leiden: E. J. Brill, I–II–III Louvain: E. Peeters, Leiden: E. J. Brill.

———. 1977 and 1980. *Avicenna Latinus. Liber de Philosophia Prima sive Scientia Divina*, 2 v., ed. S. Van Riet. Louvain: E. Peeters, and Leiden: E. J. Brill.

Bardenhewer, Otto. 1882. *Die pseudo-aristotelische Schrift Ueber das reine Gute bekannt unter dem namen Liber de causis*. Freiburg im Breisgau: Herder'sche Verlagshandlung. Rpt. Minerva, Frankfurt/Main n.d.

D'Ancona, Cristina, and Richard C. Taylor. 2003. "Le *Liber de causis*" *Dictionnaire de Philosophes Antiques. Supplément*. Ed. Richard Goulet et alii. Paris: CNRS Edition, 599–647.

Davidson, Herbert A. 1992. *Alfarabi, Avicenna, and Averroes on Intellect*. Oxford: Oxford University Press.

Gutas, Dimitri, 2001. "Intuition and Thinking: The Evolving Structure of Avicenna's Epistemology," in *Aspects of Avicenna*, ed. Robert Wisnovsky. Princeton, N.J.: Markus Weiner, 1–38.

Hasse, Dag Nikolaus, 2001. "Avicenna on Abstraction," in *Aspects of Avicenna*, ed. Robert Wisnovsky. Princeton, N.J.: Markus Weiner, 39–72.

Pattin, Adriaan, O.M.I. 1966. "Le *Liber de causis*; éd. établie à l'aide de 90 manuscrits, avec introduction et notes," *Tijdschrift voor filosofie* 28: 90–203. Also published separately, Leiden, no date.

Smit, Houston. 2001. "Aquinas's Abstractionism." *Medieval Philosophy and Theology* 10: 85–118.

Taylor, Richard C. 2000. "*Cogitatio, Cogitativus* and *Cogitare*: Remarks on the Cogitative Power in Averroes," in *L'élaboration du vocabulaire philosophique au Moyen Age*, ed. Jacqueline Hamesse and Carlos Steel. Louvain-la-Neuve and Leuven: Peeters, 111–146.

Thomas Aquinas. 1882–.*Sancti Thomae de Aquino Opera omnia*, Leonine edition. Rome, vols. 4–12, Summa theologiae; vols. 13–15, Summa contra Gentiles; vols, 22.1, 22.2, 22.3, Quaestiones disputatae De veritate; vol. 24.1, Quaestiones disputatae De anima.

———. 1882. *Opera omnia.* Paris: Vives.

———. 1887. *Opera omnia.* Parma: Fiaccadori.

———. 1929. *Scriptum super libros Sententiarum.* Vol. 2, P. Mandonnet, ed. Paris: P. Lethielleux.

———. 1933. *Scriptum super libros Sententiarum.* Vol. 3, M. F. Moos, ed. Paris: P. Lethielleux.

———. 1953. *De potentia,* P. M. Pession, ed., in *Quaestiones disputatae,* vol. 2, Turin-Rome: Mareitti.

———. 1954. *Sancti Thomae de Aquino Super Librum de causis expositio,* H. D. Saffrey, ed. Fribourg: Société Philosophique & Louvain: Éditions E. Nauwelaerts. For an English translation see *Commentary on the Book of Causes.* 1996. St. Thomas Aquinas, trans. Vincent A. Guagliardo, Charles R. Hess, and Richard C. Taylor. Washington, D.C. : Catholic University of America Press.

Wéber, Ed. H. 1978. "Les apports positifs de la noétique d'Ibn Rushd a celle de Thomas D'Aquin," in *Multiple Averroes. Actes du Colloque International organisé a l'occasion du 850e aniversaire de la naissance d'Averroes. Paris 20–23 septembre 1976,* 211–248. Paris: Les Belle Lettres (Ouvrage publié avec le concours du CNRS).

———. 1995. "Les emprunts majeurs a Averroes chez Albert le Grand et dans son École," in *Averroismus im Mittelalter und in der Renaissance,* ed. Friedrich Niewöhner and Loris Sturlese. Zurich: Spur, 149–179.

———. 1998. "L'identité de l'intellect et de l'intelligible selon la version latine d'Averroes et son interprétation par Thomas d'Aquin," *Arabic Sciences and Philosophy* 8: 233–257.

How *a priori* Is Lonergan?

Samuel B. Condic

Abstract: The debate between the "Transcendental" and "Neo-" Thomists is an ongoing concern. Specifically, Jeremy Wilkins and John F.X. Knasas differ sharply over the correct interpretation of St. Thomas, Bernard Lonergan, and the very nature of cognition itself (ACPQ 78 [2004]). This debate is clouded, however, due to a lack of appreciation for key terms, specifically, "sensation" and Lonergan's own phrase "the notion of being." Using the distinction between precisive and non-precisive abstraction, the author clarifies the relevant sense of "sensation" and its related concepts. The clarification reveals that Wilkins and Knasas use such terms in markedly different, though compatible ways. Second, the notion of being as it is presented in various texts of Lonergan is examined. Contrary to what is supposed by Knasas, the notion of being, for Lonergan, contributes no formal or constitutive element to human knowing, and is in fact a pure potency with respect to intelligibility. Accordingly, any concerns or charges of crypto-Kantianism with respect to Lonergan are unfounded.

Introduction

Far from being monolithic, the twentieth- (now twenty-first-) century Thomistic revival has produced a series of heated debates, not just with philosophers from other traditions but even among those who identify themselves as Thomists. Indeed, one of the more spirited exchanges occurred just recently within the pages of the ACPQ; namely, the exchange between Jeremy Wilkins and John Knasas over Bernard Lonergan.[1] As a subset of the more general debate between the self-named "Transcendental" and "Neo-" Thomists, this exchange ranged across a wide array of interpretive, textual, and philosophical questions surrounding the issues of objectivity and knowledge. Included among the topics of discussion was the question of the *a priori*; specifically, what, if any, contribution does the intellect make to human knowledge. For Wilkins, the agent intellect is as a mediator which renders the intelligible contents of our consciousness as objective:

Again, intelligence in act and intelligible in act are an identity; direct understanding does not attain the other as other, but as intelligible. Only mediately, through the objectifying acts of conception and reflective judgment, does one come to know that sense and sensible, intelligence and intelligible, are distinct in potency, and thus can affirm that sensation attains to external bodies.[2]

Knasas takes issue with this view, insisting that if objectivity were attained through such a mediation, such "objectivity" would only be a report on our own subjective state and would therefore tell us nothing about the real status of the object in question:

In sum, Lonergan's approach to our knowledge of the actual existence of particular things is fundamentally an indirect one. . . . The decisive moment in it is a subjective one. We first take a look and then notice if that look quiets questioning. In the crucial moment of objective knowing, we are in a sense always 'flying by instruments.' We are not noticing something about the thing but something about our reaction to the thing.[3]

Later comments by Knasas make clear that any inference from our "reaction to the thing" to the thing itself is not and cannot be warranted. The conventional view of this debate is that one must choose between the Transcendental ("*a priori*") school and the Neo-Thomist ("*a posteriori*") one, that this debate is fundamental and no *tertia via* is available. But before one chooses or even agrees to the choice, a certain effort to clarify key terms within the debate is in order.

For example, Transcendental Thomists claim that Neo-Thomists are "naïve," since the latter hold that existence is apprehended directly through sense experience. For their part, Neo-Thomists assert that a mediation is essentially crypto-Kantianism, an attempt to smuggle in an *a priori* under Thomist garb. But it is not at all clear that both sides are using these terms in exactly the same way, and accordingly there is some confusion as to whether the objections, though valid, actually apply.

In this paper I would first like to more closely examine the phrase "sense experience" and other related terms. Both Knasas and Wilkins expend considerable energy respectively defending and attacking the so-called "ocular" or "confrontational" model of knowledge, and what exactly is present in or known through "sense experience" is central to that debate. While avoiding a re-enactment of their exchange as much a possible, getting clear of the confusion surrounding this term is central to a proper appreciation of Lonergan's thoughts regarding the notion of being.

Second, I would like examine the notion of being itself, and Lonergan's treatment of it, in greater detail. In brief, whereas a lack of clarity regarding sense experience creates difficulties for an exact interpretation of Knasas's position, a corresponding lack of clarity regarding the notion of being, at precisely the critical moment in his presentation, makes Wilkins's exact position difficult to discern as well. A more lengthy analysis of the notion of being is needed to clarify what I take Lonergan's position to be.

Sense Experience

At issue for Knasas is when and through what act do we achieve our first knowledge of existence, and this is central for two reasons. First, as to the matter of "when," Knasas thinks the Lonerganian method to be something of a "labored and contrived"[4] affair. Rather than having us turn inwardly and notice a "quieting of my interrogative reactions," as he characterizes Lonergan's method, Knasas would have us turn our attention instead to the direct and immediate presence of the really existing object in our sensation. The point seems to be that the sense data is manifestly real and concrete; one need only to quickly reflect upon any given sense experience to confirm that some real object is really present to you. In contrast, the Lonerganian method, under Knasas's view, denies this: the sense data is "mushy," and the status of any sense object is in doubt until a judgment of existence occurs. Rather than living in a world of basically real objects punctuated by an occasional illusion or misapprehension, Knasas takes Lonergan's view to be just the opposite: we live in a world of existentially dubious objects, punctuated by an occasional item judged with certainty to be real.

Second, there is the more critical question of "through what act" existence is known. As Knasas succinctly states it, "a necessity of thought, no matter how absolute, does not guarantee the realism of its object."[5] Or, I think we might fairly recast the remark slightly and say that a necessity of thought only guarantees the necessity of thought. The application of that necessity to something other than thought is not warranted, unless of course some "bridge" were to be found between the thought and the other object. Hence, even if we must *think* of the objects of sense as really existing, we are not thereby justified in supposing that they, in themselves, *really are* existing. Given this, Knasas argues that only the "seeing" of real existence *in the sensed object* would warrant the claim that the sensed object really exists.

In contrast, according to Knasas, Lonergan does not discover existence directly in the sense data, but indirectly through the "profiling" of the sense data against the intention of being; real existence is grasped, not in the object sensed, but in the *relation* between the object sensed and the intention of being. But this sort of existence is an existence in thought only; the object "looks" real, but only in relation to the innate intention of being, which is not in any way included in the sense data. Unanswered is the question of how the object would "look" apart from the mediating influence of the intention. And it is precisely this unencumbered "look" that Knasas holds Lonergan must—but cannot—do and that a direct realism achieves.

Therefore, as I read him, Knasas burdens any realism with two tasks. First, it must acknowledge and accommodate the fact that we live and function in a world of "immediate" rather than "suspended" or "deferred" realism; we do not live in a state of near-perpetual doubt relieved only occasionally and laboriously through acts of judgment. And second, any claim regarding the real existence of some sensed object must be based on something apprehended *in* the sensed object. An appeal to anything *outside* the sensed object, including a mediating context, would require a justification for such an application *to* the sensed object, and this just is to require some sort of Cartesian "bridge."

In that neither of these requirements seems unreasonable,[6] the difficulty I find with Knasas's position stems from how we are to understand "sensation" as having met the challenge. And this is where a lack of precision regarding the term come in. At least since the time of Locke, the contents of an act of sensation have been construed more often than not to include *only* the proper object of the respective sense power. Locke talks of the "simple ideas" that come to us from the senses, and these "ideas" are not of "red *thing*" or "smooth *thing*," but rather simply of "red" and "smooth."[7] Simple ideas for Locke are merely sense impressions existing in the mind. Hume accepts the main line of Locke's interpretation and accordingly denies the reality of causality, e.g., because "causality" is not numbered among the proper sensibles. Kant in turn picks up where Hume leaves off and speaks of the "manifold of sensation" which is then later composed into *sensed objects* by the human intellect.[8] And finally, Lonergan himself defines sensible data as the "content of an act of seeing, hearing, touching, tasting, smelling,"[9] contents which are only *subsequently* unified together and understood as belonging to a "thing."[10] There is, then, a long history of limiting terms such as "sensation" and "sense experience" to the proper sensibles. Furthermore, this sort of understanding of the contents of "sensation" seems to be much more narrow than Knasas's use of the term. For Knasas, the sense experience which grounds his immediate realism seems to have a conscious and reflective component; it contains not only the proper sensible, but a conscious awareness of same.[11]

The point here is not to champion one view of sensation over the other, but rather to acknowledge that the difference exists. Lonergan (and Wilkins) seem to follow the more narrow meaning of "sensation" and consequently place any reflective consideration outside of the act of sensation. Such a position does not *deny* that we *know* the sensed object to be real, or that we grasp existence *in* what is sensed; rather, it merely highlights the fact that knowing or grasping existence is an intellectual, rather than sensory act, strictly understood. This, I would suggest, is the source of Wilkins's befuddlement with regard to Knasas's position: our "original grasp of *esse*" cannot come through sensation because "grasping" is inherently an intellectual (cognitive) act and is as such outside of sensation. *Esse* is not a proper sensible.

Nor is such a consideration of sensation without an intellectual pedigree within Thomism. In the first place, as Wilkins points out, St. Thomas ascribes *knowledge* of the natures of sensible qualities to the intellect and not to the senses.[12] But further, the "narrow" view of sensation would seem to be a specific application of a more general Thomistic technique; namely abstraction with and without precision. As Knasas notes, St. Thomas uses this technique in the *De Ente* to distinguish the various senses of the term "body."[13] Abstracted without precision, "body" designates a nature possessing extension in three dimensions, but not to the exclusion of other perfections which the body may also have (e.g., being an animal, being rational). "Body" understood in this sense can admit of additional modifications and determinations. To use Knasas's phrase, this sort of abstraction "does not exclude what it does not include."

On the other hand, abstraction with precision renders a term designating some specific aspect of a thing, to the exclusion of all other modifications or determinations. "Animal" and "rational" are outside of "body" understood in this way, as something added to it. It is according to this way of understanding, for example, that man can be thought of as a composition of "soul" and "body": even though the soul is the form of the body, it can be understood as a "part" composed *with* the body when each term is understood precisely.[14]

And what is possible with "body" and "soul" is also possible with "sensation." One can construe "sensation" so as to only include the proper objects of sense, to the exclusion of all else. Given this understanding, such things as "being *aware* of sensation," or "*grasping* a unity-identity-whole" or "*perceiving* existence" or even "*knowing* an object" fall outside of "sensation." Such acts are viewed as subsequent to an act of sensation, are composed with it, and additional to it. And furthermore, just as conceiving of "body" and "soul" as parts via precisive abstraction does not require the denial of the fundamental unity of man nor does it imply that "body" in reality has some actuality apart from soul or form, so too the precisive understanding of sensation does not necessarily deny e.g., the derivative nature of intelligible content with respect to sensory content. In other words, a precisive understanding of sensation does not require one to assert that what we know and what we sense are *ontologically* separate.

The proposed application of precisive and non-precisive abstraction to sensation seems then to accurately mark out the different understanding of terms like "sensation." Knasas, operating with a fundamentally non-precisive understanding, can include such things as a "perception" of existence in the sense data because the sense data includes such intelligibility implicitly. Lonergan, and the moderns for that matter, precisively abstract the contents of sensation and hence place any such intellectual appreciation of the sense data outside of the sensitive act. Both methods of abstraction are legitimate, though each one renders a rather different "spin" on human cognition. But, given the inherent compatibility of both forms of abstraction, it should follow that the understandings of cognition they produce are inherently compatible as well.[15]

Furthermore, abstraction with precision is quite useful in that it effects a very clear distinction between "knowledge" and "sensation" and highlights the fundamentally different character of the former with respect to the latter. Apprehending something as a sensible is not the same thing at all as grasping the same thing as an intelligible. It is not the case then, as Locke would seem to imply, that "ideas" come cascading into us, ready-made, through the "portals" of the senses. Rather, it becomes clear that "idea" and "proper sensible" are not synonyms and that the passive reception of the latter cannot completely account for the presence of the former in our consciousness. Ideas or concepts are the result of a subsequent human act, one that renders the *potentially* intelligible (which is made accessible *through* our sense powers but is not the proper object of them) *actually* intelligible. By making clear this distinction, abstraction with precision is an excellent first step in addressing the various forms of materialism, all of whom attempt to reduce knowledge to some physical state or process.

Intention

But acknowledging the validity of the two forms of abstraction with respect to sensation does not completely solve our epistemological puzzle. True, a solution to the problem of the bridge is made clear via the precisive/non-precisive distinction. The problem is created in the first place because Kant, e.g., operated exclusively from a "precisive only" standpoint. With sensation reduced to a "manifold" of discrete sensory inputs, and with no non-precisive approach open to him, the best Kant could do in the face of skepticism was to construe such notions as "substance" as an *a priori* framework. The contents of sense experience, precisively understood, simply could not support an alternative conclusion. Correspondingly (and to continue with the anachronistic application of Thomistic terminology to the Kantian problem), the solution is to admit the legitimacy of non-precisive abstraction and apply it to sense data. This creates the "space" required for sensation to carry along with its proper sensibles some intelligible content which another faculty can detect.

But our epistemological puzzle still remains because establishing this scenario as possibility is not the same as establishing it as fact. To put the matter a slightly different way, Wilkins rightly points out that for St. Thomas knowledge is an "intentional identity between knower and known"[16] and an "ontological perfection of the knower."[17] In other words, the knower, in some sense, *becomes* the thing known and thereby obtains objectivity. But this is still a claim for which evidence must be presented. The validity of non-precisive abstraction indicates that the isomorphism is *possible* and hence one can side-step much of the modern problem. But a precisive abstraction makes clear that the question remains whether the alleged isomorphism exists, or not.[18]

And it is this question of isomorphism that I believe Lonergan attempts to answer in his discussion of the notion of being. In these discussions, Lonergan characterizes knowing as a process consequent to the desire to know and with a term in the intention of being. In such a context, it is reasonable for Knasas or anyone else to ask whether the desire itself brings some content to the cognitional table and/or whether the intention of being settles any epistemological question in advance. It is legitimate to wonder whether the mediating intellectual acts, which purportedly work through what is properly sensed to grasp additional intelligible content, are achieving what is claimed for them. I contend that Lonergan, at least, is aware of these questions and expends a not-insignificant amount of intellectual energy addressing them.

Lonergan, Sensation, and the Intention of Being

Central to Lonergan's argument for the isomorphism of knower and thing known is his assertion that sensation, and indeed anything we know prior to judgment, should be understood as ontologically neutral or "given." Concerning sensation, Lonergan notes:

> The given is unquestionable and indubitable. What is constituted by answering questions, can be upset by other questions. But the given is

constituted apart from questioning; it remains the same no matter what the result of questioning may be; it is unquestionable in the sense that it lies outside the cognitional levels constituted by questioning and answering. In the same fashion, the given is indubitable. What can be doubted is the answer to a question for reflection; it is a 'Yes' or a 'No'. But the given is not the answer to any question; it is prior to questioning and independent of any answers.[19]

The first thing that should stand out is the stark contrast between this view and that of Kant's. For the latter, the status of such "predicates" is already established, *as phenomenal*:

> Long before Locke's time, but assuredly since him, it has been generally assumed and granted without detriment to the actual existence of external things, that many of their predicates may be said to belong not to the things in themselves, but to their appearances, and to have no proper existence outside our representation.[20]

Such an understanding already assigns a status to the contents of experience; for Kant, the matter is already decided. And as was noted earlier, such a formulation leads immediately to the problem of the "bridge"; i.e., some necessary justification for claiming that phenomena corresponds to noumena. For Kant, there is *necessarily* the issue of moving from the thing as it is to us to the thing as it is in itself; an issue that Kant considered irresolvable.

In contrast, understanding sensation as a given avoids this problem. What is present in sensation may carry with it some existential marker, or it may not; that has yet to be determined. All that can be said at this juncture is that there is data; but whether that data is, for example, a mere object of thought (i.e., phenomenal) or whether it is an existential object with an additional act of "cognitional existence" is not yet clear. Such a determination can only be made through a judgment, and that has not yet occurred. But notice that with this view, there is no need to build a bridge between a phenomenal object and an existential world since there is no inherent or necessary distance between the two in what is given in sensation. The neutrality, the "giveness" of precisive sense data sidesteps entirely the problem of the bridge.

Second, to say that sensation is ontologically neutral is *not* to say that it does not *have* an ontological status, but only that its ontological status is not *revealed* in an act of sensation considered apart from the rest of the cognitional process. As the passage states, the given is indubitable and unquestionable because it is something that occurs prior to questions and doubts; it is what questions and doubts are about. It is up to subsequent reflection and judgment to reveal the ontological status of the sensed thing to us. Upon reflection, the correct judgment may be "I am aware of something real," or it may be "sensation is phenomenal only" but in either case these are judgments made *about* something present to consciousness prior to the judgment.

Third, notice that this interpretation does *not* leave us stranded in a phenomenal world until we are liberated through an act of judgment. Prior to an intelligent act of reflection, the data is *given* and not phenomenal. Hence intelligent reflection and judgment is not a movement from phenomena to noumena, as Kant would have it, or from a "glossy" appreciation of existence to a "grainy" one, as Knasas would have it.[21] Rather, it is a movement from something whose ontological status was not considered *at all* to something whose status is affirmed as existential. This third alternative seems to meet the requirement for an immediate and direct realism in that the recognition of a thing's ontological status occurs only in judgment and is not an issue beforehand. In other words, as soon as the issue of existence arises, it can be resolved through judgment, with no hiatus in an interim, phenomenal world.

The Notion of Being

The inherent neutrality of the sense data allows Lonergan to avoid both the problem of the bridge and any concern regarding a deferred or delayed realism. Hence, the isomorphism required by Thomistic realism is preserved as a real possibility; what remains is to examine the desire to know and in what sense the intellect is a constitutive, *a priori* condition for knowledge. The precisive understanding of sensation highlights that establishing the existential character of any object will be a cognitive, and not purely sensory act, precisively understood. The precisive data is not biased in any direction; what is required is an intellectual act to uncover its status. What remains, then, is to establish the character of that intellectual act.

Now in Knasas's view, the Lonerganian desire to know plays a constitutive role in understanding by supplying what the data lacks; namely, an existential reference point, a.k.a., the notion of being. This alleged reference point is the source of Knasas's discomfort regarding Lonergan's position; being is known not by "looking" at what is in sensation but rather by "looking" at how what is in sensation "looks" against the backdrop of the pre-existing notion of being.

And Lonergan does indeed make certain comments that might lead one to conclude that this notion provides some content to the object understood. In his discussion of the notion in *Insight*, Lonergan again affirms that existence is known through judgment and yet there is a precursor to that judgmental knowledge at work in the intellect:

> Still, though being is known only in judging, the notion of being is prior to judging. For prior to any judgment there is reflection, and reflection is formulated in the question, Is it? That question supposes some notion of being and, strangely enough, it is prior to each instance of our knowing being. Not only, then, does the notion of being extend beyond the known but also it is prior to the final component of knowing when being is actually known.[22]

A quite plausible reading of this text has Lonergan establishing the notion of being as some sort of formal or objectively valid knowledge or "criteria" against which is measured the beings of experience in the act of judgment. In other words, we know what will count as "being" in virtue of the notion of being and the desire to know, which is innately in us. We affirm this or that thing as meeting that criterion through the act of judgment.

But this reading, though plausible, does not jibe with the surrounding texts. Three pages earlier, still in the discussion of the notion of being, Lonergan refers to its definition as a "second order" definition. He then goes on to clarify what that means:

> Other definitions determine what is meant. But this definition [i.e., 'being' = 'the object of the pure desire to know'] is more remote for it assigns, *not what is meant by being*, but how that meaning is to be determined. It asserts that if you know, then you know being; it asserts that if you wish to know, then you wish to know being; but *it does not settle whether you know or what you know*, whether your wish will be fulfilled or *what you will know when it is fulfilled.*[23]

This text seems carefully calculated to preclude an interpretation of the desire to know as containing any positive, formal content of any sort. Far from being the formally constitutive context (the "pencil sharpener" that modifies what it admits[24]) that Knasas criticizes, Lonergan appears quite insistent that the notion of being is, as it were, purely nominal. The notion is understood simply and only as "the objective of the pure desire to know." What a particular being might be; indeed, what "to be" might mean at all will be entirely and thoroughly a product of a reflective judgment on the "given." But the notion, in and of itself, decides nothing in advance concerning the nature or determination of being. It is, of itself and prior to judgment, neutral toward this or that possible theory of being:

> [the notion of being] leaves the materialist free to claim that to be is to be material. Equally, it allows the empiricist to claim that to be is to be experienced, the idealist to insist that to be is to be thought, the phenomenalist to explain that to be is to appear, and so forth. . . . If the strategic correct judgments are that matter exists and nothing but matter exists, then the materialist is right. If the strategic correct judgment is that there is appearance and nothing but appearance, then the phenomenalist is right. Similarly, if the propositions enunciating other positions are correct, then being is as such positions declare.[25]

Furthermore, understanding the notion of being as completely without any determinative content in itself seems *necessary* to make the notion consistent with another of Lonergan's central claims; namely, that the desire to know is completely unrestricted. Again in the context of discussing the notion of being, Lonergan states:

> Other doubts may arise, but instead of chasing after them one by one, it will be better to revert to our initial theorem. Every doubt that the

pure desire is unrestricted serves only to prove that it is unrestricted. If you ask whether X might not lie beyond its range, the fact that you ask proves that X lies within its range. Or else, if the question is meaningless, incoherent, illusory, illegitimate, then X turns out to be the mere nothing that results from aberration in cognitional process.[26]

Now this sort of "retortional" argument is one richly and frequently criticized by Knasas.[27] Basically, as we have seen earlier, Knasas holds that such arguments can only conclude to a necessity in thought, and nothing else. Hence, if one attempts to establish some particular "horizon" (e.g., the principle of non-contradiction) as absolute and concrete due to its ineluctability, then one has established only something about how we must think, and nothing about how something other than thought must be.

But notice, however, that in the above argument Lonergan does *not* attempt to establish the ineluctability of some "horizon," but in point of fact seeks to do precisely the opposite. In the above case, retortion reveals, not that there is some primitive term or concept or intelligible content (e.g., that some relation is *necessary* or is not only known, but known *with certitude*) that is inescapable, but rather that there is *no term* that escapes the possibility of questioning. Knasas characterizes all retortional arguments as claiming that any formulated question must employ a framework and this fact proves that the framework is absolute. But for Lonergan, the key observation is that, first, *anything* can be questioned, and second, prior to any formulated question there is first a *desire* to formulate the question. And such a desire is obviously beyond or outside of the "framework" and hence the "framework" is manifestly *not* ineluctable after all. The desire to question, i.e., the desire to know, reveals itself upon inspection to be absolutely devoid of any ineluctable pre-existing frameworks or constitutive elements. It shows itself to be, in point of fact, the very *tabula rasa* required for Thomistic epistemology:

> If your intellect were something that was confined within a finite range, then there could possibly be questions that you could brush aside without any reason whatever, and so a certain measure of radical obscurantism would be justified. But if no obscurantism whatever is justified, then in principle there is no finite limit to our knowing. What the effort to know heads to is unrestricted, and because it is unrestricted we name it being.[28]

Hence, we can be confident that the intellectual acts that work on the contents of precisive sensation are in fact uncovering *in*, not imposing *on*, the data. The intellect, when it honestly and objectively reflects upon the data of sensation, is not in point of fact employing some crypto-framework to create the illusion of objectivity since the intellect has no such crypto-framework to provide:

> Prior to conception and to judgment, there is the dynamic orientation of intelligent and rational consciousness with its unrestricted objective. This

orientation is man's capacity to raise questions and thereby to generate knowledge. Immanent within man, it is a spark of the divine. Cognate to God, still it is knowing, not in act but in *sheer potency*.[29]

It would appear then that in Lonergan we have not only the recognition but the requirement for the intellect's pure potentiality, *in se*. This is not to say that biases, preconceptions, and habits do not exist nor that such things can influence (for good or for ill) our understanding of reality. It is only to say that radically, in itself, the intellect is unlimited in its potential range, ready and open to accept whatever reality has to offer.

Conclusion

Earlier it was noted that the precisive and non-precisive accounts of sensation should render two different though ultimately compatible explanations. This is due to the fact that what differs in each explanation is not the underlying reality but rather what the term "sensation" is understood to designate. Knasas, I have argued, understands "sensation" non-precisively and accordingly emphasizes the direct and immediate character of our knowledge of singulars. "Sense data" understood this way includes the proper objects of sense explicitly and at the same time neither excludes nor emphasizes other potential (intelligible) objects which may be co-located with such proper objects. Building on this understanding of "sense data," "sensation" is then understood simply as that act through which sense data is acquired and accordingly the term carries with it the same implicit extension found in "sense data." Hence the coherence of Knasas's talk of "sensation" being our first grasp of being, while at the same time characterizing the grasp reflexively. Such a construal is not double-talk when one understands "sense data" and "sensation" non-precisively because on that view "sense data" implicitly includes intelligibility beyond the proper sensibles. Thus "sensation" also implicitly includes acts beyond the merely sensory. To "see" the object means to grasp both what is properly *and* what is implicitly present before our senses.

In contrast, a precisive understanding restricts "sense data" and "sensation" to their proper objects. Accordingly, such an act as "reflecting" on the "sense data" is highlighted as a separate and distinctively intellectual act. Hence any conclusion reached subsequent to an act of reflecting is also properly understood as intellectual, and specifically as a *judgment*. And while later judgments may reveal such profound things as, for example, that *esse* is an act distinct from *essentia*, even such mundane assertions as "the object before me is real" is rightly understood to be expressive of an act of judgment, though much less regal. And so it is that the very same act which Knasas understands non-precisively as an act of "reflective sensation" is appreciated precisively as an act of judgment.

University of Houston—Downtown

Notes

1. J. Wilkins, "A Dialectic of 'Thomist' Realisms: John Knasas and Bernard Lonergan." *American Catholic Philosophical Quarterly* 78 (2004): 107–130 and John F. X. Knasas, "Why for Lonergan Knowing Cannot Consist in 'Taking a Look.'" Ibid: 131–150.

2. Wilkins, "Dialectic," 112.

3. Knasas, "Look," 134.

4. For this and immediately following comments, cf. "Look," 141–143.

5. "Look," 140.

6. Nor, if I am reading him correctly, would Wilkins find them unreasonable. For example, he favorably quotes Lonergan as asserting you see a *being* when you see a color (cf. "Dialectic," 113), describes the passive intellect as "open to any intelligibility whatsoever," and the agent intellect as a "medium" in much the same way that the Medievals took physical light to be the "medium" which actuated, but did not distort, the object of sight (i.e., some color), thus implying that existence is discovered in, rather than applied to, the object of sense (cf. "Dialectic," 127. In point of fact, as I understand the Medievals, they took the *air* and not the light to be the medium of sight, with light actuating the medium and rendering it transparent. But however this is, the main point is that Wilkins does not read the agent intellect's "constitutive" role as anything more than an efficient cause actuating whatever is there.).

7. John Locke, *Essay Concerning Human Understanding*. Bk. II, chap. 3.

8. E.g., speaking of the "pure concepts of the understanding," which include substance, Kant notes: "although our pure concepts of the understanding and our principles are independent of experience, and despite the apparently greater sphere of their use, still nothing whatever can be thought by them beyond the field of experience, because they can do nothing but merely determine the logical form of the judgment relatively to given intuitions. . . . Experience must therefore contain all the objects for our concepts; but beyond it no concepts have any significance, as there is no intuition that might offer them a foundation." Immanuel Kant, *Kant's Prolegomena*. No. 43 of the *Religion of Science Library*. Ed. and trans. Paul Carus. La Salle: The Open Court Publishing Company, 1947. 77–78. Hereafter *"Prolegomena."* And on sensation as of itself unconstituted: "Our *apprehension* of the manifold of appearance is always successive, and is therefore always changing. We can therefore never determine from this alone whether this manifold, as object of experience, is simultaneous or successive, if something does not ground it *which always exists*, i.e., something *lasting* and *persisting*, of which all change and simultaneity are nothing but so many ways (*modi* of time) in which that which persists exists. Only in that which persists, therefore, are temporal relations possible . . . i.e., that which persists is the *substratum* of the empirical representation of time itself, by which alone all time-determination is possible." Immanuel Kant, *Critique of Pure Reason*. Trans. and ed. Paul Guyer and Allen W. Wood. Cambridge: Cambridge University Press, 1998. 300 (A182–3; B225–6). Hereafter, *"Critique."*

9. B. J. F. Lonergan, *Insight*, 73.

10. Ibid, 245ff.

11. "As I have written, the glory of judgment is not in being our first knowledge of existence. *Sensation is that*. The prerogative of judgment is to furnish an appreciation of that existence as a distinctive *actus*, as *esse*. What we *sensed as an existing something* is judged to be something *with* its existence. "Look," 143. Emphasis added, internal references omitted.

One page earlier, Knasas describes the reflective process whereby we come to know the real in sensation: "I know that the data of sense are real . . . because, reflect as I may, no 'ideas' in and through which I am aware of the sense data are present . . . reflection upon what I am doing right now as I look this way locates no 'ideas' and so confirms that sensation is nothing other than a direct and immediate presence of something real" ibid, 141–142.

12. *ST* I, 78.3 c.; *SCG* 4.11 §4

13. For St. Thomas, cf. *De Ente*, chap. 2; for Knasas, cf. *Being and Some Twentieth-Century Thomists*. New York: FUP, 2003. pp. 39–42.

14. For more on the use of precisive abstraction with regard to body and soul, cf. Joseph Owens, "Soul as Agent in Aquinas." *New Scholasticism*, 48: 40–72, esp. 45–53.

15. It should also be acknowledged that the precisive understanding of sensation is indeed a counter-intuitive affair. In point of fact, we do not and cannot experience just "red," "loud," "smooth" etc. Experience is always of a red, loud, smooth *thing*. But this is only to say that *awareness* of something is an intelligent, and not merely sensitive act. Awareness of sensed objects already requires an intellectual engagement with that object. We arrive, then, at a precisive understanding of sensation through reflecting on our conscious sense experience and excluding from "sensation" all things that are present through the intellectual act and limiting ourselves to what is present in the sensory act only.

Nevertheless, the precisive/non-precisive distinction is not only possible, but useful in that it provides a well-understood Thomistic context for engaging post-Lockian epistemological viewpoints. Whether consciously or not, many modern thinkers have adopted a precisive technique for the conceptualization of the contents of sensation. In Locke and those who follow him there appears to be no awareness of a second, equally-legitimate, abstractive possibility. Accordingly then, there are the modern difficulties with, for example, necessity, causality, and substance: how can such concepts be grounded *in* sensation when sensation itself only contains "color," "sound," "smell," etc.? Keeping with our use of Thomistic terminology, they have recognized one sort of abstraction, but not the other. Recognition of the second, non-precisive sort of abstraction allows one to sidestep such issues by asserting that *through* (rather than in) sensation we come into contact (directly or indirectly) with such realities, and by means of a power distinct from the sensitive.

16. "Dialectic," 109.

17. "Dialectic," 120.

18. In other words, the precisive/non-precisive distinction makes the refutation of the skeptic *possible*, but it does not accomplish the refutation on its own. The distinction makes clear that it is the intellective power *abstracting* rather than the sensitive powers *perceiving* universals co-located in the phantasms. Hence, the *de facto* nature of sensation is not a grounds for asserting the *de facto* nature of cognition. It is an open question as to whether the intellect *actually does* abstract rather than impose, and whether its abstraction is without distortion or addition. Lonergan's objection to the "ocular" model of cognition is that it masks this additional requirement. It can lead to confusion concerning exactly how objectivity is gained. One can "see" objectivity if seeing is construed non-precisively. But "objectivity" is not numbered among the proper sensibles nor any combination of proper sensibles, and a precisive abstraction makes this fact clear. We are *knowing*, not "perceiving" objectivity and the question is whether we are *knowing* accurately or not.

19. *Insight*, 382.

20. *Prolegomena*, 43. And as Kant's comments immediately following this passage make clear, he would ascribe this status to *all* predicates.

21. "Look," 143.

22. *Insight*, 353.

23. Ibid., 350, emphasis mine.

24. Cf. J. F. X. Knasas, "Transcendental Thomism and the Texts," *Thomist* 54 (1990) 81–95, pp 94–95.

25. *Insight*, 361

26. Ibid., 352.

27. Cf., e.g., "Look," 138, as well as the multiple references to his own works in n. 18.

28. B. J. F. Lonergan, *Understanding and Being: The Halifax Lectures on* Insight. Toronto, UTP, 1990, p. 149. In *The Collected Works of Bernard Lonergan*, vol. 5.

29. *Insight*, 370, emphasis mine.

Reflections on a Critical
Genealogy of the Experience of Poverty

Edward McGushin

Abstract: The persistence of poverty is one of the great problems of our times. In this paper I want to show how we can use Michel Foucault's work to recast this problem through a genealogy of the political rationality within which it appears. Foucault's genealogies present us with at least three irreducible experiences of poverty: 1) the philosophical care of the self where poverty is a goal to be attained; 2) the religious sacralization of the poor and charity; and 3) the bio-political project in which poverty is a social disease to be cured or purged or a resource to be exploited. Foucault offers us the hope of resisting the danger of bio-politics, the cynical logic that stigmatizes the poor for their poverty and places them in apparatuses that treat them like a social disease, a moral failure, or a subhuman form of life.

In *Amazing Grace*, Jonathan Kozol affords residents of "one of the largest racially segregated concentrations of poor people in our nation" the opportunity to tell their own story (Kozol, 3).[1] The narrative that emerges is startling. One of the many difficult revelations in the book comes from a group of adolescents Kozol encounters at a youth center in Harlem. Trying to best express the situation in which they find themselves, one of the kids explains that the ghetto is "not like being in jail . . . it's more like being 'hidden.' It's as if you have been put in a garage where, if they don't have room for something but aren't sure if they should throw it out, they put it there where they don't need to think of it again" (Kozol, 38–39). Another kid in the group continues the thought, "if people in New York woke up one day and learned that we were gone, how would they feel? . . . I think they would be relieved. I think it would lift a burden from their minds" (Kozol, 39). This sentiment, repeated throughout the book, is re-iterated in the epilogue by one of Kozol's most engaging and consistent interlocutors: "I think they wish we were never born" (Kozol, 246).

These statements seem to me to be achingly true of an attitude towards poverty, and to the poor themselves, that pervades and is transmitted by the political and ethical rationality framing our thinking and our action, shaping to no small degree our relation to poverty and the poor.[2] What is this basic attitude? Poverty, and the poor themselves *are a problem*. As a problem they tend to appear as burdensome, undesired, even *guilty*. The themes of sin and disease run throughout Kozol's book. The poor people Kozol meets know that to many (and sometimes even to themselves) their poverty is the outward sign of their sinfulness—public perception often paints them as lazy, drug-addicted, or criminal; inferior beings who simply cannot make it. The poor know that poverty is perceived as a social disease and that they tend to be seen as its carriers and therefore an infection risk to the city and the nation, the wealthy and the healthy (Kozol, 41).[3] According to a cynical, moralizing logic, they, and they alone, are responsible for their condition, choosing, out of what must be some hyperbolic spitefulness, to sink themselves into poverty and despair (Kozol, 21). Even programs for assistance often carry with them a moral stigma and the interminable perpetuation of social exclusion (Kozol, 101). Kozol describes this combination of stigmatization with containment in the name of welfare: "All the strategies and agencies and institutions needed to contain, control, and normalize a social plague—some of them severe, others exploitative, and some benign—are, it seems being assembled: defensible stores, defensible parks, defensible entrances to housing projects, defensible schools. . . . All these strategies and services are needed—all these and hundreds more—if our society intends to keep on placing those it sees as unclean in the unclean places" (Kozol, 135–136). The director of one assistance program puts it succinctly and dramatically: "In reality, it is a form of quarantine . . . not just of people who have AIDS but of people who have everything we fear, sickness, color, destitution" (Kozol, 136–137). In other words, the projects don't so much attempt to re-integrate the poor into society as much as to reinforce the sense that they belong in a certain place, that there is a place for them apart from the rest of us. And this place is meant to hold them in forcibly.[4]

Teaching service learning courses,[5] in combination with studying the thought of Michel Foucault, has helped me to better appreciate aspects of this 'experience' of poverty that I had not noticed before.[6] In this paper I want to use the insights and methods found in Michel Foucault's work to articulate and understand the service learning experience and to begin to recast the *problem* of poverty through a genealogy of the political rationality within which it appears.[7] My aim is to bring into the foreground some of the dangers of modern political reason, hopefully without undermining its capacities and resources. One of these dangers, as the preceding paragraphs are intended to indicate, is the very way that modern forms of power, discourse and subjectivity constitute poverty as an object of knowledge and control by making it (and by implication the poor themselves) into a *social problem*. Perhaps, it should be obvious that poverty is a social (or economic) problem that must be managed, controlled, and eventually eliminated. However, genealogical thinking maintains a skeptical attitude towards modern certainties. It shows that modern political reason not only is incapable of eliminating the *problem* of poverty, but even tends to exacerbate it—both quantitatively and qualitatively. More optimistically, genealogy shows that there are other ways of experiencing poverty. Foucault's genealogies present us with at least three different and irreducible modes of experiencing poverty: 1) the philosophical care of the self; 2) the religious sacralization of the poor and charity; and 3) the bio-political project (indicated above). Each of these experiences of poverty is a mode of spatiality (distance or nearness); a specific disclosure of the Other or Otherness; a relation to one's Self; and a fundamental relation of poverty to political power and the activity of governing (leadership). In the following I will briefly sketch these three modes. Then I will present an analysis of my student's reactions to their service learning experiences in order to show how these different modes are reflected and challenged therein.

1) Poverty and Care of the Self in Ancient Philosophy

According to Foucault, philosophy in the ancient world was not just a theoretical, or 'discursive' activity. Rather, it was first and foremost an art of living, the aim of which was to attain a higher, truer, or fuller way of being. It was an exercise or a practice through which one became capable of grasping the truth—through which one in deed became the truth. This is how Foucault understood the ancient Greek imperative, *epimeleia heautou*—take care of yourself—that he discovers in the writings of Plato, the Epicureans, the Cynics, etc. The practices of care are what Foucault called variously the practices of the self, the technologies of the self, the aesthetics of existence, or spirituality.[8] These *technés* or practices were manners of establishing a relationship to one's "self."[9] In 1983, Foucault shows that Socrates and Plato develop a philosophical care of the self as a form of resistance to the corrupt practice of politics in fifth century Athens (CdF83). Politics was dominated by flattery and rhetoric rather than by truthful, courageous '*parrhésia*'—frank speech. Socrates and Plato argued that the Athenians could not properly govern the *polis* because they did not govern themselves—they neglected the ethical work necessary to fashion themselves as effective political subjects, as *parrhésiastés*. Therefore, effective power in the city is grounded upon care of the self—one must first govern oneself and only subsequently will one be capable of governing others.

It is within this framework of power (politics), knowledge (speaking the truth) and subjectivity (taking care to maintain the right or true relation to one's self) that poverty takes on a meaning in ancient philosophy. The true relation to one's self was attained, in part, through detachment from material possession and dependence. The true life then was a practice of poverty and poverty was a form that truth took when inscribed in an individual existence. Foucault distinguished three different modalities of the philosophical practice of poverty: Socratic, Stoic, and Cynic poverty.[10]

First, Socratic or negative poverty: Socrates practices a form of poverty that is a consequence of his care of the self (CdF84 February 15). Because he cares for the truth, and because he cares for the condition of his soul and the souls of his fellow citizens, he disregards the pursuit of wealth in order to devote himself to the truth. In the *Apology*, Socrates explains that his care for himself and the other Athenians "has kept [him] too busy to do much either in politics or in [his] own affairs. In fact, [his] service to God [Apollo] has reduced [him] to extreme poverty" (*Apology*, 23b).[11] The philosophical life occupies one's time and attention to such a degree that the result is poverty. But, conversely, the care for wealth, occupying oneself with political power or material gain, results in the neglect of one's soul. Socrates makes this clear when he asks the jury rhetorically: "are you not ashamed that you give your attention to acquiring as much money as possible, and similarly with your reputation and honor, and give no attention or thought to truth and understanding and the perfection of your soul (*Apology*, 29e)?" Care is a zero-sum game: one can spend it on the soul or on wealth. If one devotes oneself to the soul one will, to that extent, neglect wealth. The poverty of the Socratic life of philosophy is evident in the *Symposium* as well where Socrates' appearance and hygiene practices are described as less than perfect or regular (for example, *Symposium*, 174a).[12] Furthermore, Diotima says that Eros, who is a philosopher and a mythical reflection of Socrates himself, is born of poverty (*Symposium*, 203b–d). In other words, the philosophical life is a life of Eros and Eros is inseparable from poverty, from lack. The poverty of Socratic philosophy is a necessary consequence of the direction of one's care towards the truth and away from material concerns. The true life, the examined life, the life devoted to care of the self, is a life of material (and spiritual) lack.

Foucault shows that the valorization of poverty runs through the work of Seneca as well—an example of Stoic poverty. For Seneca it is a matter of developing an attitude of indifference with respect to wealth. What is required for the true life is a kind of "virtual poverty" rather than an actual condition of poverty (CdF84 March 14, 48). In order to attain this attitude, Seneca recommends exercises by which one experiences, for a fixed time at regular intervals, the life of a truly poor person—denying oneself food, shelter, clothing—in order to create the necessary detachment, in order to learn the true value of things (CdF84 March 14). In other words, Seneca does not need to give up wealth in reality. Rather through these exercises one forms an *attitude of detachment*—one does not love or depend on the wealth one continues to possess.

The Cynics also practiced a life of poverty, of indifference to material wealth, but they did so in a radical way (CdF84 March 14). Cynic poverty is real: it is an actual physical and material poverty and not a temporary exercise or experiment, like that of the Stoic. It is active in that the Cynic does not just allow his fortune to dwindle away, like Socrates, but renounces what he has; he gives it away or throws it away. Foucault writes that, "Cynic poverty must be an operation which one performs on oneself in order to obtain the positive results of courage, of resistance and of endurance" (CdF84 March 14). It is both a gesture of rejection and an act of strength and self-appropriation. Poverty itself is a goal to be attained which brings tangible benefits to the one who practices it.

In each of these modes of impoverishment (of becoming poor), we can identify goals and consequences. First, there is a connection between government (or power or politics) and poverty. According to Socrates, only one who properly governs himself is qualified to govern others, and poverty is one outcome of proper self-governing or self-care. For Seneca, the spiritual guide (an essential figure in Stoic philosophy) is the one who has attained power over himself, in part, through this exercise of detachment from dependence on material wealth (even if only virtually). In the case of the Cynics, the true master of himself is the one who is completely freed from this dependence on material possessions (CdF84 March 21).[13] Poverty is the basis of true, virtuous, just power or leadership. Second, the life of poverty is Other than the ordinary life of the citizen with its attention to material wealth and productivity. For these philosophers, this Other is a goal to be achieved. Through spiritual and physical exercises and self-transformation the philosopher becomes Other than she was and other than what we might call normal. She becomes poor, and simultaneously or consequently becomes true to herself. Finally, poverty and the poor are linked to knowledge in the form of self-knowledge and to the knowledge required for effective governing. Indeed, knowledge of the highest things is connected in each of these modes of thought to the care of the self through self-impoverishment. Foucault's excavation of ancient philosophy as a way of life, consisting of deliberate practices of self-impoverishment, stands, therefore, as a stark challenge to the current professionalized, detached, and purely discursive form of academic philosophy. If there is some intimate connection between philosophical truth and the experience of poverty, then we must consider the degree to which our way of living advances or inhibits our pursuit of that truth. The professionalization of philosophy may, in important respects, inhibit philosophy and seal it off from the very truth it seeks.[14]

2) Poverty and Charity in the Christian World

Foucault showed that the philosophical art of living was appropriated by Christianity (CdF84 March 28). This is true also for the exercise of poverty, which becomes a fundamental part of Christian asceticism. The figure of the true philosopher comes to be embodied in the desert ascetic and then in the monk (CdF84 March 28). Likewise, the figure of the pastor will arise as the spiritual director whose access to the truth is linked to his practice of the true life through spiritual exercise—and in particular through poverty. But with the appropriation of the true life by Christianity, the experience of poverty comes to be split into two forms. On the one hand, the ascetics of poverty will continue as a prominent feature of Christianity modeled on the life of Jesus and his disciples. However, on the other hand, a new figure appears—the Poor. The Poor do not actively practice their poverty; they are simply poor. Thus, what the philosophers sought through *askésis*, the Poor are granted, without aiming for it, by fate.

Peter Brown has recently argued that the bishops of the early Church established themselves in Roman culture precisely through defining their relationship to a class of persons that they *invented*: the poor.[15] In so doing they reinvented the art of governing or caring for others (Brown, chapter 1). For the Greeks and Romans charitable giving meant giving to the city, not to the poor. In this way, the rich benefactor could be admired and honored as a "lover of the city" (Brown, 5). Charitable giving was a civic act and generosity was a civic virtue. In the Greco-Roman model, the poor were not likely to be the recipients of charitable giving. "There was little room in such a model for the true urban 'poor', many of whom would, in fact, have been impoverished immigrants, noncitizens, living on the margins of the community" (Brown, 5). In other words, insofar as giving was directed to the city, its benefits fell to the citizens. The poor, being largely non-citizens, then, were simply outside the domain of charity. Even where the poor clearly benefited from the generosity of the rich and powerful, they did so not because they were poor, but because they were citizens (Brown, 5). However, as Christianity came to play a more prominent role in defining ethical and political virtues civic honor was displaced by a new definition of generosity. The bishop, as opposed to the wealthy citizen or ruler, sought to be a "lover of the poor." (Brown, 1–3).

Brown argues that this transformation represented a challenge to the civic model of the Greeks and Romans, throwing "open the horizons of society" (Brown, 6). The social landscape itself was transformed through this new relationship to the poor, and to oneself as a subject of generosity. This new mode of charity produced a civic experience in which the community, no longer perceived as a unity of citizens, was seen as divided between rich and poor. This divided and wounded, and yet, for all that, more profoundly integrated community called for a new form generosity: the rich had a duty to give to the poor.

> It was now the poor . . . whose silent presence challenged the rich to give, and to give, above all, to them, the poor . . . [this] relation to the poor acted, as it were, as a symbolic clamp. It bracketed and held in place an entire society. To act as a 'lover of the poor' was to make an assertion, heavy with symbolic meaning, of one's acknowledgment of the ultimate cohesion of the entire human community. (Brown, 6)

Cleary, the poor are not see here as an essentially economic category or social problem. Much more fundamentally they are a political, ethical, and spiritual category of individuals. It was through the interweaving of the spiritual and the social that the full meaning of the Poor came to be constituted. Brown writes:

> The joining of human and divine in Christ was a charged statement of the ultimate cohesion of the universe, secured by a mighty act of *sunkatabasis*, of 'condescension' on the part of God. It could also act as a symbol of the ideal cohesion of society. Widely separated segments of society—emperor and subjects, rich and poor—were bound together by mysterious ties of common flesh and common belief. Those at the top should learn to respect these ties and 'condescend' to listen to those at the bottom. (Brown, 97)

In such a framework, one does not provide charity merely as a means to the end of improving the social-economic situation of an individual or a community. As Brown puts it, "To give alms to the poor was to find oneself, instantly, standing in the Presence of God" (Brown, 92). These remarks echo Foucault's analysis, in *Histoire de la folie*, where he claims that all through the Middle Ages, the poor continued to embody a "absolute meaning." Precisely because of their poverty they were especially close to God. The act of charity received its value from the poor themselves not from its social utility (HF, 69). Charity was an end in itself.[16]

To the extent the Church grows in influence and Christianity invests life and social practice, just government—the art of conducting individuals—becomes inseparable from care of the poor. And, again, care is not subsumed under categories of social or economic utility but rather is a sacred duty. Furthermore, the Poor are seen not just as an Other self (as in ancient philosophy), but rather as a transcendent and sacred Other; an Other who imposes an unconditional duty of charity upon subjects.

3) Poverty, Bio-politics and Normalization

Now I will briefly sketch the formation of a modern way of thinking about poverty and the poor. Foucault argues that modern subjectivity and modern political rationality are constituted on the one hand on the basis of a gesture of exclusion or marginalization and on the other hand through the deployment of mechanisms of social, economic, psychological, and biological integration or conformity. These two movements—of marginalization and of integration—are not reducible to one another even though they function together and could not exist without each other. Within this dual movement the poor come to hold an ambivalent though primarily negative value. The modern horizon of meaning against which the figure of the poor or of poverty will appear is not care of the self and it is not the sacred presence of the divine or the sacramental act of charity. It is social utility and order. The poor and poverty as such are forms of disorder and intrinsically disruptive. They are the signs of social inefficiency or failure and they contribute to that inefficiency and failure. The poor person is a burden, a drain on society who does not hold up his end or contribute his share. However, at the same time, the poor are the wealth of the nation insofar as they constitute the labor force. Their bodies are necessary for the functioning of the system and at the same time they are burden on the system. Therefore they are caught in a paradoxical situation into which they must be integrated and yet from which they must be eliminated.

First, the gesture of exclusion. I refer to Foucault's famous analysis of the "great confinement" of the poor, the immoral, the homeless, and the mad that took place across Europe in the middle of the seventeenth century (HF, chapter 2). Foucault's claim is that this gesture groups together a variety of individuals—and types of individual—that need to be excluded form the social landscape—namely those who cannot or will not conform to a new sense of social order based on an "imperative to labor" (HF, 75). In other words, the excluded are essentially the same individuals who would have been experienced as sacred in the Christian rationality of government. This act of exclusion takes place at two levels. First of all what is immediately and obviously set apart are certain individuals who are physically confined in the massive *hôpitaux généraux*. But on another level what is marginalized and even stigmatized along with these individuals is the very way of thinking within which they can take on positive meanings. In other words, a whole range of forms of life and ways of thinking are displaced. In this new framework, charity, understood as an end-in-itself and a sacred duty to the poor whose meaning is absolute, is itself disorder. Charity must become a means of creating social order and productivity (HF, 69).

Now on the other hand, this gesture of exclusion is complicit with a positive movement of integration. A new basis for community, integrity and inclusion in a whole is established. This new rationality will be manifest *positively* in the forms of human life, relation, action and discourse that are recognized as meaningful, desirable, and fulfilling and *negatively* in the forms of human being that will no longer appear as meaningful, perhaps will no longer appear as human. First of all, the positive goal and function of politics in modernity is more and more understood in terms of the extension, preservation, and cultivation of life at the level of a population understood in a biological sense.[17] As Foucault puts it in *The Birth of the Clinic*, in modernity "health replaces salvation" as the goal of government.[18] The wealth and strength of the state hinges on the health and productivity of its population. Given this task government will devote itself to knowing and controlling the biological life of the population in order to make it as healthy and productive as possible. The formation of a political practice that conceives its objective to be the management of a population results in the "development of a medicine whose main function will . . . be public hygiene, with institutions to coordinate medical care, centralize power, and normalize knowledge. And which also takes the form of campaigns to teach hygiene and to medicalize the population" (CdF76, 244). Modern political government cannot restrict itself to purely juridical, legislative, economic or even ethical problems: politics is intrinsically a medical activity dealing with the material, biological existence of the population. This is what Foucault calls bio-politics—the politic government of biological life.

Within this framework, the well-integrated, biologically and economically productive individual is defined as the *normal*. The normal is the form of integration into the social whole as well as the form of a complete and integrated, healthy personality and mode of living. Therefore, to the extent that reason is bio-political, one fundamental goal of government is the constitution of normal individuals through medicine, education, psychology, as well as the regulation of economic and legal institutions. The normal at the same time comes to mediate the relation to oneself and to others—self-worth, self-knowledge, self-discipline all come to be pervaded by the sense of the normal, the drive and the need to be normal. The term "normal" has, therefore, social, psychological, moral and medical senses that tend to overlap and become hard to distinguish from one another. The linking of the normal to the productive—both in the economic and the biological senses—goes a long way to shaping contemporary experiences not only of ethical and social value but also of the aesthetic beauty of the body and the fullness of our personal relations. Given this rationality, poverty and the poor tend to be seen as a social burden, as a political and economic problem, as a moral and medical threat and as an aesthetic blemish on society as well as an aesthetically undesirable mode of existence.

In sum, the emergence of a modern political rationality involves a transformation in the way society deals with the poor and with poverty. The poor first acquire a double meaning in terms of the wealth of the state: on the one hand, they bear a positive social value as labor; and on the other hand, a negative social value as idle and immoral source of social disorder. In either case, the poor have a meaning that is constituted in terms of social, economic and biological utility and normality. Then as government becomes bio-political, the poor are grasped in terms that are simultaneously biological and moral. The growth and concentration of the population of the poor, combined with their "immoral" and "unhygienic" pattern of living, creates a bio-medical threat to society as a whole. Government therefore develops a technology of social hygiene in order to sanitize the poor, to protect society from the threat they represent, and to attempt to order their lives in such a way as to make them useful to society. In modern political rationality the poor are constituted as an Other who are neither our better, truer self, nor a Sacred Other who give our lives meaning, but who are, instead, an inferior and threatening Other to be contained, controlled, put to work.

Conclusion

In the bio-political context the condition of poverty—material lack, misery, destitution, suffering—is grasped as a social problem that can and must be reduced and eventually eliminated. Furthermore, the bio-political state aims at easing the burden of the poor for the temporary period within which they are unable to provide for themselves. Poverty and the poor are thought of as temporary problems and the logic of bio-politics holds that the overall increase in wealth can and will make these inconveniences a thing of the past. The poor do not tell us anything true, they have nothing to say to us; they are an aberration. This logic and the social practices that accompany it are, however, contradicted by the persistence and even the increase in various forms and degrees of poverty, misery, and material lack during and despite vast increases in the overall amount of wealth and the development of the technological means of distribution of resources.[19] Furthermore, bio-political practices perpetuate and exacerbate other social problems that contribute to the isolation and suffering of the poor. For example, we have witnessed the ghettoization of urban landscapes and the general distribution of social space in economic terms: the gating-in of communities and the locking out of the anti-social or undesirable classes. In addition, the problematization of poverty in bio-politics engenders practices that tend towards the stigmatization of the poor themselves—this can take the form of a moral perception, a vaguely medical perception of the poor as contaminated or impure, or an infantilization of those who do not appear capable of conducting themselves like normal, mature, responsible adults. So long as the regime of bio-political rationality continues to guide our thinking and practices and shape institutions, poverty will persist as a moral, social, and biological disorder or disease, a *problem* that can and must be eliminated rather than a persistent theme of the human condition, what Heidegger calls the "poverty of the shepherd."[20]

What new directions might this genealogy suggest for the practice of philosophy? My recent experience in service learning suggests to me one possible way of going. As an instructor in service learning classes, I witnessed my students expressing often conflicting or contradictory reactions to their experience of service. Most, if not all of us, began the year with assumptions about the needy individuals we would be assisting and about the very nature of the service act—assumptions reflecting our modern way of thinking about poverty and the poor. Students saw themselves as the ones possessing goods to offer, such as their time, energy, and knowledge, in order to help those in need—not altogether unreasonable. By the end of the yearlong class, however, most students[21] stated that they got more out of their service than those they were ostensibly helping or serving. Perhaps they were repeating a cliché that they didn't really believe; perhaps they thought that was what I wanted to hear from them. But I wondered, if this were true (and despite my reservations I knew that for some it was clearly the case and for others it wasn't impossible), then what would this say about the relative value/usefulness of those needy, poor people, and my relatively privileged students? It would seem that some other logic of value and meaning revealed itself to my students that did not fit with the utilitarian rationality of bio-politics and normalization. Because the poor are implicitly constituted as inferior it may be that we tend to see and think of them as intrinsically unable to offer us anything of value.[22] Yet, somehow what the poor had to offer my students was in some important sense *more* than those students had to offer the poor and disadvantaged. I wondered how this happened and what had happened. Perhaps there is a virtue, corresponding to Nietzsche's "gift giving virtue," that we might initially designate as a "gift receiving virtue."[23] For if there is no virtue of receiving, corresponding to the virtue of giving, the giving virtue will be perpetually undermined, thwarted, frustrated. I may be wrong to call this receiving a virtue, but I don't think so. This gift receiving virtue may in fact be a deeper form of the gift giving virtue because it requires a more profound self-overcoming and victory over pettiness and *ressentiment*. In other words, in addition to the service rendered by *giving* food and clothes, by washing, by teaching or mentoring, by giving time and energy, there was another kind of exchange going on. While the service of physical and educational needs went mostly in one direction—from the students to those they cared for—there was something going in the other direction: some kind of spiritual value and some form of knowledge was being given to my students. The people talked to the students, told them their stories in their own words. Over time some students got to know these individuals, learned who they were, and learned about the joys and the suffering of individuals living in dire straights. In a more profound way students came to see that they didn't know these people as much as they had thought, that their ignorance of who these desperate individuals were, and what they were really like, reflected back on some lack in themselves. Moreover, they heard those people say "thanks." The *thanksgiving* of those individuals, whose suffering was so great, made deep impressions on the students. I think they came into contact with a logic of exchange, value, and utility altogether incommensurable with bio-political reason. These students who are so enclosed in a drive to validate themselves through quantitative productivity, to measure themselves against impossible standards of health and beauty (i.e., biological re-productivity); these students gained a new sense of value, meaning, and accomplishment through their exchange/encounter with the people they served. It seems to me that elements of the care of the self Foucault had discovered in ancient philosophy, and the medieval (and not altogether lost) Christian experience of sacramental charity and sacred poverty, re-emerged through this work.

The exercise of concerted and significant care for the needy combined with philosophical reflection on that care as well as its social, political, and spiritual context opens up the possibility of transformational experiences. First of all, students are asked to traverse the divisive distances defining the social landscape that function as barriers maintaining both the rich and the poor in their proper places. Service and reflection break down other more deeply ingrained elements of bio-politics as well. If we conceive of different deployments of poverty in terms of embodiment and spatialization then we can see bio-politics, pastoral charity, and care of the self as varying degrees of distance and proximity as well as different modes of embodiment. Bio-politics is a deployment of distance, isolation, and confinement. It separates bodies and it establishes the impoverished body as a figure of disease and threat. The healthy, aesthetically beautiful body is privileged as pure, productive, and desirable. Contact between these bodies is difficult—the presence of the impoverished body in spaces designated for productive bodies is experienced at best as an annoyance or inconvenience, at worst as repulsive and threatening. If the aesthetics of the productive/reproductive, healthy body is related to the bio-political concern with health, production, and reproduction, then this same aesthetics of the body might be linked to fear, intolerance, and repulsion from impoverished bodies. The sacralization of the poor on the other hand, is a deployment of proximity and contact. It is through emotional and physical touching, embracing, washing, and healing that the two different kinds of bodies realize themselves. Finally, care of the self is the deployment of an identical space in which healthy bodies and productive places are transformed into more or less impoverished ones and vice versa. Each of these modes of embodied ethical and social space induces or reflects a mode of subjectivity. In other words, by forming a relationship to bodies inscribed with different social meanings we establish our own subjectivity and our relationship to our own body. The poor become debased not by becoming poor but by being excluded and devalued. When we devalue and exclude the poor, when we fear them and find ourselves repulsed by them, we are at the same time revealing our sense of our own meaning and worth. Do we love ourselves only insofar as we are quantifiably productive, physically clean and healthy, aesthetically attractive—that is, do we hate our bodies and emotions insofar as they mark us as imperfect, vulnerable, mortal, and in a deeper more spiritual sense, impoverished and needy? Traversing those spaces of separation and coming into contact with the poor, offers the possibility of overcoming the distance and stigmatization that bio-politics projects on the social landscape. By combining such practices with philosophical analysis of the relations of power, knowledge, and subjectivity at work in the bio-political context of community service, the possibility of a transformed relation to the poor and to one's own embodied subjectivity opens up.[24]

Saint Anselm College

Notes

I would like to thank Chris Callaway for his comments, which have helped me to clarify my claims and arguments as well as to consider more thoroughly their limits.

1. Jonathan Kozol, *Amazing Grace: The Lives of Children and the Conscience of a Nation*. New York: Perennial, 1995 (hereafter Kozol). The neighborhood is Mott Haven, in the Bronx, NY.

2. This fact was revealed most recently and most shockingly in the horror of the aftermath of Hurricane Katrina.

3. The poor have their own discourse on evil—one which holds the rich accountable and which grasps "the ghetto as a 'sin' committed by society" (Kozol, 72).

4. In a recent article for *Harper's Magazine* (adapted from a forthcoming book, *The Shame of the Nation: The Restoration of Apartheid Schooling in America*, published by Crown), Kozol returns to these themes to show that things have failed to improve and in measurable ways are deteriorating. In this paper I don't give proper place to the problem of race and racial segregation. The overlap between poverty and race, and the intensification of poverty as a consequence of this overlap, is perhaps the gravest social problem of our times (see *Harper's Magazine*, September 2005, 41–54; Foucault has his own discourse on race—see CdF76). To put this in Foucault's terms: The contemporary *spatial technique* of segregation is a nefarious combination of "exclusionary" practices modeled on the "great confinement" of the poor across Europe in the middle of the seventeenth century (*Madness and Civilization* [hereafter MC]), trans. Richard Howard. New York: Vintage, 1988. 38–64; *Histoire de la Folie à l'âge classique* (hereafter HF), (Paris: Gallimard, 1972), 56–91 with "disciplinary" practices of quarantine and surveillance like those deployed in 'plague' towns in the end of the seventeenth century (*Discipline and Punish* [hereafter DP], trans. Alan Sheridan (New York: Vintage), 1979, 195–198; *Surveiller et punir*, (Paris: Gallimard, 1975), 228–233. The poor find themselves imprisoned in a stigmatizing network of discourse, power, and subjectivity, the first elements of which, were put into place not just out of humanitarian concern for the needy but also through the deployment of systems of surveillance, control, and normalization.

5. I was an instructor in the PULSE program at BC in 2003–2004 (for information on the PULSE program see: http://www.bc.edu/schools/cas/pulse/).

6. The term 'experience' in Foucault's work is notoriously slippery. One of the best recent treatments of this term can be found in Flynn, *Sartre, Foucault and Historical Reason, Volume Two: A Poststructuralist Mapping of History* (Chicago: The University of Chicago Press, 2005). See especially chapter 9, 208–229.

7. In addition, I hope to begin to fill in a gap in current Foucault scholarship. To date little attention has been paid to the central figure of the poor in his work. However, careful attention shows that the figure of poverty appears in his work, from beginning to end, and plays keys roles in each period of his career (early, middle, and late) as well as in each of his studies of power, knowledge, and subjectivity.

8. See *L'Herméneutique du Sujet:Cours au Collège de France, 1981–1982*. Ed. Frédéric Gros. 2001 I give a fuller treatment of care of the self in *Foucault's* Askésis: *An Introduction to the Philosophical Life* (forthcoming, Evanston, Ill.: Northwestern University Press).

9. It would be too difficult to go into a discussion of the notion of self in this formulation. Again, I treat this question at length in *Foucault's* Askésis.

10. These can be found in his Collège lectures of 1982–1984. For references to the 1984 course I have relied on the typescript of this course prepared by Michael Behrent for James Miller. The typescript is based upon the audiocassette recordings which are available at the IMEC in Caen, France and the Bibliotèchque du Collège de France. Behrent's typscript is available for consultation at the Boston College O'Neill Library. Hereafter reference to this course will be cited as CdF84 followed by month and day of lecture and page number in the manuscript. References to the 1983 lectures are based on the audio-transcripts held at the IMEC. All references to Foucault's Collège de France lectures in the following will take the form of CdF followed by the year and date of lecture.

11. Plato, *Apology*, translated by Hugh Tredennick, in *Plato: The Collected Dialogues*, ed. Edith Hamilton and Huntington Cairns (Princeton: Princeton University Press, Bollingen Series LXXI. 1961).

12. Plato, *Symposium*, trans. Michael Joyce, in *Plato: The Collected Dialogues*.

13. Dion Chrysostome, *IVe discours: Sur la royauté*, translated from the Greek to the French by Léonce Paquet, in *Cyniques grecs*, livre de poche, 2002 (available online at: <www.spiritual-dimension.com/dion-royaute.html>).

14. The aim of this first section is to pose this challenge to those of us in academic philosophy. Of course, the deliberate practice of impoverishment in ancient schools of philosophy is incommensurable with the poverty of those who do not choose it or desire it. And yet, as this paper will suggest, even those who suffer poverty against their will have the possibility of knowing and expressing a fundamental truth about human life and relation that remains closed to the 'privileged' classes. The poor have knowledge, and make manifest a value, that we need to recognize and respect.

15. See: Peter Brown, *Poverty and Leadership in the Later Roman Empire* (London: University Press of New England, 2002), 8 (hereafter cited as Brown).

16. In *Matthew* 25: 31–46, Jesus does not ask about the consequences of caring for the needy, nor about the intentions of the giver—he only indicates the importance of the act itself.

17. See for example: 'The Politics of Health in the Eighteenth Century'; 'The Birth of Social Medicine'; 'Omnes et Singulatum: Towards a Critique of Political Reason'; and, 'Political Technology of Individuals', in *Power*, Vol. 3, ed. James D. Faubion, *The Essential Works of Foucault, 1954–1984*, 3 vols (New York: The New Press, 2000). Also, 'Society Must Be Defended': Lectures at the Collège de France: 1975–1976. trans. David Macey (New York: Picador, 2003) (hereafter CdF76), as well as the lecture courses of the following two years: *Sécurité, Territoire, Population: Cours au Collège de France. 1977–1978*; and *Naissance de la Biopolitique: Cours au Collège de France. 1978–1979*. (Paris: Gallimard/Seuil. 2004).

18. *Naissance de la clinique*, Paris: Quadrige/Presses Universitaires de France. 1963. 201. In *Naissance de la clinique*, Foucault discusses the political meaning of the formation of clinical medicine, and the role of medicine in the development of modern power relations. At the end of the eighteenth century, doctors came to be seen as the means by which a perfect society would be constructed through the elimination of physical and spiritual suffering and disorder. However, this required not just curing individuals—it meant curing the social body. Government in this context came to be grasped in terms of biological and medical normalcy (31–36).

19. Recent studies have shown that even as the US economy grows poverty rates increase (see the US Census Bureau, http://www.census.gov/hhes/www/poverty/poverty.html). Even the Human Development Report's optimistic findings are questionable (see: http://hdr.undp.org/). The "dollar a day" standard is rather arbitrary as an indicator of the global victory over poverty (more information and statistics are available online at the Population Reference Bureau: http://www.prb.org/).

20. *Letter on Humanism*, trans. Frank A. Capuzzi and J. Glenn Gray, in *Basic Writings*, ed. David Farrell Krell (New York: HarperSanFrancisco, 1993), 245.

21. I only remember one who didn't.

22. In *The Call of Service: A Witness to Idealism* (New York: Houghton Mifflin Company. 1993), for example see, 1–9. Robert Coles goes a long way to undermining our prejudice that service extends only in one direction, from the rich to the poor.

23. Friedrich Nietzsche, *Thus Spoke Zarathustra*, trans. William Kaufmann in *The Portable Nietzsche* (New York: Penguin Books, 1976), 186–191.

24. From this point of view, one of the main critiques of Foucault, that his favoring an aesthetics of existence leads to a narcissistic self-obsession, is absurd. The aesthetics of existence practiced in this way problematizes the bio-political obsession with bodily aesthetics and its corresponding stigmatization of impoverished bodies.

"Greening" James L. Marsh's "Philosophy after Catonsville"

Jason Bausher

Abstract: American Catholic Philosophical Association President James Marsh is calling for a "Philosophy after Catonsville." This paper begins by examining Catonsville as specifically American, Catholic, and philosophical. "Wildness" is then presented as it has emerged recently as a category in environmental philosophy and is shown to necessitate a social ecology for Catonsville. Finally, Marsh's problematic relationship to ecology will be presented and resolved by discussing the necessary entailment of social ecology by his trilogy of *Post-Cartesian Meditations, Critique, Action, and Liberation*, and *Process, Praxis, and Transcendence*. By the end of this paper, wildness will have established a crucial connection between Catonsville, Marsh's "greened" critical theory, and social ecology as a necessary condition for the possibility of a "Philosophy after Catonsville."

So four of us took our own blood
and when the equipment for drawing our blood
broke down   we added animal blood
We attempted to anoint these files
with the Christian symbol of life and purification
which is blood
                              —Daniel Berrigan, S.J., *The Trial of the Catonsville Nine*

American Catholic Philosophical Association (ACPA) President James L. Marsh is calling for a "Philosophy after Catonsville." This paper begins by examining Catonsville as specifically American, Catholic, and philosophical. "Wildness" is then presented as it has emerged recently as a category in environmental philosophy and is shown to necessitate a social ecology for Catonsville. Finally, Marsh's problematic relationship to ecology will be presented and resolved by discussing the necessary entailment of social ecology by his trilogy of *Post-Cartesian Meditations* (PCM), *Critique, Action, and Liberation* (CAL), and *Process, Praxis, and Transcendence* (PPT). By the end of this paper, wildness will have established a crucial connection between Catonsville, Marsh's "greened" critical theory, and social ecology as a necessary condition for the possibility of a "Philosophy after Catonsville."

Catonsville as Philosophical Locus

This section of the paper seeks to show the relevance of Catonsville to the ACPA through its relation to the adjectives of "American," "Catholic," and "philosophical." First, the ACPA is "American," and Catonsville is a specifically American event. Catonsville occurred on American soil. Catonsville occurred with American activists. Catonsville occurred with American police, courts, media, and laws. If the ACPA is to live up to the "American" component of its name, then it must concern itself with the American social matrix of Catonsville. Second, the ACPA is "Catholic," and Catonsville is a specifically Catholic event. Catonsville occurred because of well-developed Catholic principles. Catonsville occurred because of Catholic conscience. Catonsville occurred because of a long history of Catholic struggles for social justice. If the ACPA is to live up to the Catholic component of its name, it must concern itself with the pursuit of justice at Catonsville. Third, the ACPA is "philosophical," and Catonsville provides a rich ground of critical philosophical reflection. Catonsville occurred because of the philosophical concept of praxis embedded in Catholic principles. Catonsville occurred because of philosophical theories of ethics and morality embedded in Catholic arguments about whether the "is" of Vietnam hit the mark of the "ought" of ushering in the Kingdom of God. Catonsville occurred because terms like "Viet Cong" and "American" had become one-sided, abstract reductionisms allowing their alienation to solidify into the fixed dualisms necessary for killing.[1] If the ACPA is to live up to the philosophical component of its name, it must concern itself with philosophical reflection upon Catonsville.

If Catonsville is "American," "Catholic," and "philosophical," there must be a social ecology at work in Catonsville. This paper seeks to explore the social ecology of Catonsville vis-à-vis the works of James Marsh, and "wildness" will be shown to be a key category cutting through Catonsville, Marsh, and social ecology. From the wildness of Catonsville and Marsh's social theory, this paper will argue for Marsh's need for an explicit and developed social ecology. Social ecology is the theory and practice of nurturing wildness in the world and opposing its barriers. I will argue that Marsh's social ecology is sufficient, but not adequate: his work sufficiently develops a critical theoretical framework for a Marshian social ecology, but he fails to adequately present, develop, and apply a specifically ecological conceptual apparatus. Nevertheless, Marsh's work has laid the foundation for a social ecology more structurally penetrating than the multitude of environmental philosophers who lack radical critical theory.

Wildness as Philosophical Category

Although explicit ecological concerns are largely missing in both Catonsville and Marsh's trilogy, the category of wildness can be shown to connect the two with social ecology and thereby "greened." A few definitions of terms are necessary to distinguish my use of these terms from their more frequent use. By "greening," I propose a verb denoting the rendering explicit of a necessary ecological conceptual framework implicit in the event, concept, or theory. The framework follows necessary from the logic of the arguments made. "Environment" as it is commonly understood as having to do with plants, trees, animals, etc. will be collapsed into the term "nature" or "ecology." The word "environment" will be used only in the juridical-bureaucratic sense.[2] Although the word "environmentalism" is the dominant American word for conservation and preservation of wild places, I will follow Murray Bookchin and differentiate between environmentalism (which lacks a thorough critique of capital) and ecology. Environmentalism is "a mechanistic, instrumental outlook that sees nature as a passive habitat composed of 'objects' such as animals, plants, minerals, and the like that must merely be rendered more serviceable for human use."[3] Ecology "was coined by Ernst Haeckel a century ago to denote the investigation of the interrelationships between animals, plants, and their inorganic environment."[4] "Social ecology" examines (1) the natural world of one side of a dialectic including the (2) human world on the other, explores their interrelationships, explains barriers to wildness, and works to overcome these barriers.[5]

"Wildness"[6] is a key concept evident in Catonsville and relevant to discussions today about wilderness versus wildness. With the designation of wilderness areas after the 1964 Wilderness Act, the legal obligation to "untrammeled" wilderness (Sec. 2c) resulted in the fetishization of wilderness: its prelapsarian and Edenic qualities separated it in dualistic fashion from the sinful and infernal qualities of the city. Yet Bill McKibben has argued that acid rain, aircraft over-flights, and other environmental impositions have resulted in the "end of nature."[7] Max Oelschaeger has argued that wilderness is a changing idea imposed upon place with little relation to the physical referent.[8] If the adequacy of the idea of wilderness has ended, then another concept is necessary that uncouples dead appearance from living essence: "wildness."

Having de-coupled wildness as the *spirit* of a dying body, we seek to develop the concept of wildness to work in this spirit and thereby save our dying planet. Wildness appropriates Kant's concept of self-organizing purposiveness of nature unfettered from its shackles as a mere presupposition.[9] In its human form, it gains the spontaneity of Kant's transcendental ego mediated by a Hegelian dialectic of *Logik*, *Natur*, and *Geist*. Wildness is rational in the cosmic sense of expressing the *Logos* and applicable to both human and non-human nature. Wildness thus manifests itself in conscious, personal forms and unconscious, impersonal forms.

Wildness according to Gary Snyder is "self-organizing, self-informing . . . self-authenticating, self-willed, complex, quite simple."[10] In a line about wildness descriptive of Marsh's demand for authenticity in PCM, Edward Abbey puts the following words on the lips of an eco-activist in *The Monkey Wrench Gang*: "There comes a time in a man's life when he has to pull up stakes. Has to light out. Has to stop straddling, and start cutting, fence."[11] Wildness is thus "the autonomous and self-willed."[12] Wildness is also Hegel's third moment of knowing (speculative reason) as the unity of theoretical and practical reason as praxis directed by will and motivated by desire.[13] Wildness stands in the interstices of natural law and pure spontaneity, teleology and caprice (*Willkur*), and necessity and freedom.

A social ecology of Catonsville implodes into itself the entire world of Vietnam, capitalism, deforestation, banking, the Berrigan brothers, other defendants, etc.

As we saw earlier, Catonsville is a locus through which things American, Catholic, and philosophical may be considered. This locus becomes the lens through which social ecology begins its work of uncovering the social systems at work—what one might call a "deep ecology" properly considered.[14] Wildness binds the facets of this locus together, because the Catonsville Nine acted upon their inner-purposiveness: they lived authentically by becoming actually what they were potentially inside the jaws of state violence. In Berrigan's words, "This is what it means to be a Christian/that you act on what you say you believe."[15] Justice is the *connatus essendi* of Catonsville as the fully rational concrete opposition to the fully irrational abstraction of capital.[16]

Nevertheless, we must not leave the Catonsville Nine as abstractions opposed to abstractions. As Jack Turner wrote in *The Abstract Wild*, "my enemies are abstractions, abstractions that are rendering even the wild abstract."[17] Marsh's existential orientation[18] steps forward at this point and marks his move away from Hegel and toward Kierkegaard. If we left the Catonsville Nine as merely epiphenomena of *connatus essendi*, we would abstract from the deeply personal and individual nature of wildness that transcends conceptualization yet maintains its rationality and intelligibility. She who is authentic is wild: she feels, thinks, and acts in accordance with that which she is. Although the self is not comprehended all at once and thereby maintains mystery, her intelligibility manifests itself over time. While the concept of the self appears as a tautology, the difference is one of potentiality versus actuality and essence versus appearance and is expressed temporally: I am what I am, I am what I was, and I am what I will be. Hegel points out in both *Logics* that every proposition is both analytic and synthetic, however, and the synthetic moment becomes a fixed and rigid opposition in the man who "keeps his life at arm's length."[19] Tautology now appears as contradiction, and solving the puzzle of the contradiction is personal, individual, and experiential. In Turner's words, "To create a wilder self, the self must live the life of the wild."[20]

Greening or Green-washing Marsh?

The previous section presented wildness as a category binding Catonsville and ecology. This section attempts to connect wildness to Marsh's critical theory. We must first ask whether this move is warranted, because Marsh does not appear to be an environmental or ecological philosopher. We must ask whether an ecological framework is a supplemental set of concepts that must be externally annexed to Marsh's work or whether the ecological framework is at work at a deeper level and simply requires disclosure to uncover subterranean ecological themes. This paper sides with the latter by arguing that Marsh's philosophy necessarily implies a social ecology: if Marsh seeks to overcome the logic of capital and this logic results in ecological devastation, then Marsh is seeking to overcome the logic of ecological devastation. Thus, Marsh may not wear his ecological heart on his sleeve, but an ecological heart is a necessary condition for the possibility of Marsh's radical critical theory leading toward "ecological socialism."[21]

I defined the verb "greening" as the rendering explicit of a necessary ecological framework in an event, concept, or theory. I now define "green-washing" as the use of ecological language to hide the death-dealing qualities of an event, concept, or theory. If I attempted to green the work of Milton Friedman, for example, I would fail. The necessity of its ecological destruction is conceptually consistent and empirically verifiable. Reducing the environment to commodified "resources" is necessary, because the "value" of these "goods" can only be "democratically" arbitrated by the market and disposed of by the owner. With the market as the ultimate arbiter of preservation, the environment has no necessary protections. Moreover, Marsh shows how capitalism necessarily implies devastation of human and non-human nature. The absence of necessary protections thus forbids us from "greening" Friedman. We may only green those events, concepts, or theories necessarily implying a social ecology.

Our first suggestion that Marsh may be greened emerges in his mantra of oppressions seeking liberation: racism, sexism, heterosexism, and classism. Anthropocentrism[22] and speciesism, [23] however, are missing. Anthropocentrism and speciesism are implied, nevertheless, by the connection between environmental devastation and the litany of oppressions.[24]

PCM/CAL. Second, although PCM includes no explicit ecological references, wildness involves both subjective and objective moments. Wildness or another subjective ecological concept can be explored vis-à-vis PCM. Third, whereas Hegel devoted the entirety of the second part of his *Encyclopedia* to a *Naturphilosophie*, Marsh devotes very little space in CAL to ecology. This paucity of explicit treatment of *Natur* not only results in a weaker understanding of *Geist*, but it opens the door to misunderstandings based on interpretations of Marsh's ecological thought—especially along the lines of aesthetics and anthropocentrism.

Anthropocentrism is the justification for human domination of nature as raw materials, and Marsh has given us little more than anthropocentric justifications *in his environmental discussions proper*. For example, "my environment should be a beautiful, aesthetic context and expression of who and what I am as an embodied, free, rational human being, not degraded and ugly."[25] Aesthetic appreciation is an important value, but it cannot justify ecological preservation. First, it establishes value for nature based on its utility as something aesthetically pleasing and thus establishes a simultaneously utilitarian, anthropocentric, and speciesist basis for valuation. Second, abstracting (again) from the non-ecological work establishing Marsh's assault on fascism and aestheticism, the aesthetic valuation of nature shares with fascism the glorification of that which is pleasing to the eye, e.g., blood and soil. The entire corpus of Marsh's work repudiates the elevation of the aesthetic moment to an unrestrained ground of valuation and thereby denies eco-fascism, and this renders his ecological argument sufficient. Yet the work is inadequate, because Marsh must find recourse in the non-ecological work to bail him out for a justification for what must necessarily be an explicitly biocentric philosophy. Biocentrism saves Marsh's argument by justifying ecology as an end in itself.

By "biocentric," I mean a holistic and non-hierarchical view that attributes value as intrinsic to all organic and inorganic nature.[26] Biocentrism is compatible with the humanism to which Marsh points in PPT,[27] and this may look similar to the non-anthropocentric humanism offered by William James: an anarchistic pluralism which denies hierarchy yet allows for human experience as a center of knowledge and valuation.[28] Although Marsh offers sufficient support for biocentrism and an ecological humanism, he is silent about these sources of justification.

PPT. Fourth, Marsh brings discusses more ecology in PPT than the previous two texts combined. Marsh devotes two pages[29] to describing the connection between the exploitation of humans and non-human nature, offers an almost perfect definition of anthropocentrism in capitalism without naming it as such,[30] devotes two paragraphs to ecology in the penultimate chapter,[31] and one paragraph in the final chapter.[32] Notably, he confesses weakly to the misdemeanor of which this paper seeks to indict him: "The environmental devastation is perhaps worth emphasizing because I, perhaps, have not emphasized it enough in previous works."[33] Marsh has "not emphasized it enough," and his ecological emphasis has thus been inadequate to the task of social ecology. Yet its sufficiency is gained only by reference to his non-ecological work (e.g., the inferences above about biocentrism and Jamesian humanism). We may conclude that Marsh's critical theory is *sufficient for* social ecology, but *inadequate as* social ecology.

The next section of this paper will move from this mere acceptance of ecology to an argument that Marsh's critical theory necessarily implies social ecology. In so doing, the conceptual adequacy of even Marsh's pre-greened critical theory rises above explicitly ecological philosophies. This claim follows from the argument that capitalism threatens all life on the planet. Environmentalists and ecologists offer deficient critiques of capitalism. If they offer deficient critiques of capitalism, they present deficient opposition to that which threatens all life on the planet. If they fail to present adequate opposition to that which threatens the natural world they claim to protect, then their theoretical declaration is not adequate to the practical actualization. If Marsh presents adequate opposition to that which threatens the natural world claimed to be protected by environmentalists, then his lack of a theoretical declaration of preservation does not affect his practical actualization of this end. If environmentalists fail to protect nature and Marsh succeeds, then the theoretical declaration and use of an ecological conceptual apparatus is less relevant to the objective of preserving the wild, natural world.

Marsh as Wild Philosopher

Our final task is to uncover the wild man in Marsh[34] by sketching how his critical theory leads necessarily to a social ecology. Ecological death necessarily entails the death of humanity, and a philosophy failing to address ecology continues our current trajectory toward ecological death. If Marsh's work does not necessarily entail a social ecology addressing this trajectory, then Marsh has not fulfilled his promise to present a critical-theoretical version of Absolute Spirit leading from subjective spirit (PCM) to objective spirit (CAL) to absolute spirit (PPT).[35]

Subjective Spirit: Post-Cartesian Meditations

One of the first tasks of a Marshian social ecology is to develop a systematic account of wildness into subjective spirit as implicit in the existentialist moment of Marsh's work. His definition of "authenticity" as "the self's fidelity to itself"[36] is the personal expression of wildness. His four "transcendental precepts" pull us out of idealistic and materialistic reductionisms clouding knowledge of ourselves and demands return to the world as free agents. In our knowing of wildness, Marsh prescribes a sensuous and practical form of knowing that nevertheless maintains its dialectical relationship to the ideal and theoretical.

The precept, "*Be attentive,*" necessitates attention to the particulars disclosed in phenomenological description and experienced as individuals.[37] Nature offers diverse phenomena that have been "flattened out" through their abstraction by human labor. John Muir, for example, says, "When California was wild, it was the floweriest part of the continent."[38] The deflowering of California was part of the modernist drive to tame wild nature. Modernism in general is the abstraction from the particular and erasure of the individual.[39] Whether in the architectural form of housing projects in New York, Chicago, and St. Louis, the political form of National Socialism, or in the painted forms of Kandinsky, the drive toward universalization and uniformity seeks to erase the individuality of the natural world. Diverse individuality is most evident in discussions of biodiversity: the rich manifold of species and natural inorganic forms threatened by deforestation, pollution, and decreasing urban proximity.[40]

If we may follow Maimon, Fichte, Schelling and Hegel in denying Kant's denial of intellectual intuition[41] and non-reductively identify empirical biodiversity with Kant's transcendental category of *Mannigfaltigkeit* (manifold),[42] then destroying biodiversity destroys our ability to think diversely by destroying the conditions for the possibility of thinking diversely. Preserving diversity motivates Leave No Trace practices[43] and Ken Kesey: "Before God I tell you: a man might struggle and labor his livelong life and make no mark! None!"[44]

"*Be intelligent*" demands logical rigor in explicating a social ecology inclusive of the nature that is self and the self that is nature. Deep ecology and nature mysticism argues against a fully logical world-order by asserting a mysterious unintelligibility and thereby limits phenomenological investigation of capital. Furthermore, they contradict themselves by asserting an unintelligibility that is nonetheless intelligible *as* an unintelligibility.[45] If the Absolute is intelligible, then claims by deep ecology and nature mysticism are invalid.

"*Be reasonable*" demands that a social ecology constrain itself to that which is given rather than allowing itself to create coherent belief systems with no ground in nature. Biocentrism and anthropocentrism, for example, obfuscate the relation between capital and ecological disaster; without such a critique, their arguments for "sustainability" dissolve. Coherentism needs a non-dualistic externalism requiring verification in nature and dialogue with others sharing the intuitions that prevent emptiness of coherent concepts.[46] Rousseau illustrates this in the naturalized instruction of Emile: "He receives his lesson from Nature, and not from men…Thus his body and mind are called into exercise at the same time."[47]

"*Be responsible*" recognizes the Hegelian argument that every position implies its determinate negation and must incorporate its negations through sublimation. Just as Hegel gives the highest honor to Spinoza by locating him as the Substance that has not yet become Subject,[48] responsibility demands that social ecology incorporate deep ecology and anthropocentrism. Deep ecology reveals the systemic nature of human and natural processes and must be preserved. Anthropocentrism reveals the specific difference of humanity in relation to the plurality of natural beings and must be preserved. Rather than abolish arguments for their one-sidedness, responsibility demands their dialectical abolition and preservation.

Objective Spirit: Critique, Action, and Liberation

Marsh's general critique of capital in CAL and elsewhere rotates around the same two axes as Karl Marx's critique: space and time. Marx claims that capital seeks to reduce space and time to nullity, because these are the means by which competition must take place in the marketplace.[49] For example, space between factory, warehouse, and sales room tends toward nullity. The greater the space covered in transport, the greater the time spent as capital *in potentia* rather than capital *in actu*.

Another way this drive to nullity manifests itself is the elimination of American wilderness. Eastern states retain only pockets of wilderness; the vast majority of the 643 wilderness units are in six western states. As the Olympic National Park illustrates, preservation occurred through utilitarian arguments[50] warranted by evidence that rocky sub-alpine regions were of greater economic value for eco-tourism[51] than harvestable trees.[52] Wild space tends toward nullity—saved from private capital subject to deforestation to become public capital "loved to death" by eco-tourism.[53]

Likewise, the opportunity for and prevalence of "wild time" is threatened. Wild time is determined by natural indicators,[54] but a "revolution in time" was inaugurated by clocks in medieval monasteries[55] that began the reduction of qualitative time to quantitative time. As monastic time became the time of global capital,[56] abstract time joined abstract space as a condition for capital.[57] Wilderness managers thus identify "escape"[58] as a motivator for increasing visitation,[59] and visitors see time as an enemy.[60]

Absolute Spirit: Process, Praxis, and Transcendence

Like Hegel's Absolute Spirit, Marsh's PPT preserves and abolishes both the one-sidedly subjective (PCM) and the one-sidedly objective (CAL). His dialectical religion both prevents ecology from descending into the sludge of a pluralistic naturalistic materialism and floating into the air as a mystical unifying nature spirituality. An ecological religion preserves and abolishes opposed moments of conceptual unity and experiential plurality into an absolute unity of conceptual unity and experiential plurality in praxis.

Combined with Marsh's critical theory in PCM and CAL, his "speculative-political metaphysics" of absolute spirit leads to "liberation in the center and periphery" and offers ecotheology a more secure ground. Marsh moves beyond what he calls "gentle Jesus" to "The Liberating Christ."[61] If liberating the world from capitalism liberates the world from ecological destruction, then Marsh's version of Christianity necessarily entails ecological salvation.

Conclusion

"In wildness is the preservation of the world."[62] Wildness was at work when the Catonsville activists spilled their own blood on the draft card files, and wildness is still at work in the critical theory of James L. Marsh. This paper has shown that this wild spirit must receive a more adequate flesh through an expansion of Marsh's hermeneutical circle to one that leads from Marsh's explicitly ecological work to his other critical work in greater conversation with other work in social ecology—especially the Hegelian-Marxian anarchism of Bookchin.[63] Marsh has richly developed the "social" dimension of *social ecology*, and working out the relations between his critical social theory and "ecology" is our critical task today.

Notes

1. Dave Grossman, *On Killing: the Psychological Cost of Learning to Kill in War and Society* (Boston: Little, Brown & Co., 1995).

2. For example, the National Environmental Protection Act (NEPA) signed by Richard Nixon in 1970.

3. Murray Bookchin, *The Ecology of Freedom* (Montreal: Black Rose Press, 1991), 21.

4. Ibid., 21.

5. For the most explicit working out of the simultaneously Hegelian and Marxian moments of social ecology, see Murray Bookchin, *The Philosophy of Social Ecology: Essays on Dialectical Naturalism* (Montreal: Black Rose Press, 1996). As he is wont to do, Bookchin says here that the ecological crisis is a result of a social crisis.

6. This specifically American term became a philosophical category with Thoreau and became more important after the publication of Gary Snyder's *The Practice of the Wild* in 1990. Bookchin deplores the term, because it may be interpreted as another symptom of New Age spirituality and primitivism. I retain the term because it carries a specifically American intuition of embodied, sensuous freedom while standing in for the *Geist* of German Idealism (especially Hegel) whose translation as "spirit" has long lost its rightly natural and intuitional content in the U.S.

7. Bill McKibben, *The End of Nature* (New York: Anchor Books, 1989).

8. Max Oelschlaeger, *The Idea of Wilderness: from Prehistory to the Age of Ecology* (New Haven: Yale University Press, 1991). cf. Roderick Frazier Nash, *Wilderness and the American Mind* (New Haven: Yale University Press, 1967).

9. "Hence I understand by an absolute purposiveness of natural forms such an external shape as well as inner structure that are so constituted that their possibility must be grounded in an idea of them in our power of judgment. For purposiveness is a lawfulness

of the contingent as such," in Immanuel Kant, *Critique of Pure Judgment*, trans. Paul Guyer and Eric Matthews (Cambridge: Cambridge University Press, 2000), 20.

10. Gary Snyder, *The Practice of the Wild* (New York: North Point Press, 1990), 10.

11. Edward Abbey, *The Monkey Wrench Gang* (New York: Avon Books, 1975), 93.

12. John S. Turner, *The Abstract Wild* (Tucson: the University of Arizona Press, 1996), 107.

13. G. W. F. Hegel, *The Encyclopedia Logic with the* Zusätze, trans. Theodore F. Gereats, W. A. Suchting, H. S. Harris (Indianapolis: Hackett Publishing Company, 1991), 132–133. Paralleled by Marsh in CAL, 56: "Theory without praxis is empty; praxis without theory is blind."

14. "Deep ecology goes beyond a limited piecemeal shallow approach to environmental problems and attempts to articulate a comprehensive religious and philosophical worldview," in Bill Devall and George Sessions, *Deep Ecology* (Salt Lake City: Peregrine Smith Books, 1985), 65. A Marshian social ecology would agree with this proposition, but disagree with the way it has been worked out. In Bookchin's words, "'Deep Ecology,' taken at its word, leads us into a foggy and dangerous logical realm from which there is usually no recourse but Eastern mysticism," in *The Philosophy of Social Ecology*, 138.

15. Daniel Berrigan, *The Trial of the Catonsville Nine* (New York: Fordham University Press, 2004), 65.

16. Arbitrating between competing claims of rationality appears throughout Catonsville. The Catonsville Nine appear irrational for dumping blood on files and burning them, because the action brings them neither income nor career advancement nor other profit. The dominant paradigm of "self-interest" prioritizes short-term gain for self by self over long-term gain for self through others. Turning this paradigm on its head, Berrigan levels the claim of "madness" and "insanity" against the self-contradictory and topsy-turvy military-industrial complex.

17. Turner, *The Abstract Wild*, xiv.

18. This existential orientation is most evident in his moment of "subjective spirit" expressed in PCM, esp. chapter 4.

19. Personal Interview, February 28, 2005. The same interview included his succinct rebuttal to an overly-conceptual response to a personal and existential question: "Stop talking like a philosopher and start talking like a man!"

20. Turner, *The Abstract Wild*, 91.

21. Marsh, PPT, 124.

22. "Anthropocentrism" as a hierarchical perspective of species wherein humans are accorded rights to dominate other species, and is thus a subset of speciesism. Whereas social ecology recognizes differences between species, hierarchy, domination, and speciesism are impermissible. cf. Bookchin in *Philosophy of Social Ecology* and *Ecology of Freedom*.

23. "Speciesism" as elaborated by Peter Singer in *Animal Liberation* (New York: HarperCollinsPublishers, 1975), 213–248. Singer demonstrates here the ultimately arbitrary determination of rights accorded to particular species.

24. It is conceivable that anthropocentrism and speciesism would not justify environmental devastation, but this is not the case in capitalism: justification must be reduced to the

living and dead labor constitutive of capital, and this leaves one species to take the personal form of impersonal social process resulting in ecological destruction.

25. Marsh, CAL, 319.

26. The classic proponent of this view is Aldo Leopold, *Sand County Almanac* (New York: Ballantine Books, 1949).

27. Page 125.

28. James's relation to anarchism is discussed in David Kadlec, *Mosaic Modernism: Anarchism, Pragmatism, and Culture* (Baltimore: the Johns Hopkins University Press, 2000) and Deborah Coon, Courtship with Anarchy: the Sociopolitical Foundations of William James's Pragmatism," Ph.D. Dissertation, Harvard University, 1988.

29. Pages 124–125.

30. Marsh, PPT, 105.

31. Marsh, PPT, 281.

32. Marsh, PPT, 318.

33. James Marsh, *Process, Praxis, and Transcendence* (Albany: State University of New York Press, 1999), 281.

34. Pursuing wild philosophy is not without precedents. cf. Holmes Rolston III, *Philosophy Gone Wild: Essays in Environmental Ethics* (Buffalo: Prometheus Books, 1986). Rolston's wildness proves only nominal, however, because he remains uncritically trapped by categories of capital. Marsh offers greater potential for wildness.

35. Marsh, PPT, ix.

36. Marsh, PCM, 112.

37. One fruitful elaboration of this precept would track Marsh's use of Maurice Merleau-Ponty embodied epistemology along with David Abram's use of Merleau-Ponty to develop an ecological epistemology in *The Spell of the Sensuous* (New York: Vintage Books, 1996).

38. John Muir, "Our National Parks" in *John Muir: the Eight Wilderness Discovery Books* (Seattle: the Mountaineers, 1992), 513.

39. David Harvey, *The Condition of Postmodernity* (Oxford: Blackwell Publishers, Ltd., 1990).

40. cf. David Takacs, *The Idea of Biodiversity: Philosophies of Paradise* (Baltimore: the Johns Hopkins University Press, 1996).

41. Kant, *Critique of Pure Reason*, B159, A249, and A252.

42. Ibid., A77, B139, A99, A121.

43. cf. Buck Tilton, *Leave No Trace Master Educator Handbook* (Boulder: Leave No Trace Center for Outdoor Ethics, 2003), and http://www.LNT.org.

44. Ken Kesey, *Sometimes a Great Notion* (New York: Penguin Books, 1964), 21.

45. cf. Marsh's discussion of "performative contradictions" in Chapter Four of CAL: "Rationality and Critique."

46. "Thoughts without content are empty," in Immanuel Kant, *Critique of Pure Reason*, B75/A51.

47. J. J. Rousseau, *Emile*, trans. William H. Payne (Amherst: Prometheus Books, 2003), 86.

48. cf. G. W. F. Hegel, *The Science of Logic*, trans. A. V. Miller (Amherst: Humanity Books, 1999), 580–581.

49. Although presented *in ovo* in volume one of *Capital*, the full exposition of space and time is best considered by locating Marx's critique of time in volume one, his critique of space in volume two, and his critique of the mystification of both in volume three. This architectonic maps onto Marsh's trilogy with important differences.

50. Such arguments continue today, and Ramachandra Guha offers a critique of first-world authoritarian imposition of wilderness on third-world countries that drives off the land those who are dependent on the land: "Radical American Environmentalism and Wilderness Preservation: a Third World Critique," in *The Great New Wilderness Debate*, J. Baird Callicot and Michael P. Nelson, eds. (Athens: the University of Georgia Press, 1998), 231–245. His argument parallels Marx's description of the "clearing of the commons" and "clearing of the estates" in chapter 27 of the first volume of *Capital*.

51. Similar to communism in the U.S.S.R. that used public goods for profit in state capitalism, eco-tourism is American state capitalism. A symptom of this is the distribution of propaganda to government agencies by private global consulting firm Booz Allen Hamilton claiming to be "the public sector's premier capital asset management programs" and claims that public lands require "planning the life cycle of the portfolio" through "Asset Management Plans" such as its plans for Grand Canyon and Rocky Mountain National Parks. The firm also "developed business practices for trails, structural fire, concessions, environmental, housing, and maintained landscapes." cf. http://www.boozallen.com. Literature distributed by promotional table staffed by three representatives at the 2005 George Wright Society Biennial Conference on People, Parks, and Protected Places.

52. Kathie Durbin, *Tree Huggers: Victory, Defeat, and Renewal in the Northwest Ancient Forest Campaign* (Seattle: the Mountaineers, 1996), William Dietrich, *The Final Forest: the Battle for the Last Great Trees of the Pacific Northwest* (New York: Penguin Books, 1992), and Carsten Lien, *Olympic Battleground: the Power Politics of Timber Preservation* (Seattle: the Mountaineers, 2000).

53. Ecology and economics share the Greek root *oikos*, meaning "house." We may draw upon Marsh's post-Habermasian explanation of the reduction of lifeworld to system to explain the reduction of ecology to economy, especially chapters 12 and 13 of CAL. He warrants an argument that this "house" divided within itself cannot stand.

54. Ralph Waldo Emerson writes of the farmer: "He is a slow person, timed to Nature, and not to city watches. He takes the pace of seasons, plants, and chemistry. Nature never hurries: atom by atom, little by little, she achieves her work." in *The Essential Writings of Ralph Waldo Emerson* (New York: Random House, Inc., 2000), 674.

55. David Landes, *Revolution in Time* (New York: Barnes and Noble Books, 1983).

56. Jean Gimpel, *Medieval Macine: the Industrial Revolution of the Middle Ages* (New York: Penguin Books, 1976).

57. Moishe Postone, *Time, Labor, and Social Domination* (Cambridge: Cambridge University Press, 1996).

58. This conflation of time in general with abstract time in particular is a conflation similar to Luddism in its conflation of technology in general with capitalist technology in particular.

59. For a polemical description of public land commodified by the State to provide escape from commodification outside the parks, see "Polemic: Industrial Tourism and the National Parks" in Edward Abbey, *Desert Solitaire: a Season in the Wilderness* (New York: Ballantine Books, 1968), 48–73.

60. Laura and Guy Waterman, *Wilderness Ethics: Preserving the Spirit of Wildness* (Woodstock: The Countryman Press, 1993), 162–168.

61. Marsh, PPT, chap. 9.

62. Henry David Thoreau, "Walking," in *The Natural History Essays* (Salt Lake City: Peregrine Smith Books, 1984), 130.

63. Reflection upon praxis in nature is already present in Marsh's circle, so unnecessary to mention in a new circle.

A Counterfactual Analysis in Defense of Aquinas's Inference of Omnipotence from Creation *Ex Nihilo*

James D. Madden and Louis A. Mancha, Jr.

Abstract: There is a traditional view, maintained by Aquinas and others, which holds that there is a mutual entailment between the power to *Create Ex Nihilo* (hereafter *CEN-power*) and the property of omnipotence. In his *Metaphysical Disputations*, however, Suarez attacks the traditional view by pointing out a serious flaw in Aquinas's argument. Suarez claims that there is no reason in principle why God cannot miraculously bestow *CEN-power* to creatures—albeit in a limited form—even on the assumption that God cannot make creatures omnipotent. In this paper the authors argue that the debate can be resolved in favor of Aquinas; that *CEN-power* does indeed strictly imply omnipotence. After clarifying a sufficient condition for the property of omnipotence, the authors argue that attention to a modest possible worlds semantics and some interesting properties of counterfactuals are together sufficient to show that beings with *CEN-power* are in every case beings that are omnipotent.

Introduction

Most traditional Christian theists accept as a part of doctrine that God created the universe and everything in it *ex nihilo*, or *from nothing*. The ecumenical creeds clearly accept and expound upon this theological position, and Christian philosophers from Augustine onward have consistently explained that the opening line of Genesis, "In the beginning God created the heavens and the earth [*In principio creavit Deus caelum et terram*]," properly should be understood as an affirmation of God's creation without the need for any pre-existing matter.[1]

In conjunction with the doctrine of creation, traditional theists also contend that God is an extremely powerful or *omnipotent* being, one whose power extends over the vast range and depth of all the things that can possibly be brought about. On this account, any being that is omnipotent has *CEN-power*, or the power to *Create Ex Nihilo*, thus establishing at least a one-way logical relation between both doctrines.[2]

According to Thomas Aquinas, the logical entailment goes the other way as well. That is to say, Aquinas argues that if some being has *CEN-power*, then that being is also omnipotent or has infinite power. Aquinas defends this position in several places, with the most succinct argument being in the *Summa Theologica*:

> The power of the maker is reckoned not only from the substance of the thing made, *but also from the mode of its being made*; for a greater heat heats not only more, but quicker. Therefore, although to create a finite effect does not show an infinite power, *yet to create it from nothing does show an infinite power*: which appears from what has been said (ad 2). For if a greater power is required in the agent in proportion to the distance of the potentiality from the act, it follows that the power of that which produces something from no presupposed potentiality is infinite, because there is *no proportion* between no potentiality and the potentiality presupposed by the power of a natural agent, as there is no proportion between *not being* and *being*. And because no creature simply has an infinite power, any more than it can have infinite being, as was proved above (7, 2), it follows that no creature can create. (ST I.45.5.ad3; our emphasis)

From the text, we can see that Aquinas cashes out the relation between *CEN-power* and omnipotence in terms of its *incommensurability* with natural, creaturely power. In its simplest form, Aquinas's argument appears to be as follows:

(1) *CEN-power* is incommensurable with natural, creaturely power.

(2) If *CEN-power* is incommensurable with natural, creaturely power, then *CEN-power* must be infinite.

∴ (3) *CEN-power* must be infinite, i.e., *CEN-power* implies omnipotence.

Aquinas then goes on to explain the implication this has for creatures:

(4) If *CEN-power* must be infinite, then no creature can create.

∴ (5) No creature can create.[3]

Aquinas's conclusion is important insofar as it attempts to demonstrate the view that *any* act of creation implies that the agent under consideration is omnipotent, thus preserving the traditional view that both doctrines are unique to God.

Although initially compelling, there appears to be a small fly in the ointment, particularly with regard to Aquinas's main inference. To see this, we turn briefly to Francisco Suarez, who offers one of the more penetrating objections against Aquinas's argument for the infinite nature (and thus omnipotent character) of *CEN-power*. In his twentieth *Metaphysical Disputation*, Francisco Suarez evaluates Aquinas's argument and determines that it comes up short. He contends that

> Even though [Aquinas's] argument aptly proves that a creative power, by the very fact that it is creative, is incommensurable with a power that educes [a form] from the potentiality of matter, it is wrong to infer from this that it will be an absolutely infinite power.[4]

The punch line of Suarez's observation can be seen as follows: Although creation can be shown to be incommensurable with—or of a wholly different order than—the power exemplified by creatures in ordinary acts of natural production, such a difference in *kind* does not also imply the requisite difference in *degree* to be considered absolutely infinite. If so, then there is no reason in principle why God cannot grant creatures the power to create, if only on a "limited scope."

Whether or not Suarez is ultimately correct in his analysis, we will take his observation as a direct challenge to Aquinas's argument. The purpose of our paper is to re-examine the Thomistic position from a more analytic viewpoint, and demonstrate the claim that any being that can be said to have *CEN-power* must be omnipotent. We will do this by defining and focusing in on one specific condition for omnipotence itself—which we call the *Sufficient Power Principle* (SPP)—and applying it to a counterfactual analysis of the potential limitations on that power.[5]

Some Preliminary Considerations

Let's revisit what Aquinas has in mind when he makes claims about *infinite power* or *omnipotence*. Applying this notion to God, Aquinas tells us in question twenty-five of the *Summa Theologica* that "since power is said in reference to possible things, this phrase, *God can do all things*, is rightly understood to mean that God can do all things that are possible, and for this reason he is omnipotent." Aquinas then spells out what he means by "all things that are possible" with the following remarks:

> Therefore, everything that does not imply a contradiction in terms is numbered among those possibles in respect of which God is called omnipotent; whereas whatever implies a contradiction does not come within the scope of divine omnipotence, because it cannot have the aspect of possibility. (*ST* I.q25.a3)

To translate Aquinas's point into the parlance of contemporary philosophers, one might say that an omnipotent being can bring about *any logically possible states of affairs*, i.e., the referent of any proposition that does not imply a formal contradiction. On this view an omnipotent being cannot, for example, bring about round squares because such an alleged state of affairs simply is not a possibility. This is no denigration of its power, however, for such a being can still do all that can be done.

It will be useful for our purposes if we can think about the Thomistic notion of omnipotence in a very specific way. We will state a sufficient condition for Thomistic omnipotence in terms of *compossibility*. Two states of affairs are compossible if each is possible in itself and it is possible for them to obtain simultaneously. For example, the state of affairs depicted by 'Smith is visiting Maryland' and the state of affairs depicted by 'G. W. Bush is the President of the United States' are compossible—both are intrinsically possible and they both can obtain without contradiction. Consider the states of affairs depicted by 'Smith is visiting Maryland' and 'Smith is visiting Tacoma.' These states of affairs are not compossible—although they are each intrinsically possible, they both could not obtain simultaneously without contradiction.

If a being can instantiate any compossible set of states of affairs, then it can be said that that being has fulfilled Aquinas's conditions for omnipotence. This move may seem to go beyond Aquinas's definition, for he makes no explicit mention of compossibility. All Aquinas mentions is that each possible state of affairs can be brought about by an omnipotent being. Nevertheless, the power to instantiate any compossible set of states of affairs is a sufficient condition for omnipotence in Aquinas's sense. The set that contains one and only one possible state of affairs is itself a compossible set, and a being with the power to bring about all compossible sets of states of affairs would in effect be able to bring about all such states of affairs. Bringing about non-compossible states of affairs simultaneously is logically impossible.[6] In other words, a being with the power to bring about any set of compossible states of affairs would be at least as powerful as a being that satisfied Aquinas's explicit definition of omnipotence. In this light we propose the *Sufficient Power Principle* (*SPP*) as a sufficient condition for omnipotence:

> SPP: If an agent *A* could have arranged the world to bring about any compossible set of states of affairs, then *A* is omnipotent.

In other words, if a being has enough power to bring about any collection of possible states of affairs that are non-contradictory, then we have sufficient reason to conclude that such a being is omnipotent. In what follows, we will argue that the SPP is satisfied by any agent who creates a world *ex nihilo*, insofar as such a being can be demonstrated to have the power to bring about any set of compossible states of affairs.

Before we present our argument we must make a distinction between *intrinsic powers* and *extrinsic powers*. By 'intrinsic power' we mean a natural capacity an agent has to bring about effects *that is not derivative from other entities*. By 'extrinsic power' we mean a natural capacity to bring about effects *that are derived in some way from relationships between the agent and other entities*. For instance, one's ability to deadlift a barbell loaded with six hundred pounds is determined in part by the agent's relation to other entities, e.g., his location with respect to the earth, the force of gravity, and so on. Thus, this capacity would be called an extrinsic power.

It is very important for what follows that we note that extrinsic powers and, conversely, their limitations, can be represented by counterfactuals. For instance, say that *A* has brought about an effect *e* at a time *t*, and say that *A* did so under an extrinsic limitation. This implies that there is a true counterfactual of the form:

> *A* would not have been able to do exactly *e* at *t*, if _____.[7]

In other words, there was some sufficient condition, extrinsic to *A*, such that if it had not obtained, *A* would not have been able to do exactly *e*. Furthermore, the counterfactual into which we analyze talk of an extrinsic limitation cannot be trivially true, where what we mean by "trivially true" is that the counterfactual is necessarily true either given its logical form or the metaphysical facts of the matter. Thus, we must not place in the open argument space in the above counterfactual form anything like "*A* had a different nature" or "there were round squares." The reason for this point is that the truth-maker for such a condition is either the nature of the agent itself or simply the laws of logic. In the former case, what one now has in mind is an *intrinsic* limitation rather than an extrinsic limitation. With respect to the latter case, it is simply absurd to argue that the laws of logic have some sort of real causal influence on agents—logical truths do not grant power. Thus, whatever goes into the argument place must not be a logical contradiction and its truth cannot rely entirely on the nature of the agent.

The Argument from Creation *Ex Nihilo* to Omnipotence

Suppose an agent, A, creates a world *ex nihilo* at a time t. Call this act of world creating 'C.' What is meant by a 'world' here is a composible set of states of affairs that exhausts reality, so the agent brings into existence *ex nihilo* everything that is really distinct from itself. A more technical way of stating this matter is to say that the agent creates a world by bringing about the truth-maker for a maximally consistent set of propositions. In other words, a world-creator arranges reality such that every proposition takes a truth-value without contradiction.[8] C is then a case in which an agent instantiates a maximally consistent set *ex nihilo*—without the prior existence of any causal patient or pre-existing substance to act on whatsoever. Since an extrinsic limitation requires that an agent's causal power is at least in part derived from its relation to other entities, then if the agent acts so as to bring about everything distinct from itself *ex nihilo*, we can infer that the agent acts without some extrinsic limitation. Now, as discussed above, an agent acts with some extrinsic limitation if and only if there is a true counterfactual of the form "A would not have been able to do P at t, if _____." Yet there is no extrinsic limitation on our agent, so we know that there is no non-trivial statement that can be put into the open argument space of the appropriate counterfactual form. Therefore, we may state the first premise of our argument as follows:

(1) If an agent A creates a world *ex nihilo* at t, then there is no true counterfactual of the form "The agent A would not have been able to create this world *ex nihilo*, if _____."

Given (1) and the assumption that our agent has created the world *ex nihilo*, we may obviously infer that there is no true counterfactual of the form "A would not have been able to C at t, if _____." This result implies that there is no logically possible state of affairs that could have prevented our agent from creating the world. We take it that this point is simply a truth of logic and state our second premise as follows:

(2) There is no logically possible state of affairs that could have prevented A from performing C at t.

Thus far we are committed to the claim that at t there are no possible conditions that could have obtained under which our agent would be unable to create the world *ex nihilo*. We further maintain that for any agent, if there is a time at which there is no possible condition under which the agent would be unable to perform a certain action, then that agent could perform any action of that type at such time. If we apply this thesis to our current case, we render our third premise:

(3) If there is no logically possible state of affairs that could have prevented an agent *A* from doing *C* a *t*, then at *t*, *A* could perform any action of *type-C* that is logically possible.

Prima facie this may sound quite implausible. Indeed, one will likely wonder why performing an instance of, say, ladder climbing, would imply that one can perform any other instance of such an activity. So suppose our agent is 5'8" and performs an instance of ladder climbing that satisfies the antecedent of (3). Why, one might ask, would this lead us to believe that our agent could perform some other instance of ladder climbing, which involves a ladder in which there is a distance of seven feet between each rung? Such an activity seems logically possible in itself, but it also seems impossible for our agent to perform it.

Careful attention to the conditions laid out in (3) will speak to this reservation. Notice that our antecedent tells us that "no logically possible state of affairs could have prevented *A* from doing *C*." So on analysis, any other logically possible instance of ladder climbing will be a logically possible state of affairs, and thus should be excluded by the fact that the agent's activity satisfies the antecedent of (3). Sticking to our example of ladder climbing, an agent would satisfy the antecedent of (3) if and only if there were no possible instance of ladder climbing which she could not perform. In other words, pointing out possibilities such as "what if the rungs on the ladder were seven feet apart" or any other logically possible states of affairs involving an action of this type will not serve as a counterexample to (3) since all such possibilities are accounted for by an agent that actually satisfies (3)'s antecedent.

Given premises (2) and (3) we then infer

(4) The agent *A* could have performed any *C-type* action at *t*.

With (4) we have come a long way toward showing omnipotence. We know, given our earlier discussion, that, according to (4), *A* can instantiate any maximally consistent set—the agent can provide the truth-maker for any exhaustive set of non-contradictory propositions. This capacity includes the power to bring about any set of compossible states of affairs; if a set of states of affairs are compossible then they must be referred to by the members of some maximally consistent set or other. Thus, since *A* can bring about any maximally consistent set, *A* likewise can instantiate any compossible set of states of affairs.

One may worry whether (4) shows quite enough. (4) seems only to speak to the agent's power at *t*, the initial moment of creation. Certainly it does the orthodox theist very little good to prove that God is omnipotent for only one moment. However, notice that if an agent brings about the truth-maker of any maximally consistent set of propositions at *t*, then among the propositions that the agent can arrange for at *t* include propositions that refer to states of affairs subsequent to *t*. For instance, our agent would, by virtue of providing the truth-maker of a maximally consistent set, need to arrange for the truth value of such propositions as "Jesus of Nazareth rises from the dead in 33 A.D.," and "An earthquake levels Lisbon in 1755." The agent would not merely arrange the state of the world at the moment of creation, but would need to, through its creative activity, arrange for the truth value of all propositions. We take the following principle to capture this point:

(5) For any Δ, if there is a time t at which Δ could perform any *type-C* activity (bringing about the truth-maker for the conjunction of a maximally consistent set of propositions), then Δ could arrange for any compossible set of states of affairs at anytime subsequent to t.

Furthermore, from (4) and (5) we may then infer that

(6) A could have arranged to bring about any compossible set of states of affairs.

and from (6) and *SPP* we may finally conclude that

(7) Therefore, A is omnipotent.

At this point we believe it might be useful to the reader to have the argument laid out in sequence:

(1) If an agent A creates a world *ex nihilo* at t, then there is no true counterfactual of the form "The agent would not have been able to create this world *ex nihilo*, if _____." (From the definitions of creation *ex nihilo* and extrinsic limitation)

(2) There is no logically possible state of affairs that could have prevented A from performing C at t. (From (1) and the assumption that A creates *ex nihilo*)

(3) If there is no logically possible state of affairs that could have prevented an agent A from doing C a t, then at t, A could perform any action of *type-C* that is logically possible. (Assumption based on the considerations given above.)

(4) The agent A could have performed any *C-type* action at t. (From (2) and (3).)

(5) For any Δ, if there is a time t at which Δ could perform any *type-C* activity (bringing about the truth-maker for the conjunction of a maximally consistent set of propositions), then Δ could arrange for any compossible set of states of affairs at anytime subsequent to t. (Assumption)

(6) A could have arranged to bring about any compossible set of states of affairs. (From (4) and (5).)

(7) Therefore, A is omnipotent. (From (6) and SPP.)

Replies to Two Likely Objections:

First Objection: *The notion of omnipotence provided by this argument is not consistent with orthodox theism. This concern comes along the following lines: One may worry that our argument implies an extreme form of occasionalism or determinism inconsistent with the traditional conception of freedom of the will (Wherein the creator is responsible for all of the activities of each if its creatures. Thus, if the creator has arranged for the truth of all propositions, then what work is there left for creatures to do?).*

We have two basic replies to this likely objection. First, this objection states a problem not for our argument in particular, but for orthodox theism in general. Many theists have worried, including Aquinas himself,[9] that God's omnipotence, however it might be construed, leaves very little for his creatures to do. Moreover, determinism is a worry for any theist with a strong view of foreknowledge or providence. Thus, one is no worse off with our argument and most other ways of thinking about omnipotence.

Second, notice that our argument hinges only on the *formal, logical relations* governing an act of instantiating a maximally consistent set of propositions. We have not committed ourselves to any view regarding how a being with *CEN-power* may or must carry out such an act. It may be that such a being brings about all future compossible states of affairs by endowing his creatures with causally efficacious natures that will one day even freely cause the creators plan to obtain. In short, our view may require the truth of future contingents, but it is also consistent with a concurrentist account of providence that makes room for significant creaturely activity. On Aquinas's view such a scenario is quite plausible, and we are content to rely on his account.

Second Objection: *Does this make any act of creation ex nihilo tantamount to omnipotence? One might worry that we have only shown that world-creating* ex nihilo *implies omnipotence, whereas the original debate between Suarez and St. Thomas was an issue over whether any act of creation* ex nihilo *implies omnipotence.*

The simple answer to this question is 'yes,' and the worry that it generates can be dealt with by attending a bit more carefully to the distinction between creation and ordinary "natural" production, and how we parse out action types. According to the scholastics, in every act of ordinary causation or production, there is a patient being acted upon, and thus some kind of extrinsic limitation is established for the agent. The patient thus delimits the range of effects of the agent in some way or other, i.e., it delimits the forms that might be generated or altered in it (the patient) when it is acted upon by the agent. Hence, from the perspective of the agent, anything that is naturally produced (i.e., not created) is brought about by a power the scope of which is extrinsically limited by the potentialities of its patient. Conversely, from the aspect of the patient, those same passive potentialities can be considered as active and necessary causal contributors to the natural acts of production that they participate in.[10]

Yet if we are allowed to hold that "creating *ex nihilo*" denotes an action type, then we may adjust our argument to meet this concern. Say that one has the power to create, for example, a dog *ex nihilo*. Then by definition there would be no extrinsic limitations on her doing so (since there is no pre-existing patient to act upon) and therefore she could do any logically possible act of this type. Well, since instantiating *any* maximally consistent set of compossible states of affairs is a logically possible act of the relevant type, we may then run through the same line of reasoning that we have presented above to show that one would likewise be omnipotent if she created a dog, or any entity *ex nihilo*, just as one would be if she had created a world. In this way, we can completely side-step the original Suarezian objection that was directed against Aquinas's incommensurability claim.

The final worry, of course, is whether or not finite creatures can be found to have such a power, either naturally or "superadded" *via* a miraculous act of God's. If our argument is correct, we believe that it speaks for itself on that matter.[11]

Benedictine College and Ashland University

Notes

1. For further analysis on the origins of this philosophical doctrine see Steven Baldner's and William Carroll's introduction to *Aquinas on Creation*, trans. Steven E. Baldner and William E. Carroll (Toronto: Pontifical Institute of Mediaeval Studies, 1997). For those interested in the historical/theological story behind the development of this doctrine, a good source is Leo Scheffczyk's *Creation and Providence*, trans. Richard Strachan (London: Burns & Oates, 1970).

2. This is true on the assumption that *CEN-power* is itself logically possible, of course. The Medievals were keenly aware that this claim was open to debate, and developed detailed arguments in its defense. For an overview of some of the various positions and arguments see Francisco Suarez, *Metaphysical Disputation* XX, §1.

3. For the curious, we can flesh this argument out a bit, particularly with respect to premise (2). In the beginning of the passage, Aquinas emphasizes that with regard to the act of producing or making, we ought to distinguish between *what* is made ("the substance of the thing") and *how* that thing is made ("the mode of its being made"). From either of these vantage points, Aquinas contends, can the power of the maker be "reckoned" or determined. Of course, the method of determination will be different, depending upon which part of the distinction one considers. He then introduces the following principle P: *The greater the degree of difference between (or "distance" of) the potentiality and the act, the more power is required to produce the act (i.e., the effect).* What Aquinas has in mind here is quite interesting. When an agent produces something—i.e., is an efficient cause—that agent acts so as to bring about an effect. With regard to natural creaturely power, such an act always presupposes some patient. If so, some degree of difference of being or perfection always obtains between the patient and the effect to be produced. This proportion or "distance" then, reflects the amount of power required by the agent to bring the patient from potentiality to act. For example, consider a lump of clay. If an agent were to mold the piece of clay into a sphere, it would take a certain amount of power, which would be reflected by the degree of potentiality—the degree of difference of complexity, as it were—between the "shapeless" lump and the subsequent sphere. Similarly, if an agent were to mold the clay into a human figurine, still more power would be required, given the greater complexity of the act to be obtained in camparison to the sphere. Seemingly, this kind of analysis can go on *ad infinitum*, given greater and greater degrees of complexity or distances of the potentiality from the act to be obtained. So in general there is a proportion or relation that holds between the potentiality of the effect and the power required to manifest it.

Thus, instead of trying to prove that God's pwer is infinite because God can create (or has created) infinite substances—which would be to prove the power of the maker "from the substance of the thing made"—Aquinas takes a different route. The reason for this is that Aquinas seems to accept the claim that "all created being is finite," hence when one applies principle P to any particular substance, at best, one will demonstrate really, really great power, but never infinite or omnipotent power. Thus, Aquinas approaches the problem from the second part of the distinction, which is to prove the power of the maker "from the mode of its being made."

At this point, we get Aquinas's main premise: What it takes to bring about something *ex nihilo*—to produce something "from no presupposed potentiality"—is to have a power that is radically different in degree from natural creaturely power, which always has some potentiality presupposed by it: In fact, it's infinite. By examining principle P, we can determine that such power, which is executed from no presupposed potentiality, cannot be proportioned to the potentiality which is necessarily presupposed in any act of ordinary, creaturely production, no matter how great. Now this lack of a proportion cannot imply that *no* power is required in order to produce the effect, but rather the opposite: *infinite* power is required. Therefore, *with regard to the mode or manner of acting*, if *CEN-power* is incommensurable with creaturely power, it must be infinite. Since no creature has infinite power, because no creature has infinite being, then it follows that no creature can create.

4. Francisco Suarez, DM XX.2.39, our emphasis. All quotations from DM are from *On Creation, Conservation, and Concurrence: Metaphysical Disputations 20, 21 and 22*, trans. Alfred J. Freddoso. (South Bend: St. Augustine's Press, 2002).

5. We wish to emphasize the fact that we are not attempting to historically reconstruct Aquinas's argument, nor are we attempting to object to Suarez' position directly. We are also not attempting to actually prove that God has *CEN-power*. Rather, we are arguing that on the assumption of *CEN-power* and its conditions, any being that has it is also omnipotent in the traditional sense.

6. Indeed, Samuel Clarke seems to make a similar move in the seventeenth century when he attempts to correct the Thomistic approach by claiming that not only must the state of affairs that an omnipotent being causes be intrinsically possible, but the state of affairs involving *that particular being causing such and such state of affairs* must likewise be possible. What Clarke has in mind here is a very narrow brand of compossibility. We simply expand the notion. It should be noted, however, that Aquinas can be charitably interpreted as pre-empting Clarke's analysis in his reply to objection 2 of q25: "To sin is to fall short of a perfect action; hence to be able to sin is to be able to fall short in action, which is repugnant to omnipotence. Therefore it is that God cannot sin, because of His omnipotence." (ST I.q25.a4.ad2) What Aquinas is explaining here is that if God could sin, then God could make it the case that *His nature itself* would be imperfect, which is not possible.

7. It is important to note for what follows that the analysis of extrinsic limitation into counterfactuals is a matter of logical equivalence. That is, not only does an extrinsic limitation imply the truth of the appropriate counterfactual, but the truth of the appropriate counterfactual implies an extrinsic limitation. One may put the matter as follows: For any agent μ and act ψ and time t, μ acts with extrinsic limitation in doing ψ at t if and only if there is a true and non-trivial counterfactual of the form "μ would not have been able to do ψ at t, if _____." It is crucial for our argument to notice that, given this equivalence, the lack of an extrinsic limitation implies that there is no appropriate true counterfactual.

8. We note at this point that in addition to the creation of all that is distinct from it, the agent would likewise need to be responsible or the explanation for all those states of affairs pertaining to exclusively it.

9. In fact, many of the Medievals worried about the push towards occasionalism on the assumption of God's omnipotence, or strong providential power. To give a few citations: Aquinas DP 3,7; SCG III.69; ST I.105.5; Luis de Molina, *Concordia*, 25.3–8; and Suarez, *Metaphysical Disputation* XVIII.1. For a careful assessment of the medieval objections to occasionalism in these and other passages, see A. J. Freddoso's "Medieval Aristotelianism and the Case against Secondary Causation in Nature." In *Divine and Human Action*, edited by Thomas V. Morris (Ithaca: Cornell University Press, 1988).

10. So properly understood, an extrinsic limitation doesn't really take power *away* from a creature. Rather, it delimits or demarcates the natural power the creature (the agent) actually has. This condition of ordinary production or efficient causality also applies to non-transeunt activity, where the creature is said to be acting upon itself, for example (which is to be differentiated from an immanent act like thinking). The passive powers of the agent, then, in some way delimit the range of effects that might be intra-substantially generated or altered. Yet this limitation would still be considered an extrinsic limitation, since the creature is not *per se* responsible for the passive powers it has. For more on this Medieval/Aristotelian analysis of efficient causation, see A. J. Freddoso's "God's General Concurrence with Secondary Causes: Pitfalls and Prospects." *American Catholic Philosophical Quarterly* 68:2 (Spring 1994).

11. We would like to thank Trent Dougherty for his insightful and penetrating comments on our paper, and James Pappas for helping us clarify several key points concerning the SPP and our counterfactual analysis of an extrinsic limitation.

Is Evil Really an Ontological "Primitive"?

Siobhan Nash-Marshall

Abstract: This paper regards the plausibility of rejecting the scholastic claim that the "good" is a transcendental property of being—that *ens* et *bonum convertuntur*—on the basis of two claims: (1) Stephen Cahn's claim that evil worlds created by an evil God are intrinsically plausible—i.e., that it is plausible to think of evil as a positive and instantiable property; and (2) the claim that "evil is a primitive"—that is, that evil is a primary or basic ontological property. It argues that if an "ontological primitive" must be a property which has no basic constituents other than itself—or whose definition cannot invoke concepts or constituents other than the primitive itself—evil itself cannot be considered a primitive. Nor can it be considered a positive property.

There seems to be something baffling to many contemporary metaphysicians about the scholastic claim that "good" is a transcendental property of being: that everything that is, insofar as it is, is necessarily "good."[1] I gather this not just from claims like the one Steven Cahn makes in "Cacodaemony," that evil worlds which are created by a evil Creator-God are intrinsically plausible.[2] I also infer it from what seems to be a far more common claim: that "evil is a primitive." What is meant by this claim, I take it, are two things primarily:

   (a) evil is a primary or basic ontological property—a characteristic, quality, attribute, or principle, in other words, that (a[1]) does not in any way derive from some other more basic component (a characteristic, quality, attribute, principle, or relation), that (a[2]) cannot be defined other than in terms of itself, and (a[3]) is a necessary component of reality;

and:

   (b) evil is a positive, instantiable, property that is an essential property of that in which it is instantiated—a characteristic, quality, attribute, or principle, in other words, that (b[1]) is not simply the negation of some other property (characteristic, quality, attribute, or principle), that (b[2]) intrinsically characterizes that thing or entity in which it is instantiated, and that (b[3]) is a necessary characteristic of the thing, entity, or whatever else one wants to call the non-abstract particular, in which it is instantiated.

To my knowledge, the clearest statement of the first of these two latter claims, at least in contemporary literature, is Rosamond Kent Sprague's. She defines ontological evil as "an ever present feature of reality" (564) whose "essential characteristic" is "badness" (562), and claims that evil must be a "real being"—as opposed to merely a "rational entity"—else it would "surrender" this essential characteristic (562).[3] But the belief that evil is, and should be thought of as, an ontological primitive, whether one means by this one or both of the claims above, seems also to be a presupposition common to many approaches to what has come to be known as the "problem of evil."

Consider Mackie's approach to evil in "Evil and Omnipotence." At the outset of indicating what he considers to be contradictions in classical attempts to reconcile the existence of evil and God's omnipotence, Mackie makes two primary claims with respect to evil: (1) that "evil exists" (200), and (2) that "evil is opposed—or alternatively "contrasts" to—the good" (201).[4] He seems to believe these two claims to suffice both to explain what evil is and to eliminate both the classic belief that evil is a privation and its variant that evil is an illusion—since evil could not be "really opposed to the good" if it were merely a privation or an illusion, and this would be contrary to (2). This last point clearly shows that Mackie holds (b[1]). But Mackie's definition of evil as "existing" seems to indicate that he also holds (b[2]) and (b[3]), and the fact that he believes that his claims (1) and (2) regarding evil are sufficient to explain what evil is seems to warrant claiming that he also holds at least something akin to (a[1–3]).

Similar considerations can be made with respect to many contemporary authors who engage in the "problem of evil." Rowe simply assumes that evil is a property which is instantiated in such things as "intense suffering"—a fawn dying a lingering and painful death due to a forest fire—thus apparently also treating evil both as a positive and instantiable property, which is a necessary characteristic of a state of affairs, and as something which can only be defined through itself.[5] Thus, Rowe too seems to believe something at least akin to (a[1–3]) and (b[1–3]). These same considerations also hold for Cahn, who seems to assume both that evil is to be equated with wickedness, which just seems to be a synonym of "evil," and that the existence of evil requires no explanation at all. These last points would indicate that he holds at least something like (a[1–3]). Cahn's thought project, on the other hand, indicates that he thinks (b[1–3]) to be at least plausible.[6]

Beliefs like these clearly entail that not everything that is is necessarily good: that *a priori* it is not necessary that *ens et bonum convertuntur*. If evil is a positive, instantiable, and essential property, there could exist such things as "evil worlds," and an "evil God." But if evil and goodness are mutually exclusive properties, such that anything which necessarily instantiates evil cannot thereby also instantiate goodness, this would entail that by definition there could exist some "worlds"—and a "God"—that are not good. Thus, if *cacodaemonies* are inherently plausible, "good" need not at all be a transcendental property of being.

Indeed, these beliefs seem to dismiss the very possibility of the "good's" being a transcendental property of being altogether. If ontological evil *is* indeed a "primitive," a positive and primary property—a "real being, because it cannot be taken as a rational entity without surrendering its essential characteristic, that of badness" (562) as Sprague claims—and if evil and goodness are again mutually exclusive properties, then there must *be* at least something which is not "good": the property of evil itself. This is obviously to say more than simply that it is not necessary for the "good" to be a transcendental property of being. It is to say that the "good" cannot be a transcendental property of being: that evil is a basic constituent of reality.

The questions I address in this paper regard the plausibility of rejecting the claim that the "good" is a transcendental property of being on the basis of claims such as Cahn's and Sprague's. That is, granted that the plausibility of *cacodaemonies* and the "primordiality" of ontological evil make the scholastic claim questionable at best, I wonder if such claims as Cahn's and Sprague's are really plausible. The specific questions I would like to address here are, as such, two: (a) can evil really be a primary or basic ontological property?—that is, are (a^{1-3}) plausible? and (b) can evil really characterize an entity—a non-abstract particular—both intrinsically and necessarily? that is, can God or any other existing thing really be essentially evil? or are (b^{1-3}) plausible?

1. On Evil and Primitiveness

A. Definitions—Primitives

To claim that "evil is an ontological primitive"—that is, a primary or basic ontological property—it would seem, is necessarily to claim at least three things:

(a^1) that evil is a *primary* or *basic property*, a characteristic, attribute, or principle, that does not in any way derive from some other thing, attribute, principle, or relation; a property, that is, that has no constituents other than itself;

which claim might be made more simply by saying that:

(a^{11}) that evil is an *unconditioned* or *non-composite* property, characteristic, attribute, or quality;

(a^2) that evil cannot be defined other than in terms of itself;

and

(a^3) that evil is a *necessary positive property* of reality, and not simply the privation or negation of some other attribute, principle, or relation.

All three claims, it would seem, are necessary entailments of the notion of "primitive." This is clearly true of the first two claims. Whatever an ontological primitive is, it would seem at the very least to require what we might call "ontological and conceptual independence." That is, the primitive must not have any basic constituents other than itself—this is what "ontological independence" would seem to entail. Given this first point, it is clear that no adequate intrinsic, essential, or whatever else one wants to call a definition of the primitive *an sich*, can invoke concepts or constituents other than the primitive itself. This is what "conceptual independence" would seem to entail. A primitive, it would seem in other words, should be something like a prime number: something that cannot be decomposed into two (or more) distinct factors—or constituents—of which one is not itself, and that cannot therefore be defined through factors—or constituents—other than itself.[7]

This first point might, perhaps, best be made by saying that ontological primitives must be "unconditioned" or "non-composite." For as true as it is that a conditioned, or composite reality—be it an entity or a property which has conditions or constituents other than itself—can be at least conceptually distinct from its factors—that is, its constituents or conditions—it is also true that that reality can also be decomposed into factors—constituents or conditions—other than itself. What this means, first off, is that no conditioned or composite reality can be "ontologically independent," since it has constituents or conditions other than itself. It is clearly a derived reality. But it also means that no conditioned or composite reality can be "conceptually independent." The very fact that this reality can be decomposed into factors other than itself necessarily entails that it can be intrinsically defined by invoking factors other than itself. If this is so, no conditioned or composite reality can be a primitive.

As for the third claim, it is clearly an entailment of the first two. A property which is unconditioned, it would seem, is by definition necessary. If it exists, it cannot not exist since it has no conditions other than itself. What is more, that property could not be a privation or negation of something other than itself, since this would clearly make it a conditioned or composite property: a property which could neither exist, nor be defined without invoking a concept or constituent other than itself. It would necessarily invoke that of which it is the privation or negation.

Given these qualifications, to ask our first question—can evil really be a primary or basic ontological property (an ontological primitive)?—is primarily to ask if evil is an "ontologically and conceptually independent property." That is, if it is a property that cannot be decomposed into factors, or constituents, other than itself. For if evil is indeed a primary or basic property, then clearly it must also be a positive and necessary property.

B. Definitions—Evil

Having squared away what sort of property "evil" must be in order to be a primitive—i.e., the necessary conditions of predicating "primitive" of the property "evil"—the next question clearly has to do with the nature of the property or feature which we call ontological "evil."

For the sake of the argument, I am going to assume that "evil," is that property or characteristic which all commonly recognized instantiations of "evil" have in common.[8] Thus, it is that characteristic which both murderers *qua* murderers and murder itself, which both torturers *qua* torturers and torture, which both perpetrators of genocide as such and genocide, which ebola and diseases more generally, which pain and suffering, which a fawn dying a lingering and painful death due to a forest fire, which the recent tsunami, the 1988 earthquake in Armenia, and all other such things have and which makes us identify them as "evil."

Now, the necessary requisite of calling any one of the above listed things (or things similar to them) "evil"—of claiming that it possesses the attribute or property which we would call "evil"—it would seem, is its destructiveness: the fact that it in some way negates or annihilates something, or some part or attribute thereof. Thus, a murderer is a person to whom we would ascribe the property "evil," because he has the property of "having intentionally *destroyed* human life." The same thing can be said of the act of murdering. A torturer is a person to whom we would even more readily ascribe the property "evil" because he is a being who has the property of "intentionally *destroying* a human being's integrity" and the same thing can be said of the act of torturing. Pain and suffering, which are the most common candidates used to illustrate evil—i.e., what one might call obvious *tokens* of they *type* evil—have the property "evil," it would seem, because they have the property of *negating* a being's well-being, life, or what not, and so on. The same thing can be said of ebola, or diseases more generally.[9]

Indeed, were none of these things not in any way destructive, we simply would not call them, or consider them evil. Ebola is a good example of this point. Were that virus not to be destructive of life, or well being, we would neither call it evil, nor consider it evil. We would simply consider the virus another life form. The same thing holds for all other instantiations of evil.[10]

This gives us a working definition of evil:

(1) if something is "evil," it must be in some way "destructive:" that is, it must negate, annihilate, damage, or any such similar thing.

This might be otherwise stated:

(1¹) if something has the property evil, it must have the property of being "destructive."

C. Evil and Primitiveness—Definitions

Now, for evil to be a "primitive" ontological property, it must be a property that has no constituents other than itself, and which cannot consequently be defined through factors other than itself. Thus, if our definition of evil is an acceptable one, then in order for evil to be an ontological primitive, every instance of evil would have to be destructive, and every instance of destructiveness would have to be evil—else evil would have to have constituents other than itself. Destructiveness, we have claimed, is a constituent of evil. To put the point in conceptual terms, if evil is indeed a primitive, evil and destructiveness must be coextensive—or synonymous—terms. For were "evil" and "destructiveness" not coextensive terms, then the claim that "if something is evil must be in some way destructive" would define "evil" other than in terms of "evil" itself. This would imply that the property "evil" has constituents other than itself. According to what would seem to be a self-evident definition of a primitive—i.e., that a primitive cannot have basic constituents other than itself—this would necessarily entail that evil is not an ontological primitive.

The fact of the matter is, however, that destructiveness is not always evil: evil and destructiveness do not at all seem to be co-extensive terms. Not all destruction is necessarily what we could call "evil." The destruction of a worn-down and broken bridge upon which no person is walking and upon which no one depends in any way, would not seem to be evil, despite the fact that it involves destruction. Indeed, it might even be a good thing, if the bridge endangers some innocent person's life, or if its destruction is a necessary requisite of building a safer bridge, of safe-guarding the environment, or any other such thing. Nor would cutting one's hair and burning the fallen locks, seem to be necessarily evil, although it clearly destroys the hair. There are cases in which one might indeed think that burning one's cut hair is a morally good thing. If leaving traces of your DNA makes it possible for someone to clone you, and cloning is a moral evil, then burning one's hair might be a morally good thing. If this is so, however, then not all destruction is necessarily evil. There are cases which are even clearer than these. Take the destruction of cancer cells, or of a loaded nuclear device which is about to explode in a densely populated area, or any other such instance in which what is being destroyed is the source of immanent destruction of the sort that we would deem "evil." It seems obvious that destruction of this kind is not only not evil, but is positively good. Whatever the case which one wants to use to illustrate this point, the fact remains that not all destruction is necessarily evil. If this is so, however, then not all destructiveness is necessarily evil.

This clearly entails that "evil" and "destruction" cannot be co-extensive terms. Thus, if the co-extensiveness of "evil" and "destructiveness" is a necessary requisite of the primitiveness of ontological evil, it would seem obvious that "evil" cannot be a "primitive," at least not in the sense delinated by the characteristics (a^{1-3}).

D. Destructiveness and Primitiveness

There is another and perhaps more significant way to demonstrate this point. It concerns destructiveness. For destructiveness itself cannot be a primitive. Destruction is a derived or conditioned fact. It is necessarily a function of two distinct elements:

(a)   a force which is capable of destroying,

and

(β)   an object which can be destroyed.

And a quick analysis of destruction itself indicates that:

- destruction is neither identical to either (a) or (β) alone, nor is it the necessary consequence of either (a) or (β) alone;[11]
- both (a) and (β) are necessary conditions of destruction;[12]

and

- destruction is necessarily a function of at least both (a) and (β);[13]

That destruction is neither identical to, nor the necessary consequence of (α) a force, power, or whatever one wants to call the capacity to effect a deleterious change is obvious. 500 mile-an-hour winds are not necessarily destructive. They can be, if they blow in the midst of a forest, on a city, a car, or what not. They can be, in other words, if they hit some destructible object. They are simply not destructive, on the other hand, if they do not hit some destructible object. If 500 mile-an-hour winds blow on some barren planet which only has flat surfaces—one of Jupiter's moons, let's say—or if they blow on a windproof skyscraper, or again if one attempted to use them to destroy an immaterial being, they would simply not be destructive. As this is true of winds, it is clearly true of any other force which is capable of destroying. Thus:

(2)   destruction is not identical to, or the necessary consequence of, (α) a force, power, or whatever one wants to call the capacity to effect a deleterious change.

This point might be better expressed:

(2¹)   (α) a force capable of destroying is neither identical to, nor the sufficient condition of, destruction.

Nor is destruction identical to, or the necessary consequence of, (β) a destructible object. This too is obvious. Any object which is not its own sufficient condition, or which has necessary conditions which are distinct from it and of which it is not the sufficient condition, is necessarily destructible. Thus, a tree, which has necessary conditions which are distinct from it and of which it is not the sufficient condition—water, light, and so forth—is necessarily destructible, precisely because it has necessary conditions which are distinct from it and of which it is not the sufficient condition. A tree cannot continue to exist as a tree without water and light. But water and light are not the tree, and need not subsist simply because the tree does. Thus, a tree can be destroyed. All one needs to do in order to do so is deprive it of one of the necessary conditions of its subsistence. Destruction, however, is not the necessary consequence of the destructibility of such an object. It cannot be, precisely because the destructible object is distinct from its necessary conditions and is not the sufficient condition of these conditions. For what this distinction entails is that the necessary conditions of a destructible object need not themselves be destructible: that they need not themselves have necessary conditions from which they are distinct. They could be their own sufficient conditions. And this could entail that an object which is inherently destructible not ever be destroyed. This is, for instance, what Aquinas claimed was the case with the human soul. Aquinas did not question that the human soul was *per se* destructible. It was clear to him that it necessarily was: the human soul is not a sufficient condition of its own subsistence—it is not the condition of the possibility of its own existence—which means of course that it has necessary conditions other than itself and of which it is not the sufficient condition. He nonetheless argued that the human soul is immortal, because the sufficient condition of the soul's existence—God—is both His own sufficient condition—and consequently is not destructible—and will not cease to sustain the soul.[14] As the destructibility of the human soul does not necessarily entail the destruction of the human soul, this could be true of any destructible object. The point here is that:

> (3)   destruction is neither identical to, nor the necessary consequence of, (β) a destructible object.

This point might be better expressed:

> (3¹)   (β) a destructible object is neither identical to, nor a sufficient condition of, destruction.

Implicit in conclusions (2) and (3) is a third conclusion:

> (4)   both (α) a force capable of destroying and (β) a destructible object are necessary conditions of destruction.

This conclusion is a direct consequence of (2) and (3). The reason why (α) a force capable of destroying is not a sufficient condition of destruction is that destruction necessarily involves a destructible object. This point is illustrated by our example. 500 mile-an-hour winds can be destructive *only* if they hit a destructible object. What this means, of course, is that a destructible object is a necessary condition of the destruction wreaked by 500 mile-an-hour winds. As this is true of winds, it is clearly true of any other potentially destructive force. Indeed, the very claim that something is destructive without actually destroying something seems contradictory, unless it is intended in something other than a literal sense. Thus, if a potentially destructive force is a necessary condition of destruction, then so too must a destructible object be. But it would seem obvious that a potentially destructive force is a necessary condition of destruction, precisely because destruction is not the necessary consequence of an object's destructibility. Thus, both a potentially destructive force and a destructible object are necessary conditions of destruction.

Now, if destruction is (2, 3) not a necessary consequence of either (α) force capable of destroying or (β) a destructible object, and yet (4) both (α) force capable of destroying and (β) a destructible object are necessary conditions of destruction, then:

> (5)   destruction must be a function of at least both (α) force capable of destroying and (β) a destructible object.[15]

Destruction, in other words, must be what in scholastic language is called a transitive act. It is an act through which something effects some change upon something other than itself. The particular characteristic of transitive acts is that they must involve both an act and an object upon which that act effects a change. If what could be a transitive act does not involve both an object upon which some change is effected and something which effects that change, then it simply does not take place. Indeed, a transitive act can only be said to take place once the object upon which the act effects the change is changed.[16] Kicking is a good illustration of this point. One actually only kicks something when one's foot strikes an object. Should there be no object to be struck, or should one to miss this object, one simply would not kick. One would swing one's leg.

But if (5) destruction is necessarily a function of at least two elements (α) force capable of destroying and (β) a destructible object, then:

(6)　destruction must be a derived, conditioned, or composite fact.

After all, the very definition of a derived, conditioned, or composite fact is that it has distinct factors—constituents or components—neither of which is itself, and can therefore be defined invoking two distinct factors—constituents or conditions—neither of which is itself. If this is so, then destruction itself cannot by definition be an ontological primitive. For as we saw, a primitive cannot be decomposed into two distinct factors of which one is not itself.

The consequences of this point with respect to the claim that "evil is a primitive" are obvious. For if destruction is a composite fact, then by definition being destructive cannot be a non-composite fact. Thus, if something evil must by definition be destructive, that is, if it is true that:

(1)　if something is evil, it must be in some way destructive: it must negate, annihilate, damage, or what not,

and that:

(6)　destruction must be a derived, conditioned, or composite fact,

then evil is necessarily not an ontological primitive.

This is an important conclusion. It entails that evil cannot be (or be thought of as) a basic and necessary property, but rather must be a derived property. This point has enormous consequences. For if evil is a derived property, then that from which evil is derived can not itself be evil. If this is so, however, then all basic and necessary properties—all ontological primitives—are necessarily not evil.

2. On the Instantiability of Evil

A. Definitions—Conditions of Instantiation

This brings us to our second question: can God, or any other existing thing, really be essentially evil? To claim that "evil is a primitive" in this second sense," it would seem, is necessarily to claim at least two things:

(b²)　evil is a property which *intrinsically* characterizes that thing, entity, or non-abstract particular in which it is instantiated, as opposed to characterizing that thing in virtue of some relation it has to things other than itself;

and:

(b³)　evil is a *necessary* characteristic of the thing, entity, or non-abstract particular in which it is instantiated.[17]

These points seem merely to delineate some of the obvious requisites of the instantiation of an essential property. Indeed, they seem to be just the sort of requisites which Cahn himself adopts in his characterization of the evil Creator of the *cacodaemony*. When Cahn claims that it is possible to think of a world as the product of a "maximally evil demon"—an evil God—he does not mean merely to claim that it is plausible to think of the Creator as appearing to be "maximally evil" to some bystander who cannot make sense of such things as "separating the sheep from the goats," or even that the Creator is evil because he "maltreats" his creations. Rather, he seems to suggest that we can treat the property "evil" as a property that the Creator has independently of his relations—cognitive or otherwise—to things other than himself: a property that characterizes Creator intrinsically. Cahn seems to think that that property is wickedness. Nor does Cahn's thought project involve thinking of evil as a property which is not essential to the *maximally evil demon*, as an accidental property: one, that is, that it might be possible for the Creator to acquire to a maximal degree, but that the Creator does not need to instantiate. Cahn does not claim that God could perhaps become "evil," and if He did it would be a very scary evil indeed. On the contrary, Cahn seems to think that it is possible for "evil" to be a property which the Creator instantiates necessarily: a property which the Creator of the universe cannot not have.

Given these requisites, determining whether evil is a primitive in the sense in question is primarily to determine if evil can really characterize an entity—a non-abstract particular—(c) independently if its relations to things other than itself, and (d) necessarily.[18]

B. Evil and Essential Instantiation

Whatever evil is, one of the necessary requisites of calling something evil is that it be in some way destructive. Thus, in our working definition we claimed that:

(1) if something is evil, it must in some way be destructive: it must annihilate, damage, or what not.

Thus, if to claim that for something to instantiate a property essentially is for that property to characterize that non-abstract particular in which it is instantiated both necessarily and independently of its relations to things other than itself, and then it must be true that:

(7) if something is "essentially evil," it must be necessarily destructive independently of its relations to things other than itself.

If (7), however, then:

(8) there can only be one thing with respect to which something which is essentially evil, insofar as it is essentially evil, can be necessarily destructive: itself.

There are a number of interesting considerations to be made at this point. To begin with, if something can be destructive only if it actually engages in actual destruction, then (8) would entail that:

(9) something essentially evil must engage in the actual destruction of itself in order to be evil.

In itself, this is an odd thing to believe. But the corollaries of this point are even more odd. For if that which is essentially evil is also necessarily evil—which is to say that that which is essentially evil cannot exist without being evil—then if (9) is true, we have that:

(10) something essentially evil cannot exist without engaging in the actual destruction of itself;

or again that:

(11) something essentially evil must actually engage in the destruction of itself in order to exist.

There seems to be something contradictory about these conclusions. They would require the negation of a given thing's existence to be a condition of its existence. Thus, it seems credible to claim that:

(12) something essentially evil cannot exist.

C. Evil and the Instantiation of Composite Properties

There is another way of making this point. It has to do with destructiveness. Destruction, as we saw above, is (6) a composite fact. What this means in terms of thinking of evil as a property is that:

(13) if evil were a property, it would necessarily be a composite property.

This, in essence, is the reason why evil cannot be a primitive in the first sense. The point has bearing on this present argument too. For it would seem evident that:

(14) it is necessary for that which instantiates a composite property to instantiate all of the elements of which that composite property is composed.

Thus, if a cup instantiates whiteness, the cup must instantiate all of the colors of which the color white is composed. Indeed, a cup could not instantiate whiteness if it did not instantiate all of the colors of which the color white is composed. By definition, if it were to instantiate only some of these colors of which the color white is composed, it would be some other color.

This is not quite right. Although instantiating all of the elements of which a composite property is composed is a necessary condition of instantiating that composite property, it is not a sufficient condition of instantiating that composite property. What is lacking here, of course, is the fact that the elements of which the composite property is composed must themselves be composed in their instantiation in order for an instantiation to be of the composite property. To continue with our example, a cup could instantiate all of the colors of the rainbow, but this would not necessarily entail that that cup be white. The cup could instantiate each of the colors of the rainbow distinctly: it could be a harlequin sort of cup. In order for the cup to instantiate "whiteness," the colors of which the "white" is composed must themselves be composed in the cup. Thus, it is perhaps best to reformulate (14) above to read:

(14¹) that which instantiates a composite property must instantiate all of the elements of which that composite property is composed in a property which is a compound of these properties.

Now, if (14^1) is true, then it must be true that:

(15) that which instantiates "evil" must instantiate all of the elements of which "evil" is composed in a compound property.

Two of the elements which destruction necessarily involves, as we saw above, are: (α) force capable of destroying and (β) a destructible object. For:

(5) destruction is necessarily a function of both (α) a force capable of destroying and (β) a destructible object.

Thus, if (15) a being which instantiates a composite property must instantiate all of the elements of which the composite property is composed in a compound property:

(16) whatever instantiated "evil" would necessarily instantiate at least both (α) a force capable of destroying and (β) a destructible object in a compound property.

The point here is obvious in light of the arguments we formulated above. For an object which instantiates evil must instantiate destructiveness: it must necessarily be destructive. But if an object were only to instantiate (α) a force which is capable of destroying, it would not necessarily be destructive, precisely because (2^1) such a force is not a sufficient condition of destruction. Thus, an object which only instantiated (α) could not instantiate destructiveness, and could not instantiate evil. Nor would an object be necessarily destructive if it only instantiated (β) a destructible object, because (3^1) a destructible object is also not a sufficient condition of evil. In this case too, as such, the object would not instantiate destructiveness and could not consequently instantiate evil. The only way in which a being could necessarily instantiate destructiveness would be for it to instantiate the compound of both (α) a force capable of destroying, and (β) a destructible object .

But:

(17) if a being instantiated the compound of both (α) a force capable of destroying and (β) a destructible object, the being would necessarily destroy itself.

This being would certainly instantiate destruction. It would, however, also not exist. If this is so, however, then:

(18) no existing being can instantiate destructiveness or destruction.

But if no existing being can instantiate destructiveness or destruction, then:

(19) no existing being can instantiate evil.

Thus, it would not seem possible to think of evil as an essential property of things.[19]

Conclusion

Where does this leave us? To demonstrate that evil can neither be a primitive in the two senses in which we have intended this proposition is to demonstrate two things: (1) that one cannot think of evil as a basic constituent of reality, and (2) that one cannot think of it as a basic constituent of things, entities, non-abstract particulars. These are certainly important things. They are a far cry from demonstrating that the scholastic doctrine of transcendentals is sound. At most they allow us to claim that all that is might be good. This is important in its own right, however. It demonstrates that that doctrine can at least be plausible.

University of St. Thomas, St. Paul, MN

Notes

1. In contemporary analytic terms, the claim that being and the good are convertible terms is: that the good is intentionally distinct from being, but is extensionally identical to being. It is not just a scholastic claim. Aristotle coined the phrase.

2. Steven M. Cahn, "Cacodaemony," *Analysis*, 37,2 (1977), 69–73. Cahn's claim is that "evil" worlds created by an "evil" God—a "maximally evil" demon—are just as plausible as "good" worlds created by a "good" God.

3. This definition would imply that Sprague believes that evil has at least the attributes (a^2) and (a^3). But granted her take on (a^2), one can surmise that she also holds that evil has the attribute (a^1). She claims as much in the body of her article. See Rosamond Kent Sprague "Negation and Evil," *Philosophy and Phenomenological Research*, 11 (1951), 561–567.

4. J. L. Mackie, "Evil and Omnipotence," *Mind* 64 (1955), 200–212. Mackie does not actually list the second requisite at the beginning of the article. It is, however, clear that he assumes it as one of his opening premises. He claims as much. "This solution denies that evil is opposed to the good in our original sense" (204).

5. See, e.g., William Rowe, "The Problem of Evil and Some Varieties of Atheism," *American Philosophical Quarterly*, 16 (1979), 336.

6. Nor is there anything mysterious about the reasons why those contemporary authors, who wish to claim that God does not exist because evil does, would want evil to be a primitive. That reason, simply put, is that evil's being a primitive would make their claims very much stronger. This is not difficult to see. For their arguments, whether logically or evidentially based, seem always to involve the claim that there is something irreconcilable—I am using this word purposely, since I don't believe that contemporary thinkers believe that the claims result in a contradiction—about the combination of propositions that: (1) God is good, (2) God is omnipotent, and (3) evil exists. The irreconcilability, it seems, is two-fold: (a) the irreconcilability of God's goodness and evil; and (b) the irreconcilability of God's omnipotence and the existence of evil. Thus, if God is good, God is necessarily "opposed to" evil. If God is omnipotent, or so the claim goes, then God can ensure that His opposition is felt—i.e., that evil will not exist. By combining these claims, as such, we have the premise: if God is good and omnipotent, then evil necessarily does not exist. Assuming, then, that one does want to ensure that the conclusion that God does not exist is drawn from this premise—which I believe is a fair assumption with respect to the thinkers in question—then one must find the strongest possible way of affirming that evil necessarily does exist. Now, the strongest possible way of doing this would seem to involve the claim that evil is a primitive, i.e., an irreducible and necessary part of reality, since this would make evil indestructible. Indeed,

this claim would make these authors' basic argument run thus: God exists iff God is good and omnipotent. But if God is good and omnipotent, then, evil would necessarily not exist. But evil cannot necessarily not exist. Evil exists necessarily. It is an irreducible and necessary component of reality. Thus God cannot be good and omnipotent. If this is so, however, then God does not exist.

7. I am using Borevich and Shafarevich's definition of a prime number in this definition of a primitive: "An element p of the ring D, nonzero and not a unit, is called *prime* if it can not be decomposed into factors $p=ab$, neither of which is a unit in D."

8. The reason for my focusing on "all" instantiations of evil, as opposed to just one, stems from contemporary approaches to evil itself. Most thinkers who deal with the problem of evil in contemporary literature focus solely on pain and suffering. The reason for this is not just historical, i.e., the fact that Hume seems to focus on these instances of evil. Pain and suffering also seem to be the closest case of what might qualify as instances of "evil" *qua* primitive. This seems to have led to thinkers to believe that they can hold that evil is a primitive forthright, rather than demonstrating that it is. Thus, I thought it best to return to the drawing board to see if the claim could be substantiated. This return should in principle not alter the case for the primitiveness of evil in any way. For if evil is indeed a primitive, it should make no difference what instances of evil we use to analyze it. Indeed, if the case is made that considering all instances of evil does alter the case for the primitiveness of evil, then one would have to posit either that there are different types of evil, or that there is a difference in "evil," as it is instantiated in different things. But positing this sort of thing would inevitably indicate that evil cannot be an ontological primitive. For if "evil" admits of different types, or varies from instantiation to instantiation, then the "evil" must be a composite property. This claim is true for a variety of different reasons. The fact remains, however, that a composite property cannot be a primitive.

9. Hence the classical definition of evil as a privation: that is, as (1) that which negates being, or (2) the negation of being. See, e.g., Boethius, *Consolatio Philosophiae*, III.12.80–82. The definition seems rather commonplace in modern philosophy too. When, for instance, Hume lists the evils of the world, he includes such things as "unhappiness," and "corruption," "pain," and so forth, all of which seem to be privations.

10. To get back to pain, serious thinkers have given serious reasons for holding that it should be thought of as a "positive property"—i.e., that cannot be thought of merely as "destructive," or "privative." I am thinking here, for instance, of Suarez. See Jorge Gracia, "Evil and Goodness: Suárez's Solution," in Scott MacDonald, *Being and Goodness: the Concept of the Good in Metaphysics and Philosophical Theology*, Ithaca: Cornell University Press, 1991, 151–178). The case Suarez makes for pain's being positive evil is that pain cannot be reduced to a privative relation with respect to pleasure: "pain is something positive we experience and cannot be analyzed negatively in terms of the privative or preventive functions it may have with respect to pleasure" (135–136). Nor can it be reduced to a "mental phenomenon without objective reality" (136). Thus, it seems to be an "intrinsic evil" (157). This point seems to be a barrier to the claim that all things are evil because they are destructive. For if pain is an "intrinsic evil"—i.e., something that is evil independently of its relations—then it would seem that pain cannot be evil because it is destructive. Destruction involves a relation. Yet, I wonder if it is true that pain is evil independently of any relations at all. If it were, then it would seem plausible to claim that all pain is necessarily evil. But this does not seem to be true. There are some pains which are not evil. I am thinking here of the pain that one feels when one's body is healing. If this is so, however, then it does not at all seem necessary

for pain to be evil independently of all relations. Thus, I find it difficult to accept that pain can be evil independently of all relations. Another consideration which would lead to this same conclusion might be this: if pain is evil independently of all relations, then it must be evil independently of its being felt, since feeling a pain seems to be relational. But this too does not seem plausible. Why should pain be an evil independently of its being felt? I doubt anyone would consider unfelt pain to be evil. This being so, I do not believe that pain is necessarily an "intrinsic evil," or that it cannot be thought of relationally. Thus, I do not think that it is a counterexample to my point.

11. That is, $\{(d \neq a) \text{ and } (d \neq b)\}$.

12. That is, $\{\text{if } d, a \wedge b\}$

13. That is, $\{d = ab\}$.

14. See, for instance, *Summa Contra Gentiles*, 2, 55 § 14.

15. The reason for the qualification is that there could presumably be factors other than a destructive force and a destructible object involved in that destruction which we call evil. One might think that intentionality is one such factor.

16. Hence the scholastic claim that for transitive acts is *actio est in passo*. The source of the doctrine is Aristotle. See, e.g. *Physics*, III., c. iii.

17. The reason why one might want to define "evil" in this second sense as primitive is that it too can fall under the definition of primitive we gave above. After all, if something can be counted as ontologically primitive if it has "no components other than itself," and as conceptually primitive insofar as "its adequate essential definition cannot invoke factors other than itself," then since a thing's being essentially evil implies that it is "intrinsically and necessarily evil," a thing's "evil" seems not to have factors other than the thing itself.

18. One's response to these questions is not necessarily determined by one's stance with respect to the "primordiality" of the property evil itself—i.e., its being a primary or basic ontological property. The reason for this is simple: a property need not be "primitive" in order to characterize a non-abstract particular intrinsically and necessarily. Consequently, the fact that evil cannot be a primitive in the first sense—a primary or basic ontological property—does not in principle preclude its being a primitive in the second sense.

19. This last point has an added advantage of meeting a possible objection to our first argument. For the argument with which we demonstrated that destruction is a composite fact, presupposed that the two elements involved in destruction—i.e., that (a) a force capable of destroying if that force (b) a destructible object—were distinct. This present argument grounds that presupposition. For if (a) the potentially destructive force were one and the same thing as (b) the destructible object, the destructive force would necessarily destroy itself. But something which necessarily destroys itself cannot exist, let alone destroy anything. It would cease to exist the moment it existed. Thus if there is such a thing as a destructive force: then the (a) a force capable of destroying must be distinct from (b) a destructible object.

Natural Law, Natural Rhetoric, and Rhetorical Perversions

Jeffrey J. Maciejewski

Abstract. Observers, including the Catholic Church, have consistently demonstrated a keen ability to identify instances of rhetoric, such as advertising, that are distasteful or offensive. Although they have not necessarily characterized such endeavors as immoral, I submit that a developing notion of "natural rhetoric" may permit such criticism by contextualizing rhetoric as natural, unnatural or even perverse. Following this approach I assert that natural rhetoric, in service to reason, makes possible the apprehension of the basic good of *societas*. Consequently, rhetoric of the unnatural variety undermines this teleological purpose; when conceived as a perversion it might not only undermine the mission of natural rhetoric, but it might do so in such a way that it harms one or more individuals. After articulating and testing this exploratory thesis with two exemplars, I offer implications for Thomistic natural law and for those who formulate the Catholic Church's positions on social communications.

As perhaps the most visible form of modern rhetoric, advertising is subject to an endless stream of criticism. Among its critics is the Catholic Church's Pontifical Council for Social Communications who has regularly commented on the role of advertising in economic and social life.[1] However, despite the usefulness of this discourse it has been mostly unable to account for the human propensity to employ rhetoric in the pursuit of social and economic relationships.[2] Indeed, it seems that the use of rhetoric is a necessary element of fruitful human associations, be they economic or purely social.[3] Recent research on this topic has asserted that the ability of rhetoric to enable human associations can be sourced to the manner in which reason supports rhetoric and within the context of natural law, the manner in which reason moves the will in order to precipitate action and apprehend our dispositions. If rhetoric services reason, which in turn services the dispositions in natural law, and if rhetoric is particularly adept at apprehending of the basic good of living with one another in society (*societas*), then it might be said that rhetoric is intrinsic to the basic good of *societas* itself. Therefore, in view of its ability to affect the apprehension of a basic good, rhetoric might be viewed as "natural."[4]

If one can accept the possibility that in their ability to apprehend *societas* rhetorical endeavors might be conceived as natural, then I believe that one useful feature of "natural rhetoric" is its use as a paradigm in which to criticize rhetorical artifacts, such as advertising, in a unique way: It might be used to identify particular rhetorical practices as unethical especially for the manner in which they violate the teleological purpose of rhetoric in apprehending *societas*. If one purpose of rhetoric is to secure the good of *societas* and if this might in some way constitute natural rhetoric, then it would seem that rhetorical endeavors that in some way negate the good of *societas* might be seen as unnatural; if such endeavors go so far as to harm individuals then they might well be considered *perversions*. I believe that being able to assess the "naturalness" of rhetorical endeavors in this way, including the ability to identify some as perversions, can precisely assess rhetorical practices based on their "natural" ability to apprehend *societas*.

Therefore the purpose of this paper is to continue the exploration into the possibility of a natural rhetoric by examining the way in which it might be used to uniquely implicate certain persuasive practices as immoral. After briefly describing the thesis of natural rhetoric, I will advance the idea that rhetoric may in some cases be considered unnatural and possibly even perverse. I then test these conceptions with two exemplars, after which I suggest implications for those in the Catholic Church responsible for formulating the Church's position on social communications as well as some implications for Thomistic natural law.

While advancing my thesis, I will be making a number of assumptions that should be explained at the outset. First, although in the classical or skeptical rhetorical traditions were understood by Aristotle, Plato, Sophocles, and Euripides to be "art[s] of persuasion and belief, of deception and proof, of image-making and communication,"[5] I have chosen to adopt a postmodern conception of rhetoric that sees both persuasion and rhetoric as somewhat indeterminate elements that are inherent in discourse.[6] In this idiom, the once disparately treated practices of rhetoric and persuasion are held to be interchangeable forms of discourse that are oftentimes employed imperceptibly. Brummett has characterized this conception of rhetoric as "a complex concept comprising reason-giving discourse which seeks to influence people symbolically."[7] Although this position is certainly controversial among some rhetorical theorists[8] I, like Scott, believe that "rhetoric is present and is sensed as a part of the normal experiencing of one's environment"[9] and that as such, "an enlarged conception of rhetoric is necessary if we are to comprehend the substantial and dynamic senses in which rhetoric functions to generate continuous validation of ways in which communities act together."[10]

Second, my application of natural-law ethical theory will be based on a theory of human nature articulated by Aquinas.[11] It is not my intent to offer natural law as a completely defensible means of moral inquiry or to suggest that Thomistic natural law is without fault. Indeed, a number of writers have recently taken up the charge of reconstructing and analyzing Aquinas's theory of natural law, often coming up with different results.[12] Rather, I believe that Aquinas's conception of natural law can serve as a starting point for an exploration of natural rhetoric.

I.

On the Possibility of Natural Rhetoric. I have previously expressed the belief that reason serves as a nexus of natural law and rhetoric based on the manner in which reason supports rhetoric and based on the way that reason precipitates the pursuit of the dispositions.[13] To see this as a possibility, one must first revisit Aquinas's conception of the three dispositions that define our essence: a disposition towards living, towards sensory apprehensions and towards rational cognitivity. Although rationality might appear to be limited to the last of these dispositions, Lisska writes that human nature has rationality as an essential property: "Hence, the ends which make up the human essence, determined by theoretical [or speculative] reason and pursued by practical reason, establish the obligatory actions for human beings."[14]

This would imply that the ends prescribed by our dispositions must be in accordance with reason. Crowe takes up the matter more directly:

> Man is not made up of three natures, substantial, sensitive and rational, successively superimposed one upon the other. The nature of man is one, and the single rational soul performs, *eminentiori modo*, the functions of man considered as a substance or as an animal. Reason, then, enters at all three levels of natural inclination.[15]

Although Lisska and Crowe do not elaborate on the structural relationship between reason and the dispositions, one might assert that reason nonetheless in some way "services" Aquinas's dispositions.

This brings us to a most important proposition: If reason services all three of Aquinas's dispositions, and if "rhetoric [is] the handmaiden to reason,"[16] then it would follow that rhetoric has some bearing on the servicing of all three dispositions such that Reason > Rhetoric > Dispositions. Although the precise character and magnitude of this bearing is a topic for further exploration, it seems rather clear that if rhetoric services reason and if reason in some way services the dispositions, then rhetoric in some way makes the attainment of the dispositions possible.

One way to visualize this relationship between rhetoric and the dispositions is to consider how rhetoric might apprehend one disposition: the good of living with one another in society, or *societas*. Rhetorical theorists such as Burke have made clear that "rhetoric [is] an important tool of socialization"[17] whose utility is derived from its ability to forge a collective sense of meaning among individuals living in society with one another. Brummett asserts that rhetoric therefore finds itself at the center of the creation of meaning: "Reality is what experience *means*. This meaning is taken from personal experience and communication about it with others, the sharing of meaning."[18] Moreover, "since meanings are formed and changed socially through rhetorical dialogue with others, the reality which is grounded in meaning is also formed and changed rhetorically."[19] Brummett illustrates the point through the following example:

> People have no difficulty seeing as rhetorical a speech arguing that we should try to conserve our trees. But through the more diffuse, everyday

rhetoric experienced by living in a culture, the speaker and audience have been led to regard trees as a distinct category of objects (plants), worth conserving, also worth squandering, not able to help themselves, a material resource, etc., and it is through those rhetorically induced meanings that we have the tree in the first place.[20]

Thus, he holds that "participation in shared meanings are requisites for participation in society."[21]

The moral implication behind this "requirement" can be sourced to *societas*. Recall that Lisska described the third of Aquinas's dispositions as "dispositions or inclinations towards rational cognitivity."[22] Under this heading he included the disposition "to understand (rational curiosity)" and the disposition "to live together in social communities," or *societas*. If indeed "part of the 'rational disposition' [of which *societas* is a part] is to engage in language with other persons,"[23] then it would follow that "language" (or in our case "rhetoric") is somehow one constituent of *societas*. Finnis illuminates this possibility by claiming that truthful, authentic "communication is central to the good of *societas* and is a requirement of love of neighbour as self."[24] If we can assume the position of Scott who saw rhetoric as giving rise to truth,[25] we can see the possibility that rhetoric, as a form of communication that in a sense "creates" truth, is intrinsic to or services the good of *societas* itself. Brummett once observed, "the most ethical world view is one with rhetoric at its center."[26] If so, then I believe that the rhetoric he was referring to was, in essence, *natural rhetoric*.[27]

II.

On the Possibility of "Unnatural" Rhetoric. Having made my case for natural rhetoric, I now turn to the "unnatural." Within the context of natural-law theory, the unnatural is not only situated as the ideological opposite of the natural, it is possessed of a moral connotation, which "has to do with a threat to the exercise of some essential property of human nature (or 'basic value')."[28] Aquinas believed that human goods, as ends, "may be hindered in either of two ways—by being totally excluded or by being made more difficult or less becoming of attainment."[29] Therefore, "an unnatural act is one that denies a person (oneself or another) one or more of the basic human goods without necessity."[30]

To be considered unnatural *and immoral*, the act must be considered as a sin against nature (by way of an obstruction of a natural inclination). This is mainly determined by choice, or the decision to pursue one basic good at the expense of another. Finnis characterizes the matter as a "distinctive concern with the *form* of one's choices."[31] May situates "form of choice" as a process by which practical reason is brought to bear in an examination of "the various contingencies or circumstances in which the act is done," fully cognizant that "a contingency can inwardly change the moral object that the agent must intend as the proximate end of his act."[32] Since we are "summoned to love the basic values where they directly and immediately fall under [our] choice by reason of the form of [our] choice,"[33] to be considered unnatural, choice must reject the call of human value.

An important subclass of the unnatural is the perverted, a condition in which an agent has "turned away from a condition that is naturally proper or right."[34] This "turning away" need not be immoral as Kainz and Williams point out. Generally, acts that might be classified as perversions are those that: involve some sort of aesthetic disparity in which "taste" is brought into question;[35] or deny a person, whether herself or another, "one of the basic human goods (or the capacity for it) and no other basic human good is seen as resulting thereby, and when pleasure is the motive of the denial."[36]

Amoral Rhetorical Perversions. Following these conceptions of perversion, it is posited that *rhetoric* is subject to *perversion* when it runs afoul of aesthetic judgment and when, as it takes the form of natural rhetoric, it is misused. These, I shall argue, represent "rhetorical perversions" of the amoral variety. First, an elaboration of amoral perversions is in order. Hume believed that "the judgment of taste as an effect characterizes the aesthetic response as essentially passive and nonintellective."[37] As "passive" and "nonintellective" such judgments are amoral, precisely because no one has been harmed or more specifically, because no basic human goods have been denied or violated. However, aesthetic judgments might still be perverted since they are "psychological incapacities." Williams notes this by claiming, "the possibility of perversion and the possibility of beauty are related to each other in our psychology."[38] Given this relationship, perversion might be thought of in aesthetic terms:

> An aesthetic response, for the purposes of this discussion, is a response directed to an object that is imaginatively and emotionally satisfying because it is a perceptual object. In this light, a perversion is to be understood as a type of attraction that reveals a defectiveness or incapacity in aesthetic response and is subject to a recognizably aesthetic style of criticism.[39]

Therefore, I maintain that a rhetorical perversion might be considered amoral if it not only fails to do harm to a person or violate any basic human goods, but employs natural rhetoric to produce some form of an aesthetic deviation.

Immoral Perversions of Rhetoric. Similarly, it is proposed that for a persuasion to be immorally perverse, it must deny one or more persons one or more of the basic human goods (or the capacity for them) without necessity in the pursuit of an attraction, thereby degrading or corrupting these persons.[40] To better envision such a case, it is necessary to define attraction and degradation as they relate to immoral perversion. Williams writes that, "for perversion to be possible, a desire should be regarded as responsive to something that has considerable attractive power in its own right, that allures and captivates, and that disposes the person who has the desire to dwell on, linger over, or interact with, the attracting object."[41] For Levy, attraction is "pleasure"—whatever pleasure is being serviced by the perversion is itself perverted. Degradation, on the other hand, deals with a "sort of damage" that is rendered to someone while in the pursuit of pleasure, which might be considered a "traumatization" or a "corruption."[42]

III.

Exemplars. To test the thesis outlined in the foregoing, it is first necessary to establish advertising (as rhetoric) as a candidate for perversion. Williams offers a useful framework for making such a determination:

> Where X ranges over responses to attractive things, and where the de facto attractive is at least a provisional indicator of the attraction-worthy, (i) a perversion if X presupposes a teleological framework for thinking about Xs. (ii) Some Xs do have a natural purpose, and so are intelligible within a teleological framework. Therefore, (iii) such Xs are (potential) candidates for perversion. According to this argument, a perversion of X is more circumspectly regarded as a perversion of X's natural purpose.[43]

One might immediately be able to substitute "rhetoric" with "X" and substitute "pursuit of sales" or "acquisition of profit" in place of "attractive things" in the above argument. But a more rigorous application of Williams's framework is necessary in order to claim that advertising (as rhetoric) is subject to perversion. To begin, it certainly seems that the pursuit of sales or the acquisition of profits (which is generally believed to be advertising's main purpose, at least in capitalist societies) would meet Williams's definition of an "attraction," if not Levy's more ephemeral concept of "pleasure." Within the context of Williams's framework, in this paper I have asserted the notion that (i) a perversion of rhetoric presupposes a teleological framework for thinking about rhetoric. This framework is rooted in a natural inclination to use rhetoric in the pursuit of *societas*; such is the concept of natural rhetoric. Similarly, (ii) the natural purpose of rhetoric is to positively affect human associations or apprehend the good of *societas*. Therefore, (iii) rhetoric is a potential candidate for perversion (but not necessarily an *immoral* perversion).

An Amoral Rhetorical Perversion. Having made the determination that advertising is susceptible to perversion, it is now possible to probe two exemplars to more fully apply the thesis. As suggested, some perversions are amoral. One example might be the Benetton ad presented in Figure 1. I believe that this exemplar represents an *amoral rhetorical perversion* based on the following:

1. The imagery used in the ad fails to harm a person or violate a basic human good; and

2. The ad utilizes natural rhetoric in such a way as to result in an aesthetic deviation or to simply run afoul of good taste.

Italian clothier Benetton has gained a reputation for producing controversial ads that promote social and cultural diversity using the theme "United Colors of Benetton." Although this particular execution does not harm anyone or violate a basic human good, I assert that the ad nonetheless embodies questionable aesthetic judgment, which classifies it as a perversion.

I believe this ad's status as a perversion is due mainly to a misuse of rhetoric. Morrow wrote that persuasion may be accomplished by "fair means" or may consist

Figure 1

of a "talking over by foul means."[44] Since the apparent intent of this ad was to shock and titillate in order to convey Benetton's support of social or racial diversity, and since it would seem that other less aesthetically dubious options were available to convey the same message, I believe that this ad constitutes a "talking over by foul means." The "foul means" in this case are means that would seem to have been purposely left unrestricted, thereby demonstrating a concern for "the efficacy of bringing about [an] end" in preference to the "standards" involved in "choosing among means."[45] Employing rhetoric in literally any manner necessary in order to bring about an end might constitute "foul means" and indicate a clear misuse of natural rhetoric.

An Immoral Perversion of Rhetoric. Now consider the advertisement for Audiovox electronic equipment presented in Figure 2 (see next page). I believe that this ad meets the criteria for an *immoral perversion of rhetoric* based on the following:

1. The imagery used in the ad might well contribute in some way to the objectification of women and as such undermines *societas*; and

2. The undermining or limiting of this capacity was done so without necessity in the pursuit of sales or in the acquisition of profits, thus degrading women.

Objectification and Sociability. First, I assert that since the ad objectifies the female form it objectifies females, thereby limiting the capacity for the attainment of the basic good of *societas*. There is widespread agreement in the literature that the gratuitous use of sexual imagery of women (and even the not-so gratuitous) is in some way responsible for their objectification in society. Kilboure writes that women's "bodies are routinely used as objects to sell every imaginable kind of product, from

Figure 2

chainsaws to chewing gum."[46] In many cases, women's bodies are decontextualized. Like the Audiovox ad, "many ads feature just a part of a woman's body—a derriere, a headless torso."[47] When women's bodies are presented as though they've been "dismembered"[48] or represented in a fragmentary manner "as if their bodies were made up of spare parts,"[49] the images certainly affect women. Dickey believes that they "teach [them] to know [their] place, to make [them] feel disempowered, inadequate, second-rate."[50] Thus, as Haineault and Roy claim, "it is absolutely justifiable to assert that such images degrade the female body and perpetuate an ineluctable phantasm of female submission."[51]

Beyond affecting just women, such imagery might indeed have a profound impact on society. Kilbourne believes that such an objectification of women influences sex and desire:

> It is becoming clearer that this objectification has consequences, one of which is the effect that it has on sexuality and desire. Sex in advertising and the media is often criticized from a puritanical perspective—there's too much of it, it's too blatant, it will encourage kids to be promiscuous and so forth. But sex in advertising has far more to do with trivializing sex than promoting it, with narcissism than with promiscuity, with consuming than with connecting. The problem is not that it is sinful, but that it is synthetic and cynical.[52]

Dickey believes that objectification affects the relationship between men and women:

> We grow up with this voyeurism and it has deep psychological effects on us. It means we learn to see ourselves as men see us. We see with their eyes, not our own. Men look at women. Women watch themselves being looked at. This determines not only most relations between men and women but also the relation of women to themselves. The surveyor of woman in herself is male, the surveyed female. Thus she turns herself into an object and most particularly an object of vision: a sight.[53]

Given the cumulative effect that objectified images such as used in the Audiovox ad might have on women's self-perceptions and on men's perceptions of women, it seems rather clear that objectification undermines the human good of sociability, the attainment of positive human relationships, and more broadly, the apprehension of *societas* itself.

Unnecessary Objectification. Second, I assert that this objectification and related social harm was done without necessity. As much as women's bodies are "used to attract attention to the product in increasingly absurd ways, as when a nude woman is used to sell a watch or breasts are used to sell fishing line,"[54] one might wonder what a woman undressing (or sex with a woman, for that matter), has to do with portable DVD players, flat panel televisions, or cell phones. Apparently, the "eye opening" response to seeing a woman undress was used as a metaphor for the "eye opening" features offered by the Audiovox products featured in the ad. But clearly, other choices were available to whomever conceived or executed the ad. One might readily imagine other metaphors, equally legitimate as "eye openers," that could have been depicted in the ad instead. That this *particular choice* was made suggests that the "attraction" alluded to by Williams was compelling enough to disregard the aversion to using an image of a woman undressing to sell personal electronic products and pursue sales by whatever means possible.

IV.

Implications for Catholic Social Communications Policy. One implication of the foregoing is how it might inform Catholic social thought. Here, I believe that the concept of natural rhetoric comports with moral principles espoused by the Church and that this concept may offer those who articulate policy an important way to characterize manifestations of rhetoric in a manner that is consistent with the law of human nature. I believe also that this manner of characterizing rhetoric will permit more precise moral assessments based on the extent to which rhetoric supports or denigrates the pursuit of our dispositions.

Foley and Pastore have made clear that those who work in the media must know the principles of the moral order and apply them faithfully: "The moral order to which this refers is the order of the law of human nature, binding upon all because it is 'written on their hearts' and embodies the imperatives of authentic human fulfillment."[55] This is, of course, a direct reference to natural-law theory. But this seems to prompt two important questions: How is the law of human nature manifested specifically in the media? And how might those who work in the media come to know this moral order?

I submit that the answers to both questions is natural rhetoric. If indeed "rhetoric services reason, which in turn services the dispositions, it can [then] be seen as a natural, morally praiseworthy concomitant of the exercising of reason which helps to reveal the potentiality of reason itself."[56] The role of rhetoric in securing the basic good of *societas* as but one example, I believe this conception of rhetoric helps to codify the linkage between the law of human nature and rhetoric (as one concomitant of the media). Similarly, I submit that if practitioners understood their endeavors in terms of their ability to bring about the positive human relationships that help define *societas*, that they might have a better understanding of how their work relates to the law of human nature.

Finally, I believe also that conceiving of rhetoric as having the potential to be natural, unnatural or possibly even perverse, permits more precise moral criticism, consistent with natural law, by focusing on the manner in which rhetorical artifacts are executed. One example is being able to cite ads that objectify women as being morally perverse. Foley writes:

> It frankly surprises me that, as women rightly fight for equality of treatment in politics and in business, they are still so often exploited in the media in general and in advertising in particular as objects, as sex symbols. Such exploitation has now apparently been extended to men as well.[57]

Although he notes that such ads fail to recognize the dignity of the human person (as in the persons portrayed and the audience members reached), one might also say that such ads are morally problematic because the stereotypes and depictions used have the ability to erode the basic good of *societas* by hindering or making more difficult its attainment. All this, I believe, helps to sharpen the moral criticism of advertising (as rhetoric) using a stronger philosophical link to natural-law theory.

Implications for Natural Law. Another implication of this essay is what it might suggest for natural-law theory, which has heretofore merely hinted at some relationship between communication and natural law. Accounting for those conditions necessary for the expression of human authenticity, Maritain writes "by the very fact that each of us is a person and expresses himself to himself, each of us requires communication *with other* and *the others* in the order of knowledge and love."[58] Similarly, Fuller writes "if we were forced to select the principle that supports and infuses all human aspiration we would find it in the objective of maintaining communication with our fellows."[59] Ryan articulates a more specific role for communication in natural law, claiming the "good of human communication"[60] is one of three important dispositions that human beings are inclined to pursue. Although certainly more specific, I believe that Ryan's conception of communication (like Maritain's) is susceptible to the same criticism leveled at Fuller, who Lisska claims, "[did] not develop this insight."[61]

Nevertheless, if communication serves as an important human disposition (i.e., Ryan), enables the development of the person (i.e., Maritain), or functions as the keystone of human aspiration (i.e., Fuller), then I believe that it does so in its service to reason in the apprehension of at least one basic good, *societas*. And so it seems that if one admits to the possibility of Reason > Rhetoric > *Societas*, then one may wonder about the role of rhetoric in apprehending practical reasonableness itself. Finnis asserts that practical reasonableness can only amount to virtue "when it is integrated with the other elements of good character: justice, courage, and self-control: each of these four cardinal virtues is a strategic way of instantiating the good of practical reasonableness, in one's deliberations (*prudentia*), one's dealing with others (justice), and one's inner integration of emotions with reasons (temperance)."[62] Now consider the important role that rhetoric plays in moderating one's deliberations, one's dealings with others, and in one's integration of emotions with reasons. Since rhetoric is in some way necessary in order to moderate the relationship between reason, will and action, it would seem that rhetoric plays an important role in successfully completing one's deliberations and one's dealings with others, and as such rhetoric would therefore seem necessary in order to instantiate the good of practical reasonableness itself.

V.

Conclusion. It might be said that describing an act as a perversion is to make one of the worse possible condemnations. Although the word is often used to describe deviant sexual behavior, I assert that when rhetorical discourse (such as advertising) runs contrary to its intended function, and when the viability of human goods is affected without any visible means of restraint it, too, can be morally denounced as a perversion.

It is my hope that this paper has contributed to the literature in two ways: First, I hope that the conception of natural rhetoric and its application to morally problematic advertising has enlivened the thinking of those responsible for formulating the Church's positions on social communication. I hope also that this paper has contributed to our understanding of natural law by exploring, philosophically and practically, a linkage between rhetoric and natural law by way of the developing notion of natural rhetoric.

McShea writes that "men do not become men but in some culture and an understanding of human nature requires the study of how that nature has expressed itself in a variety of times and places."[63] Similarly, Macquarrie believed that "natural law changes, in the sense that the precepts we may derive from it change as human nature itself changes, and also in the sense that man's self-understanding changes as he sharpens his image of manhood."[64] In view of these observations, "it would follow that the free-market consumer culture in which we find ourselves constitutes circumstances that warrant a second look at those inclinations that manifest themselves in economic relations"[65] such as the production of rhetorical discourse. Having the ability to criticize some of these manifestations as *perversions* certainly places them in a new light.

Creighton University

<h2 style="text-align:center">Notes</h2>

1. See John P. Foley and Pierfranco Pastore, *Ethics in Advertising* (http://www.vatican.va/roman_curia/pontifical_councils/pccs/documents/rc_pc_pccs_doc_22021997_ethics-in-ad_en.html, February 22, 1997); John P. Foley, *Ethics in Advertising* (http://www.vatican.va/roman_curia/pontifical_councils/pccs/documents/rc_pc_pccs_doc_20031028_foley-advertising_en.html, October 28, 2003). See also Martin O'Connor and Augustine Ferrari-Toniolo, *Communio et Progressio* (http://www.vatican.va/roman_curia/pontifical_councils/pccs/documents/rc_pc_pccs_doc_23051971_communio_en.html, March 23, 1971).

2. See Jeffrey J. Maciejewski, "Reason as a Nexus of Natural Law and Rhetoric," *Journal of Business Ethics* 59 (2005): 247–257; Jeffrey J. Maciejewski, "Can Natural Law Defend Advertising," *Journal of Mass Media Ethics* 18 (2003): 111–122.

3. See Scott, who asserted that rhetoric is "the possibility of bringing reason together with passion so that in action humans may civilize themselves" (Robert L. Scott, "The Forum: Between Silence and Certainty: A Codicil to 'Dialectical Tensions of Speaking and Silence,'" *Quarterly Journal of Speech* 86 [2000]: 109) and Burke, who believed that "rhetoric is an important tool of socialization" (Karen Watson, "A Rhetorical and Sociolinguistic Model for the Analysis of Narrative," *American Anthropologist* 75 [1973]: 75).

4. J. Maciejewski, "Reason as a Nexus of Natural Law and Rhetoric," 254.

5. Richard McKeon, "The Uses of Rhetoric in a Technological Age: Architectonic Productive Arts," in *Rhetoric: Essays in Invention and Discovery*, ed. Mark Bachman (Woodbridge: Oxbow Press, 1987): 1.

6. See, e.g., James Kastely, *Rethinking the Rhetorical Tradition: From Plato to Postmodernism* (New Haven: Yale University Press, 1997): 1–3; Robert L. Scott, "On *Not* Defining Rhetoric," *Philosophy & Rhetoric* 6 (1973): 81–96.

7. Barry Brummett, "A Defense of Ethical Relativism as Rhetorically Grounded," *The Western Journal of Speech Communication* 45 (1981): 288.

8. See William D. Harpine, "What Do You *Mean*, Rhetoric Is Epistemic?" *Philosophy & Rhetoric* 37 (2004): 335–352. Although Harpine has called for more precision in operationalizing the terminology used in discussing postmodern rhetoric, he nonetheless advocates Scott's notion that rhetoric is epistemic and that one assessment of this thesis may call for a definition of rhetoric that is constructively broad.

9. R. Scott, "On *Not* Defining Rhetoric," 84.

10. Ibid., 94 (see also n. 25, n. 27).

11. St. Thomas Aquinas, *Treatise on Law* (*Summa Theologica*, Questions 90–97) (Washington, D.C.: Regnery Publishing, 1996).

12. Cf. John Finnis, *Aquinas: Moral, Political, and Legal Theory* (Oxford: Oxford University Press, 1998); Anthony Lisska, *Aquinas's Theory of Natural Law* (Oxford: Clarendon Press, 1996).

13. J. Maciejewski, "Reason as a Nexus of Natural Law and Rhetoric."

14. A. Lisska, *Aquinas's Theory of Natural Law*, 109.

15. Michael Crowe, *The Changing Profile of the Natural Law* (The Hague: Martinus Nijhoff, 1977): 178.

16. Arthur E. Walzer, "Rhetoric and Gender in Jane Austen's *Persuasion*," *College English* 57 (1995): 688. The notion that rhetoric is "the handmaiden to reason" is espoused by Bacon, whose rhetoric Walzer uses as a conceptual framework in which to analyze Austen's text.

17. K. Watson, "A Rhetorical and Sociolinguistic Model for the Analysis of Narrative," 75.

18. Barry Brummett, "Some Implications of 'Process' or 'Intersubjectivity': Postmodern Rhetoric," *Philosophy & Rhetoric* 9 (1976): 29.

19. Barry Brummett, "The Forum: On to Rhetorical Relativism," *Quarterly Journal of Speech* 68 (1982): 425.

20. Ibid., 426.

21. B. Brummett, "Some Implications of 'Process' or 'Intersubjectivity': Postmodern Rhetoric," 31.

22. A. Lisska, *Aquinas's Theory of Natural Law*, 101.

23. Ibid., 105.

24. J. Finnis, *Aquinas: Moral, Political, and Legal Theory*, 161.

25. Robert L. Scott, "On Viewing Rhetoric as Epistemic," *Central States Speech Journal* 18 (1967): 9–16. Although this view might seem controversial, Scott writes that truth in human affairs "can arise only from cooperative critical inquiry," (14) by individuals engaging in debate and dialectic, collectively forging accepted "truth." From this perspective, "truth is not prior and immutable but is contingent. Insofar as we can say that there is truth in human

affairs, it is in time; it can be the result of a process of interaction at a given moment. Thus rhetoric may be viewed not as a matter of giving *effectiveness* [emphasis added] to truth but of *creating* [emphasis added] truth" (13).

26. B. Brummett, "Some Implications of 'Process' or 'Intersubjectivity': Postmodern Rhetoric," 32.

27. I will concede that in the foregoing I do not offer any succinct definition of what it is I mean by "natural rhetoric." This is both intentional and reflective of the ongoing development of the concept. I, like Scott, believe that "definitions are like belts. The shorter they are, the more elastic they need to be. A short belt reveals nothing about its wearer: by stretching, it can be made to fit almost anybody. Yet the hope of hitting on some definition which is at one and same time satisfactory and brief dies hard: much can be learned by seeing just how much elasticity is ultimately required of such portmanteau definitions" (R. Scott, "On *Not* Defining Rhetoric," 82–83). Thus, I believe that we are in the process of learning how much elasticity is necessary for the concept of natural rhetoric; this essay can be seen as but one step in this learning process. See also J. Maciejewski, "Reason as a Nexus of Natural Law and Rhetoric."

28. Howard Kainz, *Natural Law: A Reexamination* (Chicago: Open Court, 2004): 60.

29. M. Crowe, *The Changing Profile of the Natural Law*, 180.

30. Donald Levy, "Perversion and the Unnatural as Moral Categories," *Ethics* 90 (1980): 200.

31. John Finnis, "Natural Law and Unnatural Acts," *Heythrop Journal* 11 (1970): 377.

32. William E. May, "The Natural Law and Objective Morality," in *Natural Law and Theology*, ed. Charles Curran and Richard McCormick (New York: Paulist Press, 1991): 353.

33. J. Finnis, "Natural Law and Unnatural Acts," 379.

34. Christopher Williams, "Perverted Attractions," *The Monist* 86 (2003): 116.

35. See e.g., Noel Carroll, "Hume's Standard of Taste," *The Journal of Aesthetics and Art Criticism* 43 (1984): 181–194; James R. Shelley, "Hume and the Nature of Taste," *The Journal of Aesthetics and Art Criticism* 56 (1998): 29–38; C. Williams, "Perverted Attractions."

36. D. Levy, "Perversion and the Unnatural as Moral Categories," 201.

37. N. Carroll, "Hume's Standard of Taste," 185.

38. C. Williams, "Perverted Attractions," 123.

39. Ibid.

40. See e.g., D. Levy, "Perversion and the Unnatural as Moral Categories," 200–201.

41. C. Williams, "Perverted Attractions," 122.

42. D. Levy, "Perversion and the Unnatural as Moral Categories," 202.

43. C. Williams, "Perverted Attractions," 116–117.

44. Glenn Morrow, "Plato's Conception of Persuasion," *The Philosophical Review* 62 (1953): 235.

45. Eugene Garver, "Aristotle's Genealogy of Morals," *Philosophy and Phenomenological Research* 44 (1984): 471.

46. Jean Kilbourne, *Deadly Persuasion: Why Women and Girls Must Fight the Addictive Power of Advertising* (New York: The Free Press, 1999): 258. It should be noted that Kilbourne is not alone in mounting this criticism. See e.g., Anthony J. Cortese, *Provocateur: Images of Women and Minorities in Advertising* (Lanham: Rowman & Littlefield, 2004); William Leiss, Stephen Kline and Sut Jhally, *Social Communication in Advertising* (New York: Routledge, 1990); and Judith Williamson, *Decoding Advertisements* (New York: Marion Boyers, 1984).

47. Ibid.

48. Ibid., 259

49. Gerald Dyer, *Advertising as Communication* (London: Methuen, 1982): 107.

50. Jean Dickey, "Women for Sale—The Construction of Advertising Images," in *Out of Focus: Writings on Women and the Media*, ed. Karen Davies, Jean Dickey, and Tina Stratford (London: The Women's Press, 1987): 77.

51. Doris-Louise Haineault and Jean-Yves Roy, *Unconscious for Sale: Advertising, Psychoanalysis, and the Public* (Minneapolis: University of Minnesota Press, 1993): 125.

52. J. Kilbourne, *Deadly Persuasion*, 260.

53. J. Dickey, "Women for Sale," 76.

54. J. Kilbourne, *Deadly Persuasion*, 259.

55. J. Foley and P. Pastore, *Ethics in Advertising*.

56. J. Maciejewski, "Reason as a Nexus of Natural Law and Rhetoric," 254.

57. J. Foley, *Ethics in Advertising*.

58. Jacques Maritain, *The Person and the Common Good* (Notre Dame: University of Notre Dame Press, 1966): 41–42.

59. Lon Fuller, *The Morality of Law* (New Haven: Yale University Press, 1969): 185.

60. Columba Ryan, "The Traditional Concept of Natural Law: An Interpretation," in *Light on the Natural Law*, ed. Iltud Evans (London: Compass Books, 1965): 28.

61. A. Lisska, *Aquinas's Theory of Natural Law*, 25.

62. J. Finnis, *Aquinas: Moral, Political, and Legal Theory*, 84.

63. Robert McShea, "Human Nature Ethical Theory," *Philosophy and Phenomenological Research* 39 (1979): 398.

64. John Macquarrie, "Rethinking Natural Law," in *Natural Law and Theology*, ed. Charles Curran and Richard McCormick, (New York: Paulist Press, 1991): 243.

65. J. Maciejewski, "Can Natural Law Defend Advertising?" 120.

The Ancients, the Moderns, and the Court

Bernard G. Prusak

Abstract: This paper examines the case of *Lawrence v. Texas* to bring out the philosophical commitments of Justices Anthony Kennedy and Antonin Scalia. It is proposed that Justices Kennedy and Scalia, while both Catholics, represent fundamentally different visions of the "ends and reasons" of democratic law. A close reading of the Justices' opinions in *Lawrence* indicates that Justice Scalia belongs to the tradition of the "ancients" and Justice Kennedy to the tradition of the "moderns." The paper focuses in particular on the Justices' interpretations of the Due Process Clause of the Fourteenth Amendment. It is claimed that the interpretation of this clause turns on a philosophical commitment regarding the ends and reasons that the Constitution should be understood to serve, and thus that justices cannot help acting as "philosopher kings" here. Which of the two Justices is more consistent with the Catholic tradition is proposed as a question for another day.

The case of *Lawrence v. Texas*, decided by the U.S. Supreme Court on June 26, 2003, is worthy of attention in several respects: socially, legally, and philosophically. To begin with, the Opinion of the Court attests to a major change in attitudes toward homosexuality over the last several decades: in Justice Antonin Scalia's terms, "the moral opprobrium that has traditionally attached to homosexual conduct," while still common, is now no longer the rule, both figuratively and literally.[1] It may or may not be true that, as David Cole claimed in *The Nation*, "[t]he Court is simply catching up to the rest of society on the issues of gay rights and sexual freedom"—does public opposition to gay marriage tell another story?—but it is certainly true that times have changed.[2]

Legally, *Lawrence* raises the now regularly-recurring question of how to interpret the Due Process Clause of the Fourteenth Amendment: more precisely, to quote Justice Byron White in the 1986 precedent that *Lawrence* overturned, *Bowers v. Hardwick*, whether this clause concerns only "the processes by which life, liberty, or property is taken," or has "substantive content, subsuming rights that to a great extent are immune from federal or state regulation or proscription," even "rights that have little or no textual support in the constitutional language."[3] The relevant sentence of the Fourteenth Amendment reads: "No state shall make or enforce any law which shall abridge the privileges or immunities of citizens of the United States; nor shall any State deprive any person of life, liberty, or property, without due process of law [the Due Process Clause]; nor deny to any person within its jurisdiction the equal protection of the laws [the Equal Protection Clause]." On its face, the Due Process Clause is open to two readings, neither of which necessarily excludes the other. On the one hand, it may be read as requiring the state to have legal authority enacted through the proper bodies and according to the rules of democracy ("due process of law") before depriving any person of life, liberty, or property. On this reading, the clause is emphatically about "process," and the import of the clause is "formal." On the other hand, the clause may be read as placing restrictions upon what kinds of laws may be properly enacted ("due process of law") in a constitutional democracy. On this reading, the clause is emphatically about what is "due"—what is due to persons in our democracy—and the import of the clause is "substantive."[4]

The philosophical question raised by *Lawrence* is closely related and may be put simply: What kinds of laws are legitimate in a constitutional democracy? To be sure, this question is also a legal question, one that judges have to reckon with in the practical task of interpreting and applying the Constitution to disputed cases. As, however, legal scholar Frank I. Michelman has nicely remarked, this task proves hard to do "without getting into speculative questions concerning . . . the ends and reasons for which a country's basic law [that is, constitution] imposes limits and requirements on ordinary political rule."[5] In other words, judges must try to determine *for what end* the Fourteenth Amendment limits the power of the states and imposes the requirement of "due process." Since the language of the amendment does not by itself answer this question, and since the relevant precedents and analogies are controversial, it follows that judges sometimes cannot help but "do philosophy" here: they must consider the "ends and reasons" that the Constitution serves and so doing try their hand at interpreting what John Rawls called the "fundamental ideas seen as implicit in the public political culture of a constitutional regime."[6] In other words, it turns out that the legal question of how to interpret the Fourteenth Amendment is also a philosophical question about the "ends and reasons" of democratic law.

Obviously, an adequate treatment of these legal and philosophical questions would require a very lengthy discussion. I limit myself here to an analysis of *Lawrence*, and more specifically to bringing out the philosophical commitments of Justice Anthony Kennedy's Opinion of the Court and Justice Scalia's dissent, both of which prove uncommonly revealing in this regard. Since the Supreme Court will likely often be in the news over the next several years, it is worth spending some time trying to understand how the present justices think. Justices Kennedy and Scalia, while both Catholics, represent fundamentally different visions of the rule of law.

§1. Kennedy v. Scalia

According again to Rawls, "in considering whether to make homosexual relations between citizens criminal offenses" in a constitutional democracy, "the question," properly formulated,

> is not whether those relations are precluded by a worthy idea of full human good as characterized by a sound philosophical and nonreligious view, nor whether those of religious faith regard [those relations] as sin, but primarily whether legislative statutes forbidding those relations infringe the civil rights of free and equal democratic citizens.[7]

Both Justice Kennedy and Justice Scalia agree with this formulation of the question, but disagree "whether legislative statutes forbidding those relations infringe the civil rights of free and equal democratic citizens." For they disagree on the interpretation of the "rights of free and equal democratic citizens" under the Constitution. Yet more fundamentally, they disagree on the ends and reasons that the Constitution should be understood to serve.

This last claim may be substantiated by a close reading of the Justices' opinions. According to Justice Kennedy, "Liberty presumes an autonomy of self that includes freedom of thought, belief, expression, and certain intimate conduct" (Kennedy 1). The controversial item in Justice Kennedy's list is obviously "certain intimate conduct." For where does the Constitution discuss it? And can a right to it credibly be interpreted as a fundamental idea in our political culture?

Justice White's Opinion of the Court in *Bowers* rejects the claim that homosexual conduct, and sodomy more generally, qualify for protection from the state. To be sure, he acknowledges that the Court has many times recognized "rights that have little or no textual support in the constitutional language" and that, in doing so, "the Court has sought to identify the nature of the rights qualifying for heightened judicial protection." Citing *Palko v. Connecticut* (1937), he notes that "it was said that this category includes those fundamental liberties that are 'implicit in the concept of ordered liberty,' such that 'neither liberty nor justice would exist if [they] were sacrificed.'" Justice White also cites a "different description of fundamental liberties" in *Moore v. East Cleveland* (1977), namely, as liberties "'deeply rooted in this Nation's history and tradition.'" He concludes, however, that "[i]t is obvious to us that neither of these formulations would extend a fundamental right to homosexuals to engage in acts of consensual sodomy." For "[p]roscriptions against that conduct have ancient roots," reaching back to English common law and "the laws of the original 13 States when they ratified the Bill of Rights." Even "[i]n 1868, when the Fourteenth Amendment was ratified," Justice White remarks, "all but 5 of the 37 States in the Union had criminal sodomy laws." Accordingly, "Against this background, to claim that a right to engage in such conduct is 'deeply rooted in this Nation's history and tradition' or 'implicit in the concept of ordered liberty' is, at best, facetious."[8]

Justice Kennedy begins to counter this line of argumentation by claiming that the Court in *Bowers* failed "to appreciate the extent of the liberty at stake." According to Justice Kennedy, "To say that the issue in *Bowers* was simply the right to engage in certain sexual conduct demeans the claim the individual put forward, just as it would demean a married couple were it to be said marriage is simply about the right to have sexual intercourse" (Kennedy 6). Though "the laws involved in *Bowers* and [*Lawrence*] . . . purport to do no more than prohibit a sexual act," Justice Kennedy claims that "they seek [rather] to control a personal relationship that, whether or not entitled to formal recognition in the law, is within the liberty of persons to choose without being punished as criminals." Justice Kennedy also challenges the "historical grounds" relied upon by Justice White's Opinion of the Court. Drawing upon academic writings and scholarly *amicus* briefs, Justice Kennedy observes that "early American sodomy laws," from colonial times through the nineteenth century, "were not directed at homosexuals as such but instead sought to prohibit non-procreative sexual activity more generally" (Kennedy 8). Sodomy laws directed at homosexuals as a distinct category of persons originated only in the twentieth century.

This observation, however, does not refute the claim that laws against homosexual conduct have long standing in our nation's "history and tradition." As even proponents of the majority opinion concede, the fact that sodomy laws were not specifically directed to homosexual conduct until the last century does not change the fact that they nevertheless prohibited such conduct.[9] Justice Kennedy, too, may be read as implicitly conceding this point when he turns to "our laws and traditions in the past half century [as] of most relevance here" (Kennedy 11).[10] According to Justice Kennedy, "These references show an emerging awareness that liberty gives substantial protection to adult persons in deciding how to conduct their private lives in matters pertaining to sex." The phrase "emerging awareness" is critical. With it, Justice Kennedy rejects in advance the accusation that the Court is engaged in "making" law in the sense of drawing it up, that is, doing the job of a legislative body. Instead, he suggests, the Court comes to be aware of new dimensions of the Constitution's promise of liberty.

Justice Kennedy traces this "emerging awareness" principally through five cases: *Griswold v. Connecticut* (1965), having to do with married couples' use of contraceptives; *Eisenstadt v. Baird* (1972), having to do with the distribution of contraceptives to unmarried persons; *Roe v. Wade* (1973); *Carey v. Population Services Int'l* (1977), having to do with the distribution of contraceptives to persons under the age of sixteen; and finally *Planned Parenthood of Southeastern Pa. v. Casey* (1992), substantially upholding *Roe v. Wade*.[11] He draws especially from *Casey*. For example, after challenging the historical grounds relied upon in *Bowers*, Justice Kennedy acknowledges that the Court

> was making the broader point that for centuries there have been powerful voices to condemn homosexual conduct as immoral. This condemnation has been shaped by religious beliefs, conceptions of right and acceptable

behavior, and respect for the traditional family. . . . These considerations do not answer the question before us, however. The issue is whether the majority may use the power of the State to enforce these views on the whole society through operation of the criminal law. [Quoting *Casey*:] "Our obligation is to define the liberty of all, not to mandate our own moral code." (Kennedy 10)

According to Justice Kennedy, "The *Casey* decision again confirmed that our laws and tradition afford constitutional protection to personal decisions relating to marriage, procreation, contraception, family relationships, child rearing, and education." He goes on:

> In explaining the respect the Constitution demands for the autonomy of the person in making these choices, we stated as follows: "These matters, involving the most intimate and personal choices a person can make in a lifetime, choices central to personal dignity and autonomy, are central to the liberty protected by the Fourteenth Amendment." (Kennedy 13)

Griswold, recognizing only "a right of marital privacy,"[12] does not yet provide the grounds for such a statement, or for Justice Kennedy's description of our "laws and tradition." *Eisenstadt*, however, begins to clear the way: according to Justice William Brennan's Opinion of the Court, "If the right to privacy means anything, it is the right of the *individual*, married or single, to be free from unwanted government intrusion into matters so fundamentally affecting a person as the decision whether to bear or beget a child" (italics in the original).[13] As former solicitor general Charles Fried has observed, drawing attention to both the use of the term 'individual' and the reference to childbearing, "Thus was the seed planted from which *Roe* grew," or more precisely what Justice Harry Blackmun called "a right of personal privacy, or a guarantee of certain areas or zones of privacy," which right he located in the Fourteenth Amendment's Due Process Clause and judged to be "broad enough to encompass a woman's decision whether or not to terminate her pregnancy."[14] Justice Kennedy's opinion in *Lawrence* represents an extension (and, to be sure, a yet deeper entrenchment) of this reasoning.

It must be noted, however, that Justice Kennedy does not explicitly say that engaging in homosexual conduct is a "fundamental right," as the right to abortion has been declared to be. By not doing so, he invites Justice Scalia's counter-argument. As Justice Scalia observes, "Not once does [the Court] describe homosexual sodomy as a 'fundamental right' or a 'fundamental liberty interest,' nor does it subject the statute to strict scrutiny," which is typically the appropriate standard of review for cases implicating a fundamental right: an analysis of whether the statute is precisely drawn to further a legitimate state interest, or significantly interferes with the exercise of a fundamental right. Instead, "the Court concludes that the application of Texas's statute to petitioners' conduct fails the rational-basis test," namely, whether the statute is rationally related to a legitimate state interest, a point that Justice Scalia substantiates by quoting a sentence toward very the end of Justice Kennedy's opinion: "The

Texas statute furthers no legitimate state interest which can justify its intrusion into the personal and private life of the individual" (Kennedy 18, Scalia 10).

As Justice Scalia observes, the *Bowers* Court roundly rejected the argument that such laws lack a legitimate basis. According to Justice White:

> Even if the conduct at issue here is not a fundamental right, respondent asserts that there must be a rational basis for the law and that there is none in this case other than the presumed belief of a majority of the electorate in Georgia [where *Bowers* originated] that homosexual sodomy is immoral and unacceptable. This is said to be an inadequate rationale to support the law. The law, however, is constantly based on notions of morality, and if all laws representing essentially moral choices are to be invalidated under the Due Process Clause, the courts will be very busy indeed. Even respondent makes no such claim, but insists that majority sentiments about the morality of homosexuality should be declared inadequate. We do not agree.[15]

Neither does Justice Scalia: "Countless judicial decisions and legislative enactments have relied on the ancient proposition that a governing majority's belief that certain sexual behavior is 'immoral and unacceptable' constitutes a rational basis for regulation" (Scalia 5). Moreover, it is impossible, he holds, to distinguish "homosexuality from other traditional 'morals' offenses" (Scalia 6) such as "bigamy, same-sex marriage, adult incest, prostitution, masturbation, adultery, fornication, bestiality, and obscenity" (Scalia 5). The Court is correct, he acknowledges, that the Texas statute "seeks to further the belief of its citizens that certain forms of sexual behavior are 'immoral and unacceptable,'" yet he adds with a dash that this "same interest [is] furthered by criminal laws against fornication, bigamy, adultery, adult incest, bestiality, and obscenity" (Scalia 15). In other words, "If, as the Court asserts, the promotion of majoritarian sexual morality is not even a *legitimate* state interest, none of the above-mentioned laws can survive rational-basis review." What is more, we should not believe, he claims, the Court's statement "that the present case 'does not involve whether the government must give formal recognition to any relationship that homosexual persons seek to enter'" (Scalia 20). According to Justice Scalia, a close reading of the Opinion of the Court belies "this bald, unreasoned disclaimer." Instead, such a reading shows that "[t]oday's opinion dismantles the structure of constitutional law that has permitted a distinction to be made between heterosexual and homosexual unions, insofar as formal recognition of marriage is concerned" (Scalia 20–21). In future cases, judges will be compelled to "carry things to their logical conclusion" (Scalia 20).

But is he right? Though some of his own logic is dubious—*pace* Justice Scalia, it seems right to say that a person is not and even cannot be a bigamist, prostitute, adulterer, masturbator, or fornicator in the same sense that a person is homosexual; the fact that the indefinite article may be omitted here calls for consideration[16]—Justice Scalia is right at least that the Court does not provide any *reasons* that would lead to the conclusion that *Lawrence* does not have any bearing on laws against same-sex marriage. Perhaps it could be argued that, since marriage obviously has to do with more than sex, the Court's recognition that adult persons have substantial protection "in deciding how to conduct their private lives in matters pertaining to sex" is not relevant to the question of whether adult persons have a right to marry whomever they like. Yet Justice Kennedy also writes that "[t]he *Casey* decision again confirmed that our laws and tradition afford constitutional protection to personal decisions relating to *marriage*, procreation, contraception, family relationships, child rearing, and education" (Kennedy 13, my italics). Unless the term "marriage" is stipulated to mean a heterosexual union, how does this sentence *not* bear on the question of same-sex marriage?[17] Such a stipulation, moreover, would seem to run against ordinary language. Justice Kennedy studiously avoids speaking of same-sex or homosexual marriage, but Justice Scalia refers to it freely. He also thereby gives ammunition to the "culture war" that he accuses the majority of fighting (Scalia 18).

§2. Whose Justice, Whose Morality?

What, then, do we learn about the two Justices' philosophical commitments?

Justice Scalia's use of the word 'ancient'—he affirms, as we have seen, "the ancient proposition that a governing majority's belief that certain sexual behavior is 'immoral and unacceptable' constitutes a rational basis for regulation" (Scalia 5)—is worth picking out. To be sure, this word seems to mean here only that the "proposition" in question is very old, or of long standing. Yet this proposition may also be qualified as "ancient" in another, more technical sense: that of the nineteenth-century philosopher Benjamin Constant when he compares, famously, "ancient liberty" with "modern liberty." As Rawls has remarked, Constant's contrast of these two forms of liberty is highly "stylized," but useful nonetheless.[18] For Constant is not indulging some antiquarian interest, but drawing attention, in Rawls's words again, to a "conflict within the tradition of democratic thought itself, between the tradition associated with Locke, which gives greater weight to what Constant called 'the liberties of the moderns,'" and "the tradition associated with Rousseau, which gives greater weight to what Constant called 'the liberties of the ancients.'"[19] This conflict, historians have shown, was present even at the origins of the American Revolution.[20]

To be "ancient," in Constant's lexicon, is to value first and foremost what he calls "political liberty": "an active and constant participation in collective power"; or, the "sharing of social power among the citizens of the same fatherland."[21] The aim is to organize life together according to an idea of the good. To this end, "the authority of the whole" is allowed to overrule "individual independence."[22] By contrast, to be "modern," in Constant's lexicon, is to value first and foremost "the enjoyment of security in private pleasures" (or, "peaceful enjoyment of private independence"). From this perspective, "liberty" is the name for "the guarantees accorded by institutions to these pleasures."[23] These guarantees include the rule of law; freedom of expression, association, and religion; and property and voting rights.[24] In brief,

"Individual liberty . . . is the true modern liberty." To be sure, "Political liberty," in the form of the vote, "is [individual liberty's] guarantee," and so "political liberty is . . . indispensable"; but it is valued instrumentally.[25]

Justice Scalia's dissent exemplifies the tradition of the "ancients," Justice Kennedy's Opinion of the Court the tradition of the "moderns." That is, Justice Scalia gives greater weight to the liberties of the ancients; Justice Kennedy, greater weight to the liberties of the moderns. Like the "ancients" on Constant's account, Justice Scalia is an advocate of "political liberty": in the present case, the right of the majority to regulate sexual behavior according to its conception of what is moral and what is not (or, its idea of the good). While certainly recognizing the individual rights protected by the Constitution, he believes in maximizing the opportunities for the people to rule themselves and limiting the role of the judiciary to protecting the rights *unambiguously* articulated in the Constitution.[26] Like the "moderns" on Constant's account, Justice Kennedy is an advocate of "private independence": in the present case, the right of an individual to conduct his or her sexual life as he or she pleases. In more contemporary terms, Justice Kennedy appears to subscribe to a limited version of what Ronald Dworkin calls (rather peremptorily) "the constitutional conception of democracy," which is distinguished by an interpretation of equality according to which each individual enjoys what Dworkin calls "moral independence" in "the fundamental ethical choices that define each individual's sense of why his or her life is valuable and what success in living it would mean."[27] Advocates of this conception of democracy read the Constitution as articulating abstract principles whose extension advances (or at least changes) with the times.[28] In Justice Kennedy's words, "As the Constitution endures, persons in every generation can invoke its principles in their own search for greater freedom" (Kennedy 18). Thus it can be claimed that "[l]iberty presumes an autonomy of self that includes" not only "freedom of thought, belief, expression," as has traditionally been acknowledged, but "certain intimate conduct," which has come to be realized only over the past half century (Kennedy 1).

Both of these conceptions of liberty belong to "the tradition of democratic thought itself"; in other words, they are both "implicit in the public political culture of a constitutional regime" (to quote Rawls again). Relevant to present purposes, they also both reflect philosophical commitments regarding the "ends and reasons" that the Constitution should be understood to serve: for Justice Scalia, *ceteris paribus*, the will of the people; for Justice Kennedy, *ceteris paribus*, the freedom of the individual. With these different commitments come different conceptions of legitimacy, or, more obviously, illegitimacy. For Justice Kennedy, a law is illegitimate if it mandates a sectarian moral code, whether it be religious or philosophical in nature. As he writes in the present case, "The issue is whether the majority may use the power of the State to enforce these views"—views with which some people may reasonably disagree—"on the whole society through the operation of the criminal law. [Quoting *Casey*:] 'Our obligation is to define the liberty of all, not to mandate our own moral code'" (Kennedy 10). For Justice Scalia, by contrast, the Court exercises its power illegitimately when it stretches the Constitution to give "the liberty of all" the bounds that the Court thinks that it should have. In so doing, it is true, the Court does not mandate a moral code: that is, it does not decide what is right or what is wrong, but only gives individuals the right to make this decision themselves. But, from Justice Scalia's perspective, the Court illegitimately restricts the right of the people as a whole to organize our life together, or to determine its character. The majority's distaste for a form of behavior certainly is not a good reason for prohibiting it—Justice Clarence Thomas, recalling Justice Potter Stewart's dissent in *Griswold*, calls "the law before the Court [in *Lawrence*] 'uncommonly silly'" (Thomas 1)—but, according to Justices Scalia and Thomas and Chief Justice William Rehnquist, that the morality of a law is open to challenge does not *thereby* make the law illegitimate under the Constitution. Remarkably, a law may be based upon disputed or even objectionable "notions of morality," to use Justice White's phrase, yet be constitutional nonetheless.

By way of conclusion, it is worth noting that Justices Kennedy and Scalia agree in insisting that the job of a justice is not the job of the proverbial philosopher king who has insight into the good and thus is able to determine what is just. Instead, both Justices separate questions of constitutionality from questions of morality. According to Justice Scalia, the Court's proper role is that "of assuring, as neutral observer, that the democratic rules of engagement are observed" (Scalia 18). The Court acts illegitimately when, "impatient of democratic change," it takes it upon itself to reshape the law to reflect its own judgments of what is moral. For "it is the premise of our system that those judgments are to be made by the people, and not imposed by a governing caste that knows best," i.e., philosopher kings exercising power surreptitiously and undemocratically through the judicial system (Scalia 19). Similarly, for Justice Kennedy, considerations of traditional morality, though deserving of respect, "do not answer the question before us" (Kennedy 10). For the business of the Court is "to define the liberty of all" under the Constitution, "not to mandate our own moral code," i.e., not to act as philosopher kings seeking to bring light into the darkness of our cave.

Now, if it is right, as I have claimed, that the interpretation of the Due Process Clause of the Fourteenth Amendment turns on a philosophical commitment regarding the ends and reasons that the Constitution should be understood to serve, it follows that justices cannot help acting as philosopher kings here. In other words, if the interpretation of the Due Process Clause turns on a vision of the *good* that the Constitution is supposed to serve—for the tradition of the "ancients," "political liberty"; for the tradition of the "moderns," "private independence"—it is baseless, even bad faith for one party to accuse the other of acting the philosopher king while claiming innocence for itself. It is probably naïve to think that our *Kulturkampf* could be diffused by more honesty. Arguably, however, Supreme Court justices do our political discourse a disservice by pretending to a purity in interpreting the law that is not to be had. In a word, they infuriate, as reactions to *Lawrence* have shown.

It would be worthwhile to consider further which of the two Justices is more consistent with the Catholic tradition and its re-articulation in such Vatican II documents as *Dignitatis Humanae* and *Gaudium et Spes*. I wonder if the answer is neither.

Villanova University

Notes

1. *Lawrence v. Texas* No. 02-102, slip op. at 18 (U.S. June 26, 2003), hereafter cited in the body of my text as follows: (Scalia 18). The same style is observed for Justice Anthony Kennedy's Opinion of the Court and Justice Clarence Thomas's dissent.

2. David Cole, "Court Watching," *The Nation*, July 21/28, 2003, 5. Compare the editorial "A Moderate Term on the Court," *The New York Times*, June 29, 2003, 12 ("Week in Review").

3. 478 U.S. 186, 191 (1986).

4. Compare, among the vast literature on this question, Cass R. Sunstein, *One Case at a Time: Judicial Minimalism on the Supreme Court* (Cambridge, Mass.: Harvard University Press, 1999), 75. Contrast Justice Scalia, "Common-Law Courts in a Civil-Law System: The Role of United States Federal Courts in Interpreting the Constitution and Laws" in *A Matter of Interpretation: Federal Courts and the Law*, ed. Amy Gutmann (Princeton: Princeton University Press, 1997), 24: "By its inescapable terms, [the Due Process Clause] guarantees only process." For yet another perspective, see Ronald Dworkin, *Life's Dominion: An Argument about Abortion, Euthanasia, and Individual Freedom* (New York: Alfred Knopf, 1993), 160: "The right of procreative autonomy follows from any competent interpretation of the due process clause and of the Supreme Court's past decisions applying it."

5. Frank I. Michelman, "Rawls on Constitutionalism and Constitutional Law" in *The Cambridge Companion to Rawls*, ed. Samuel Freeman (Cambridge: Cambridge University Press, 2003), 394.

6. John Rawls, *Political Liberalism* (New York: Columbia University Press, 1996), 13 and "The Idea of Public Reason Revisited," *The University of Chicago Law Review* 64 (1997): 776. This paper appears as chapter 26 of Rawls's *Collected Papers*, ed. Samuel Freeman (Cambridge, Mass.: Harvard University Press, 1999); see 584.

7. Rawls, "The Idea of Public Reason Revisited," 780. See his *Collected Papers*, 588.

8. 478 U.S. 186, 191, 191–192, 192, 192–193, 194 (1986).

9. So Adam Goodheart, for example, writes that Justice Kennedy's "dismissal of conservative arguments that laws against same-sex intercourse had deep roots in Anglo-American tradition" represents a "well-intentioned evasion"; see "The Ghosts of Jamestown," *The New York Times*, July 3, 2003, A25. See also Richard Posner, *Sex and Reason* (Cambridge, Mass.: Harvard University Press, 1992), 343.

10. It is also possible, however, to read Justice Kennedy as implying that traditional attitudes toward sexuality in general and homosexuality in specific have fallen into "desuetude"; for this concept, see Sunstein, *One Case at a Time*, 109.

11. For a more detailed account of the issues presented in these cases (excepting, because of its date, *Casey*), see Posner, *Sex and Reason*, 324–341.

12. 381 U.S. 479, 486 (1965).

13. 405 U.S. 438, 453 (1972).

14. Charles Fried, *Order and Law: Arguing the Reagan Revolution—A Firsthand Account* (New York: Simon & Schuster, 1991), 77 and 410 U.S. 113, 152, 153 (1973).

15. 478 U.S. 186, 196 (1986).

16. See further Ian Hacking, "Making Up People" in *Reconstructing Individualism: Autonomy, Individuality, and the Self in Western Thought*, ed. Thomas C. Heller, Morton Sosna, and David E. Wellbery (Stanford: Stanford University Press, 1986), 222–236, and David M. Halperin, "Forgetting Foucault: Acts, Identities, and the History of Sexuality" in *The Sleep of Reason: Erotic Experience and Sexual Ethics in Ancient Greece and Rome*, ed. Martha C. Nussbaum and Juha Sihvola (Chicago: The University of Chicago Press, 2002), 21–54.

17. A writer in *The Economist*, July 5, 2003, 27, shows no doubts: "Five of the six justices in the majority signed an opinion broad enough to open the way eventually to homosexuals' claiming all the rights enjoyed by heterosexuals, including marriage and adoption." Writing in *The Nation*, John Kim sees more "radical possibilities," namely, "an elaboration of sexual rights under the Constitution that could protect sexual dissidents of all stripes," including "sex workers." See "Queer Cheer," *The Nation*, July 21/28, 2003, 5–6.

18. Rawls, *Political Liberalism*, 5.

19. Rawls, *Political Liberalism*, 4–5. See also 299.

20. See, for example, Bernard Bailyn, *The Ideological Origins of the American Revolution* (Cambridge, Mass. Harvard University Press, 1967), 22–54. See also Charles Taylor's *Varieties of Religion Today: William James Revisited* (Cambridge, Mass.: Harvard University Press, 2002), 90–91.

21. Benjamin Constant, "De la liberté des anciens comparée à celle des modernes" (1819) in *De la liberté chez les modernes. Écrits politiques*, ed. Marcel Gauchet (Paris: Librairie Générale Française, 1980), 501, 502; English trans., "The Liberty of the Ancients Compared with That of the Moderns" in *Political Writings*, ed. and trans. Biancamaria Fontana (Cambridge: Cambridge University Press, 1988), 316, 317.

22. Constant, *De la liberté chez les modernes*, 495–496; English trans., *Political Writings*, 311.

23. Constant, *De la liberté chez les modernes*, 501, 502; English trans., *Political Writings*, 316, 317. Fontana translates "la jouissance paisible de l'indépendance privée" as "peaceful enjoyment *and* private independence" (my italics). Admittedly, however, I have used a different edition of the French text from hers (1820), which I have not been able to acquire.

24. Constant, *De la liberté chez les modernes*, 495; English trans., *Political Writings*, 310–311.

25. Constant, *De la liberté chez les modernes*, 509; English trans., *Political Writings*, 323.

26. *Hence* Justice Scalia's "more or less originalist theory of interpretation," which in his view best serves the goal of democratic freedom. See Justice Scalia, "The Rule of Law as a Law of Rules," *The University of Chicago Law Review* 56 (1989): 1184 and "Originalism: The Lesser Evil," *University of Cincinnati Law Review* 57 (1989): 849–865, especially 862: "[O]riginalism seems to me more compatible with the nature and purpose of a Constitution in a democratic system."

27. Dworkin, *Freedom's Law: The Moral Reading of the American Constitution* (Cambridge, Mass.: Harvard University Press, 1996), 17, 25 and "The Arduous Virtue of Fidelity: Originalism, Scalia, Tribe, and Nerve," *Fordham Law Review* 65 (1997): 1264. Interestingly, Dworkin associates this conception of democracy with the natural law tradition: the

"constitutionalist" and the natural lawyer share a commitment to "the rule of principle." See "'Natural' Law Revisited," *University of Florida Law Review* 34 (1982): 187.

28. See Dworkin, *Freedom's Law*, 7: The First, Fifth, and Fourteenth Amendments "must be understood in the way their language most naturally suggests: they refer to abstract moral principles . . . as limits on government's power."

Hylomorphism and Mental Causation

William Jaworski

Abstract: Mind-body problems are predicated on two things: a distinction between the mental and the physical, and premises that make it difficult to see how the two are related. Before Descartes there were no mind-body problems of the sort now forming the stock in trade of philosophy of mind. One possible explanation for this is that pre-Cartesian philosophers working in the Aristotelian tradition had a different way of understanding the mental-physical distinction, the nature of causation, and the character of psychological discourse, which was not liable to generating problems of a post-Cartesian sort. If so, it might be possible to recover and redeploy parts of that pre-Modern conceptual apparatus to resolve contemporary mind-body problems. I will argue that at least one such problem can be solved in this way.

1. Dual-attribute Theories and the Problem of Mental Causation

Dual-attribute theory—'DAT' henceforth—is distinguished by two claims: first, *Psychophysical Property Dualism*, the claim that there are mental properties and physical properties; that they are distinct, and that all properties are either of one sort or the other; and second, *Psychophysical Coincidence*, the claim that some substances have both mental and physical properties; that mental substances—*persons*—are also physical substances. DAT faces a problem with mental causation which can be expressed as an inconsistent pentad:

(1) Mental events cause actions;[1]

(2) Actions are physical events;

(3) Every physical event that has a cause has a physical cause.

(4) Mental events are not physical events.

(5) Actions are not causally overdetermined.

Consider an example: Madeleine has learned that Eleanor plans to tell Alexander everything. To avoid a scandal (something she very much desires), she decides to communicate Eleanor's intention to Gabriel posthaste, and believing a letter the best means, she writes. What are the relations between Madeleine's beliefs and desires, on the one hand, and her actions and physical events such as neural impulses and muscular contractions, on the other? It seems that her writing is caused by her desire, as per (1); and that her action is a physical event, as per (2); so according to (3) her action must have a physical cause. The mental and the physical cause of her action will either be identical or not. If they are identical, statement (4) will be false: mental events will be physical events. If, on the other hand, they are *not* identical, the action will have multiple causes, and (5) will be false instead: Madeleine's action will be causally overdetermined. Statements (1)–(5) are therefore inconsistent: they jointly imply both that the mental and physical cause of Madeleine's writing cannot be identical, and that they cannot be distinct. I will call this inconsistent pentad simply *the problem of mental causation.*

There are, broadly speaking, two strategies for solving it. The first seeks to deny a premise, and comprises a number of solutions including the following:

A. The Overdetermination Strategy (denies 5): Mental and physical events are each independent causes of actions.

B. The Identity Theory (denies 4): Mental and physical events are identical.

C. Cartesian-style Interactionism (denies 3): Mental events, not physical ones, cause actions, which are physical events.

D. The Dual-Explanandum Strategy (denies 2): Mental events, not physical ones, cause actions, which are *not* physical events.

E. Epiphenomenalism (denies 1): Physical events, not mental ones, cause actions.

F. The Joint Psychophysical Sufficiency Strategy (denies 1): Mental and physical events are jointly sufficient but by themselves insufficient for causing actions.

G. The Collective Neutral-Psychophysical Sufficiency Strategy (denies 1): Mental events, physical events, and something else are jointly sufficient but by themselves insufficient for causing the action.

H. The Neutral Sufficiency Strategy (denies 1): Actions are caused exclusively by something other than mental or physical events.

I. Acausalism (denies 1): Actions are uncaused.

DAT is compatible will all of these solutions except B, which is ruled out by Psychophysical Property Dualism together with a theory of events I'll discuss momentarily.

The second strategy seeks to deny the argument's validity. It claims the argument equivocates on, say, the notion of causation or the notion of a physical event. This is the approach I want to explore. I want to suggest the argument equivocates on both of these notions. Actions might be physical events in one sense, but they are not physical events in the sense covered by statement (3). Likewise, mental events might cause actions, but they don't cause actions in the sense in which events described by the natural sciences cause each other.

Establishing either equivocation by itself would be sufficient to dispense with the problem, but there are certain theoretical advantages to endorsing both, so I will outline a type of DAT that implies both, and that therefore provides dual-attribute theorists a solution which is consistent with option D.

2. Organic Dual-attribute Theories

DATs claim that some substances have both mental and physical properties. This is what distinguishes them from various forms of substance dualism, which endorse Psychophysical Property Dualism, but reject Psychophysical Coincidence. I want to consider an *organic DAT* in particular, one which claims persons are organisms, physical composites composed solely of physical proper parts. In this sense, organic DATs resemble standard forms of retentive physicalism more than substance dualism. We can make matters clearer if we assume a substance-attribute ontology committed to the following claims.

First, there are substances and properties, and every substance instantiates some property.

Second, *events* are property instances: n-tuples of objects standing in n-adic relations at times (Kim 1973, 1976). An event, x's *being F at t*, occurs on this view iff x instantiates F at t, where x, F, and t are the event's *constitutive object, property*, and *time*, respectively. Events A and B are identical iff their respective constitutive objects, properties, and times are.

Third, events are categorized as mental or physical depending on the properties constituting them. Hence, x's being F at t is a *mental event* iff F is a mental property, and it is a *physical event* iff F is a physical property.

Fourth, *mental properties* are those expressed by the predicates of psychological discourse, ones applicable truly only to persons and suggestive of either intentionality, consciousness, or subjectivity. By contrast, physical properties of a *narrow, natural scientific* sort—call them *N-physical properties*, are those expressed by the non-logical, non-purely-mathematical predicates deployed in the natural sciences, paradigmatically physics. Those predicates are not tied logically either to persons or to intentionality, consciousness, or subjectivity. Knowing that x weighs eighty kilograms, for instance, tells us nothing *a priori* about whether or not x is a person or has intentional, conscious, or subjective states. The term 'physical' is also taken in a broader sense that countenances things such as automobiles and baseball games, which although not postulated by the natural sciences nevertheless depend on things that are. *Being an automobile*, for instance, might not be a property expressible in natural scientific terms, but its instantiation nevertheless depends in a robust sense on the instantiation of properties that *are* thus expressible: nothing can be an automobile without also instantiating a range of natural scientific properties. Hence, the property of *being an automobile* qualifies as a physical property in a broad sense even if not in the narrow natural scientific one. Call properties of this broad physical sort, *B-physical properties*.

Using this framework, I want to consider a *hylomorphic DAT*. It differs from other organic DATs in several respects. I will focus on one respect—though by no means the only respect—which proves helpful vis-à-vis the problem of mental causation.

The hylomorphic theory I want to consider is committed to a certain understanding of the relations between *forms of discourse*, on the one hand, systems of predicates, terms, and rules for their deployment, and *families of properties* on the other. The basic idea is that predicates belonging to different forms of discourse express properties belonging to different property families. Mental and physical properties belong to diverse families, the differences between which are reflected in differences between psychological and natural scientific forms of discourse. The gist of the solution I want to develop is that differences among properties and events are reflected in differences among the rules governing different forms of discourse. Causal relations, for instance, obtain between events; on this view, those relations are mirrored in language as explanatory relations. The idea, then, is that because psychological explanation differs from scientific explanation, mental causation must differ from physical causation, and so the problem of mental causation must commit a fallacy of equivocation.

3. Anomalous Monism

To develop this solution I want to consider Davidson's (1970) anomalous monism since its contours are similar in many respects to those of the hylomorphic theory that interests me. In Davidson's ontology, events are the basic entities—concrete, datable particulars individuated by their causes and effects. A given event is categorized as mental or physical on this view depending on whether or not it is describable in psychological or natural scientific terms; and the very same event might be describable both ways—as, say, Alexander wanting money or as Alexander having temporal lobe activity; as Eleanor reaching for a glass of water or as such-and-such neural impulses and muscular contractions. According to Davidson all events are describable in natural scientific terms; all are physical, but some are also describable in psychological terms; they are mental as well.

On Davidson's view psychological discourse and natural scientific discourse are governed by different rules for the deployment of predicates and terms—rules that differ from each other, he thinks, in a way that precludes psychophysical reduction. I want to consider his argument for this because it can help us understand the solution to the problem of mental causation I'm proposing.

According to Davidson, psychological discourse is reasons-related discourse; psychological descriptions conform to a "constitutive principle of rationality" (223); natural scientific descriptions do not. The difference is clearly illustrated by considering how we go about revising psychological and natural scientific descriptions in light of countervailing evidence. Suppose we describe Gabriel psychologically as wanting to light the grill, and as believing the use of lighter fluid the best means. If we see him begin dousing the coals with water, we do not immediately conclude that he must be suffering from some sort of neural malfunction; more likely we revise our description by saying he believes mistakenly that the water bottle is filled with lighter fluid. If this description is challenged—if, for instance, he says, "Why yes, I did know it was filled with water"—we revise our description yet again in a way that renders his behavior rational: we describe him as, say, feeling too embarrassed to admit his mistake, or as not really having wanted to light the grill, but as having wanted only to seem to be doing so, or something of the sort. We revise our psychological description of his behavior, in other words, to accommodate the claim that he is a rational being.

Suppose by contrast that I observe a number of falling bodies, and formulate a hypothesis implying that terrestrial bodies fall at a rate of 7 m/s^2. If repeated experiments indicate a rate of 9.8 m/s^2 instead, I could revise my description of the situation in a number of ways: by discarding my hypothesis, by discarding the experimental results as somehow flawed, even by discarding the gravitational constant of the universe. But whatever I choose to do, however I choose to alter my description of the situation, *my choice does not depend on considerations of rationality*; I do not alter my overall set of scientific assumptions to render the behavior of falling bodies more rational. The same is true of any branch of natural science. Natural scientific descriptions are not revisable in the same way as psychological ones; rationality is not a consideration with the former as it is with the latter.

According to Davidson, psychological discourse is discourse in terms of reasons; natural science is discourse in terms of causes. To describe how events are causally related to each other, we use the latter; to describe what people do, their actions, and why they do them, we use the former. The Wittgensteinians from whom Davidson inherited this dichotomous understanding of psychological discourse and natural science claimed that on account of these discursive differences reasons could not be causes: my beliefs and desires, they claimed, do not cause my actions.[2] Davidson was able to reject this awkward claim on account of his ontology: psychological and natural scientific forms of discourse describe the very same events. All events are physical, on Davidson's view, all are part of the network of causal relations described by natural science, so any events that count as reasons by virtue of being describable psychologically, also count as causes by virtue of being describable physically. So on Davidson's view, reasons must be causes. Nevertheless because psychological and natural scientific forms of discourse are irreducibly distinct, because they are governed by completely different types of rules, it is impossible to provide exhaustive explanations for human behavior in purely scientific terms.

According to Davidson, explanations are underwritten by laws. Explaining human behavior in natural scientific terms would require appeal to psychophysical laws, ones expressed by statements featuring both psychological and natural scientific predicates. Providing a natural scientific explanation of why, say, Caesar crossed the Rubicon would require a law statement to the effect that necessarily, whenever such-and-such psychological conditions were met, such-and-such physical effects would result. Davidson argues, however, that psychological and natural scientific predicates cannot co-occur in this way. Their deployments are governed by different rules—rules *constitutive of* their respective forms of discourse. Trying to formulate psychophysical law statements would be like a playing a game in which opponents sat at a chess board and then leaped across it to tackle each others' kings: a game with elements of football and of chess, but which was neither football nor chess, and which violated rules of both.

Davidson's analogy is that the resulting statements would be like the following:

(H1) All emeralds are grue.

Something is grue just in case it is either observed before, say, October 29, 2005 and is green, or is not observed before that time and is blue. Although (H1) has the look of a genuine law statement, it is not. We can tell, because it is not confirmed by its positive instances the way law statements are. If we discover that this particular piece of copper conducts electricity, that gives us some reason, however slight, to suppose that *all* copper conducts electricity. Likewise, every observation of a green emerald lends credibility however slightly to the following generalization:

(H2) All emeralds are green.

But every positive instance of (H2) is also a positive instance of (H1); every emerald observed to be green is also observed to be grue. So if our emerald observations confirm (H2), they should also confirm (H1), but they *don't*, for (H1) predicts (falsely we suppose) that unobserved emeralds are blue! Since law statements are confirmed by their positive instances, and (H1) is not, it follows that (H1) is not a genuine law statement.

Goodman (1956) took this result to show that some predicates, such as 'is grue,' were simply unsuitable for inclusion in law statements. Davidson argued, however, that this unsuitability was a feature not of predicates taken in isolation, but in combination with other predicates, something illustrated by another example:

(H3) All emerires are grue.

Something is an emerire just in case it is observed before October 29, 2005 and is an emerald, or is not observed before that time and is a sapphire. This statement does not result in the false prediction that unobserved emeralds are blue; it predicts (truly we suppose) that unobserved sapphires are blue. This shows that the problem with statement (H1) is not a function of the predicate 'is grue' all by itself, but of that predicate in combination with the predicate 'is an emerald.' In combination with other "gruesome" predicates such as 'is an emerire,' it doesn't generate the problems associated with (H1).

Davidson took the foregoing considerations to support the idea that certain predicates are "made for each other" (218), while others are not. The predicate 'is grue' is not made for predicates like 'is an emerald,' but it *is* made for predicates like 'is an emerire.' Davidson suggests that combining psychological and natural scientific predicates is like combining 'is grue' and 'is an emerald': those predicates not made for each other, and consequently, any attempt to juxtapose them in a psychophysical law statement would result in a bastardized non-lawlike generalization such as 'All emeralds are grue.'

Moreover, says Davidson, whether or not predicates are made for each other in this way is something we can know *a priori*. The claim that all emeralds are green may turn out false, but it at least has a shot at confirmation: it is an empirically respectable hypothesis capable of standing before the tribunal of experience. The claim that all emeralds are grue, on the other hand, isn't even a *candidate* for law-like status. Likewise, psychological and natural scientific predicates are not even candidates for co-inclusion in law statements; the rules constituting their respective forms of discourse rule this out.

4. Van Fraassen on Explanation

One way of developing Davidson's idea about the disparity between psychological and natural scientific forms of discourse is in terms of van Fraassen's (1980) account of explanation. According to van Fraassen, explanations are answers to why-questions. So understanding the nature of explanation requires first understanding the logic of why-questions.

A natural-language sentence can express numerous diverse why-questions. The sentence 'Why did Adam eat the apple?' for instance, could express any of the following:

i. Why did Adam eat *the apple* (as opposed to having eaten something else)?

ii. Why did Adam *eat* the apple (as opposed to having done something else with it)?

iii. Why did *Adam* eat the apple (as opposed to someone else having eaten it)?

This shows that a why-question always presupposes a *contrast class*, a class of alternatives which might have obtained but do not, and which thereby allow the question to arise. Question (i), for instance, assumes that the statement 'Adam ate the apple' is true, and the statements 'Adam ate the pear,' and 'Adam ate the steak,' and the like are all false. Why-questions therefore have the following form:

Why is it the case that p in contrast to (other members of) X?

where p is a statement—the *topic* of the question—which is assumed in the context to be true, and X is the contrast class, the set of statements including p, all of which except p are assumed to be false. In addition to the topic and contrast class, every why-question assumes a certain *relevance relation* to them. Not just any true statement regarding them can count as an answer to the question. This is illustrated by an example van Fraassen adopts and adapts from Aristotle:

Suppose a father asks his teenage son, 'Why is the porch light on?' and the son replies, 'The porch switch is closed and the electricity is reaching the bulb through that switch.' . . . [Y]ou are most likely to feel that the son is being impudent . . . because you are most likely to think that the sort of answer the father needed was something like: 'Because we are expecting company.' But . . . imagine a less likely . . . context: the father and son are re-wiring the house and the father, unexpectedly seeing the porch light on, fears that he has caused a short circuit that bypasses the switch. (131)

In van Fraassen's second case, the son's remark counts as an answer; it is relevant to the question; in the first case it is not. A why-question may therefore be identified with a triple <p, X, R>, where p, X, and R are the question's topic, contrast class, and relevance relation respectively.

One way of articulating Davidson's point about psychological and natural scientific explanation is to say that psychological why-questions, ones the topics of which describe intentional actions, say, cannot be answered by natural scientific statements because the latter are not relevant to their topics.[3] The idea is not new. Consider, for instance, Plato's Socrates:

My wondrous hopes were swept away, my friend, when I proceeded to read, and saw [Anaxagoras] neither appealing to thought, nor citing any of the causes responsible for the ordering of things, but instead citing air, and aether, and water, and many other absurdities as causes. To me it seemed exactly the same as someone saying that Socrates does everything he does with thought, and then in undertaking to state the causes of each thing I do were to say that I am sitting here now because, first, my body is composed of bones and sinews, and the bones are hard and have joints separating them, while the sinews for their part contract and relax, and cover the bones along with the flesh and skin that contains them, and that because the bones move freely in their joints, the contracting and relaxing of the sinews somehow enables me to bend my limbs now, and this is the cause of my sitting here in a bent position. . . . But to call such things causes is most absurd. If someone were to say that without having bones, and sinews, and such, I would not be able to do what I believe best, that would be true. But to say that I do what I do *because* of these, and therein act with thought, but not on account of choosing what I believe best—*that* would be an extremely careless way of speaking. (*Phaedo* 98c–99b)[4]

According to Socrates, the problem with Anaxagoras's account is not that he gets the physiology of human action wrong, but that he assumes a physiological story of this sort is *relevant* to explaining why people act as they do. Actions can only be explained psychologically, Socrates thinks, by appeal to thoughts and choices based on beliefs about what is best.[5] (Putnam (1975b, 297–298) has argued for a similar point.)

The basic idea here is that the natural sciences elucidate the conditions that make action possible: muscular contractions, membrane depolarizations, and the like; but they do not and cannot describe and explain *actions*. The latter are not natural scientific postulates governed by the conceptual rules of scientific discourse; they are postulates of vernacular psychology, and for that reason are beholden to the constitutive rules of psychological discourse, rules that govern the asking and answering of questions, that place constraints on what counts as a legitimate question or answer, and that in particular prescribe relevance relations which only other psychological statements can satisfy.

5. A Substance-property Analogue

The hylomorphic theory I want to develop has several features in common with anomalous monism. Hylomorphic theorists can agree with Davidson's characterization of the difference between psychological and natural scientific discourse; they can agree that it rules out psychophysical reduction, and can agree with the clarification I've offered of it à la van Fraassen. The principle difference between the theories concerns their ontologies: Davidson endorses an ontology of events; the hylomorphic theory, an ontology of substances and properties in which events are understood as substances having properties at times. So on the hylomorphic account substances not events are the basic entities. Yet the role of substances in that account is analogous to that of events in Davidson's: they are concrete particulars which are describable by different vocabularies. Because their ontology includes properties, hylomorphic theorists add that these vocabularies, or forms of discourse, as I've called them, express different types of properties which substances can instantiate. Thus Gabriel, a substance, can undergo or be the agent of both mental and physical events because he can instantiate both mental and physical properties.

Like Davidson's theory, the hylomorphic one is committed to reasons being causes, but because of the different ontology, this claim cannot be formulated in terms of event identity as it is on Davidson's view. The alternative formulation involves a commitment to a certain type of *explanatory realism*, which I will take here as an assumption. It claims that causation is the ontological correlate of explanation in something analogous to the way properties are the ontological correlates of predicates. On this view, the relation of explanans to explanandum mirrors that of cause to effect. Different types of explanation correspond to different types of causation, and these differences are revealed in various relevance relations that might obtain between a statement and the topic and contrast class of the why-question it purports to answer.

Explanatory realism of this sort implies that understanding the relation between a cause and its effect requires understanding how the one explains the other. As N. R. Hanson (1954) says in a passage quoted by van Fraassen (1980, 125):

> There are as many causes of x as there are explanations of x. Consider how the cause of death might have been set out by a physician as 'multiple haemorrhage,' by the barrister as 'negligence on the part of the driver,' by a carriage-builder as 'a defect in the brakeblock construction,' by a civic planner as 'the presence of tall shrubbery at that turning' (54).

In each of these cases understanding how something operates as a cause involves understanding how it contributes to an explanation of the effect. The prototype for this approach to causation is Aristotle's four *aitiai* (194b16–195a26) which Aristotle identifies as those things appeals to which answer the question 'Why?' or 'On account of what?' (*dia ti*). This type of explanatory realism implies that we can understand mental causation only by understanding psychological explanation.

Our discussion of Davidson suggested, however, that there is a categorical difference between psychological explanation and explanation in the natural sciences, a difference which rules out the possibility of providing explanations for human action in natural scientific terms; natural scientific claims are simply not relevant to explaining why people act as they do. The foregoing explanatory realism conjoined with Davidson's characterization of the difference between psychological and natural scientific forms of discourse suggests part of our solution to the problem of mental causation: *If psychological explanation is categorically different from natural scientific explanation, and causation mirrors explanation, then mental causation is categorically different from physical causation.* The foregoing considerations suggest, in other words, that there are at least two distinct types of causation, call them *M-causation* and *P-causation*, which are reflected in two distinct types of explanation, psychological and natural scientific. If that is the case, then the problem of mental causation trades on an equivocation. Claims (1), (3), and (5) must be reinterpreted, the former pair as follows:

(1') Mental events M-cause actions;

(3') Every physical event that has a P-cause has a physical P-cause.

Standard approaches to the problem of mental causation have assumed there is only one type of causal relation; on those approaches, an event's status as mental or physical is irrelevant to its status as a cause, and so statement (5) is taken to rule out multiple causes of any type. If there are multiple types of causal relations as I've suggested, however, statement (5) can be understood in any of the following senses, or as a combination of them:

(5a) Actions do not have multiple P-causes;

(5b) Actions do not have multiple M-causes;

(5c) Actions do not have both M-causes and distinct P-causes.

The considerations advanced hitherto imply both (5a) and (5c), for those considerations imply that actions cannot be explained in physical terms, and hence cannot have physical causes.

But the solution I want to develop involves more. It claims that the problem of mental causation equivocates not just on the notion of a cause, but also on the notion of a physical event. Earlier we distinguished N-physical properties and events from B-physical ones. This distinction suggests two ways of understanding (2) and (4), and four ways of understanding (3):

(2a) Actions are N-physical events;

(2b) Actions are B-physical events;

(3a) Every N-physical event that has a P-cause has an N-physical P-cause;

(3b) Every N-physical event that has a P-cause has a B-physical P-cause;

(3c) Every B-physical event that has a P-cause has an N-physical P-cause;

(3d) Every B-physical event that has a P-cause has a B-physical P-cause.

(4a) Mental events are not N-physical events;

(4b) Mental events are not B-physical events.

Dual-attribute theorists are committed to (4a), but they are not committed to (4b), and are free to claim that the instantiation of mental properties depends in certain ways on the instantiation of N-physical properties. In addition, I want to argue that they should reject (2a), and should endorse (3a). I'll consider these claims in reverse order.

Statement (3), or something like it, has been called *causal closure* or *causal completeness* of the physical domain.[6] The argument for (3a) over against other interpretations of (3) concerns the type of evidence available to support it. However (3) is interpreted, it must be supportable by whatever evidence there is for thinking something like it is true, and that evidence derives in at least two ways from the methods and results of the natural sciences. The first concerns its role as a working hypothesis. If scientific research is investigation into causes, the tacit assumption of scientific method is that there are causes to be investigated, that every type of event the natural sciences investigate is a type for which they could discover a cause. Scientific practice is therefore tacitly committed to something like (3), and denying (3) would be tantamount to revoking the methodological license the natural sciences in fact enjoy. Second, as a methodological assumption of this sort, (3) has very strong inductive credentials. Consider just the case of neuroscience, which has provided a detailed map of functional structures in the human nervous system (Kandel, et al. 2000). Its history, which is one of providing progressively more detailed descriptions of and explanations about those structures, their operations, and the nomological relations among them, gives us strong reason to expect any remaining gaps in the story of how components of the nervous system are causally related to each other will at some future date be filled. And this is just one example among many of a science in which successful research has provided evidence supporting (3).

The foregoing considerations suggest the evidence supporting a claim like (3) concerns the natural sciences, and this suggests N-physical events are the sort for which it makes sense to suppose (3) is true. So (3a) seems the interpretation of (3) best supported by our current knowledge and scientific practice.

The idea is now to show that actions are not N-physical events, and are therefore not covered by (3a). This claim follows from DAT in conjunction with the premise that actions are mental events. DAT implies Psychophysical Property Dualism, and this in turn implies that mental properties are not N-physical properties. Consequently, if act properties are mental properties, it follows that they are not N-physical properties either, and therefore actions are not N-physical events.

Since DAT is being taken here as an assumption (our goal is not to argue for *it*, but only for *its compatibility* with a certain approach to mental causation), the crucial premise is that actions are mental events.

Given our substance-property ontology, actions are mental events precisely if their constitutive properties, *act properties* henceforth, are mental properties. Act properties are mental properties, moreover, precisely if they are expressed by psychological predicates. The question, then, is this: Are action predicates psychological predicates? Do they apply truly only to persons, and imply intentionality, consciousness, or subjectivity? It seems clear that the answer to both these questions is 'Yes.' Intentional actions manifest intentionality just as beliefs and desires do.[7] This is clear if we consider that the psychological content descriptions which individuate beliefs and desires also individuate actions. Whether my action is one of biking home instead of biking to the pub, for instance, depends on whether I intend in my action to go to the one place instead of the other. If I suddenly change my mind in mid-ride and resolve to visit the pub instead of home, my action changes as well. The same is true in legal contexts: whether the crime I committed was murder or some other type of homicide depends in part on what I intended in committing it. Likewise, the question "What is s/he doing?!" often arises precisely because we cannot discern the agent's motives, i.e., the beliefs, desires, intentions, and other propositional attitudes the contents of which make the action what it is. So, just as there cannot be a belief that is not *about* some propositional content or other, there likewise cannot be an intentional action that is not aimed at an end specified by some propositional content or other. As Davidson says, "intentional actions are clearly included in the mental domain along with thoughts, hopes, and regrets" (1970, 211).

Action predicates imply intentionality the same way that paradigmatic psychological predicates such as 'believes,' 'desires,' and 'hopes' do. They are therefore psychological predicates, and that means the properties they express are mental properties. But according to DAT mental properties are not N-physical properties, and so on that account, act properties are not N-physical properties either, and hence actions are not N-physical events. The DAT I've been developing is therefore committed to rejecting (2a). That DAT is nevertheless still compatible with (2b): if actions are not N-physical events, they might still be B-physical events provided only that the instantiation of act properties depends in a suitable sense on the instantiation of N-physical ones.

6. The Solution

The solution I've been developing claims the problem of mental causation is invalid; that it equivocates on both the notion of a physical event and the notion of a cause. In statements (3) and (4) 'physical' is best understood in a narrow sense proper to the natural sciences; in statement (2), by contrast, it is best understood in a broader sense. Actions might be physical events, therefore, but not in the sense countenanced by (3). When Madeleine is writing, there occurs *something* describable in natural scientific terms; what that something is, however, is not the action, but physiological correlates which, though related to it in empirically-specifiable ways, are nevertheless not identical to it. Likewise, the notion of causation is ambiguous: mental events cause actions, but not in the sense that physical events cause each other. Hence there can be no issue of mental and physical causes overdetermining a single effect. Physical causation pertains to membrane depolarizations, muscular contractions, and the like; mental causation pertains to thought and action. The apparent inconsistency among the five claims therefore dissolves. Dual-attribute theorists are free to endorse various, mutually consistent interpretations of (1)–(5):

(1') Mental events M-cause actions;

(2b) Actions are B-physical events;

(3a) Every N-physical event that has a P-cause has an N-physical P-cause;

(4a) Mental events are not N-physical events;

(5ac) Actions do not have multiple P-causes, and they do not have both M-causes and distinct P-causes.

These statements yield a solution that can be represented visually as follows:

Figure 1

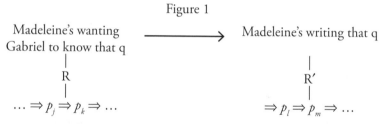

The action and mental event at the top part of the figure are type-distinct from N-physical events (p_j, p_k, etc.) at its bottom. The single arrow represents an M-causal relation; the double arrows represent P-causal relations, and the ellipses represent unbroken causal chains from earlier events to later ones. (For simplicity I am assuming there are no uncaused physical events.) R and R' are non-causal dependence relations of a sort that would qualify Madeleine's writing as a B-physical event, but that would not determine its occurrence. Madeleine's action has a mental cause, and although it has no overdetermining N-physical causes, it and its mental cause are strongly dependent in certain ways on N-physical events that *do* have N-physical causes—intuitively, events that might include the muscular contractions responsible for pushing her pen, neural events in her brain, spinal cord, etc. Hence, the action has a mental cause, as per (1'); actions are B-physical events, as per (2b); every caused N-physical event has an N-physical cause, as per (3a); mental events—thoughts *and actions*—are not N-physical events, as per (4a), and actions do not have overdetermining mental and physical causes, as per (5ac). Dual-attribute theorists can resolve the inconsistency, therefore, without endorsing either epiphenomenalism or psychophysical overdetermination.

7. Psychophysical Relations

What the account so far does not include is a positive story of the relation between thought and action, on the one hand, and N-physical events on the other. There are two things to be said here.

First, according to the hylomorphic theory I'm suggesting there is a good reason why the solution would leave out certain details about psychophysical correlations: those details involve more than we can say philosophically. Philosophically we can say that Madeleine's writing is related in certain ways to N-physical processes involving her proper parts; that it requires the occurrence of those processes; that those processes would not have occurred had Madeleine not acted as she did; that we can observe some of those processes but not others without the use of special equipment, and that all of them are open to further scientific investigation. But *which* organic parts are implicated in which actions, *which* microphysical processes are implicated in the changes in those parts, and *which* microphysical conditions are needed in order for them to occur are *all empirical questions*: we need science to provide the answers. Indeed, without empirical data of the right sort it is a mistake to assume that the correlations between mental and N-physical events are in any way systematic. It is therefore unreasonable to demand such an account without first having concluded the relevant scientific work.

Second, an account of how mental phenomena are related to physiological conditions is a complicated one. It includes (i) a story about how being a human, or an organism of any kind, consists in the possession and exercise of certain capacities such that (ii) those capacities can be possessed and exercised only if the organism is composed of certain proper parts which are (iii) individuated by the performance of certain sub-activities which (iv) contribute to the activity of the whole. Points (i) and (ii) imply that human psychological capacities are dependent on having a certain organic composition, which depends in turn on certain N-physical conditions. Points (iii) and (iv), however, imply a dependence that runs the other way: what counts as an organic part depends on its contribution to the activity of a whole—the organism. A story along these lines implies, then, that psychophysical dependence relations do not run in one direction only, and are not of only one type. Articulating this sort of story in greater detail, however, is something that would take us beyond the scope of this paper.

Regarding the *problem*, however, the important points still stand: natural science does not describe the causes of thought and action, but conditions which are necessary for them to occur, and which are related to them in ways it belongs largely to the natural sciences to describe. There is no issue, then, no threat of epiphenomenalism or overdetermination facing dual-attribute theorists who endorse the line of reasoning I've suggested.

Problems with mental causation have been a concern among philosophers of mind since Descartes. I have argued that it is possible to solve one problem of mental causation by redeploying one part of a hylomorphic conceptual apparatus.[8]

Fordham University

Notes

1. Paradigmatically, the actions in question are *intentional actions*. Digesting food, blinking (involuntarily) and the like, while arguably things we *do* nevertheless do not concern us since they are not among the events for which (1) would appear to be true.

2. For instance Anscombe 1957, Melden 1961.

3. Another point it is possible to make using van Fraassen's account is that questions regarding actions do not even *arise* in a physiological context. Questions always arise against a background of knowledge, and only if that background implies the presuppositions of the question: the truth of the topic, the falsity of other members of the contrast class, and the assumption that there is at least one true statement relevant to the topic and contrast class. Deriving '*Fa*' from a set of statements, K, requires that the predicate '*F*' occur in at least one member of K. The vocabulary of the natural sciences is devoid of action predicates, so if the natural sciences are taken as the sole source of background knowledge, why-questions concerning actions cannot arise. They arise only in a context which takes the deployment of psychological predicates for granted.

4. Translations from the Greek are my own.

5. Consider also Aristotle on the (efficient) causal explanation of action: "The principle of action (the source of movement, not the goal) is choice, and that of choice is desire and reasoning . . . what moves us is thought directed toward a goal" (*NE* 1139a31–5).

6. Whatever the label, it should not be confused with two other claims: first, the claim that every physical event has a physical cause, and secondly, the claim that physical events that have causes have *only* physical causes. Formally, (3) amounts to $\forall x \forall y \exists z((Py \ \& \ Cxy) \rightarrow (Czy \ \& \ Pz))$; whereas the others are, respectively, $\forall x \exists y(Px \rightarrow (Cyx \ \& \ Py))$, and $\forall x \forall y((Py \ \& \ Cxy) \rightarrow Px)$. Statement (3) is compatible with there being uncaused physical events; it merely places a condition on caused ones. It is also compatible with physical events having non-physical causes: it says that in relating the causal history of any physical event, one need never advert to non-physical causes; it does not say one *can* never advert to such causes. Statement (3) also has the advantage of being both sufficient and necessary to generate the problem of mental causation. Its sufficiency is shown by the example of Madeleine's writing; and its necessity, by the fact that its denial resolves the inconsistency among (1)–(5). The same cannot be said of alternative formulations of causal closure.

7. Searle's (1983) discussion of intentional action makes the intentionality of action manifest as well.

8. Many thanks to my colleagues John Greco and Bryan Frances for helpful comments on an earlier draft of this paper.

Bibliography

Anscombe, G. E. M. 1957. *Intentions*. Oxford: Blackwell.

Davidson, Donald. 1963. Actions, Reasons, and Causes. *Journal of Philosophy* 60: 685–700. Reprinted in Davidson 1980, 3–19

———. 1970. Mental Events. In *Experience and Theory*, ed. L. Foster and J. W. Swanson. Amherst: University of Massachusetts Press. Reprinted in Davidson 1980, 208–227.

———. 1980. *Essays on Actions and Events*. Oxford: Clarendon Press.

Goodman, N. 1956. *Fact, Fiction, and Forecast*. Indianapolis, Ind.: Bobbs-Merrill.

Kandel, Eric, et al. 2000. *Principles of Neural Science*. 4th Edition. New York: McGraw-Hill.

Kim, Jaegwon. 1973. Causation, Nomic Subsumption and the Concept of Event. *Journal of Philosophy* 70: 217–236. Reprinted in Kim 1993a, 3–21.

———. 1976. Events as Property Exemplifications. In *Action Theory*, ed. Myles Brand and Douglas Walton, 159–177. Dordrecht, Holland: D. Reidel Publishing Co. Reprinted in Kim 1993a, 33–52.

———. 1993a. *Supervenience and Mind*. Cambridge University Press.

———. 1993b. The Non-Reductivist's Troubles with Mental Causation. In *Mental Causation*, ed. J. Heil and A. Mele. Oxford: Clarendon Press. Reprinted in Kim 1993a, 336–357.

Melden, A. I. 1961. *Free Action*. London: Routledge & Kegan Paul.

Pereboom, Derk and Hilary Kornblith. 1991. The Metaphysics of Irreducibility. *Philosophical Studies* 63: 125–145.

Putnam, Hilary. 1975a. *Mind, Language, and Reality: Philosophical Papers, vol. 2*. Cambridge University Press.

———. 1975b. Philosophy and Our Mental Life. In Putnam 1975a, 291–303.

Searle, John. 1983. *Intentionality: An Essay in the Philosophy of Mind*. New York: Cambridge University Press.

Van Fraassen, Bas C. 1980. *The Scientific Image*. Oxford: Clarendon.

Thomas Aquinas and Nonreductive Physicalism

Kevin W. Sharpe

Abstract: Eleonore Stump has recently argued that Thomas Aquinas's philosophy of mind is consistent with a nonreductive physicalist approach to human psychology. I argue that by examining Aquinas's account of the subsistence of the rational soul we can see that Thomistic dualism is inconsistent with physicalism of every variety. Specifically, his reliance on the claim that the mind has an operation *per se* spells trouble for any physicalist interpretation. After offering Stump's reading of Aquinas and her case for the supposed consistency with nonreductive physicalism, I use Aquinas's discussion of the mind's operation *per se* to argue that the human mind is incapable of being physically realized. To support this general argument, I offer a detailed examination of Stump's use of two criteria of physicalism drawn from contemporary functional analyses of the mind and argue that both are inconsistent with Aquinas's theory.

I. Introduction

Recent work on Thomas Aquinas's contribution to the philosophy of mind has produced a variety of approaches to his account of the mind's relation to the body. Though commentators have historically stressed his dualistic tendencies, recently some philosophers have begun to emphasize the seemingly physicalistic strands of his thought. In her recent book *Aquinas*, Eleonore Stump argues that Aquinas's position is consistent with a physicalist psychology, properly understood. Specifically, she argues that "a certain kind of (restricted rather than global) materialism—one that takes mental states to be implemented in bodily states—is compatible with a certain sort of dualism—one that is non-Cartesian in character."[1] Yet, as I read Aquinas, this is clearly mistaken. Though certain features of his theory of mind seem to resonate with nonreductive physicalism of a functionalist character, it can be seen, or so I shall argue, that the consistency of Thomistic dualism with any variety of physicalism is merely apparent rather than real.

Given the *prima facie* similarity between Aquinas's conception of the rational soul as the form of the human being and contemporary functionalist analyses of mental states and properties in computational or causal terms, it is especially ironic that he argues against the possibility of the physical realization of minds on broadly functionalist grounds. To make my case for the inconsistency of Thomistic dualism and nonreductive physicalism I begin by developing Stump's reading of Aquinas and then offer a general argument against this reading in light of Aquinas's claim that the mind possesses an operation *per se*. To reinforce my general argument, I consider two possible criterions of physicalism suggested by Stump and argue that Aquinas's theory cannot satisfy either.

II. Stump's Reading of Aquinas

Aquinas's account of the human person as a living organism with rational capacities falls within his general hylomorphic theory of material objects, according to which each material object is a composite of both form and matter. Stump's chapter on human persons, "Forms and Bodies: The soul," constitutes a major attempt by a contemporary philosopher to explain Aquinas's metaphysical views of persons and their bodies. Her admirable exposition and defense of Aquinas's position focuses on the Thomistic conception of the rational soul as a "configured configurer" and presents his theory of mind as a way of carving out a conceptual space between Cartesian substance dualism and nonreductive physicalism.

Stump begins her exposition of Aquinas's views with an account of substantial form in general. I follow her in doing the same here. The substantial form is that in virtue of which some matter composes a material object and what makes the object belong to a given kind or species. By arranging or configuring some portion of matter in a substance-composing way, a substantial form confers on that matter a specific range of natural causal powers unique to its kind. For medievals, such as Aquinas, a substance is a member of its natural kind in virtue of possessing the causal powers distinctive of that kind, where an object's causal powers are a consequence of the substantial organization of its matter. As Aquinas says, "the nature of a thing is revealed by its operation."[2] That is, to be an F is to have the causal powers or natural dispositions characteristic of Fs and for Aquinas causal powers and dispositions are grounded in or supervene on actual structural features of the object. So while contemporary taxonomies of natural kinds focus on compositional features, the medieval tradition characterizes kinds functionally.[3]

The functional nature of kinds together with the fact that a substance is a member of its kind in virtue of its substantial form entails that an object is a member of its kind in virtue of the powers conferred on the object by its substantial form. We can label such a view hylomorphic functionalism. Thus, the hylomorphic functionalist claims that in virtue of organizing matter F-wise, on which F-powers supervene, an F-type substantial form makes it true both that the matter composes a substance and that the substance is an F. Though Stump does not define it as such, this characterization of substantial form suggests the following definition:

x is a substantial form of some material substance S of kind F = df. (i) x is an intrinsic feature of S and (ii) x makes it true that S's matter is in a state of dynamic structural complexity, y, and S's F-powers supervene on y.

One of the key benefits of this definition is that it defines substantial forms functionally in terms of the role they play in Aquinas's hylomorphic analysis of material substances, and so allows for multiple types of entity to fill this role and therefore count as substantial forms. For example, as Stump points out, the substantial form of a non-human material object is "the arrangement or organization of the matter of that object in such a way that it constitutes that object rather than some other one and gives that object its causal powers,"[4] while, as we will see, at least one type of substantial form of a living organism is an immaterial particular.

This potential for multiple realization is also exhibited by Aquinas's abstract functional characterization of the soul as "the first principle of life in the things that are alive around us."[5] Characterized functionally, the soul is simply that which makes the organism alive and capable of performing a characteristic range of activities, or that which functions as the internal cause of the living activity characteristic of its kind. For living things these characteristic causal powers will include either a capacity for movement or cognition. While plants are capable of only the most basic forms of movement in the broadest sense of that term, animals have a natural capacity for self-propelled motion and additional cognitive capacities for processing information. Thus, the sensitive soul will account for both the basic mechanical activities of nutrition, reproduction and the like and also those responsible for the organism's mental life involving sensory cognition. As with substantial forms in general, the functional characterization leaves as unspecified what plays the required causal or explanatory role with respect to motion and cognition. For both the vegetative and sensitive soul, Stump quite rightly notes that what fills this explanatory role is a complex "configuration of matter" (i.e., a configurational state or property) in virtue of which the organism possesses its kind-defining activity.[6]

The rational soul, the intellectual aspect of which is equivalent to our notion of the mind, is that which explains the distinctive cognitive and volitional capacities characteristic of the human mental life.[7] While it might be tempting to think of the rational soul simply as a type of *property*, it is best not to yield to temptation. The human soul, in a way reminiscent of God and the angels, exists as a particular subsistent entity. Unlike a mere configuration of matter, which depends on that matter for its existence, the soul is capable of existing and functioning independently of the matter it informs. This forms the basis of Aquinas's proposal that the rational soul is not a mere configurational state or property of the body, but rather is an immaterial configured particular more akin to an angel than a sensitive soul. Summing up Aquinas's complex views of the mind Stump says, "In the middle [of the metaphysical hierarchy of forms] are human souls, the amphibians of this metaphysical world, occupying a niche in both the material and the spiritual realm. Like an angel, the human soul is itself a configured subsistent form; but like the forms of material things, the human soul has the ability to configure matter."[8]

The soul's amphibian character as a configured configurer underlies Aquinas's rejection of the Platonic (or, Cartesian) thesis that thinking, and the other higher cognitive activities, occurs only in the soul and not in the body. The rational soul, Stump claims, is "that configuration of matter on the basis of which something exists [and acts] as this living human body"[9] and since the power to engage in intellectual cognition is conferred on the human in virtue of being configured in this way, Stump says "there is something misleading about attributing cognitive functions just to the soul itself. Rather, even such higher cognitive functions as understanding are to be attributed to the whole material composite that is the human being."[10]

This distinctively anti-Cartesian thesis distances Aquinas from the more radical substance dualists by allowing that *material* substances themselves (i.e., hylomorphic compounds) can engage in cognitive activity. This, in conjunction with a view of the human mind as the complex configuration of a material object, leads Stump to claim that "all human cognitive functions can be implemented in the body."[11] Mind, on this reading of Aquinas, is both a subsistent entity, hence the dualism, and also a complex configuration of a material organism realized or implemented in living matter, hence the physicalism.[12] Aquinas, Stump proposes, offers us a nonreductive physicalist theory of human persons that is consistent with holding the mind to be a non-Cartesian subsistent entity.

III. Against Stump's Reading: Subsistence and the Mind's 'Operation Per Se'

For all its philosophical attractions, this reading of Aquinas overlooks a central feature of his theory of mind. In the midst of arguing for the soul's subsistence Aquinas appeals to the mind's possession of an operation *per se*, a cognitive function it performs on its own apart from the activity of any bodily organ. To argue for the subsistence of the soul and the necessity of a unique and nonphysically realized cognitive process, Aquinas relies on his brand of functionalism. If the mind were to depend on a bodily organ for all of its activities, then, according to his metaphysical commitments, it must exist as a non-subsistent material form. In this case, the rational soul would depend for its existence on the matter it informs. If, on the other hand, there is some cognitive function that the mind performs that does not rely on a bodily organ or any physical process, then the mind does not depend on matter for its existence.

It follows from Aquinas's hylomorphic functionalism that "a thing operates in the same manner that it exists"[13] and also that "as a thing exists, so it operates."[14] This means that for any given thing, its mode of operation and mode of existing are mutually entailing and so, if the thing functions on its own, then it must exist on its own. The argument for this claim is that nothing can function on its own unless it exists as an independent particular thing; i.e., as a subsistent being. Aquinas says, "Every operation belongs to something actually existent."[15] Since something must exist in order to function, if the mind performs some cognitive act independently of the body, then its existence and powers must not depend on the matter it informs. Thus, for Aquinas, if the mind has an operation *per se*, then it is a subsistent entity.[16]

While the specific details of the argument are difficult to establish, Aquinas employs a familiar dualist strategy to argue for the mind's possession of an operation *per se.* The general structure of his argument is that the mind has certain representational capacities that would be impossible if it were to either be a physical entity or be entirely functionally dependent on a physical entity. He takes it as a given fact that the mind, in principle, can think about every kind of material object. As he sees it, if the mind were related to a physical object in either of the ways specified above, then its cognitive activity could only be directed toward the kind of stuff that composes it and so rendering it impossible to think about any other kind of material substance. Clearly the mind is not limited in this way and so, Aquinas thinks, it operates independently of every bodily organ.[17] The general problem this creates for Stump's reading should be clear. As she reads Aquinas he holds that "all human cognitive functions can be implemented in the body,"[18] but as we have just seen there is an important range of intellectual activity for which this is not true. For any thought whose intentional content concerns a material species cannot, for that reason, be or be realized by a neural event or process. If so, then assuming that the physicalist must hold to the physical realization of all mental activity, Aquinas's position is inconsistent with a physicalism about the mind. The development of this general line of thought into a complete criticism of Stump's reading is the task of the next section.

IV. Applying the General Criticism: Two Failed Proposals

A. Patricia Churchland's Implementation Criterion of Physicalism

Stump draws on the work of both Patricia Churchland and Richard Boyd in arguing that Aquinas's dualism is consistent with a functionalist version of nonreductive physicalism. Her goal is to show that the criteria of physicalism offered by Churchland and Boyd allow Aquinas to be counted among the physicalists. She begins by citing Churchland's claim that "one of the main characteristics of physicalism [is] to hold that 'mental states are implemented in neural stuff.'"[19] This suggests the following criterion of physicalism:

> Churchland's Implementation Criterion (CIC): (i) a mental state M is physical if and only if M is implemented in physical stuff and (ii) every mental state is a physical state.[20]

By introducing CIC, Stump hopes to show that if CIC is our criterion of physicalism, then Aquinas should be counted among the physicalists. As we have seen, she understands the mind to be a dynamic organization of matter and, as such, Thomistic minds are implemented in neural stuff. As this is sufficient for a Thomistic mind being physical, Aquinas's dualism should be considered consistent with this form of physicalism.[21]

For this strategy to work, Aquinas must hold that the mind is implemented in matter in the same sense as intended by our criterion, CIC. Evidently Stump would have us understand Aquinas as arguing that mental states are functional types (and that minds are functional entities) realized by token physical states (and entities).[22]

While there is a sense in which this is true, since I have argued that Aquinas holds to a sort of hylomorphic functionalism about the mind, his analysis of the mind does not count as physical according to CIC. Let me explain why: Following the standard functionalist analysis, let's say that what is essential to a mental state is its abstract causal role within a given cognitive system and so, as functional kinds, mental states are defined by what they do (esp. their role as causal intermediaries between stimuli, other internal states and behavior). Some state's being a pain or belief, then, is a matter of that state's playing the right causal role in a cognitive system by being properly connected to a given range of stimuli (including both external and internal stimuli) and behaviors (including both bodily behaviors and internal states, such as beliefs and desires).

Putting this a bit more precisely, some property F is a second-level property if and only if F is a property of instantiating or possessing some distinct property G that satisfies condition C.[23] In the case of functional properties, understood as second-level properties, the condition satisfied by G will be a causal condition specifying a role in a given system. This allows us to say that a second-level property F is physically realized in some entity S by a first-level property G just in case S is F in virtue of the fact that S is G and G satisfies C. Where F is some mental state, and G is the appropriate neural state, S is in F in virtue of the fact that it in G and G is causally connected to the appropriate internal states, stimuli, and behaviors.

Our question, then, is whether Aquinas's theory of the mind as a functional entity satisfies CIC so developed. It seems on any plausible interpretation of his argument for the subsistence of the soul it cannot satisfy the required condition. To satisfy CIC, it must be the case that every mental state or property is physically realized by complex neural configurations. Though Stump characterizes the mind as a configuration of matter, we have also seen that Aquinas argues against the possibility of the physical realization of the mind's representational capacities; i.e., no disposition of a physical mechanism can satisfy the causal condition characteristic of a representational property. This means that the mind has a capacity for functionally specifiable processes, the mind's operation *per se*, for which there can be no "neural correlate." Aquinas's argument for the subsistence of the soul requires him to hold that a given range of intentional states cannot be realized by a first-order token physical state. One should conclude, therefore, that Aquinas's theory of mind cannot be characterized as a physicalist theory according to CIC.[24]

B. Boyd's Compositional Physicalism

Stump's second proposed criterion fares just as poorly. Again, by focusing on contemporary functionalism, Stump looks to Richard Boyd's nonreductive physicalism according to which mental states are essentially "computational" or, what comes to the same thing, constituted by "information-processing" roles within a system. He says,

> For each type of mental or psychological state, event, or process there
> are certain configurations of information-processing systems, or internal

"programs," such that their manifestation in the body of an animal is . . . sufficient to constitute a manifestation of the mental or psychological event, state, or process in question.[25]

As a type of computational state, mental or psychological states display what Boyd labels "maximal compositional plasticity."[26] By "plasticity" Boyd means a state-type's "capacity to be realized in more than one way." "Compositional" plasticity is exhibited by a type of state to the degree that there are possible token realizations of that type which differ in the "sorts of substances or causal factors that constitute them."[27] Hence "maximal" compositional plasticity:

> in any particular possible world, only the causal laws governing that world limit the possible composition of realizations of such . . . states; such states have no essential properties that constrain the sorts of substances or causal factors that can be constituents of their realizations.[28]

If we let "purely configurational state" stand for those states that (i) possess maximal compositional plasticity and (ii) are realized by tokens whose only essential properties are configurational, then we can say that mental states are purely configurational. Since such states do not have any compositional properties essentially, Boyd takes it that it is logically possible for mental states to be nonphysically realized. Boyd's materialism, then, amounts to the view that as a matter of contingent fact, mental states and processes are composed of, and therefore are nothing over and above, the particular molecular processes that realize them.[29] We can call this version of physicalism, compositional physicalism.

Parallels with Aquinas's account are easily drawn. As Stump claims, both characterize the mind in purely configurational terms and both hold that it is possible for a mind to exist and function without being physically realized.[30] Yet, despite the seeming parallels, Aquinas cannot be classified as a compositional physicalist. Two problems arise for such a reading: (i) if Thomistic minds were purely configurational, then the only difference between subsistent and nonsubsistent minds would be that the former actualize a possibility that the latter do not and (ii) Aquinas does hold that there are compositional constraints on what is a potential realizer of the mental.

Consider (i). The purely configurational nature of mental states and minds, or total functional systems, entails that a cognitive system may be realized by a nonphysical mechanism as long as that system is able to realize the appropriate causal factors. Physically realized minds, then, are only contingently realized by physical mechanisms. For this argument to be useful to Aquinas, it will have to be the case that one and the same mind is both physically realized and possibly nonphysically realized. Boyd seems to grant this possibility when he argues both that every token mental state has a possible nonphysical realization and that it is (at least) logically possible for a complete functional system that is in fact realized by some neurobiological system to be realized by a completely synthetic nervous system.

Not only would this establish that functional systems, in addition to their constituent states, are purely configurational, it would establish also that any token system can be nonphysically realized. Accordingly, Boyd and Aquinas (as Stump would have it), hold the following general realization principle:[31]

> GRP: For any cognitive system S, S is physically realized by some physical system whose elements bear the appropriate causal relations to each other and external factors, and possibly, S is realized by some causally appropriate nonphysical system.

Stated in its full generality, Aquinas obviously rejects GRP. Take the cognitive system of some rabbit. As Aquinas sees it this functional system is physically realized by a set of first-order physical properties within a given biological structure. Our token rabbit is a subject of mental properties in virtue of the fact that it has a set of configurational properties that structure its body in such a way that the configurational properties realize the rabbit's mental properties.

If Aquinas held to GRP he would be required to claim that the rabbit's cognitive system (or sensitive soul) is possibly realized by some nonphysical system and is therefore subsistent in the same sense that the human mind is subsistent. But this is the very thing that Aquinas is committed to denying; he argues, "every operation of the sensory soul belongs to the compound. From this it follows that since the souls of brute animals do not operate on their own, they are not subsistent."[32] In fact, Aquinas holds to a principle of physical realization for nonhuman cognitive systems. On his view, material forms are essentially physically realized. This allows us to formulate the following principle concerning the physical realization of nonhuman cognitive systems:

> PPR: For any nonhuman cognitive system S', S' has its configurational properties essentially and, necessarily, if S' is realized, then there is a material substance M and M realizes S in virtue of the fact that M instantiates a complex biological configuration that realizes S' in M.[33]

PPR shows us where GRP goes wrong. Aquinas is committed to denying the possibility of the nonphysical realization of a nonhuman cognitive system, because as nonsubsistent material forms they depend on the matter they inform for their existence. If Aquinas were to hold to GRP, rather than PPR, and therefore that nonhuman cognitive systems are subsistent, the only difference between a human and nonhuman cognitive system would be that as a matter of contingent fact the human but not the nonhuman cognitive system is nonphysically realized in the actual world. But then given his claim that "a thing operates in the manner that it exists," this would commit Aquinas to holding that the sensitive soul has an operation *per se*, and given his views of sensory cognition this is not the case.[34]

Now consider (ii), my claim is that while it is true that Aquinas offers a functional account of the mind, he does not offer an account of the mind as purely configurational. For a system or state to be purely configurational is for it to possess maximal compositional plasticity. Remember that states or systems display compositional plasticity to the degree that they are multiply realizable and so those with maximal compositional plasticity have no essential properties that constrain the types of causal mechanisms that can realize the state or system in question as long as its token realization possesses the appropriate configurational properties.[35]

As we saw in connection with Churchland's criterion of physicalism, certain states of the mind do possess essential properties that constrain their range of possible realizers. If we allow that the intentionality of the mind's representational states are essential features of those states, which seems plausible, such states cannot be realized in any physical system because the first-order physical properties of a complex neural system cannot satisfy the causal condition required to realize the intentional properties of the mind. Putting this in Boydian terms: if the mind is essentially computational, in that the nature or essence of the mind is located in its cognitive capacities and these capacities can be entirely represented by computational or 'information-processing' models, then the nature of mental computation will itself rule out physical realization. The key point is that the essential properties of these representational states are themselves functional properties of the cognitive system (or its states) and their functional nature precludes even contingent physical realization by a first-level physical system (or its states). This restriction in compositionality entails that Thomistic minds do not exemplify maximal compositional plasticity and so are not purely configurational. Though the rational soul informs the matter composing a living human organism, it is not the case, as it is for Boyd, that the mind is purely configurational and contingently composed of matter.

I have argued in this section that Stump's proposed analogy between Aquinas and Richard Boyd fails due to the compositional constraints placed on what can realize a human mind due to its representational capacity or the intentionality of mental states. Generally, we can say that in so far as any plausible physicalist account of the mind must be committed to denying this key feature of Aquinas's theory, I propose that his theory of mind is inconsistent with physicalism *tout court*. While Stump's version of Thomistic dualism, understood as a variety of nonreductive materialism, may be an attractive option to those of us who have grown weary of the traditional options available to the contemporary philosopher of mind, it is not Aquinas's own view.[36]

Purdue University

Notes

1. Eleonore Stump, *Aquinas* (London: Routledge, 2003), 215.

2. ST Ia.76.1

3. The following principle adequately captures the functional nature of kinds: Necessarily, for any kind F, there is a set of causal powers C, such that, for any x, x is an F if and only if x instantiates the members of C.

4. Stump, 194.

5. ST Ia 75.1. All quotations are from *The Treatise on Human Nature*, trans. Robert Pasnau (Indianapolis: Hackett, 2002).

6. Stump, 201.

7. That the mind is equivalent to the intellective aspect of the rational soul is suggested by Stump, 212.

8. Stump, 200.

9. Ibid., 201–202.

10. Ibid., 203.

11. Ibid., 210.

12. Ibid., 210.

13. ST 1a.75.2 reply.

14. ST 1a.75.3 reply.

15. ST 1a.75.2 reply.

16. For a similar reconstruction of the argument see Robert Pasnau's *Thomas Aquinas on Human Nature* (Cambridge: Cambridge University Press, 2002), 50–51.

17. As Aquinas sees it, the independence of the mind's *operation per se* from any bodily process is consistent with the mind's causal dependence, in its natural state, on the body for the content of thought though sensory representations (i.e., phantasms).

18. Stump, 210.

19. Ibid., 213.

20. The replacement of "neural" with "physical" in my formulation is to broaden the range of possible states that can implement the mental. In what follows I will alternate between discussion of minds and mental states, even though CIC speaks only of mental states.

21. Stump, 213.

22. For ease of exposition I will only refer to mental states or properties.

23. Though this is the standard way of developing functional properties, e.g. Kim's development of functionalism in *Mind in Physical World* (Cambridge: MIT Press, 1998), following John Heil, I distinguish between second-level and second-order properties and take functional properties to be second-level properties. A second-order property is a property of a property and a second-level property is a property possessed by a substance in virtue of a distinct 'first-level' property. See Heil's "Properties and Powers" in *Oxford Studies in Metaphysics: Volume One*, ed. Dean Zimmerman (Oxford: Oxford University Press, 2004), 232 footnote 11.

24. This section presupposes the so-called functional state identity formulation of functionalism, according to which a mental property is identified with a second-level property or causal 'role'. The criticism could easily be recast in terms of functional specification varieties of functionalism, where mental properties are first-level properties satisfying a causal condition (i.e., the occupants of causal roles).

25. Richard Boyd, "Materialism without Reductionism: What Physicalism Does Not Entail," in *Readings in Philosophy of Psychology*, vol 1, ed. Ned Block (Cambridge, Mass.: Harvard University Press, 1980), 91.

26. Ibid., 88.

27. Ibid., 88.

28. Ibid., 88.

29. As stated, physicalism is obviously consistent with the possible nonphysical realization of minds.

30. Stump, 214.

31. For Aquinas this principle will exclude both the Divine and angelic minds.

32. Ia.75.3.

33. Again, this excludes the minds of supernatural agents. The first clause is intended to rule out the claim that something which is in fact a cognitive system could fail to be physically realized by failing to be a cognitive system.

34. See ST 75.3 reply. Jason Eberl has suggested that if we substitute "intellectual" in GRP for "cognitive" the resulting principle is one that Aquinas would accept. The amended principle is consistent with PPR and so human minds, as intellectual cognitive systems, are contingently realized by brains and this contingency is restricted to intellectual systems. While such a view is both interesting and worth developing, the proposed restriction of contingent physical realization to intellectual cognitive systems must be justified; that is, there must be some principled difference between intellectual and nonintellectual cognitive systems such that the first but not the second are only contingently physically realized. While Aquinas's theory of intellectual cognition allows for the possible disembodiment of human minds it does so only by forfeiting physical realization (as I briefly discussed in Section III) and so will only support the second half of the amended GRP. Thus, Boyd's functionalism supports both conjuncts of the proposed amendment, but not the restriction of possible disembodiment to intellectual systems, and Aquinas's functionalism supports the restriction of possible disembodiment but rejects the first conjunct of both the original and the amended versions of GRP. This means to justify the proposed amendment to GRP one cannot look to either Boyd or Aquinas.

35. Boyd, 88.

36. I wish to thank my commentator Jason Eberl for his stimulating comments and criticism. I also wish to thank Jeff Brower, Winship Varner, and Chris Martin for their comments on prior drafts.

Karl Marx and the Critique of Bourgeois Philosophy

Patrick Murray and Jeanne Schuler

Abstract: Marx launched a revolution in social thought that has been largely ignored. We locate this revolution in the context of two major reassessments of modern philosophy, Heidegger's *Being and Time* and Donald Davidson's new anti-subjectivism. We argue that the philosophical significance of Marx's critique of the capitalist mode of production—his critique of the bourgeois horizon—has been overlooked. The paper exposes the bourgeois mindset that runs through political economy, "traditional" Marxism, and much of modern and postmodern philosophy. Bourgeois thinking is marked by a series of "purist splits," conceptual distinctions that are mishandled as actual separations: conceptual vs. empirical, conceptual scheme vs. thing in itself, individual vs. society, production vs. distribution, preference vs. the preferred object, and subjective vs. objective. Marx shows how capitalist social forms that produce the notion of "value added" inculcate the purist, bifurcating bourgeois horizon.

Marx's critique of capitalism has been called the "scientific revolution in nineteenth century social thought."[1] But this revolution quickly stalled since basic dimensions of Marx's critique remain out of reach of even sympathetic readers. Marx names the array of obstacles to understanding capitalism "the bourgeois horizon." The bourgeois horizon describes a familiar mindset inculcated by many sources. Its power lies in its apparent self-evidence. Thinking is assumed to follow set patterns. These patterns run throughout modern philosophy and trace back to Hellenistic philosophy. They underlie sociology and neoclassical economics. Most forms of philosophical analysis presuppose them. The pervasiveness of this horizon destines Marx, ironically, to be read through the lens of that thinking he endeavors to displace.[2] Like a horizon, the bourgeois mindset conceals as well as reveals. It is the ideology of commercial societies, disguising its origin so that its mode of thinking appears as generic. With this mindset in place, Marx's effort to disclose the forms of capital is systematically thwarted.

Marx is not commonly credited for his command of philosophy. However, his disclosure of the bourgeois horizon involves a sophisticated critique of philosophy. Because that critique has been overlooked, the bourgeois horizon isn't left behind but is replicated—often in the guise of radical thought. From Hegel, Marx inherits the critique of *Verstand*, the predominant mode of thinking in modern philosophy. However, Marx faults Hegel for falling prey to the dualisms that he had exposed in modern philosophy. For the purpose of the present inquiry, we will not challenge how Marx characterizes Hegel's defects. We will address three topics. First, drawing on Hegel and Marx, we develop in greater detail the basic features of bourgeois thought. Second, we consider how commercial life or capitalist society makes these patterns plausible. Finally, we sketch how Marx's critique of capitalism presupposes an adequate phenomenology that goes beyond the bourgeois horizon. In our view, only an adequate phenomenology makes the critique of capitalism possible.

The Bourgeois Mindset

Exposing the failures of bourgeois thought was a lifelong project for Marx. Writing to his father at the age of nineteen, Marx conveyed excitement at discovering Hegel and abandoning the bifurcations of Kant and Fichte. "The mistake lay in my believing that the one (form) could and must be developed in separation from the other (matter), and consequently I obtained no actual form, but only a desk with drawers in which I then strew sand."[3] Drawers are designed to pull out of desks, but separating form from matter serves no purpose. Marx characterized bourgeois thought as a knot of unworkable bifurcations: form vs. content, mind vs. world, *a priori* vs. *a posteriori*, passive vs. active, immediate vs. mediated, sensation vs. concept.

These dualisms arise from the root conviction that what can be distinguished in thought can exist separately. For analysis to dictate the terms of existence is deeply mistaken. What Hume calls a "distinction of reason" shifts, without experiential warrant, into a "matter of fact."[4] A distinction of reason describes what can be separated for the purpose of analysis but can't exist separately. In analysis, we focus on the color, shape, or texture of something. The mistake arises with the further assumption that clear apprehension insures separate existence. Clarity comes to mean independence: distinctions signify distinct existents. Color supposedly exists independently of shape and texture if it is conceived separately. This slide from "distinguished aspect" to "separate element" fuels the bourgeois mindset and its characteristic dilemmas. What must exist together—such as action and its consequences—are split apart and treated as separable things. Splitting apart what exists only together—or makes sense together—yields thinking that never makes its way back to experience. Analysis of a sort ensues, but it doesn't get at reality—not because it is abstract, but because its abstractions are false: they posit as independent what experience shows to be inseparable.

While Hume acknowledges "distinctions of reason," he doesn't leave room for these distinctions when he divides knowledge into relations of ideas and matters of fact. Relations of ideas, found in logic and math, are inseparable in thought. To deny such a relation, described as "analytic" by Kant, results in contradiction.

Matters of fact, by contrast, are founded on experience. Hume construes experience as a stream of distinct perceptions. The route from experience to knowledge requires establishing necessary connections, such as causality, between perceived events. As Hume construes perception, this linkage doesn't exist. Perception excludes necessity, since perception is stipulated as discrete. Since necessity is not directly given in perception, argues Hume, it must arise subsequently from our habits or customs of perceiving; humans respond to repeated perception and project necessity on to the world.

Arrived at in this way, necessary connections are only subjective. Custom tells us about human nature, not about the external world. Once necessity is removed from experience, what remains of a "distinction of reason"? Hume's skepticism pulls the ground out from under distinctions of reason, since it supposes that nothing *must* exist together. What is pulled apart in analysis doesn't come back together again. Getting beyond the bourgeois horizon restores distinctions of reason to their role in achieving knowledge.

The bifurcations that constitute the bourgeois horizon presuppose *purist* conceptions of terms.[5] Purism and bifurcation go hand in hand to make up the bourgeois mindset. A purist conception pushes difference to the extreme of dualism or disjunction. For example, form and matter are *different* aspects of things. When these differences emerge within the bourgeois horizon, form becomes pure (contentless) form and content becomes pure (formless) content; the subjective becomes the exclusively subjective and the objective the exclusively objective. Rather than distinguishing aspects of the thing, these categories cordon off rival territories. The bourgeois mindset is stymied by meditation. Radical oppositions make mediation between the extremes unthinkable. The dilemma faced by Descartes in comprehending the unity of mind and body resounds from other corners. So long as concepts are isolated from each other, a semblance of order appears. To maintain this semblance, thinking is reined in. If thinking persists, then questions such as these arise: how are perceptions and concepts related? Do *a priori* structures of knowledge change over time? If so, are these changes provoked by experience?[6] Questions that force purist concepts together undermine the fundamental stance. A semblance of order quickly dissolves into nagging doubts. The clear and distinct oppositions that characterize the bourgeois horizon are often one question away from a slide into skepticism.

Marx's dissertation and notes reveal his fascination with the Hellenistic philosophies of Epicureanism, Stoicism, and Skepticism. He called them the key to the whole history of Greek philosophy and judged these bifurcating philosophies to be the forerunners of modern bourgeois thought, just as he saw in much modern philosophy a revival of Hellenistic ideas. Moneylenders and traders inhabit the fringes of a traditional society. Marx considered Hellenistic thought to be occasioned by the breakdown of traditional, "substantial" societies and the rise of private property and commercial life. Bourgeois philosophy is the shape that thought is likely to assume when traditional, communal societies give way as private property and commercial forms take hold.

The main moves of Hellenistic philosophy are the staples of bourgeois thought. Epicureanism and Stoicism stipulate as essence a single element that is supposedly self-evident and needs no defense. This element—pleasure or detachment—signifies the sole measure of worth. Hellenistic thinkers may quarrel about what constitutes the essence, but they agree that a single abstraction underlies the diversity of experience—like a common currency that expresses all prices. A further hallmark of Hellenistic thought is the split between the inner and outer realm. This line, drawn by Stoicism, separates what is mine—perceptions and judgments—from what lies beyond my control, a matter of indifference. This division between inner and outer, what is essential and inessential or subjective and objective, is the original purist split. Further bifurcations are replicated from this. With Epicureanism, the disjunction is posited between what is pleasurable in the world and what is not. With Stoicism, bifurcation retreats inward, separating external uncertainties from what falls entirely under my control, my thoughts and choices. Skepticism appears to escape bifurcation by exposing all claims to essence as flawed. Skepticism can make the case that purist concepts are empty without much trouble. However a split persists within skepticism between failed doctrines, on one hand, and the unmet criteria on the other. Like purist concepts, stipulated criteria that have never been tested by experience are hollow. Like the Epicurean and the Stoic, the Skeptic asserts criteria for the essential, though these criteria are not realized. Dogmatism and skepticism oscillate throughout philosophy, without a hint that this is a deadlock, let alone how it might be broken.

What is missing from bourgeois philosophy is an understanding of human activity. Hegel's great contribution to philosophy, in Marx's view, was recognizing the importance of activity, even if the paradigmatic activity was wrongly taken to be thinking itself. Figuring out how to think about activity moved Hegel beyond the standoffs of modern philosophy to grasp how *mediation* gives concepts their content. The dynamic process that constitutes human activity inspires the core categories of Hegel's philosophy, the concept and the idea. Philosophy arrives at an adequate grasp of its own activity slowly through its history. In the *Encyclopedia Logic*, Hegel describes three attitudes towards objectivity: traditional metaphysics, empiricism and Kant's critical philosophy, and the idea of immediate or intuitive knowledge found in Schelling. In each case, how philosophy reckons with its own activity shapes the conception of objectivity.

Traditional metaphysics, in Hegel's view, doesn't trouble about its own activity; it assumes that human thought is capable of grasping its object, whether God, the soul, or the universe. Instead of determining its object through a reasoning process, traditional metaphysics borrows from popular conceptions and fashions its predicates accordingly. This naïve confidence issues its predicates as disjunctions: God is either one or many, the universe is either created or uncreated, the soul is either simple or composite. These categories behave as labels, in Hegel's view; they lack content and remain unfit for the task of metaphysics. Disjunction reflects the absence of awareness of the relation between mind and its object. Traditional metaphysics leaps into speculating about God *because* it is naïve and never considers how its own activity as thinking matters.

Like traditional metaphysics, empiricism and critical philosophy represent a distinctive approach to human activity. Empiricism rejects metaphysics as otherworldly; it turns against thinking and claims to find truth in sensing and sensuous, earthly reality. The empiricist acknowledges that humans must act in order to determine scientific laws; the regularities of nature are grasped through research and experiment. But empiricism treats activity as neutral, as if thinking disclosed truth in a transparent, hands-off way without determining it; truth is "discovered." Sensing and subsequent analysis, for empiricism, are conduits to its object. This externality defines empiricism; categories, such as cause and effect, are handled as independent entities. Categories are connected in ways that do not alter their fundamental status as separate. Distrust of thinking is the hallmark of empiricism for Hegel.

Critical philosophy is painfully aware of its own thinking and the difference it makes. The naïve transparency of empiricism is gone. Since human activity makes knowledge possible, truth is qualified in relation to a particular set of knowers: the framework is constituted by the human activities of both thinking *and* sensing. Humans supply the categories or universal framework, while the particular content is contributed by the world outside consciousness. Nature exists apart from these activities as an unknowable residue. Human activity for critical philosophy acts like a curse: success breeds a kind of failure. Since objectivity is constituted by human synthesizing, it is subjective to some degree. We know how things appear, but not how they are in themselves. Objects not filtered by human consciousness tantalize but remain unknowable. What results from attending to human activity—whether thinking or sensing—is a subjectivism that spells skepticism. The more we acknowledge our activities, the longer grows our shadow, until it envelops reality. Under certain assumptions, self-awareness and skepticism go hand in hand.

Marx's theses on Feuerbach acknowledge idealism's edge over traditional materialism in grasping the importance and meaning of human activity.

> The chief defect of all hitherto existing materialism...is that the thing, reality, sensuousness, is conceived only in the form of the object or of *contemplation*, but not as *human sensuous activity*, *practice*, not subjectively. Hence it happened that the *active* side, in contradistinction to materialism, was developed by idealism—but only abstractly.[7]

This serves as a concise statement both of Marx's identification of (traditional) materialism and idealism as opposing branches of bourgeois philosophy—which is characterized by its purism and bifurcations—and of Marx's post-bourgeois phenomenology, which rejects the separability of the passive and the active, the objective and the subjective. Materialism takes a contemplative approach to the bodies in motion that constitute reality. Its standpoint is theoretical, not practical. It endeavors to know what exists in the passive manner of empiricism: perceptions built up into knowledge in mechanical ways. How to change the world is not its concern; space for human initiative is lacking from this map of reality. Humans, like all species, are just part of the furniture of the universe. "The materialist doctrine that men are products of circumstances and upbringing . . . forgets that it is men who change circumstances and that it is essential to educate the educator himself."[8]

It is the idealist Hegel, not the materialist Feuerbach, who grasps the importance of activity. For Hegel, purism and bifurcation signal a defective mindset that he labels understanding (*Verstand*) or abstract identity. Abstract identity separates what cannot exist independently. What replicates these defects is an inability to acknowledge the active involvement of thinking without jeopardizing truth or objectivity. The bourgeois horizon bifurcates relentlessly. Action of any sort—whether moral deeds, labor, consuming, or thinking—resists bifurcation. To grasp action takes us back to Hume's distinctions of reason. Intention, consequences, acting, interacting, recognition, personal history, and the broader cultural context are inseparable aspects of action. Thinking about action threatens the bourgeois horizon. It is safer to ignore the topic.

To grasp action, in Hegel's view, reveals how reason functions. Rather than a thinking *thing*, reason is better construed as laboring through the evidence of nature to arrive at its valued property, knowledge. Like action, reason breaks through the bifurcations of the bourgeois horizon. For example, Hegel criticizes Kant's account of moral intentions as empty because intentions are comprehensible only in relation to the purpose, ends, and context of particular kinds of action. It is not up to the individual to decide the intention expressed by an action. Intentions are not settled *prior* to actions in any sense. According to Hegel, I come to understand my intention—what I *mean* by acting in this way—through the action itself. What I insist was *my* intention must yield to the meaning of the action as recognized by myself and others. Splitting off consequences from actions in order to determine moral worth runs into similar objections from Hegel. The meaning of consequences can't be understood apart from the actions from which they flow. The attempt to vector action into intention and consequence is futile.

In the end, Marx regards Hegel less as a critic of the bourgeois horizon than its fullest embodiment. The activity largely missing from other philosophy surfaces in Hegel's work as the activity of thinking. Hegel endeavors to recover the world lost to bifurcating analysis only to have it slip away. For Marx, Hegel's focus on thinking as paradigmatic signifies a betrayal of sensuous human activity. Recall that Marx wrote that idealism developed the active side of human sensuous activity "only abstractly." Hegel does not subordinate knowledge to the actually existing world, but turns to pure knowing as the fulfillment and replacement of sensuous actuality. The shadowy realm of pure concepts—logic—emerges as the centerpiece of Hegel's system. Not sensuous human activity but the *concept* of activity captivates Hegel. Thinking reconciles subject and object, only because the "object" turns out to be a creature of the subject. The work of thinking makes everything its property: what we took to be *other* actually conceals the thought as its source of value. "*Logic therefore coincides with Metaphysics, the science of things set and held in thoughts*—thoughts accredited able to express the essential reality of things."[9]

In Marx's view, Hegel reinstates the divide between objectivity and subjectivity, with sensuous reality dismissed in favor of rational forms or logic that are then imposed on the world. This thinking does not transform sensuous immediacy; it abandons it for logical forms. This logic presupposes that conceptual content can be distilled out of knowledge and experience. While abstractions arising through a dynamic development differ significantly from lists of categories, these abstractions still signify opposition to concrete existence. In the end Hegel diagnoses the bourgeois mindset but doesn't escape it. With the culmination of reality in absolute thought, the purist splits are more entrenched than ever. Hegel turns to abstractions as the ultimate embodiment of freedom. What Hegel calls freedom, suggests Marx, actually expresses the replacement of sensuous reality by abstractions: the freedom of absolute idealism turns out to be a form of domination that foreshadows the domination of modern society by capital.

Hegel advances Marx's critique of the bourgeois mindset in another way. For Hegel, all philosophy is "its time grasped in thoughts." No philosophy is adequately understood apart from its historical context. Marx approaches Hegel on these terms when he christens Hegel the bourgeois thinker *par excellence*. The movement of Hegel's abstractions evokes the action of the real abstraction that increasingly dominates modern society, capital. Identifying modernity with the power of capital was not Hegel's intent—indeed, the concept of capital is absent in Hegel—but we are not masters of our own intentions. In spite of his objectives, Hegel's thought offers a glimpse into how modern reality is driven and fashioned by the unending expansion of capital. The domination of concrete existence by abstractions unwittingly evokes the moves of capital, revealing Hegel to be not the critic of the bourgeois mindset but its most profound exponent.[10]

For the bourgeois mindset, activity is dismissed, disdained, diminished, or driven to subjectivism and skepticism. The purist opposition between the subjective and objective governs bourgeois thinking and makes it impossible to grasp human activity as a condition of truth without qualifying truth. Either way breeds dilemmas. A student expressed the skeptical impasse this way: "Truth cannot lie in concepts, since they are of our own making. Thus truth must lie in sensation itself." We want to know what exists, but as soon as we think, we interfere with the object in more ways than we can account for. So a hopeless choice sums up our options. Either we know only what we construct, or we aim for the "given" in ways that won't distort it, such as through sensation, feeling, or intuition. If we opt for construction, then the thing-in-itself lingers as a tease: "knowledge just represents your framework and not reality itself." If we pedal steadily after the given, we end up speechless, since "saying" what is given throws us right back on concepts or constructions. Given the dilemmas associated with human activity, bourgeois philosophy is forced either to turn against thinking in order to arrive at knowledge or to settle for thoughts of its own fabrication.

Kant seemingly has the last word where truth is concerned: everything we touch turns into us. A Midas curse haunts the standoff between construction of truth and the given. The curse won't be broken until we figure out how to comprehend our own activity as an indispensable ingredient of truth that cannot be pigeonholed as merely subjective. We break free of the impasse by recognizing that there is no sorting the objective out from the subjective—when we free ourselves from what Donald Davidson called "the myth of the subjective."[11] The very idea of the purely subjective proves false. Human existence is a condition of knowledge, but, as Heidegger observed in *Being and Time*, humans exist in the world. Knowing doesn't fall on either side of the line, because the line—in its purist formulation—is our imposition. Donald Davidson captures the dilemma well.

> There is the idea that any language distorts reality, which implies that it is only wordlessly if at all that the mind comes to grips with things as they really are. This is to conceive language as an inert (though necessarily distorting) medium independent of the human agencies that employ it, a view of language that surely cannot be maintained. Yet if the mind can grapple without distortion with the real, the mind itself must be without categories and concepts. This featureless self is familiar from theories in quite different parts of the philosophical landscape. There are, for example, theories that make freedom consist in decisions taken apart from all desires, habits, and dispositions of the agent; and theories of knowledge that suggest that the mind can observe the totality of its own perceptions and ideas. In each case, the mind is divorced from the traits that constitute it; an inescapable conclusion from certain lines of reasoning, as I said, but one that should always persuade us to reject the premises.[12]

Bourgeois thought takes stock of a remarkable range of human activities from sensing, doubting, desiring, and conceiving to voting and laboring, but always against the backdrop of the subjective/objective divide. Economics, like epistemology, speaks of the active subject who constitutes value through labor or preferences. For the most part, the passive dimension belongs to sensing or to "untouched nature," before the workmanship of the mind gets involved. What is valuable about knowledge or property comes from the activity that confers form on what is formless. Value must come from us, since the result of labor—scientific knowledge or the commodity—acquires worth that doesn't exist at the onset of the process. Activity is no neutral conduit that exposes value to public view. It constitutes or adds value with each move. This bourgeois, value-added model of knowledge becomes self-evident when the only seeming alternative requires knowledge to be available like ripe fruit ready to drop. Hume demanded that necessary connections appear immediately in the collision of his billiard balls. Since this doesn't occur, Hume concludes that custom is responsible for the value or knowledge. What we purport to find, we actually have deposited.

The Social Basis of Bourgeois Thought

The abstract social forms characteristic of modern capitalism powerfully encourage the purist and bifurcated thinking not only of philosophy but also of the social science called economics. What Marx conceives of as the bourgeois mindset, then, encompasses philosophy and economics.[13] Marx wrote repeatedly of the "bourgeois horizon" of classical political economy, and he did not hesitate to apply that phrase to Left Ricardian socialists or Marxists. He referred not to the fact that classical political economists were apologists for the rising capitalist order; rather, he was criticizing philosophical features of their thinking such as their inattention to form[14] generally and historically specific social form in particular. It is not surprising that Marx identifies John Locke, whose *Essay Concerning Human Understanding* he once described as demonstrating "that the bourgeois way of thinking is the normal human way of thinking," as the philosopher *par excellence* for classical political economy.[15]

Why are purism and purist splits congenial to bourgeois thinkers and what could Marxian value theory have to say about the question? The intricacies of capitalism unfold by examining the commodity, the most immediate and everyday form that capitalism takes. The subject-object divide and the asocial conception of the person familiar from bourgeois thinking capture aspects of the situation of individuals who must sell their labor in order to purchase commodities. Persons in capitalist social relations appear stranded and cut off, lending credence to the notion of a subject/object dichotomy.[16] In the marketplace we alternate between the roles of buyer and seller. Here the buyer is judged sovereign, searching out the maximum satisfaction of privately determined desires. Consequently, a market society appears free of social constraints and collective purposes; "it's up to me" to settle on choices and initiate exchanges that shape my life.[17] The ways in which choices, labor, consumption, education, leisure, relationships, etc. are actually constrained for the collective purpose of expanding capital are less obvious. Domination and exploitation are hidden behind the real though limited freedom of the market. Here the appearance of bare individuals over against objects holds sway. A freewheeling subject set directly against commodities is captured in an abstract way by bourgeois philosophy. The bifurcation between subject and object is fostered by market activities.

A trademark of the bourgeois horizon is its obliviousness to historically specific social forms. This ahistorical outlook is germane to capitalism. The peculiar abstractness of the purpose of production under capitalism, namely, endless profit making, encourages a conception of the production process as simply the creation of wealth to serve human needs (through the mediation of the exchanges that take place in the market, of course). This promotes a picture of the capitalist production process as a *generic* activity, thereby deflecting attention away from any examination of it as a particular mode of production with specific purposes and consequences.[18] Needs, labor, and the production process as a whole appear to be without definite social form and purpose, creating "the illusion of the economic."[19] Here we see the match between the standpoint of "economics" and the enthusiasm within bourgeois social and political theory for state of nature and social contract theories, right down to the present affinity for rational choice theory.[20]

To see what light Marxian value theory can shed on the bourgeois mindset, we do well to begin where Marx begins, with the commodity.[21] The generalization of the commodity form involved in the spread of the market promotes a purist and bifurcating mentality. How? Marx pointedly begins his treatment of the commodity form by calling attention to the double character of the commodity: it is a *use value*, and it has an *exchange value*. He goes on to argue that exchange value is the necessary form of appearance of *value*. Regarding use value Marx observes, "It is conditioned by the physical properties of the commodity, and has no existence apart from the latter."[22] That seems plain enough. Nonetheless, Marx insists that the commodity "is a very strange thing, abounding in metaphysical subtleties and theological niceties."[23] What is so strange about the commodity—and by implication about the labor that produces commodities—is that "the commodity reflects the social characteristics of men's own labor as objective characteristics of the products of labor themselves, as the socio-natural properties of these things."[24] In other words, use values in the commodity form appear not to have any social character; instead they are endowed with value, a strange, "suprasensible" property that appears to be a natural feature of the commodity. Marx is quick to observe that this oddness of the commodity is a consequence neither of its use-value character nor of the bare fact that labor is involved in the production of use values. "So far as it is a use value, there is nothing mysterious about it, whether we consider it from the point of view that by its properties it satisfies human needs, or that it first takes on these properties as the product of human labor."[25] The fetishism of the commodity has nothing to do with the mere fact that labor is involved in the production of use values. Yet the commodity abounds in "metaphysical subtleties"; it is a "thing which transcends sensuousness."[26] If the "mystical character of the commodity" has nothing to do with its use value or the simple fact that labor was involved in its production, what is its source? Marx answers that the source is the commodity form itself, and he goes onto say that use values take the commodity form because of "the peculiar social form of the labor which produces them."[27]

It is important to see that one consequence of this oddly asocial social form of labor is that its products are socially validated only through market exchanges. For "it is only by being exchanged that the products of labor acquire a socially uniform objectivity as values, which is distinct from their sensuously varied objectivity as articles of use value."[28] The practice of commodity exchange, then, is an essential moment in the movements of a capitalist society that result in the purism and bifurcation involved in the double character of commodities.[29]

Simple exchanges of commodities, which take the form: x (amount of) commodity A exchanges for y (amount of) commodity B, force the problematic of value and disclose the basis for purism and bifurcation in capitalist social practices. They suggest an equation, but what is it that is being equated? The difficulty of this question is compounded by the recognition that, on the assumption of generalized commodity circulation, any amount of each commodity can be equated with some amount of every other commodity. Each commodity has multiple exchange values, but each of those expresses some identical magnitude. What on earth could they all have in common?[30] Value is the usual answer, but *what is value*? When the problem is not dodged by identifying value with exchange value,[31] the two chief answers that have been given to this question are *labor* (by classical economics and Left Ricardianism) and *utility* (whether absolute or marginal, whether construed hedonistically or in terms of personal preferences). Each answer involves us in *purism*—whether pure labor or pure preference, each expresses the idea that value comes purely from the subject—and *bifurcation*: labor and preference are separated out from the means and materials of labor and the objects of preference, respectively.[32]

Marx's analysis of simple commodity exchange exposes the purism involved in this social practice. Marx considers what sort of thing could be the common element among commodities.

> This common element cannot be a geometrical, physical, chemical or other natural property of commodities. Such properties come into consideration only to the extent that they make the commodities useful, i.e., turn them into use values. But clearly, the exchange relation of commodities is characterized precisely by its abstraction from their use values. Within the exchange relation, one use value is worth just as much as another.[33]

What remains once we have abstracted from all the useful properties?

> If then we disregard the use value of commodities, only one property remains, that of being products of labor. But even the product of labor has already been transformed in our hands. If we make abstraction from its use value, we abstract also from the material constituents and forms that make it a use value. It is no longer a table, a house, a piece of yarn or any other useful thing. All its sensuous characteristics are extinguished. . . . Let us now look at the residue of the products of labor. There is nothing left of them in each case but the same phantom-like objectivity; they are merely congealed quantities of homogeneous human labor, i.e. of human labor-power expended without regard to its form of its expenditure. . . . As crystals of this social substance, which is common to them all, they are values.[34]

Value is like Descartes' material substance—supersensible, phantom-like.[35]

Beyond the Bourgeois Horizon

Phenomenology describes the kind of thinking that leaves behind the bourgeois horizon and makes a critique of capitalism possible. Phenomenology develops the basic distinctions that analyze the world without engendering stupefying polarities. This sense of phenomenology is close to that of the young Heidegger. Each structure of human existence in *Being and Time* unknots a familiar opposition from bourgeois philosophy, such as the opposition of theoretical vs. practical, feeling vs. reason, language vs. object, or individual vs. group. If humans exist as being-in-the-world and being-with, then all knowledge presupposes these conditions. We can't raise any question, except as a being-in-the-world. Thinking thus situated doesn't lead to skeptical standoffs, such as the Cartesian dualism of mind and world. We can question whether our understanding is correct, but we can't question whether our faulty understanding exists in the world. There is no other setting for it. To situate ideas *inside a mind* is

misleading. Humans never exist as mind separated from body and world. Such knowing is not an option for our species. What *must* be presupposed can't be doubted. We
can't rid ourselves of the world even if we try. In short, "mind" constitutes a distinction
of reason, an aspect of human existence that is not a separable element.

For an adequate phenomenology, Marx draws from Aristotle and Hegel. For
these thinkers, *action* signifies the fundamental mode of human existence, and it won't
neatly factor out into subjective and objective components the way that Hume and
Kant purport to factor experience.[36] Endeavoring to sort out the objective from the
subjective is philosophy's boondoggle, in Hegel's view. He gets at this in a startling
passage from the *Encyclopedia*, "Laying aside therefore as unimportant this distinction
between subjective and objective, we are chiefly interested in knowing what a thing
is: i.e., its content, which is no more objective than it is subjective."[37] An adequate
phenomenology no longer asks what is objective or subjective; it asks what is true
or false. This is the Hegelian lesson rediscovered by Donald Davidson.

Activity is not a bridge linking subjects and object; it is not transparent, neutral,
or immediate. Activity brings about change or mediation in the world. In places, Marx
contrasts the objective conditions of production—raw materials and means of production—with the subjective or personal conditions of production—living labor.

> The same elements of capital which, from the point of view of the labor
> process, can be distinguished respectively as the objective and subjective
> factors, as means of production and labor-power, can be distinguished,
> from the point of view of the valorization process, as constant and vari-
> able capital.[38]

But Marx intends not an exclusive opposition but rather a distinction of reason,
since human labor, tools, and raw materials do not function independently within
the production process; they are inseparable.

Thinking and working are undertaken by humans in society and in the world;
knowledge and wealth result from these activities, but this does not make either one
purely subjective; it does not leave humans entirely responsible for their products. It
does not even enable us to sort out and quantify the "value-added" by our activity,
as John Locke was fond of doing and neo-classical economists revived with their
theories of marginal productivity.[39] While knowing depends upon human activity, it
doesn't follow that knowledge represents what is "true for us" as opposed to "what is
true." Human activity is a necessary condition for knowledge, but to say that human
nature determines what is known—along the lines of Feuerbach's supposition that
"theology is anthropology"—reenacts the conceptual split between "active" and "passive" or the "given" and the "constructed" with their predictable skeptical outcome.
An adequate phenomenology directs philosophy toward good concepts, not skeptical
dilemmas. Breaking the hold of bourgeois philosophy and appreciating the role of
phenomenology is difficult, since purist splits exert an often unacknowledged pull
on our thinking. But to conclude that anthropomorphism taints every cognitive
effort begs the question and makes a dogma of skepticism.

In light of these considerations, the list of philosophical false moves that Quine and Davidson named the "dogmas of empiricism" may be reconceived as the "dogmas of bourgeois philosophy," for each of the three dogmas relies on the purist splits that characterize bourgeois philosophy.[40] The list may be expanded to include nominalism or wholesale anti-essentialism, which agrees with bourgeois philosophers like Francis Bacon that "forms are figments of the mind" and John Locke that "nominal" essences are nothing but the "workmanship of the understanding." Like the other three dogmas, anti-essentialism presupposes a purist split between subjective and objective: forms are *purely subjective*—sheer *value added* by the mind.

Conceiving of activity as human, though not purely subjective, opens up new possibilities. Instead of snipe hunting for the purely given, we come, with Hegel, to appreciate how the "more subjective" can coincide with the "more objective." Good thinking doesn't diminish human engagement; active cognition opens up the actual world. Nor do skepticism's worries vanish without a trace from this way of thinking. Fallible beings who set out to understand the world will be proven wrong. But cosmic doubts should be dropped for specific doubts that begin and end. The insistence that a knowledge claim is "constructed" is either idle—what knowledge claim is not?—or it is a skeptical jeer that truth lies hopelessly beyond reach. Good judgments must contend with multiplicity, vagueness, uncertainty, stress, and the absence of most human voices from places of power and decision. Must they labor under skepticism as well? Real doubts abound in an era of capitalism's global reach. Philosophy's energies could serve more fruitful ends than cycling through the worn paths of dogmatism and skepticism. What are needed are good concepts that take us back into the world to recognize the real possibilities that are present.

While phenomenology calls into question the familiar dualisms of philosophy, Marx's critique of capitalist society reveals a double-sidedness that characterizes production, circulation, and social life generally.[41] The opening chapter of *Capital* identifies this double-sidedness as the commodity's use value and exchange value. The analysis of exchange value leads to the more abstract concept of value or congealed socially necessary abstract labor. But the duality between the material process and social abstractions persists, as abstractions become more determinate and complex. This duality between the material and the abstract is pervasive and the source of instability in capitalist society—witness the tremendous loss of value that occurs with the bursting of a stock or real estate bubble. But the double-sidedness at the core of Marx's critique differs from the familiar dualisms of bourgeois philosophy. This is not a dualism founded on a purist opposition, where one entity excludes the other. The duality of use value and exchange value is unstable because the elements cannot be separated. We can not determine human needs without considering what makes money. Capital signifies a *purely* social and abstract relationship—socially necessary average labor time—that responds to numerous factors and depends upon the material conditions of human needs, usefulness, and the physical conditions of labor. The duality between use value and exchange value is not a general feature of human existence but a specific feature of being-in-the-capitalist-world. Phenomenology does not split apart what exists together. The duality of the material and the abstract in capitalist society exists as a real and determining opposition.[42]

Conclusion: Toward Better Concepts

What are some marks of good concepts? Criticism starts from the negativity of the victim, says Enrique Dussel. Good concepts get at the specific forms of suffering that characterize the existing world and its possible transformation. Analysis begins with accessible features of the world, such as the commodity, and works through its determinations to arrive at abstract underlying processes, such as capital. As concepts develop, they become more determinate and draw us closer to the actual world. Thinking advances to the concrete, hence we claim that the more subjective (the more determinate), the more objective. It is not good enough to claim that phenomenology begins with experience and returns to experience. All sorts of dualistic doctrines make that claim. Just what counts as experience is decisive. Marx doesn't focus on "getting back" to experience, as if the truth lay somewhere behind us, waiting to be snapped up. Instead, he looks ahead to the concrete understanding that arises as we advance to more encompassing knowledge. Good concepts sound out experience in ways that are never apparent at the start. Donald Davidson was wrong to identify empiricism so completely with dogmatism that the history of empiricism ends when the last dogma is unveiled. The thinking that moves beyond the bourgeois horizon can be called empiricist; it endeavors to understand the world as revealed through human experience. Efforts to get at experience have been riddled with bifurcations, but a dogmatic or skeptical mindset is not inevitable. Why sacrifice the noble cause of empiricism to bad ideas? Freeing our concepts from the dogmas of bourgeois philosophy and undertaking a critique of capitalism are inseparable tasks.

Creighton University

Notes

1. Simon Clarke in *Marx, Marginalism, and Sociology* (London and Basingstoke: The Macmillan Press Ltd., 1982), 240. Clarke argues that, regrettably, neoclassical economics, not Marx's innovations, set the horizon of sociology. In this article, we extend Clarke's claim to philosophy.

2. A good example is the charge made by Juergen Habermas and Seyla Benhabib that Hegel and Marx hold an asocial, "monological" conception of labor, when in reality they were profound critics of the bourgeois standpoint of classical political economy on precisely that point. See Jeanne Schuler's "The Legend of Hegel's Labor Theory of Reason," *Social Philosophy Today*, vol. 14, 2000.

3. Karl Marx, "Letter to his Father: On a Turning-Point in Life" (1837) in *Writings of the Young Marx on Philosophy and Society*, ed. Easton and Guddat (New York: Anchor Books, 1967), 43.

4. Hume explains "distinction of reason" in relation to color and form, which are inseparable in terms of existence. "After a little more practice of this kind, we begin to distinguish the figure from the color by a *distinction of reason*; that is, we consider the figure and color together, since they are in effect the same and indistinguishable; but still view them in different aspects, according to the resemblances, of which they are susceptible." *Treatise of Human Nature*, ed. L. A. Selby-Bigge (Oxford: Clarendon Press, 1967), 25.

5. We adopt this notion of purist concepts from James Collins, who introduces the term "purist split" in his *Interpreting Modern Philosophy* (Princeton: Princeton University Press, 1972), 14.

6. C. I. Lewis developed the notion of the *a priori* as changing in opposition to Kant's understanding of the unchanging *a priori*. Lewis seeks to maintain the meaning of the *a priori* as independent of experience by claiming that the *a priori* changes in the presence of new experience but not in response to it.

7. Marx, "Theses on Feuerbach," in Karl Marx and Frederick Engels, *Collected Works*, vol. 5 (New York: International Publishers, 1976), 3.

8. Ibid. The third thesis on Feuerbach.

9. G. W. F. Hegel, *Logic, Part I of the Encyclopedia of the Philosophical Sciences*, trans. William Wallace (Oxford: Clarendon Press, 1975), 36.

10. See Patrick Murray, *Marx's Theory of Scientific Knowledge* (Atlantic Highlands, N.J.: Humanities Press International, 1988) and Chris Arthur, *The New Dialectic and 'Capital'* (Leiden; Boston; Koeln: Brill, 2002).

11. Donald Davidson, "The Myth of the Subjective," in his *Subjective, Intersubjective, Objective* (Oxford: Oxford University Press, 2001).

12. Donald Davidson, "The Very Idea of a Conceptual Scheme," in *Inquiries into Truth and Interpretation* (New York: Oxford University Press, 1984), 185–186.

13. There is a great deal of evidence to support this contention that Marx was involved in a lifelong investigation of the bourgeois mindset shared by philosophy and economics. Here is a brief look at some of that evidence. Marx's editors were on the right track in classing Marx's Paris manuscripts of 1844, "economic and philosophic," though it may be even more illuminating to think of them as joint critiques of (bourgeois) philosophy and economics. Particularly telling is Marx's critical observation in the final Paris manuscript that "Hegel's standpoint is that of modern political economy," *Collected Works*, Vol. 3 (New York: International Publishers, 1975), 333. Marx regarded Hegel as the consummate bourgeois philosopher, a judgment we do not share. In the tenth thesis on Feuerbach, Marx wrote, "the standpoint of the old materialism is bourgeois society," a judgment that, in his mind, surely could be extended to idealism. The thrust of the *Theses*, stated in the first thesis, is that both mechanistic materialism and idealism are caught in the purism and bifurcation that stamp them as bourgeois. The point of the *Poverty of Philosophy* is that Proudhon is the complete expression of the bourgeois mindset, as a philosopher and as an economist (a Left Ricardian one). Thus, writing in a letter to Annenkov, Marx says of Proudhon that he "does not rise above the bourgeois horizon" (*"ne s'eleve pas au-dessus de l'horizon bourgeois"*) Karl Marx, "Letter to P. V. Annenkov," *Poverty of Philosophy* (New York: International Publishers, 1936), 190. In that same letter he writes, "Really he [Proudhon] does nothing other than what all good bourgeois 'people' do. . . . They all want the impossible, that is, the conditions of bourgeois life without the necessary consequences of these conditions" (*Poverty*, 190).

In *Capital* I Marx speaks of the "bourgeois skin" of classical political economy (682), of the "limited (*beschraenktes*) brain" of the bourgeois economist (714), and of the "bourgeois field of vision" (*buergelichen Horizonts*) Karl Marx, *Capital* I, transl. Ben Fowkes (London: Penguin Books, 1976), 737. In this regard, it is very telling that Adam Smith identifies the subject of his masterwork as the "wealth" of nations whereas Marx calls his book *Capital* and insists from the opening sentence of the book that his subject matter concerns wealth having a specific social form.

14. The inattention to (social) form on the part of the economists reveals their attachment to the bourgeois mindset both in their nominalist empiricism (which bifurcates form and content) and in their failure to see how the social and social form go all the way down in human life. In pointing up the failure of the classical political economists on this score, Marx calls special attention to how the bourgeois mindset provides ideological cover to bourgeois society: "It is one of the chief failings of classical political economy that it has never succeeded, by means of its analysis of commodities, and in particular of their value, in discovering the form of value which in fact turns value into exchange-value. Even its best representatives, Adam Smith and Ricardo, treat the form of value as something of indifference, something external to the nature of the commodity itself. The explanation for this is not simply that their attention is entirely absorbed by the analysis of the magnitude of value. It lies deeper. The value-form of the product of labor is the most abstract, but also the most universal form of the bourgeois mode of production; by that fact it stamps the bourgeois mode of production as a particular kind of social production of a historical and transitory character. If then we make the mistake of treating it as the eternal natural form of social production, we necessarily overlook the specificity of the value-form, and consequently of the commodity-form together with its further developments, the money-form, the capital-form, etc." (*Capital* I, note 34, 174).

15. Karl Marx, *Contribution to the Critique of Political Economy*, trans. S. W. Ryazanskaya and ed. Maurice Dobb (New York: International Publishers, 1970), 77. "On the whole, however, the early English economists sided with Bacon and Hobbes as their philosophers, while, at a later period, Locke became 'the philosopher' *par excellence* of political economy in England, France and Italy" (*Capital* I, note 27, 513).

16. "Men are henceforth related to each other in their social process of production in a purely atomistic way" (*Capital* I, 187).

17. F. A. Hayek contended that a market society was the only free society precisely because it imposed no compulsory collective goals on its members. Hayek was mistaken in this belief because the endless accumulation of capital is a compulsory collective goal imposed upon the participants in a market society.

18. In *Capital*, Volume II, Marx points out how a one-sided attention to the circuit of *productive capital* (as opposed to the circuits of money capital and commodity capital), which begins and ends with the *use values* requisite for the production process, misled the classical political economists into thinking that the capitalist production process was production in general: "The general form of the movement P . . . P' is the form of reproduction, and does not indicate, as does M . . . M', that valorization is the purpose of the process. For this reason, classical economics found it all the more easy to ignore the specifically capitalist form of the production process, and to present production as such as the purpose of the process" Karl Marx, *Capital* II, trans. David Fernbach (Harmondsworth: Penguin, 1978), 172. See also Patrick Murray, "Beyond the 'Commerce and Industry' Picture of Capital," in *The Circulation of Capital*, ed. Chris Arthur and Geert Reuten (London: Macmillan, 1998), 33–66.

19. See Patrick Murray, "The Illusion of the Economic: The Trinity Formula and the 'religion of everyday life,'" in *The Culmination of Capital: Essays on Volume III of Marx's "Capital,"* ed. Martha Campbell and Geert Reuten (Basingstoke, Hampshire: Palgrave, 2002), 246–272.

20. This linking of state of nature/social contract theories with capitalism goes back to "On the Jewish Question," and it was with the critique of this bourgeois thinking that Marx began the *Grundrisse*. There he writes, "Only in the eighteenth century, in 'civil society', do the various forms of social connectedness confront the individual as a mere means towards his private purposes, as external necessity. But the epoch which produces this standpoint, that of the isolated individual, is also precisely that of the hitherto most developed social . . . relations" Karl Marx, *Grundrisse*, trans. Martin Nicolaus (Harmondsworth: Penguin Books in association with the *New Left Review*, 1973), 84.

21. "The problem of commodities must not be considered in isolation or even regarded as the central problem in economics, but as the central, structural problem of capitalist society in all its aspects" Georg Lukacs, *History and Class Consciousness*, trans. Rodney Livingstone (Cambridge, Mass.: MIT Press, 1971), 83. This enthusiasm for the explanatory power of the commodity, which Lukacs may have inherited from his teacher Georg Simmel, should be moderated by the recognition that, in Marxian value theory, the generalization of the commodity form is a consequence of the spread of the capitalist mode of production. For a critique of Lukacs' understanding of Marxian value theory, see Moishe Postone's *Time, Labor, and Social Domination* (Cambridge: Cambridge University Press, 1993), 72–75.

22. Ibid., 126.

23. Ibid., 163.

24. Ibid., 164–165.

25. Ibid., 163.

26. Ibid., 163.

27. Ibid., 165. Here lies the gulf separating Marxian value theory from Ricardian (including Left Ricardian) value theory: Marx's theory of value is a theory of the peculiar social form of labor in capitalist society.

28. Ibid., 166, translated slightly amended.

29. In his book *Intellectual and Manual Labor*, translated by Martin Sohn-Rethel, Alfred Sohn-Rethel emphasizes, somewhat one-sidedly, the role the abstraction involved in a system of commodity exchange plays in establishing the bourgeois mindset (London: Macmillan, 1978).

30. Compare this to the situation of the bit and the blob of wax in Descartes' second meditation. That episode involves the bifurcation not only of primary and secondary qualities but also of our powers of imagination and understanding—Descartes insists that we know the wax through the understanding alone.

31. On this, see Marx's protracted refutation of Samuel Bailey, who criticized Ricardian theory of conceiving of value as something "absolute," different from and more fundamental than exchange value. See Marx, *Theories of Surplus Value*, Part 3, trans. Jack Cohen, ed. R. Ryazanskaya and Richard Dixon (London: Lawrence and Wishart, 1972), 124–168.

32. Marx contradicts the Gotha Programme's claim that labor is the source of all wealth, writing: "Labour is *not the source* of all wealth. *Nature* is just as much the source of use values

(and it is surely of such that material wealth consists!) as is labor." He identifies this plank of the nominally socialist programme with "bourgeois phrases," and he goes on to say that the bourgeois attribute *"supernatural creative power* to labour" Karl Marx, *Critique of the Gotha Programme*, ed. C. P. Dutt (New York: International Publishers, 1938, 1966), 3. In an overlooked passage from the beginning of *Capital*, Marx rules out the very idea of utility or pure preference, "the usefulness of a thing makes it a use value. But this usefulness does not dangle in mid-air. It is conditioned by the physical properties of the commodity, and has no existence apart from the latter" (*Capital* I, 126). See also Patrick Murray, "Redoubled Empiricism: The Place of Social Form and Formal Causality in Marxian Theory," in *New Investigations of Marx's Method*, edited by Fred Moseley and Martha Campbell (Atlantic Highlands, N.J.: Humanities Press, 1997), 38–65.

33. *Capital* I, 127.

34. Ibid., 128.

35. See Murray, *Marx's Theory of Scientific Knowledge*, 149, and Postone, *Time, Labor, and Social Domination*, 142.

36. Hegel's emphasis on action comes through powerfully in *the Phenomenology of Spirit*, Chapter Five, Section C, on the spiritual animal kingdom.

37. Hegel, *Logic*, Part 1 of the *Encyclopedia*, trans. William Wallace (Oxford: University Press, 1975), 71.

38. *Capital* I, 317.

39. Thus, Locke writes, "it is *labour* indeed that *puts the difference of value* on every thing . . . the improvement of labour makes the far greater part of the value . . . if we will rightly estimate things as they come to our use, and cast up the several expences about them, what in them is purely owing to nature, and what to labour, we shall find, that in most of them ninety-nine hundredths are wholly to be put on the account of labour" John Locke, *Second Treatise of Government*, ed. C. B. Macpherson (Indianapolis: Hackett Publishing Company, 1980; originally published in 1690), 25. The American neoclassical economist John Bates Clark wrote in *Essentials of Economic Theory*, "Each man accordingly is paid an amount that equals the total product that he personally creates" (New York: The Macmillan Company, 1907), 92.

40. The "dogmas of empiricism" are, briefly, the myth of the given, the analytic-synthetic distinction, and the conceptual scheme/world distinction. Since the dogmas noted by Quine and Davidson obviously encompassed doctrines held by rationalists and by Kant, the term "empiricism" was misleadingly narrow from the start.

41. Heidegger's account of being-in-the-world and being-with falls short by not indicating how "the with-world" always takes a particular form. Human existence is thoroughly social, but the *kind* of society always mattes. In short, Heidegger offers a *dehistoricized* account of historicity. Marx's historical materialism is a needed complement to *Being and Time*.

42. Moishe Postone describes this inherent tension in capitalist society as "sheering pressure," *Time, Labor, and Social Domination*, 348.

The Concept of Work in Maria Montessori and Karl Marx

Madonna R. Adams

Abstract: Surprising as it may appear, the philosophical writings of political econo-mist Karl Marx (1818–1883), and those of philosopher, educator Maria Montessori (1870–1952), show thematic resemblances that invite further exploration. These resemblances reflect both keen awareness of the historical period they shared, but also important common threads in their philosophical anthropology, ethical and political values, and goals. In this paper, I examine one central thread which both take as fundamental, namely, the centrality of work in achieving the harmonious development of humankind. I critique Marx's description of the dynamic process leading to his classless society, because he fails to supply the proximate, efficient cause or middle term that effects this goal. My thesis is that Montessori supplies this missing causal link through her scientific demonstration of the work and function of the child and her holistic understanding of the human person in its full historical dimension, and human and cosmic *telos*.

The outstanding achievement . . . of Hegel's Phenomenology . . . is, first, that Hegel grasps . . . the self-creation of man as a process . . . and that he . . . conceives objective man as the result of his *own labour.*—Karl Marx[1]

The work of the child is to make the man.—Maria Montessori[2]

Surprising as it may first appear, the philosophical writings of political economist Karl Marx (1818–1883) and those of philosopher educa-tor Maria Montessori (1870–1952) show thematic resemblances that invite further exploration. These resemblances reflect not only a keen awareness of the historical period that to some extent they shared, but also important common threads in their philosophical anthropology with its ethical and political values and goals.

In this paper, I shall examine one such common thread in their philosophical thought, which both take as fundamental to the development of the individual and the social relationships of humankind, namely, the centrality of work in hu-man life. I shall examine Montessori's analysis of work in *Education and Peace* and her other major writings in relation to Marx's analysis of labor in his *Political and Economic Manuscripts of 1844*, *The German Ideology*, and later works. My thesis is that Montessori supplies the missing link in Marx's practical philosophy, by her causal explanation of the work of the child and her philosophical understanding of the human person in its full historical dimension and *telos*. I begin by considering aspects of their shared historical context and philosophical goals, their assumptions, and methods, and then by setting forth the likenesses and differences in their approaches to the analysis of human work within their philosophical thought.

Historical Context

Marx and Montessori belonged to different generations—she was thirteen in 1883, the year Marx died—but their creative thought and life efforts arose within a shared historical matrix, the age of the industrial revolution and the rise of political socialism: in its early and socially violent and disruptive phases for Marx, and in its subsequent period of vigorous nationalism and world war for Montessori. She was born in 1870, the year that marked the unification and birth of the modern Italian state, her native country. Their thought, like other intellectual currents of the time, such as Hegel's emphasis on the dialectical character of human history with its economic and social institutions, and Darwin's evolutionary theory, reflects a modern awareness of dynamism in both the social and the physical order that is open-ended rather than determined, yet one in which certain natural principles of "laws" operate.

Marx's Goal

Marx's goal was straightforward as well as revolutionary. He was outraged by the oppression and violation of human beings in the person of wage laborers, whom the new capitalism of the industrial revolution had reduced to an expendable quantity and alienated from the products of their labor, from their fellow human beings, and from themselves. His goal was practical: to free human beings from this individual and social alienation to which they had been subjected, and to show how their full, human emancipation might be realized within a transformed industrialized economy.[3]

His criticism of the "heavenly" philosophy of Hegel springs from his rejection of Hegel's method of intellectualizing the human condition and historical experience.[4] For example, Hegel ranks the political state, wherein individual differences are transcended through the equality of citizenship, above the level of mere civil society. But equality under the law is an abstraction that ignores the dominant economic and social relations among citizens with all their inequities. Marx insists that merely saying that wealth, class, race, and gender are irrelevant to one's status as a citizen leaves all these inequalities intact. In real life, political emancipation alone is inadequate. Since civil society is the real basis of the state or political society, it is civil society that needs to be transformed, and it is only social emancipation that brings human emancipation.[5]

Montessori's Goal

As the first woman in Italy to become a medical doctor, Maria Montessori, citizen, physician, scientist, and educator, confronted the dilemma facing human beings at the end of the nineteenth and in the twentieth century: unprecedented scientific discovery juxtaposed with unprecedented human destructiveness and misery. She observed that, on the one hand, technological achievement had moved the human race into what she calls the "third dimension," the age of space,[6] an experience she describes with a keen sense of the historical moment when she writes: "we, the last earthbound men . . . ."[7] But just as vividly, she saw human beings in the twentieth century suffering from the very achievements that their intelligence and work had produced: nationalistic and economic domination, world wars, an international military economy, human devastation, and pollution of the environment.

Montessori traces this dichotomy to a pathology endemic to the entire educational process, in which a fundamental misunderstanding of human nature and its humanistic and social ends is operative.[8] This pathology begins with a failure to understand the natural capacities and agency of the child, and the significance of its work in developing a healthy psyche that, according to Montessori, is the basis of individual and social integrity.[9] This pathology marks all phases of the current educational process, resulting in the alienation of human beings from themselves, from each other, and from the natural principles of life in the universe. According to Montessori, such alienation is a human product, an artifact, and not a "natural" state of affairs. She considers it a type of barbarism and an absurdity, one that future generations will recognize as such.[10]

I note here that for Marx, who bases his analysis on the dynamic of labor and capital, the child has only potential value, until such time as s/he is able to exercise a role within the economic system—a role that came all too soon for children of wage-laborers in his era, as it still does today in the suffering areas of our world.

Like Marx, Montessori's goal is practical: to free human beings from a self-destructive and alienated state, and to show how human development, freedom, and peace can be achieved by a radical transformation of the educational process based on a true science of human nature.[11]

Marx's Anthropological Assumptions

Marx's diagnosis of, and prescription for, the alienated human condition of his time reveal an anthropology that reflects Aristotelian principles of nature as these apply to human beings. In *Physics* 2.1, Aristotle defines "nature" as "a source or cause of being moved and of being at rest in that to which it belongs primarily, in virtue of itself and not in virtue of a concomitant attribute."[12] According to Aristotle's analysis, the continual change characteristic of living, natural beings shows itself as a process by which individual and species realize their natural *telos* over time, thereby actualizing their innate potentiality so as to attain their natural end or "rest." For Aristotle, the goal proper to human nature is "activity of soul according to excellence," i.e., moral and intellectual excellence, and such activity forms his definition of happiness.[13] Like Aristotle, Marx understands the human *telos* in this dynamic sense, but he focuses primarily on its intrinsic social character. The emphasis is not original with Marx. Witness Plato's *Republic* with its famous definition of justice in *Republic* 433, and Aristotle's *Politics* in which he dubs the human being a *politikon zoion* (*Politics*, 1253 a 1). But Marx stresses the universal character and implication of this concept by asserting the necessity of the transformation of social relationships based on the dignity of free, self-directed, and self-actualized individuals whose relatedness transcends not only all social classes and divisions, but all national and political boundaries.[14]

He strives to express this with a new terminology when, echoing Feuerbach, he defines us as a "species-being" (*Gattungswesen*).[15] This term speaks to our intrinsic social nature as well as our ability to know ourselves *as* members of the human species. Marx struggles to affirm these two dimensions as a single reality with such phrases as: "The individual is the *social being*" and "In his *species-consciousness* man confirms his real *social life*."[16] But to actualize this full and true nature of human beings as "*species beings*," the primary, efficient cause in practice is work.

Montessori's Anthropological Assumptions

Like Marx, Montessori's anthropology reflects an Aristotelian understanding of nature as dynamic and teleological. This is not surprising, since like Aristotle, Montessori was a highly trained, natural scientist. In addition, she articulates the dynamic teleology of human life beginning with its earliest embryonic stages through its social and technological achievements, all within an environmental and cosmic context. Like Marx, she argues that attaining the goal of human life requires the development of the individual in all of his or her dimensions: physical, psychological, intellectual, and, for her, spiritual aspects, and for Montessori the direct means for this development is human activity or work. Her specific contribution is that 1) she provides a causal explanation of the dynamic process of human activity, or "work" and 2) uncovers the paradigm of this process in early childhood, a process which unfolds on a continuum embracing all stages of individual and social life.

Methodology

Marx and Montessori have much in common with respect to their methods of analysis and synthesis which shape their diagnosis of, and prescription for, the human condition. Both use empirical methods based on longitudinal, historical, and scientific observation; both are dialectical, following Hegel; both have positive social change as their goal; and both communicate their arguments and discoveries in a personal, rhetorical style. Marx stresses this empirical approach in *The German Ideology*:

> The premises from which we begin are not arbitrary ones, not dogmas, but real premises from which abstraction can only be made in the imagination. They are real individuals, their activity and the material conditions

under which they live, both those which they find already existing and those produced by their activity. These premises can thus be verified in a purely empirical way.[17]

These "real premises," rather than a desire to construct an abstract philosophical system after the pattern of German idealism, undergird his intellectual work.[18]

Montessori's empirical method is that of the natural scientist: systematic, empirical observation of data, analysis, longitudinal experimental trials, and synthesis. In the Italy of her youth, the educational system followed a two-track system: one could choose either a course of studies in the humanities or one in the scientific and technical disciplines. From childhood, Montessori chose the latter. This prepared her well for her life work as a medical doctor, a research scientist, and eventually an international researcher and reformer of educational theory and practice.

In his Foreword to the *Grundrisse*, Martin Nicolaus describes the challenge of analyzing any object considered in its dynamic aspects:

the problem of grasping a thing is firstly the problem of grasping that it is in motion. This step of logic is rendered more difficult by the fact that in the ordinary course of events it is by no means obvious that this is so. Only when things suddenly crack and break apart does it become obvious that there was a dynamic within these all the time; but ordinarily, things present an appearance of rest.[19]

In meeting this challenge, both Marx and Montessori share a gift for radical insight into the fundamental dynamics of individual and social work, one that facilitates their reinterpretation and redirection of human energies. The world-wide impact they have had to the present affirms their insights. With these preliminary remarks, I turn to Marx's analysis of work.

Marx's Analysis

In the classical period, intellectual activity and contemplation mark the ideal of human life (*otium*), and other activities or labor (*negotium*), the absence of that ideal or a mere means to achieve it. These distinctive activities are located, however, in distinct social classes, with *negotium* assigned to those of lower social status (women, servants, slaves). Marx is quick to point out that this class dichotomy springs from the nature of their economic system. In keeping with classical concepts of work (*negotium*) and leisure (*otium*), he recognizes some activities as means, others as ends, the latter representing what is most human. But departing from the classical model, he redefines work as the essential means (efficient cause) for every individual—not just some classes—to realize the proper goal of human life, individual/social development and integration. According to his prescription, this demands a different economic structure, the abolition of the *division* of labor, so that within the communist society, human work may function as the means of development of individuals—physical, psychological, mental, and above all social and ethical—as *species-beings*. Marx thus roots the source and quality of the desired social relations in the appropriate structure or mode of production, which alone can generate such relationships or *superstructure*, i.e.,

> the connection of individuals, . . . in the universal solidarity of the free development of all, and finally, in the universal character of the activity of individuals on the basis of the existing productive forces.[20]

Making a living for Marx means far more than earning what we need to survive. It means making a life.[21] For him, human work in any productive form reveals the true character of human life. As natural beings, humans stand within nature and yet relate to nature in a specifically human mode: as free, intelligent, self-aware beings, able to make nature itself an object of study and science. Involvement in the world in solidarity with others is not alien to the achievement of human happiness and fulfillment. Rather, it is the natural and proper mode of human life, individually and as a species. This way of being in the world, and not just contemplative activity, represents for Marx full human actuality, because for him labor is not an extrinsic activity, but one expressing the "capacity of a living being."[22] Indeed, if informed with an intrinsic and comprehensive awareness of the full meaning of nature and life, such work itself has a contemplative aspect.

When Marx viewed the economy spawned by industrialization, he saw that scientific progress and the new capitalism had not brought true human progress, development, and liberation. Instead it held human labor hostage in a system that destroyed the humanity and nature of the workers as *species-beings*. He concludes that capitalism as an economic system is therefore unethical and must be replaced.[23] The question for Marx is how the task of "replacing the domination of material conditions over individuals," with "the domination of individuals over chance and circumstances" is to be accomplished. His answer is through the appropriation of the forces of production by the workers.

Marx's Thesis: A Missing Link

Marx's critique of capitalism lay precisely in the contradiction he saw between an economic system that supplied far more needed goods than before, and the dehumanizing conditions to which this system subjected the wage-laborer. This contradiction, which Marx strove to elaborate scientifically in his writings, seemed to be endemic to the system. The practical question, as well as the logical question, arising from his dialectical method, lay in whether the contradiction—an economic system that supplied an excess of goods while subjecting wage-laborers to dehumanizing conditions—was an absolute contradiction, or whether it allowed for a mediating element. Nicolaus states the issue in these logical terms:

> Given that every unity . . . is composed of contradictory poles or aspects, are we to understand that the unity of these opposites is absolute, immediate and unconditional, or is it rather the case that the opposites require

an intermediary in order to form a unity, and that the effectiveness of this intermediary (and hence the maintenance of the whole) is dependent on certain conditions which may or may not be present?[24]

Marx's challenge was to answer this question with respect to capitalism.

Marx had already completed the first logical step with his identification of the contradiction in the present state of affairs. The second step was to determine whether a middle term existed, and, if so, to identify the practical middle term that functioned as the efficient cause in the dynamic process of development. Keeping in mind that Marx is trying to analyze a dynamic process proceeding from capitalism to the ideal society which he describes in *The German Ideology*, let us look closely at his argument.

According to Marx, the contradictions of the class society with its division of labor which subjects individuals to "material conditions" and "chance," i.e., the threefold alienation from one's work, self, and fellow human beings, constitute **Stage A** in the dialectical process. This sets "the task of replacing the domination of circumstances and of chance over individuals by the domination of individuals over chance and circumstances" which "coincides with the task of the communist organisation of society"[25] (**Stage C**). This later stage of development (**Stage C**) depends on "the abolition of private property" and "the division of labor." The abolition of private property, however, requires one indispensable condition, namely, individuals that "are developing in an all-round fashion" (**Middle Term, Stage B**). Only such well-rounded persons can appropriate the means of production, and abolish private property and the division of labor, so that the forces of production serve human development.[26]

What Marx describes, but does not explain, however, is how the requisite *all-round development of a sufficient number of people* takes place prior to, and leading up to, the abolition of private property. He merely states that *it is a necessary factor in the process.*

> [T]his development is determined precisely by the connection of individuals, a connection which consists partly in [1] the economic prerequisites and [2] *partly in the necessary solidarity of the free development of all*, and finally [3] in the universal character of the activity of individuals on the basis of existing productive forces.[27] [italics mine]

In this transformed order, Marx states, "The individuals' consciousness of their mutual relations will . . . become something quite different, and, therefore, will no more be the 'principle of love' . . . than it will be egoism."[28] The universalized form of economic activity made possible with the evolution of "modern productive forces" will bring with it the advent of a form of interrelated and interdependent human activity that is the proper, connatural form of human society.[29]

Marx seems to assume that since the superstructure (the network of human relationships) reflects the structure of the economy, the universalized economy effected by the "indispensable communist revolution" will yield a developmental stage in which there will be no need to deprive some for the sake of others, and the ideal goal will be realized: "from each according to his ability; to each according to his needs."[30]

This follows if Marx's fundamental thesis is correct, namely, that the economic structure is the primary and proximate cause of the superstructure. But I challenge this. A plenitude of means for supplying human needs on a universal scale does not insure that these products will be made available to all, since, following his argument, the distribution of goods depends on the political and social superstructure of society, which is itself the product of the economic system.

It appears that Marx takes this higher level of human development and consciousness as a *cause* as well as an *effect*. First he sees it as a necessary condition in bringing about the communist society with the abolition of private property, and therefore a proximate cause of the new set of human relationships emerging from these universalized conditions of production. Secondly, he sees it as a product or function of the same economic productive system that has over time reached a universal level. But if an economic system on a universal scale can generate such a consciousness, Marx has not shown how. Thus a challenge to Marx's logic seems to remain, and it lies in the question concerning the prior achievement of all-round development of individuals that is required precisely for the transformation leading to the communist society.

Montessori's Analysis

As mentioned earlier, Montessori shares Marx's anthropological assumptions and goals for human flourishing which she, too, sees as inseparable from human activity in the world. Like Marx also, she begins her analysis dialectically by confronting the stark contradiction between the extra-ordinary technological developments of the nineteenth and twentieth centuries, and the violence and unparalleled destruction of world wars and other social conflicts of this period which reveal a primitive level of human development and social relationship.[31] But whereas Marx traces human alienation to contradictions resident in the economic system, Montessori identifies a more primary causality.

She traces the destructive use of power in the political/economic order, with its domination and greed, not primarily to economic structures, but to a widespread pathology in the process of human development, a process logically prior to the formative causality of the economic structure.[32] The roots of this pathology lie in an ignorance and violation of the true nature of human beings, a pathology that the educational system of her time reinforces.[33] Her diagnosis is that while the science of technology has been highly developed, the science of human nature has not, and without the development of a new kind of individual, human beings will self-destruct.[34]

The negative aspect of the technological advances and the global interdependence human beings have attained and which Montessori addresses is all too familiar: pollution of land, air, and water, threats to food supplies from ecological change, radiation danger, and the spread of contagious disease through world travel and the rise of stronger viruses through overuse of antibiotics. Such effects reflect, in its negative moment, to borrow a Hegelian term, the arrival of Marx's third condition for a communist society, "the universal character of the activity of individuals on the basis of existing productive forces."[35] Unlike Marx, however, she does not see this development taking place in its positive moment as a corollary of the evolution of economic structures, but far more fundamentally through a revolutionary and scientific approach to the educational process, beginning with its earliest stages. Like Marx she sees society's problems not as primarily economic but as rooted in an alienation within the human psyche. And going beyond Marx, she sees human emancipation as rooted in the emancipation of the powers of the child.[36]

Just as Marx confronts alienation and the need for a redemption of humanity based on his analysis of the oppression of the proletariat, an unrecognized social class, Montessori identifies the same need, but traces it to ignorance about, and neglect of, children as an unrecognized but vital class in the society, an unnamed and powerless class but one with unsuspected powers. When properly nurtured in the educational process, the child, like Marx's proletariat, comes to self-consciousness through its own activity or "work," and is capable of radically transforming human relationships at their source. Here is the proto-typical human being whose unfolding, self-development holds the possibility for that peaceful, well-related *species-being* that Marx envisions. Montessori's prototype, the young person, has a universal character as does Marx's *species-being*, but she differs from him in the causal explanation she gives as to how the desired social reality will emerge. While Marx bases the requisite change on "modern productive forces and world intercourse,"[37] Montessori grounds it in recognition of the child's potentiality and agency. According to Montessori the social reality that both she and Marx envision can and will emerge organically of itself if sufficient care is given to the child taken as a universal class.[38]

Montessori and Education

Montessori's method of education marks a profound shift in understanding the nature of human beings who develop as children the resources needed as adults. Her articulation of just what Marx's "all-round development of individuals" entails, and how it occurs, supplements what Marx refers to only in general terms. For Montessori, understanding and supporting the natural, developmental process is the only way to insure a healthy, human development in keeping with the intrinsic principles of the human organism. Montessori's thesis, based on her practice of the new pedagogy, which she developed throughout some fifty years in the laboratory of the classroom, is that the proper insight into, and nurture of, the normal developmental process fosters the emergence of human beings with a "healthy psyche" who are in harmony with self, others, and their environment.[39] She sees that such individuals are urgently needed to meet the needs of society at this historical juncture. Most importantly, she emphasizes that the fully developed human being is not a "product" carefully managed through adult manipulation in order to achieve the desired outcome. Rather, such an individual emerges from their natural developmental process understood scientifically and supported by adult caretakers and teachers. It is the person with such a healthy psyche who forms the necessary basis for the enlightened, responsible, and ethical adult.[40]

Contrary to traditional adult assumptions about "molding" children as if they were objects,[41] she shows that the child accomplishes its distinctive work of "making the man" through its own self-directed and age-appropriate activity. She stresses that the role of adults in education is strictly collaborative. It consists in understanding the self-directing role of the child, in providing the proper environment where the child can develop the power given him by nature,[42] and in introducing the requisite learning materials when the child is ready for them. In contrast to this approach, she observes that in the current practice of her time, the adult and child relationship often played out as a kind of war—analogous to that identified by Marx between the proletariat and the capitalist—a war in which adults use the most destructive and repressive pedagogical methods to "create healthy, socially well-adapted" adults, and thereby violate the primary agency of the child in its own growth. What results from such "poisonous pedagogy"[43] is a possessive, asocial, controlling, and power-oriented adult who presents a pathology rooted in damage to the its natural developmental process.[44]

Work and Normalization in Montessori

In terms quite similar to those of Marx, Montessori defines work within a well-developed "philosophy of movement" as directed or *purposive movement or activity* involving actualization of one's potentiality.[45] She goes even further and extends her analysis to the ecosystem.[46] Montessori observes that each living organism has such a proper activity or work, with individual, social, and cosmic dimensions. She does not define human agency solely in terms of physical activity, nor does she define the person as an abstract, spiritual form. Rather, she understands a human agent or being as a dynamic whole, and she uses the term "spiritual" to affirm the multiple dimensions of the human personality with its powers of freedom, self-determination, creativity, and love which she takes as irreducible to biology or physiology. She demonstrates that the need for, and love of, work and its positive effects is natural to the child and occurs definitively at early stages under the laws of the child's own being. This "work of the child" forms the basis for what she calls the *science of peace*. It is the child's work that brings about a balanced and well-related personality, a result Montessori terms *normalization*.[47] This achievement is the child's irreplaceable contribution to society, because such personality is the fundamental requirement for all successful social life. She notes that children who achieve this through their own creative activity exhibit immense sympathy, tolerance, understanding, and patience with the often disturbing traits of younger children who have not yet experienced this growth. They also show insight and good judgment in dealing with peers and with adults. Having grappled with the challenge of their own need to learn by their own efforts and guided by their inner sense, and having experienced in themselves the freeing and empowering effect of success in attaining age-appropriate goals, they show a self-possession, confidence, and innate understanding of this process, and its possibility for others to attain as well. It is this healthy, normalized personality, creative, free, and well-related, that is the basis for positive social relationships in family, nation, and world.

Finally, going beyond the human social sphere, Montessori sees the ultimate goal of human activity as the "creation of the environment."[48] She names this product a "supernature."[49] and discerns in it an evolutionary and cosmic function unique to humans. For her, human work cannot be fully grasped apart from this cosmic function.[50] Thus where Marx uses superstructure to refer to the form of human society that emerges from particular forms of labor and economic systems, Montessori broadens the concept to include as well the impact of the work of human beings on the cosmic environment. She sees the entire realm of human activity, including technological creation, as a normal part of the evolutionary process in which human beings have a unique function, and, in keeping with their free and self-aware nature, a unique responsibility.

Conclusion

Montessori thus supplies the missing link in Marx's analysis, namely, the causality of the work of the child and young adult in developing a healthy psyche through their proper activity, and she also transcends Marx in interpreting his superstructure to include the impact of human work on the cosmic environment. The following diagram expresses their complementary contributions.

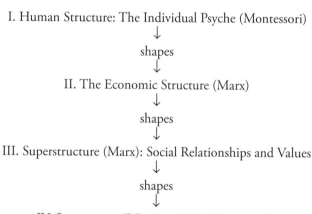

I. Human Structure: The Individual Psyche (Montessori)
↓
shapes
↓
II. The Economic Structure (Marx)
↓
shapes
↓
III. Superstructure (Marx): Social Relationships and Values
↓
shapes
↓
IV. Supernature (Montessori) Environmental,
Cosmic Relationships and Values

Montessori provides the practical philosophy that Marx proposes but fails to achieve, one which aims, as did his, not only to understand the world but to change it. She does this through a holistic philosophy of the human person, which respects its dynamic and hylomorphic nature, its historical dimension, and human and cosmic *telos*.

Caldwell College

Notes

1. *Karl Marx: Early Writings*, trans. and ed. T. B. Bottomore, *Manuscripts of 1844, Third Manuscript , XXIII* (New York: McGraw-Hill Book Company, 1964), 202.

2. Maria Montessori, *The Absorbent Mind*, trans. Claude A. Claremont, Clio Montessori Series, v. 1 (Oxford, England: Clio Press, 1988,1995), 15.

3. Karl Marx and Frederick Engels, *The German Ideology*, trans. and ed. C. J. Arthur, Editor's Introduction (New York: International Publishers Co., Inc., 1970), 12.

4. *Karl Marx: Early Writings*, "On the Jewish Question," 30–31.

5. Ibid., 31.

6. Maria Montessori, *Education and Peace*, trans. Helen R. Lane, Clio Montessori Series, v. 10 (Oxford, England: ABC-Clio Ltd., 1995), 22.

7. Ibid., 22.

8. Ibid., 37.

9. Ibid., 18, 38.

10. Ibid., 8, 14.

11. Ibid., 30.

12. Aristotle, *Physics* 2.1 (192 B 22–24), trans. by W. D. Ross.

13. Aristotle, *Nicomachean Ethics*, 1.7 (1098 a 8–17).

14. Karl Marx, *Manuscripts of 1844*, III. 6, in *Early Writings*, trans. Bottomore, 158.

15. *Early Writings*, "First Manuscript," [XXIV], 126.

16. Ibid., 158.

17. *German Ideology*, 42.

18. "Communism is for us not a *state of affairs* which is to be established, an *ideal* to which reality [will] have to adjust itself. We call communism the *real* movement which abolishes the present state of things. The conditions of this movement result from the premises now in existence" (Marx, *The German Ideology*, 56–57). Marx's approach is later called "historical materialism" (Editor's Introduction, 21).

19. Martin Nicolaus, Foreward to *Grundrisse* by Karl Marx, trans. M. Nicolaus (New York: Vintage Books, 1973), 30.

20. *German Ideology*, 118.

21. "So much is this activity, this unceasing sensuous labour and creation, this production, the basis of the whole sensuous world as it now exists, that, were it interrupted only for a year, Feuerbach would not only find an enormous change in the natural world, but would very soon find that the whole world of men and his own perceptive faculty, nay his own existence, were missing" (*German Ideology*, 63).

22. Martin Nicolaus, Foreward to *Grundrisse*, 1st ed. (New York: Vintage Books, 39).

23. "In all revolutions up till now the mode of activity always remained unscathed and it was only a question of a different distribution of this activity, a new distribution of labour to other persons, whilst the communist revolution is directed against the preceding *mode* of activity, does away with *labour*, and abolishes the rule of all classes." (*German Ideology*, 94)

24. Marx's "all-round human individual" corresponds precisely with what Montessori means by the person with a "healthy psyche," as we will discuss below.

25. *The German Ideology*, 117.

26. Ibid. Marx's "all-round human individual" corresponds precisely with what Montessori means by the person with a "healthy psyche," as we will discuss below.

27. Ibid., 118.

28. Ibid.

29. Ibid., 117.

30. *Critique of Gotha Program* (1875), published by Engels in "Neue Zeit," 1890, and trans. and ed. By T. B. Bottomore in *Karl Marx: Selected Writings in Sociology and Social Philosophy* (New York: McGraw-Hill Book Company, 1956, 1964), 258. In the paragraph containing this conclusion, Marx echoes the same points he makes earlier in *The German Ideology* about the necessary coincidence of the development of productive forces and the all-round development of individuals in the highest stage of the communist society.

31. Maria Montessori, *Education and Peace*, 8.

32. Ibid., 13.

33. Ibid., 17.

34. Ibid., 32–33.

35. *German Ideology*, 118.

36. *Education and Peace*, 18.

37. *German Ideology*, 117.

38. *Education and Peace*, 32–33; 48–49, 58–59.

39. "The man with a sound psyche is such a rare creature today that we almost never meet one, just as men with sound bodies were few and far between before the concept of personal hygiene helped mankind recognize the basis of physical health," *Education and Peace*, 18–19.

40. The further distinction in medieval thought between a passive potency, that is, a receptivity for acquiring a power, and an active potency, that is, a present ability not actually being exercised or "in act," would be helpful here.

41. *Education and Peace*, 49–50.

42. *The Absorbent Mind*, 80–89.

43. Term and concept from the thesis of Alice Miller in *For Your Own Good: Hidden Cruelty in Child-Rearing and The Roots of Violence*, trans. Alice Miller from *Am Anfang war Erziehung* (Toronto, Canada: Collins Publishers, 1983–1984), 3.

44. Montessori herself identifies the cause and effect of disordered and a social personality through the early violence done to the child by preventing or failing to nurture the child's inner self-direction and "work " (*The Absorbent Mind*, Chapters 19–21).

45. *The Absorbent Mind*, 146.

46. *Education and Peace*, 95.

47. *The Absorbent Mind*, 186.

48. *Education and Peace*, 95.

49. Ibid., 97.

50. "The fundamental goal of human existence is neither the survival of the individual nor that of the species. The individual adult's efforts to ensure his own survival and that of the species is only a means and a part of the task he must complete to fulfil [sic] his mission, to achieve his essential goal, to justify his reason for being—the creation of the environment" (*Education and Peace*, 95).

Towards a Phenomenology of Gratitude:
What Is 'Pleasing' in the *Euthyphro*

Peter R. Costello

Abstract: In this paper, I examine Plato's *Euthyphro* phenomenologically, reading the dialogue as manifesting the posture and activity of gratitude as an essential moment of piety. This phenomenon of gratitude appears directly through Euthyphro's own remarks and indirectly through Socrates's interaction with Euthyphro. Other recent commentators, notably Mark McPherran, David Parry, James Brouwer, and William Mann, have noted the importance of the *Euthyphro* as a dialogue that offers a great deal to the discussion of piety through the shape of the relationship between Socrates and Euthyphro. In building my argument, I follow Parry's examination of the notion of *therapeia* or care in order to mark out my own emphasis on *charis* or gratitude. And I note that, when gratitude is taken as an important phenomenon in the dialogue, what also appears to the reader is the pious possibility of authentic gift-giving and mutual recognition, something Brouwer, Mann, and McPherran have also noted indirectly. Finally, in addition to its synthesis of previous scholarship around a new theme, this paper applies to the dialogue the arguments of Melanie Klein's "Envy and Gratitude," Martin Heidegger's lectures entitled *What Is Called Thinking*, and Jacques Derrida's *Given Time*.

I n this paper, I argue that there is something important about piety revealed in Plato's *Euthyphro*. The dialogue does not simply fail to articulate piety at all, nor does the dialogue reveal piety only in terms of what piety is *not*.[1] Rather, the dialogue implies, and Socrates demonstrates, that gratitude is the posture that is required for piety, that it is gratitude that most pleases the gods and that it is gratitude that allows humans to give and receive real gifts (and not simply to exchange commercial benefits).[2]

Definition of Gratitude

Since I am going to speak about this dialogue in terms of gratitude, let me first by way of introduction say a bit about that term.[3] Authentic gratitude, or thankfulness, according to Martin Heidegger in *What is Called Thinking?* "*never* consists in that we ourselves come bearing *gifts*, and merely repay *gift* with *gift*. Pure thanks is rather that we simply think—think what is really and solely *given*, what is there to be thought" (Heidegger, 143, my emphasis). And according to the psychologist Melanie Klein in her well-known essay entitled "Envy and Gratitude," gratitude is "essential in building up the relation to the *good object* and underlies also the appreciation of *goodness* in others and in oneself" (Klein, 187, my emphasis). In my own words, linking Klein and Heidegger, gratitude involves both an individual and a communal (or mutual) act and experience of recognition.[4] That is, gratitude is an ongoing meditation central to each individual person's ability to relate to the givenness of good objects and to one another.

For each individual, gratitude is a preservation of what one is thankful for based on the fact that one recognizes that that object, situation, or person has attempted to enlarge or coalesce one's experience. In gratitude, one keeps something in mind because it has opened one onto a particular (and particularly relevant) stream of experiences, because it has provided an organizing route through the multiplicity that had previously receded from view as undifferentiated. In being grateful, one recognizes one's vulnerabilities, one's limits, and uses them in order to allow more sophisticated appearances to appear within one's home.[5]

Within one's individual enactment and experience of gratitude, one maintains a certain posture, that of at-homeness, of reflection, of relaxation and of freedom from anxiety. When grateful, one is at home with the world and with oneself and attributes that at-homeness to a well-maintained tension between self and other, to the others whom one still bears in mind. When one is grateful, one is open towards acting—one *could* act if it were necessary—and one is incapable of acting out of compulsion—since one is engaged precisely in a kind of reflective awareness upon experience that allows for time to show itself as a meaning that one participates in rather than a measure that constrains.[6]

However, one cannot be grateful on one's own. A communal or mutual act of recognition is implicit in and required by the individual act.[7] In gratitude, one's individual posture *is* one's response to the other, one's preservation of that other. What this means is that in real thanks one recognizes the other as another self, as a co-participant in experience who has the right to her own paths. Gratitude thus involves my seeing you or your words or your actions as *recognizing me* as valuable; that is, I see you as valuing me in a way that corresponds explicitly and appropriately to the way I value you.

Moreover, authentic gratitude acknowledges, by means of the mutual recognition that founds it, that *what* appears as given to us, what appears as gift and goodness, appears within the relationship itself. The objects that appear as good, therefore, appear and sustain themselves as good only within a good, mutually recognizable relation-ship. If the communal act of recognition is missing, concealed, or only implicit, what is left in my act of preserving, of holding you and the co-determined world in mind is *not* good. Instead, this non-recognized holding-in-mind easily tends towards acts of envy,[8] aggression or self-abnegation, acts that often produce serious errors in the way I approach myself or the world.[9] If the communal act of recognition is explicit and appropriate, however, all parties concerned have the possibility of revealing and offering something meaningful and good to one another, the possibility of approaching and revealing both good objects and goodness itself.[10]

Gratitude thus is not used in this paper as meaning simply a subjective feeling that comes and goes. Rather, gratitude is named as a structure, an attitude, a posture of human experience that also allows for particular emotions of thankfulness to be felt to various degrees of authenticity. In short, gratitude is the way in which consciousness always already negotiates givenness and otherness, embraces them, and has the possibility of continuing to direct its own notice of givenness in its bringing more and more of what is implicit to the fore.[11]

Euthyphro's Offerings

After Euthyphro has failed at least twice (at 5e and at 7a) to offer Socrates a definition of piety that can withstand scrutiny, Socrates asks Euthyphro to assume that there is a relationship between piety and justice. This assumption proves helpful for Euthyphro, who has all along been trying to define piety in the way that would justify his prosecution of his father. And he quickly determines with Socrates' assistance that "the godly and pious is the part of the just that is concerned with the care of the gods, while that concerned with the care of men is the remaining part of justice" (12e). This is an interesting attempt by Euthyphro to separate justice into parts so as to allow him the possibility of doing one thing to the gods and another to people while still remaining pious. Socrates' response, however, is not immediately to challenge the idea that justice could be fragmented or to ask whether piety would have to answer the charge of inconsistency. Instead Socrates asks Euthyphro what he would "mean by care" (13a).[12]

The word Euthyphro has used, and the word that Socrates uses to focus his question, is *therapeia*.[13] As David M. Parry has noticed, this discussion of *therapeia* in which Euthyphro and Socrates engage ultimately suggests that piety means "exhorting others and oneself to care for their soul with the realization that we mortals do not *fully* understand what the soul *is*, what care for this soul *means*, or *why* the god is concerned for the souls of human beings" (Parry, 537, my emphasis).[14] Parry's argument, which I find compelling, is that the dialogue, and Socrates, can offer this as a definition of piety because Socrates takes the notion of care seriously and continues to recollect Euthyphro's offering as the discussion progresses.[15]

I will now follow Parry's analysis of the notion of care that begins with Euthyphro's introduction of the term at 13b in order to draw out from it the notion that piety must comprise a stance of mutual recognition. First, I agree with Parry that, when Euthyphro first offers the notion of *therapeia*, Euthyphro does not yet seem to know what he means by it. When Socrates offers three examples of care at 13a–b (the care of horses by the breeder, the care of dogs by the hunter, and the care of cattle by the farmer) as to what *therapeia* could mean, Euthyphro does not immediately understand that in these Socratic examples piety would only be determined by the one who is the caregiver: "in each of Socrates' examples *therapeia* results in the good or improvement of the care-giver rather than the recipient of the care" (Parry, 531–532). That is, in Socrates' examples, the care stays internal to the care-giver. Care only reaches out in order to return and enhance the internal richness of the caregiver's life.

Moreover, the examples Socrates offers are ones in which the recipients of the care "do not ask to be recipients of therapeia. Their wishes are not consulted, not really even considered by the care-giver" (Parry, 532). What is lacking, one might say, in Euthyphro's offering of *therapeia* as a definition of piety is a way to acknowledge that piety is a kind of caring that produces a mutual recognition of what it is good for and for whom it is good. What is lacking is a recognition of who the gods are and how that recognition matters to the gods themselves and to those who care for and about them. Euthyphro's *therapeia* does not reach into the soul of another.

To compensate, presumably for the lack of mutuality in his definition, Euthyphro then offers that piety is like the care a servant has for a master. This definition does indeed inaugurate care as an action that occurs within a relationship, which offers to each person involved some kind of recognition of the other and of how the other sees her or him. The servant explicitly sees the master seeing him as a servant; the master implicitly acknowledges the servant's recognition of her as master. However, such an activity or experience of care is not a fully mutual one, since not all that characterizes the relationship is either explicit for or appropriate to all concerned.[16] The soul of the slave is considered only insofar as the benefit of the master is concerned. There is no crucible of care in that relationship, no mutual reception of the latent internality of one another in an external and explicit welcoming.

As Parry has noted, Socrates then "introduces the term *hyperetike* to characterize this service" of servant to master (Parry, 532). I would argue that it is Socrates' introduction or substitution of terms, as Socrates had also done previously at 13b by changing *therapeia* to *eusebeia*,[17] that serve as further tests to determine the manner in which Euthyphro gave the term *therapeia*. Socrates is trying to tease out what is in Euthyphro's answers, to allow the real Euthyphro to come out. Because of such care, because of such attempts to prod Euthyphro to reconcile his internal commitments to his external utterances, Socrates' counter-offers note the increasing tension between Euthyphro and Socrates as their own relation (as an echo to the discussion of piety itself) becomes bound up in the quest to discover how far mutual recognition is possible.[18]

As Euthyphro is unhappy to discover, to claim that 'care of the gods' is the service of a servant is to have to account for what it is that such service accomplishes. The asymmetrical nature of the relationship, the lack of explicit and appropriate mutual recognition implied in the kind of service (and force) required, ensures that it is the master who is guiding the service towards its appropriate end. The servant by herself presumably could not be expected to know what the service is for, and the project of abject service could not be one that on its own leads to more sophisticated relations. That is, neither the divine nor the human could reveal itself further in menial service. Presumably with such thoughts in mind, Socrates confronts Euthyphro, the priest, who acts as if he himself were more perspicacious than a servant, as to what the gods use our services for (13e).[19]

At this point, Euthyphro is on a precipice. If he answers precisely what the goals are of the gods, if he says what our service is *for*, he commits himself to what appear to *him* to be one of two unpalatable alternatives. Either he commits himself to claiming that the gods use our service in order to create something else that they need—though Euthyphro has stated that the gods lack nothing. Or he commits himself to admitting that we do not simply serve the gods and that they use our services to benefit us, which would make the practices of the gods more transparent, reaching into our very souls, committed to our education and welfare and thus to our power of involving ourselves explicitly within the sacrifices and prayers of religious tradition.

As Parry argues, "the gods' work cannot be thought of as benefiting a third party because no third party exists without some sort of economic transaction" (Parry, 534).[20] Not wishing to reduce the gods to economic partners, the only choice left for Euthyphro is to acknowledge that the gods require piety *from us* to benefit *us* (Parry, 534ff.).

Euthyphro then describes to what use the gods put our piety when he defines piety as what someone does when she knows "how to say and do what is pleasing to the gods at prayer and sacrifice, those are pious actions such as preserve both private houses and public affairs of state" (14b). On the first read of this, it might seem that Euthyphro means that it is the gods who preserve our institutions when we say and do what they would like. The worthiness of one's offering to the divine should then be judged indirectly, in a somewhat Calvinist manner, by the state of one's familial and political fortunes.

However, it is not at all clear that Euthyphro intends it to be the gods alone that directly preserve private houses and public affairs of state. To say so would be to argue that humans' pious speech and actions have no internal link to the function of preservation. That is, the acts would not on their own by virtue of their inner goodness institute lasting good relations among the faithful as a community.

But this is precisely what brought Euthyphro to court, namely, to prove that his prosecution of his father truly was in itself pious and, contrary to appearances, was not designed to tear apart his family and Athenian society but instead was designed to uphold these august institutions.[21] If such is the case, then Euthyphro means that it is not the gods working apart from our words and actions that preserve us; rather it is the divine working *through* those words and actions, helping us to connect ourselves to ourselves, which preserves us. Our words and actions are pious when we have recognized and done what the gods would do for us. It is most 'pleasing' to the gods when our acts and words mark out the proper, divine course on their own. It is not that the gods would not act for us; it is that they are most pleased when we work with them and come toward the good together.

Indeed it is here, when Euthyphro says that piety is to say and do what is 'pleasing,' that I see the main argument about piety come into play. The word for 'pleasing' that Euthyphro uses is *kecharismena*. It is this word, which can mean pleasing or gracious, that will move the dialogue toward the authentic recognition that piety is about gratitude,[22] the recognition that the divine recognizes us as important and worth caring for, and the recognition that we respond most appropriately by opening ourselves up to that gaze that cares for us, by treading that path which would structure our institutions according to the divine Logos.

The 'pleasing' or 'gracious' actions that make up piety are those that 'preserve.' They therefore keep in mind what is important, namely the proper means—i.e., which words to put together in prayer, which objects and gestures to put together in sacrifice—and the proper goals—i.e., the divine, home and the state. To say and do what is 'pleasing' or 'gracious' therefore demands a certain kind of character, one that holds things together.[23]

The 'grace-filled' words and actions must therefore arise out of some internal, synthetic power, some internal virtue, some internal organizational principle that answers to and imitates the external patterns of harmony and unity put into being by the gods. Words and actions are not sufficiently pleasant if they are enacted in a kind of indifferent deference; they are not pleasant merely if they do not offend. Rather, these words and actions must translate the internal into the demands of the external, in order to reflect back to the gods (and ourselves) their care of this our house and our state.

One of the most important steps in moving towards those pleasing words and actions Euthyphro proposes is, therefore, the realization that human life is not simply a multiplicity of relations to private houses and to public affairs, to self and to the divine, as if these relations were in isolation from or in addition to each other. Rather, what is implicit in Euthyphro's latest definition, what is implicit in these pleasing words and actions, is the desire for or drive toward a unitary relation of private to public, of internal to external, of human to divine life as such, within the same person and the same polis.

What the words and actions offer, then, must be something like self-revelation in a relationship of love, something like a quest for union. And Socrates, sensing this, as one who has tried all his life to make his personal life completely transparent in his service to Athens, leaps onto this opportunity that Euthyphro has offered him.

Like a "lover," Socrates wants more, wants to uncover what is concealed behind or implicit in the meaning of the words of his "beloved" (14c).[24] He asks Euthyphro if the kind of 'pleasant' actions and words would be those that demonstrate one's ability "to make a gift to the gods" and "to beg from the gods" (14c). As Euthyphro agrees, it is almost as if Socrates now interrogates the possibility of giving itself. For what could the gods 'need' from us, and how could a gift be possible unless it addressed some need?[25]

Thus, Socrates becomes concerned to ask whether or not Euthyphro's previous avoidance of the economic partnership model is in fact possible. Doesn't Euthyphro really remain committed, even with this excessively 'pleasing' looking piety, to advocating "a sort of trading skill between gods and men" (14e)?[26] In other words, Socrates asks Euthyphro whether or not humans and gods are equal partners, whether they are merely *trading* gifts, merely within a political economy?[27] At stake here, I find, is the kind of mutual recognition that is possible between the human and the divine.

In Socrates' question I hear others: Does the economic model assume all internal value and incommensurability to be externalized and commensurate in the exchange of coin? Is the most powerful act of mutual recognition that which commits us *either* to an unsuccessful attempt to bring the gods down to the sweat and smells of the marketplace *or* to an unsuccessful attempt to make ourselves gods? Can we enact a mutual recognition in which we accept our differences, accept that we are unable fully to reveal, to expose either ourselves or the gods and yet still form a kind of unity of love? Can there be an authentic act of welcoming each other's private selves to the public table?

Euthyphro carefully responds to Socrates' trading skill question by conditionally agreeing, with the proviso that Socrates should take responsibility for the characterization of the relationship as a kind of 'trading.' Euthyphro then maintains that the gifts that he has in mind that would be pleasing (*kecharismena*) would be "honour, reverence, and what I mentioned just now, gratitude [*charis*]" (15a).[28] The word Euthyphro offers here that is translated as gratitude is *charis*, which in its multiple meanings in Greek can mean favor, grace, homage, a gift, gratitude, and even kindness or charity.[29]

Now I take Euthyphro's final offering, here, to be a valid one. He is insisting on the difference between the divine and the human. Gratitude is the posture that remains necessary when in relation to the divine. And Euthyphro *appears* to agree that the internal posture must match the external characterization of the act by those whom it is purported to serve as pious—this is apparent in the etymological connection between the words he uses for pleasing exterior and for gratitude. But Euthyphro, again, is unclear what he means by this offering, does not pay enough attention to the appearance of his own words, and so Socrates and the reader must help again to clarify.

When Euthyphro names gratitude or 'charity' as one of the major gifts we offer to the gods, he assumes that gratitude means the same thing as what is pleasing. In fact he claims to have mentioned 'gratitude' just before. What Euthyphro cannot see, therefore, is the work needed to establish the isomorphism of a pleasant or gracious exterior and an internal posture of gratitude.[30] Euthyphro thinks, in other words, that to be bound up with the gods (and with Socrates) is simply a matter of saying and doing the customary things. But this attempt to conceal real work through the surface of tradition betrays a lack of true care, a lack that, ironically, demands real therapy.

It is not the traditional sacrifices and prayers that on their own constitute gratitude; it is in fact gratitude that opens one up to the divine, that allows the divine to bestow meaning upon, and breathe life into the tradition and thus into oneself as engaged with *others* in that tradition. It is in gratitude that our actions are not merely the external manifestations of effort, of a struggle to make or to purchase, for example, bread and wine. It is in gratitude that our actions become possible as holy.

Ultimately, what I believe the dialogue as a whole and the person of Socrates suggests is that what is 'pleasing' to the gods, what is gracious, is not a practice but a posture, not a specialized, separate role but a *person*, a person who is grateful, who is open to grace, who makes herself or himself so permeated by the divine that there *is no distinction between private and public, between inside and outside*.[31] What is pleasing is the person who holds nothing back in order that the gods may call him or her towards the highest and the best by being called towards *others*. The grateful, gracious person acts, much as Kierkegaard's knight of faith does, in an ordinary way but in extraordinary depth. And so *ultimately* Euthyphro is not wrong to note the similarity between *kecharismena* and *charis*. However, the authentic recognition of this union between internal and external, between pleasing acts and preserved institutions, is still one that is lived from within a relation to the divine other and bestowed together with that other upon one's actions. One's separate, secret actions themselves by themselves do not necessarily confer anything.

One only attains the 'pleasant' or 'gracious' exterior that 'preserves' by being the kind of person who can internalize first of all the very way in which he or she *stands* towards the divine, towards others, *as those others view that stance*. That is, only the one who first attempts to understand the demands of mutual recognition as a demand to acknowledge others' role in shaping one's own identity—only such a person can develop, through this focus and openness, a truly gracious appearance. The gods do not deserve fawning, servile servants any more than they desire arrogant, domineering ones, since this demeans all concerned. Rather, the gods deserve—and demand—persons who engage the divine, persons who recognize what of their finite selves appears as valuable *to the divine*, persons who recognize their finitude itself as appearing *both* as incommensurate with *and* as simultaneously striving toward (because welcomed by) the divine.[32]

By naming *charis* as one of the gifts we are to give the gods, Euthyphro thus at first seems to imply simply that the gods and people *do* have a relationship of mutual recognition. For, if it is gratitude that the gods want from humans, then the gods and humans are viewing each others as partners in a relationship where the point *is the maintenance and growth of the relationship*, the power of the relationship itself to reveal the goodness of what *already is divine*, and not the production or purchase of some further thing. Thus, while gratitude would recognize the distinction in kind between the divine and the human, it would not do so by negating the one who offers gratitude. Rather, accepting the very notion of gratitude as our gift would ensure that people see themselves as *wise* because they recognize that the *only true givers are the gods*. In accepting gratitude as their calling, people would be thereby restored to their true possibility—namely, to making relationships among themselves that have the echo of this gratitude as its focus, creating institutions in which, for example, they would agree to rule and be ruled in turn.

Implicit (for a short time at least) in Euthyphro's mention of *charis* is the awareness that the gods would find us pleasing because in gratitude we see the gods truly, we acknowledge that they welcome our humility, our limited power to act on behalf of the divine.[33] Again, this provides a step forward for Euthyphro, this mention of gratitude, since the kind of gift that it brings to light seems to undermine the idea that we and the gods are trading partners in a political economy.[34]

If gratitude were possible, and if gratitude were considered piety by the gods, then giving a gift to others, on *behalf of the divine*, would be possible. We could give that which was not ours to begin with. If gratitude were a gift, then we could describe the possibility of other gifts—a gift would be that which propels us toward one another in such a way as to open us onto something more sophisticated than either of us had been, more sophisticated than that relationship itself had been prior to its being offered. But such a step forward and such a possibility is not something Euthyphro by himself achieves in the dialogue. And indeed its erasure and the true concealment of the dialogue occur in the next line.

Earlier, by substituting other terms for care, Socrates allowed Euthyphro to choose to make the notion of *therapeia* disappear, thus allowing the division between the gods and Euthyphro to settle into the background. After Euthyphro mentions gratitude as one of our gifts to the gods, Socrates asks Euthyphro whether or not the definition of piety, with the addition of *charis*, has returned to what is "pleasing to the gods" (15b). In fact, Euthyphro's previous line has ended with the word *charis* only for Socrates to begin his own next sentence with Euthyphro's previous word *kecharismena*. That is to say, Socrates asks whether the evocation of the posture of gratitude is really authentic, truly a reflection of Euthyphro's soul, or if Euthyphro is instead continuing to skate along the surface. It seems clear that Euthyphro has not really been grateful and that he has instead simply assumed that *charis* is concealed within the word *kecharismena*.

What stood out in the conversation as offering a significant advance, namely the posture of gratitude, the offering of an attitude from which what would be given would *not* be immediately put within the economic system of exchange, is now in danger of being immediately covered over. If gratitude is to be taken up further, it must be taken up by us who read and respond in ways that Euthyphro did not.

All care, all therapy, if indeed *therapeia* can be made to resound toward the care for our own souls—all therapeutic care for Euthyphro would be cut short if Euthyphro leaves in anger never to revisit his decision to prosecute his father. However, I would note that, even if Euthyphro's therapy is ended prematurely, still it appears as written to us that Socrates has demonstrated care, has been graceful and demonstrated gratitude throughout the dialogue. By holding onto Euthyphro's own words, that is, by Socrates' own gratitude for what Euthyphro offers, by Socrates following the necessary obedience to his beloved, while simultaneously submitting Euthyphro and his words to critique, Socrates has clarified the true manner of givenness of Euthyphro's words, has shown the horizon on which they appear, and we can be the beneficiaries of such phenomenological work.[35]

Conclusion

In conclusion, I take away from the *Euthyphro* much of what Euthyphro offered, but only insofar as Socrates was able to change the manner of its givenness or to make explicit what these offerings of Euthyphro actually entailed through the example of his (Socrates') own life and action. For the care of people and of the gods *are* both parts of justice. Euthyphro was right, in a sense. These parts are not isolated from one another, however. Building off of what I find in the dialogue, I believe that we are called to provide a kind of therapy, a kind of social justice, that heals the divisions brought between God's people by those same people, to heal these divisions by both our own posture of gratitude and, through it, knowing by divine grace how to say and do what is necessary to provoke persons to further reflection on holiness and justice, even if our words and actions appear to be unpleasant.[36]

If we are grateful, we remain oriented towards the origin of being, towards the one *in whom we and our pleasure and suffering exist*, toward the one who calls us towards plenitude by valuing gratitude, by allowing for questions, for lack and need to appear within our relationship.[37] To be grateful is to be free of resentment—and the gratitude that piety entails is the freedom from resentment insofar as the divine has not fully revealed itself to me, the one for whom it cares.[38] To be grateful is to realize that the political economy is not the place for such gifts or offerings but to realize that we create spaces for such gifts and offerings by opening up new non-economic space in our recognition of one another.

Much as an infant's first object, the breast, can lead to the infant's first experience of intimacy, of mutual recognition, our ongoing enactments of mutual recognition and gratitude can lead to our ability to see objects as meaningful insofar as they spring from the source of givenness, from the Good itself, from the divine. Our gratitude would further our ability to think what we are given to think in a way that is thankful for such an opportunity. Our gratitude would allow us to pass beyond the care for material objects or the commodities of our individual lives toward the care for the relationships of our community, the relationships that those objects always already (at least potentially) embody.

Providence College

Notes

1. James Brouwer, in his insightful article "The Inverted Nature of Plato's *Euthyphro*, concludes that the dialogue ends with the fact that the pious is defined both positively and negatively as "its resistance to being confidently known and quantified by humanity . . . its nature is bound up in this 'not,' in this philosophical discovering of one's own ignorance in regard to it" (61).

2. See Jacques Derrida's *Given Time: I. Counterfeit Money*. Here Derrida interrogates the very possibility of a gift and suggests that, although 'gift' might be an unavoidable term and demand within experience, the act of giving initiates immediately and automatically a system of exchange that destroys the very possibility of the gift to appear within the community that demands and offers it. This revealing and concealing of 'gift,' however, does not eradicate the necessity of gratitude. And it is just such a discussion that I see Plato offering here in the *Euthyphro*. Piety is, in a real sense, learning how to "give to, and beg from, the gods" (14d). But that does not mean that such knowledge should immediately become "a sort of trading skill between gods and men" (14e).

3. In Lecture III of Part II of *What is Called Thinking?* Heidegger reminds us that the etymology of thinking, at least in Old English, is rooted in thanks: "the Old English noun for thought is *thanc* or *thonc*—a thought; a grateful thought, and the expression of such a thought; today it survives in the plural *thanks* (139).

4. The notion of authentic gratitude as mutual recognition is something I find given in Hegel's discussion of mutual recognition in the *Phenomenology of Spirit* particularly as read by John Russon in *The Self and Its Body in Hegel's Phenomenology of Spirit*.

5. For Klein "a particular cause of envy is the relative absence of it in others. The envied person is felt to possess what is at bottom most prized and desired—and this is a good object, which also implies a good character and sanity" (Klein, 203). In light of Klein's discussion, it would seem that all of Athens suffers from a bad relationship to the mother and to the breast. For when they confront Socrates, who it seems is not envious at all, they envy all the more his relation to the Good. In this light, I find it noteworthy that Socrates says in the *Euthyphro* that Meletus accuses Socrates "to the city as to their mother" (2c).

6. Again, I turn to Heidegger's lectures on thinking. There, before discussing thinking directly as thanking, Heidegger discusses how thought involves the cessation of *ressentiment*: "The will becomes free from its revulsion against time, against time's mere past, when it steadily wills the going and coming, this going and coming back of everything" (104). Gratitude towards one's own finitude means that one can appreciate the meaning that time bears within experience.

7. Gregory Vlastos in "Socratic Piety" argues that it is precisely the vision of piety or of the divine as concerned with gift that Socrates needs to overcome his own tendency to see the arc towards virtue as simply self-interested: "In Socratic piety that link between our good and that of others is made non-contingent through devotion to a disinterestedly benevolent god who, being already perfect, does not require from us any contribution to his own well-being but only asks each of us to do for other persons what he would be doing for them himself if he were to change places with us" (65).

8. Klein notes that the tendency to fall from gratitude into envy is a given part of human experience: "The very ease with which the milk comes—though the infant feels gratified by it—also gives rise to envy because this gift seems something so unattainable" (Klein, 183). Gratitude is thus not a completely automatic relationship, but it must be continually re-introduced, continually worked on.

9. T. F. Morris in "Plato's *Euthyphro*" suggests the way in which Euthyphro needs mutual recognition: "But he is not looking to the gods for this salvation; it is in the eyes of other people that he would have it established that he is not good for nothing" (318). Morris goes on to talk about how the way Euthyphro goes about attempting to achieve recognition is fundamentally flawed because of Euthyphro's ingratitude: "Ingratitude is a sort of deprivation; something that should be there is not there" (319). Morris notes that Socrates "does not refute" Euthyphro's mention that gratitude is the gift we give to the gods (319).

10. That I maintain the dialogue to offer something important to the discussion of piety, and that that discussion is implicit in the discussion of *relationships* is something that William E. Mann in "Piety: Lending a Hand to Euthyphro" has already outlined. As Mann says, the failure to produce a completely valid definition is not to say that the dialogue fails: "An account of piety need not be a definition but rather an *explanation* of piety, something that outlines its religious dimensions, something that may in fact require *embedding* piety in

a more comprehensive theory about the human, the divine and *the relations between them*" (131, my emphasis).

11. My emphasis on phenomenology in this paper is also partly derived from Edmund Husserl's discussion of the phenomenological reduction, which occurs throughout his works. There, Husserl demands that "everything originarily (so to speak in its 'personal' actuality) offered to us in 'intuition' is to be accepted simply as what it is presented as being, but also only within the limits in which it is presented there" (44). This attentiveness to givenness, the holding it in view on the thing's own terms—this evinces a posture of gratitude.

12. The question as to what something means, as to how it presents itself to Euthyphro, is an important one. The question allows what Euthyphro is saying to have its full weight, to be preserved, to be 'stood up for' by the one who gives it. Euthyphro can offer the manner in which he gives the word.

13. An earlier work, *Therapeia*, by Robert E. Cushman, pays attention to this term not in the *Euthyphro* specifically but throughout Plato's corpus. For Cushman, *therapeia* is Plato's entire attempt to heal the division between the individual and herself, between the individual and the polis. However, Cushman argues that there is a problem that is insoluble for Plato: "The real question is how long a man can endure unresolved contrariety in his own spirit. The insoluble problem of Plato's *therapeia* is identical with the unanswerable question: How long can a man live at odds with himself and with his deepest presentiments of truth?" (300). It is interesting that Cushman acknowledges that this notion of *therapeia* leads Platonic philosophy to admit that "great as it is both in its diagnosis of the human plight and in its scheme of *therapeia*, [it needs to look] beyond itself to a larger conception of divine grace" (301). This move from therapy to gratitude is precisely what I mark out here in the *Euthyphro*.

14. Notice that phenomenology also is reluctant to proclaim fully what something is, what it means, and why it occurs. Phenomenology rather allows for what something is to appear as a meaning that is correlative to the acts of consciousness that intend it (and not therefore expressible on its own); this meaning that appears is then full of latent or implicit (attendant) meanings that need further (even infinite) examination; and the engagement in this process is for phenomenology the only answer to the 'why' that is possible. Why do essences like piety appear as resisting a simple definition? Because meaning happens (and demands for us to take it up) as this polyvalent givenness—this is the answer that phenomenology offers. Because I was called to explicate, because I have a (transcendental, for Husserl) vocation, I *must* fix my eye on piety and continue to describe it as it shows itself to me.

15. That Socrates recollects what Euthyphro says and that Socrates thereby performs a therapeutic service for Euthyphro is noted by Mark L. McPherran in his "The Aporetic Interlude and Fifth Elenchus of the *Euthyphro*." McPherran notes that Socrates demands Euthyphro "accept his full measure of responsibility for the inadequacy of his definitions by adopting and developing Euthyphro's own image of moving *logoi*" (6). It is also interesting to note that when McPherran focuses on how Socrates addresses Euthyphro's accusations at 11d4 he discovers significance in Socrates' mention of Tantalus. Though McPherran only mentions the story of Tantalus without any further explanation, I believe that it can be inferred from McPherran's presentation that just as Tantalus "betrayed these secrets and so was punished" so too could Socrates and Euthyphro be said to be in danger (8). To discover piety is in some sense to be awakened to "a raging thirst and hunger" that calls for God (8). Piety would demand gratitude for that hunger and for the "ever-receding water and food"

that surrounds the pious person (8). Piety is gracious withdrawal of the beloved in order for the lover to temper his desire with openness.

16. The master, as "the recipient of this service is both the initiator of the service relationship and its main beneficiary" (Parry, 532). The servant's power in connecting the master to the good that the service produces is concealed, kept from sight. And the servant's claim to be recognized in a way appropriate to her power is also suppressed, as Socrates reveals to Meno in his education of the slave in the *Meno*.

Hegel in the *Phenomenology of Spirit* describes the master-slave dialectic as demanding to be resolved into more sophisticated shapes of self-consciousness. John Russon reveals this as follows: the "whole master-slave relation [is] a *development* of spirit that makes it possible for the same spirit-self which entered into this relation to enter now into more sophisticated relations. Growing up through this whole *Gestalt* thus develops a *hexis* for spirit, and precisely what this *hexis* is is a potential for a new relation" (op. cit., 159–160, note 52).

17. See Laszlo Versenyi's *Socratic Humanism* where he remarks on Socrates' exploration of *eusebeia*: "*Eusebeia* means proper reverence, awe, fear, and respect toward whatever is truly venerable, awesome, fearful, and respectable, be it human or divine. If, as Socrates believes, the gods happen to be good and are therefore to be respected, then proper reverence is their due, and *eusebeia* includes our relationship to them too" (107). By means of *eusebeia*, Versenyi notes, Socrates equates piety with wisdom and thus becomes guilty of at least unorthodox piety.

18. See McPherran's discussion, 6–32, of the way in which the accusations made by Euthyphro and Socrates as to who is the Daedalus in the dialogue, and therefore as to who prevents the *eidos* from becoming visible—how these accusations do more than attribute blame. It is clear that this discussion of Daedalus that begins at 11b is the rather destructive but latent way in which Euthyphro acknowledges mutuality in his discussion with Socrates. For as McPherran notes, Euthyphro is trying to suggest that "the inability to achieve a stable and thus adequate definition of piety is a *mutual* one" (6, my emphasis). Beyond blaming, however, this break from the direct pursuit of piety thus allows Socrates to manifest "a concern for the well-being of Euthyphro and his extended family" and allows Plato to rehabilitate the worth of Euthyphro and "remotivate readers sympathetic to Euthyphro to continue to follow the discussion" (10).

19. According to McPherran, it is here that the dialogue is calling attention to the asymmetry not only of the relation of gods to humans but of Socrates to Euthyphro. Euthyphro's inability to navigate either relation well is that he mistakes (and indeed manufactures) the nature of the asymmetry that he says appears in each. Euthyphro assumes that his father, Socrates, and the gods are masters. In doing so, Euthyphro believes that they are all simply to be fought off. An incredible envy burgeons. Euthyphro will not submit, and he assumes that all relationships of asymmetrical character require self-defamation or self-aggrandizement. See also Parry 532ff., especially the following: "the gods are *naturally* superior to human beings, not merely politically or conventionally superior. That Euthyphro recognizes this point is not clear" (532).

However, Socrates shows that it is not true that an act of mutual recognition cannot appear within an asymmetrical relationship. People can have different roles, just as a teacher and a student have different levels of responsibility, without trying to silence or demean one another. However, what is true is that a relationship of mutual recognition, if it includes an element of asymmetry or hierarchy, must see itself as pushing toward full equality. In Socrates' words and actions, both the gods and Socrates appear more like good parents, who have the child's interest and potential in mind in everything they say and do and who even allow the child to open up questions about human existence, the discussion of which requires real work and creativity on both the parent's and the child's parts. Euthyphro cannot see the discussion with Socrates as a 'loving' discussion because Euthyphro has not first dwelled within and been grateful for the relationship with his own parents.

McPherran takes up this point at length in his discussion of how Socrates and Euthyphro's father are conflated by Euthyphro. See especially McPherran's intriguing suggestion of how Euthyphro's father is also to blame for Euthyphro's own failure to relate to the gods and Socrates: "for again it was arguably Euthyphro's father who somehow encouraged him and taught him to fly towards the heavens in the search for an understanding of divinity that exceeds the comprehension of the multitude. It was thus the conceit that this influence had nourished which led Euthyphro to usurp the role of [exegntai] and prosecute his own father" (17). A parent-child relationship can at first appear to be freeing the child for higher things, but its acts of recognition can still on closer inspection appear as dangerous denials (in this case of finitude) or vacillations that cause great harm.

Following the kind of therapy of Melanie Klein, I would argue that it is thus Euthyphro who commits transference from the statues of his own imagination onto the living gods and people he encounters. It is Euthyphro who insists on an asymmetry that is inappropriate to the relationship Socrates desires, and it is Euthyphro who cannot acknowledge the appearance of mutual recognition on the horizon of the conversation.

20. Notice that in economic transactions the 'gazes' of each participant are directed toward some third thing—money, the object being constructed, etc. They are not directly looking at one another except insofar as each one fulfills the exchange of the object. Economic transactions are barely more sophisticated than the servant-master relationship, though it is true that in economic transactions, the players can in principle switch places. See Derrida's *Given Time*: "there is no gift without bond, without bind, without obligation or ligature; but on the other hand, there is no gift that does not have to untie itself from obligation, from debt, contract, exchange, and thus from the bind" (27).

21. Michel Despland researches the way in which Euthyphro's prosecution affects Athenian custom and law in *The Education of Desire*. Despland then develops a vision of Plato that shows how Plato is aware that "dialectical conversation" and "the intervention of the philosophic friend" are needed to help Euthyphro overcome his fundamentally bad choices (119). Ultimately for Despland, there is a logic to how Plato's descriptions of religion in every dialogue, the logic of desire that educates itself, the logic of a concept of eros that moves toward creativity. This logic appears to me to be Hegelian and to be rooted in mutual recognition and gratitude: "By redefining eros and making it an aspiration Plato makes it a movement of the soul that is capable of educating and orienting the desirous part of the soul and directing it to ever worthier objects" (236).

22. *Kecharismena* is etymologically linked to *charis* or gratitude, which Euthyphro uses at 15b. I would then, in translation, link gratitude to grace and gracefulness, as implied by the root *gratia*, in order to emphasize the connection between interior and exterior that I use below.

23. Euthyphro implies here the notion of a well-ordered soul or character. However, Parry, citing Blits and Strauss, notes that "oddly enough, the word soul is never mentioned in the dialogue. The failure to mention the soul leads to the failure to arrive at an adequate definition of the holy" (535).

24. Notice how mutual such a love relationship is, how concerned with mutual recognition of the kind that propels both the lover and the beloved further towards higher things. Contrast this with the relation of servant to master.

25. Mann notes that the act of giving implied here could be that of a contribution to the divine plan: "There is nothing in the concept of omnipotence that precludes an omnipotent being from letting another, much less powerful being contribute to a project that the omnipotent being could have carried out alone" (op cit., 133). In addition, Mann notes that "the real gift *is* the act of giving itself, the object given functioning merely as a token for what the act conveys" (133).

Mark McPherran notes that "Socrates' question forces Euthyphro confront the issue of whether offering gratifying but *non-beneficial* (non-*eudaimonia*-furthering) gifts to the gods would require expert knowledge of piety" (op. cit, 22). For McPherran, Euthyphro makes the mistake of leaving behind his idea that gratitude is part of piety because Euthyphro believes that giving gifts that the gods do not need is not an "artful (*technikon*; 14 E 3)" type of giving (22). However, that is not true and Euthyphro should have said otherwise, as McPherran shows.

26. The danger that is in this dialogue is apparent to Brouwer. For it is not simply that the possibility of the gift will *again* devolve into commerce. Rather, it is that the very possibility of piety, like the possibility of family, will be destroyed. Brouwer compares Euthyphro with Meletus and notes that both men begin their interaction with Socrates by being focused on achieving "a dis-inheritance": "The respect that mortals ought to show the gods, that sons ought to show their fathers, and that youth ought to show to elders is instead replaced by a type of destruction of the former by the latter, a type of dis-inheritance that serves also to sever the present from the past" (op cit., 49). Notice that it is gratitude that preserves time and the possibility of honoring what appears in time.

27. For this issue, it is interesting to refer to Heidegger's essay again: "thanking enacted by itself, as payment and repayment, remains too easily bogged down in the sphere of mere conventional recompense, even mere business" (141). See also Derrida's *Given Time*, which I take to be simply a longer version of Heidegger's meditation: "The gap between, on the one hand, thought, language and desire and, on the other hand, knowledge, philosophy, science, and the order of presence is also a gap between gift and economy" (29).

28. Mann also devotes some time to considering the notion of gratitude or 'charity.' He notes that gratitude is *itself given* by God: "But love of God, or Charity, is a theological virtue, not subject to natural acquisition but bestowed on those who have it by the supernatural activity of God" (op cit., 135).

29. Aristotle in *Rhetoric* II.7 discusses *charis* at length. Here he focuses on it as meaning something like kindness: "Hence those who stand by us in poverty or in banishment, even if they do not help us much, are yet really kind to us, because our need is great and the occasion pressing. . . . The helpfulness must therefore meet, preferably, just this kind of need; and failing just this kind, some other kind as great or greater" (1385a25–30).

30. In fact, Euthyphro inverts the relation between the internal and external. I am indebted to Brouwer's article for this recognition. There, Brouwer maintains throughout that "Euthyphro does not merely misunderstand the notion of piety, rather, he understands it in *reverse*" (op cit., 46). In this sense, Brouwer claims, Euthyphro is "the *inversion* of Socrates, a figure in which virtually all of what belongs to Socrates is stood on its head" (47). Socrates' focus on knowing himself, his focus on the internal is thus turned around. Yet it is noteworthy

that it is only with some of Euthyphro's assertions that we come to understand how it is that Socrates 'preserves' and is 'grateful for' the words that Euthyphro offers. By focusing on how Euthyphro is attuned only to the external, we know to look past the 'external' character of Socrates' words to the way they 'give off' an *internal* graciousness.

31. Parry notes Euthyphro's insistence on the distinction "between private and public rather than the division of the human being into the physical body, the political or honor-seeking part, and the soul proper" (535). Not recognizing the soul, or in the phenomenological sense, one's own perspective on and implication in intersubjectivity, prevents the recognition of piety as such.

32. Kierkegaard's discussion in *Fear and Trembling* as to how Abraham held the contradictions together, plunged into the absurd in order to remain both an eternal, infinite consciousness and the finite, aging recipient of Isaac—this discussion seems to be peculiarly relevant. Piety is a movement, a kind of dance. See David Wisdo's "Kierkegaard and Euthyphro" for a discussion of how Kierkegaard might explore the problem of the gift and of whether the pious is pious because the gods love it.

33. Mann focuses on gratitude as a mutually recognizing act of humans and God when he describes how Aquinas views piety. Aquinas, Mann argues, would not agree that piety could be sufficiently accounted for by gratitude, since piety is a divine gift. However, Aquinas would agree "that supernatural piety involves loving God in a way that presupposes God's love of us as finite, created beings" (op. cit., 136).

34. McPherran in "Does Piety Pay?" argues that in fact Socrates does undercut the economics of traditional piety: "I want to argue, however, that Socrates did manage to retain and recast the internal, non-mercantile dimension of the tradition, emphasizing the petitioner's intentionality and piety over his or her particular material gift-offerings and requests" (97–98).

35. Parry notes that it is Socrates' willingness to hold onto Euthyphro's offerings that pushes the dialogue further: "Thus, we need not assert that Socrates had complete wisdom or the *eidos* of holiness before him at the beginning of the *Euthyphro*, but we can leave open the possibility that his analysis of the remembered conversation could yield such an *eidos* or wisdom" (531).

36. Citing Brickhouse and Smith, McPherran notes that Socrates, despite Eutyphro's vacillations, "may none the less hold that buried far beneath Euthyphro's façade of shifting shapes there is within him—as in all of us—a stable self possessing a stable account of piety and other truths on such fundamental topics" (31). Socrates then recognizes that in Euthyphro that is most respectful and therefore most capable of authentic, mutual recognition.

37. Mann notes the mutuality of piety here: "What makes an act of acknowledging God as Father an act of supernatural piety is the act's being lovingly accepted by God. We might say that supernatural piety *supervenes* on the relevant complex of activities undertaken by the worshipper and God" (141). And again, "piety is what God loves in us when we love God as Father" (142). The issue of supervening seems to me to be a recognition that piety is a way in which the relationship as mutual institutes itself in the participant. Piety is what I have when I recognize that I am intersubjective, that I am not just myself but myself-with-for-and-in-God.

38. Brouwer notes that "Thus the negative or aporetic nature of the *Euthyphro* is at the same time a positive: the pious is, in a sense, defined by its resistance to being confidently known and quantified by humanity" (op. cit., 61).

Bibliography

Barnes, Jonathan, ed. *The Complete Works of Aristotle: The Revised Oxford Translation.* Princeton: Princeton University Press, 1991.

Brickhouse, Thomas C. and Smith, Nicholas D. *Plato and the Trial of Socrates.* New York: Routledge, 2004.

Brouwer, James. "The Inverted Nature of Plato's *Euthyphro" Dialogue* XLI.1 (Winter 2002): 45–70.

Cushman, Robert E. *Therapeia: Plato's Conception of Philosophy.* Westport: Greenwood Press, 1958.

Derrida, Jacques. *Given Time: I. Counterfeit Money.* Chicago: University of Chicago Press, 1994.

Despland, Michel. *The Education of Desire: Plato and the Philosophy of Religion.* Toronto: University of Toronto Press, 1985.

Heidegger, Martin. *What is Called Thinking?* New York: Harper and Row, 1968.

Husserl, Edmund. *Ideas Pertaining to a Pure Phenomenology and a Phenomenological Philosophy.* Netherlands: Kluwer, 1982

Kierkegaard, Soren. *Fear and Trembling and Repetition.* Princeton: Princeton University Press, 1994.

Klein, Melanie. *The Psycho-Analysis of Children.* Delacorte, 1975 *E.*

———. *nvy and Gratitude and Other Works.* London: Hogarth, 1984.

Mann, William. "Lending a Helping Hand to Euthyphro." *Philosophy and Phenomenological Research* 58.1 (March 1998): 123–142.

McPherran, Mark L. "Does Piety Pay? Socrates and Plato on Prayer and Sacrifice" in Smith and Woodruff, *Reason and Religion in Socratic Philosophy*: 89–114.

———. "The Aporetic Interlude and Fifth Elenchus of Plato's *Euthyphro"* in *Oxford Studies in Ancient Philosophy* Volume XXV Winter 2003. Oxford: Oxford University Press, 2003.

Morris, T. F. "Plato's *Euthyphro."* *The Heythrop Journal* XXXI.3 (July 1990): 309–323.

Parry, David. "Holiness as Service: *Therapeia* and *Hyperetike* in Plato's *Euthyphro." Journal of Value Inquiry* 28.4 (December 1994): 529–539.

Russon, John. *The Self and Its Body in Hegel's Phenomenology of Spirit.* Toronto: University of Toronto Press, 1997.

———. *Human Experience: Philosophy, Neurosis, and the Elements of Everyday Life.* Albany: State University of New York Press, 2004.

Smith, Nicholas D., and Woodruff, Paul B., eds. *Reason and Religion in Socratic Philosophy.* Oxford: Oxford University Press, 2000.

Versenyi, Laszlo. *Socratic Humanism.* Westport: Greenwood Press, 1979.

Vlastos, Gregory. "Socratic Piety," in *Reason and Religion in Socratic Philosophy,* 55–74.

Wisdo, David. "Kierkegaard and Euthyphro." *Philosophy* 62 (1987): 221–226.

Divine and Human Agency in the Work of Social Justice: Liberation Theology Responds to Radical Orthodoxy

Donald J. Musacchio

Abstract: Radical Orthodoxy (RO) accepts the post-structuralist critiques of autonomous human agency while liberation theologians embrace Enlightenment ideals of subjectivity and the secular political space where agency is exercised. RO theologians think that by accepting these premises, liberation theology fails to resist violence and nihilism that are the inevitable fruit of secular autonomy. I want to formulate a liberationist response to these objections. Liberationists do not see human and divine agency as fundamentally opposed, but rather the deepest strivings of the human spirit for justice are on the same trajectory as the Kingdom of God. Human and divine agency are tied together through the notion of a utopia whereby these strivings for justice are expressed in a finite and historical way. This emancipative use of reason in the construction of a utopia provides a means for divine and human agency to interact without destroying the human autonomy of the secular sphere.

The ideal of human agency as free, rational and autonomous is the fruit of the Enlightenment's rejection of a religious conception of the world. Medievals saw the world as the handiwork of God and divine providence was everywhere at work in the world sustaining it in existence and influencing its course. Enlightenment thinkers came to see the natural world as independent and self-sufficient—a place for humanity to exercise rational productivity. The liberal political theory which developed from such considerations championed a secular public space in which free autonomous rational human agents could interact without the imposition of some external authority—authority that medievals derived ultimately from God. No longer would some humans lord over others in the name of God. Rather everyone possessed of an equal human nature could enter the public secular space free of domination by the rigid institutional structures of the past. Human persons finally had a space where they could work together to realize justice based on reason alone. Religion was relegated to private life and had no place in a secular public domain.

Obviously, religious institutions such as the Catholic Church did not recognize such a development as a positive one. However, reflections on the dignity of each human person culminating in the documents of Vatican II have lead many theologians to welcome this approach to political life: Liberation theology is an important expression of these developments. Gustavo Gutiérrez,[1] one of liberation theology's leading figures, has welcomed such secularization because, through it, humans are able to free themselves from oppressive forces which have in the past limited human reason and freedom (TL 42). While this secularization involves a break from religion as a human cultural institution, it does not exclude God but rather "necessarily brings in its wake a different way of conceiving our relationship with God" (TL 42). Gutiérrez argues that secularization "coincides perfectly with a Christian vision of human nature, of history, and of the cosmos" because it "favors a more complete fulfillment of the Christian life insofar as it offers human beings the possibility of being more fully human" (TL 42). The autonomy of the natural and human worlds is "a necessary condition for an authentic relationship between humankind and nature, among human beings themselves, and finally, between humankind and God" (TL 42). Thus Gutiérrez has profound sympathy with attempts to promote a free secular political space for public life but, unlike the Enlightenment thinkers, does not see this as essentially incompatible with Christian faith. I will return later to describe how Gutiérrez works out the relationship between a secular political space and the expression of divine agency in the world.

The movement toward secularization has recently been called into question by post-structuralist thinkers through a critique of autonomous human agency. These thinkers reject the idea of a human agent as an independent unified center of activity but rather see human agency as the result of many competing influences—from repressed desires to social forms of power and control. Human agency has become de-centered and fractured: rather than being an agent of one's own destiny, personal identity is constituted by all sorts of external forces. These thinkers tend to reject politics conceived of as a free secular space and see the public sphere as the realm where anonymous forces of power play against each other. Human agency is replaced by the operation of technologies of power and government.

Radical Orthodoxy (RO) is a theological movement that celebrates this deconstruction of human agency—these theologians sense the opportunity to assert the primacy of God's ultimate agency over and against human agency. Once the fallacies of Enlightenment epistemology and the political theory it founds are exposed, once the autonomous human agent is deposed from its throne, then the radical dependence of the world on God will be apparent once again. RO theologian John Milbank[2] explicitly critiques liberation theology as being excessively humanistic and naturalistic—suggesting that liberation theologians have "naturalized the supernatural" (TST 207) with their insistence on the autonomy of human agency. It will be my purpose in this paper to formulate a response to the objections of RO from a liberationist perspective.

At the heart of this debate are different conceptions of the relationship between nature and grace that have developed in Catholic theology over the last century and a half. One approach to this relationship, know as extrinsicism,[3] was embraced by Neo-Scholastic theologians at the end of the nineteenth century. This position held that grace is absolutely extrinsic to nature—there is some state of pure nature which exists separately from God and operates autonomously without interference from God except in special cases. Grace supervenes on nature from the outside rather than being embedded within nature. Human nature is seen as possessing two separate and distinct ends: (1) a pure natural end which is penultimate, less perfect, and to be achieved by human activity and (2) an independent supernatural end which is ultimate, more perfect, and can only be fulfilled by grace, the gift of God. Human nature, while having a certain degree of natural autonomy, is impotent to fulfill its own ultimate end without the help of grace. An important motive for this theory is to protect the gratuitous nature of grace—if humanity has only one supernatural end then it would seem that grace would no longer be a free gift of God, but rather a requirement for the fulfillment of human nature. While this conception of human nature guarantees some autonomy to human agency in the natural and political sphere, it ultimately seems to reduce these domains to secondary perfections which can never bring about the ultimate fulfillment of human nature. Extrinsicism implies that working for political justice is secondary and less perfect because it is purely natural and outside of the realm of grace.

This extrinsic approach to the nature and grace debate was countered in the middle of the twentieth century by the movement know as *nouvelle théologie*[4] which argued that the state of pure nature was an abstraction and a conceptual fiction. These theologians saw nature as always already graced and therefore human nature could only ever have one end: the beautific vision of God given by grace but as a free gift and without any obligation. While the need for grace to achieve one's end seems to impose a limit on human agency, *nouvelle théologie* understands that grace is already written into nature as created by God. Grace and nature are not two fundamentally distinct levels of meaning but rather are reciprocally interdependent and interpenetrating—human and natural autonomy can be affirmed without denying an ultimate dependence on God. It is these debates that lay the ground for what is at issue between liberation theology and RO. Gutiérrez's liberation theology can in many ways be seen as the culmination of the project of *nouvelle théologie* because it unites nature and grace, creation and salvation into an integral whole. Milbank, while not an extrinsicist, maintains a more traditional Augustinian approach which understands the Kingdom of God as fundamentally opposed to the Kingdom of the World. While not a true extrinsicist because he does not believe that nature would have its own proper end independent of grace, the political implications of RO are similar: human activity is absolutely impotent without the aid of grace.

RO is fundamentally opposed to granting the world and human agency any kind of autonomy and claims that human reason without reference to God, what Milbank refers to as "secular reason," cannot be in any way congruent with the Gospel message and the Kingdom of God; an independent secular realm can only be a place of conflict and violence (TST 279). Milbank proposes to get "beyond secular reason" by rejecting the autonomous use of human reason and relying on faith alone to achieve political harmony and peace: faith is the only norm for social relations because one must explicitly accept the Kingdom of God to ensure true social harmony. A theological program that grants the secular sphere any autonomy will have a tendency to reduce the infinite grace of God into a natural setting—"naturalizing the supernatural" (TST 207). It is this naturalizing tendency that Milbank objects to in Gutiérrez (TST 234–237). Daniel Bell,[5] working within this same movement, takes a different approach, but ends with essentially the same critique as Milbank. Bell understands the ultimate fruit of liberal political theory to be the triumph of a capitalist consumer society that is antithetical to the claims of Christianity and the plight of the poor. If liberation theologians accept the premises of enlightenment political theory—for example, the autonomy of the secular political realm—then they will have no theoretical resources able to resist the "savage capitalism" of modern culture (Bell 42). The fundamental project of liberation theology—to find a means of resistance to the capitalist oppression of the poor—is doomed from the start because it accepts as normative the very premises of the Enlightenment project it seeks to resist. The problem, for both Bell and Milbank, is that liberation theology grants an autonomy to the secular realm which, according to them, inevitably leads to nihilism, violence, conflict, and "savage capitalism." Work for justice independent of grace is doomed to end in violence.

Milbank launches his attack against liberation theology by criticizing the way it incorporates the arguments of *nouvelle théologie* and he identifies two distinct currents within this movement. The first derives from French figures like Henri DeLubac, who argues that human nature has a single supernatural end which is a gratuitous gift of God (TST 219–220). Grace perfects and elevates human nature without being extrinsic. Milbank refers to this approach as "supernaturalizing the natural" and intends to argue for some version of this position. The second, and according to Milbank more toxic, tendency is exemplified by Karl Rahner who starts from within human experience and looks for ways in which human experience itself opens out to the infinite (TST 220–223). Because Rahner identifies the supernatural by exposing natural experience to its limits, Milbank calls this "naturalizing the supernatural." It is naturalizing because it starts within human experience and conceives of the supernatural only in terms of what is beyond the limits of such experience; the supernatural has no positive content in itself, as it does for DeLubac, but is reduced to what is merely beyond the limits of natural experience. Rahner's attempt to capture the infinite within the categories of the finite world results in a form of conceptual idolatry. Milbank links Gutiérrez with this movement of *nouvelle théologie* because liberation theologians start with natural human experience of the political world and try to show how this experience can be congruent with the Kingdom of God. For Milbank, the acknowledgement of the legitimate autonomy of the secular exemplifies this naturalizing tendency because it accepts political theories which are the products of finite human reason as in some way expressive of the infinite gift of the Kingdom of God.

According to Milbank's analysis, secular space is never simply a neutral place for rational expression but is founded on an ontology of violence that inevitably leads to conflict, violence and, ultimately, nihilism and is never congruent with the demands of the Gospel. Bell's work takes this critique further: the recognition of neutral secular space for politics reduces politics to statecraft—operations of instrumental reason that anonymously and impersonally regulate power (Bell 9). Such statecraft can only be complicit in the "savage capitalism" that both he and the liberationists hope to resist. Liberation theology fails, according to Bell, because it concedes political operations to statecraft and thus has no resources to resist capitalist oppression.

For RO, human autonomy and divine autonomy are always opposed. In a fundamentally Augustinian gesture, Milbank conceives of the social realm as a conflict between the City of God and the City of the World (TST 380). By granting any autonomy to the secular realm, one cannot but capitulate to the City of the World with its conflict and violence. True political peace and harmony will only be realized by making manifest the Kingdom of God where Christian faith becomes normative for all social relations. Bell further specifies how this might play out by offering a reading of Deleuze and Foucalut whereby both capitalism and Christianity are described as two fundamentally opposed technologies of desire (Bell 30). Christianity is a therapy for the capitalistic technology of desire. Christian faith and not human reason provides the only resources to resist an oppressive capitalist culture.

The beginning of a liberationist response to these objections can be forged by examining the way in which Gutiérrez understands the relationship between nature and grace, human agency and divine agency. These elements are not opposed to each other, but rather they are interwoven in one process of liberation which manifests "three reciprocally interpenetrating levels of meaning" (TL 24). First, "liberation expresses the aspirations of the oppressed peoples and social classes" (TL 24). This is the concrete economic, social and political situation where human persons find themselves oppressed by powerful institutions that favor a minority group at the expense of the masses. Second, liberation means the historical process by which "humankind is seen as assuming conscious responsibility for its own destiny" (TL 24). This represents the ongoing striving for human fulfillment throughout the course of history. The third level is more theological and relies on the "Biblical sources which inspire the presence and action of humankind in history" (TL 24). On the deepest level, liberation provides freedom "from sin, which is the ultimate root of all disruption of friendship and of all injustice and oppression" (TL 25). Ultimately for Gutiérrez "Christ makes humankind truly free, that is to say, he enables us to live in communion with him; and this is the basis for all human fellowship" (TL 25). Gutiérrez understands these three aspects as part of "a single, complex process" where these levels are not isolated, but are interwoven into each other and "interdependent." The process of liberation is a complex interaction of human strivings and the providence of God.

In order to explicate this process of liberation, Gutiérrez must answer this question: if the world is ultimately dependent on God—*theonomous*—then how can human persons assert their autonomy and freedom? As Gutiérrez puts it: "We are faced on the one hand with the affirmation of an ever more autonomous world, not religious, or in more positive terms, a world come of age. On the other hand, we are also faced with this single vocation to salvation which values human history in Christian terms, although in a different way from that of the past" (TL 46). How can human autonomy have meaning within the context of the divine plan for salvation?

Gutiérrez begins to answer this question by providing an account of salvation and creation which does not conceive of them as two distinct acts of God which can be understood in isolation from each other. Creation inaugurates the process of salvation, and salvation is the ultimate fulfillment of what is begun in creation. Salvation penetrates into the life and history of humanity: "Salvation is not something otherworldly. . . . Salvation—the communion of human beings with God and among themselves—is something which embraces all human reality, transforms it, and leads it to its fullness in Christ" (TL 85). However, the unity between creation and salvation is not complete due to the presence of sin as an existential and historical reality. "Sin is not only an impediment to salvation in the afterlife. Insofar as it constitutes a break with God, sin is a historical reality, it is a breach of the communion of persons with each other" (TL 85). The ultimate goal of salvation is not found in some transcendent world beyond but rather in "the transformation and fulfillment of the present life." Gutiérrez concludes: "The absolute value of salvation—far from devaluing this world—gives it its authentic meaning and its own autonomy, because salvation is already latently there" (TL 85). Creation, the natural world, is not complete in itself but rather needs grace, needs salvation to become complete. Human agency is a fundamental part of this process.

If the path between creation and salvation is disrupted by the presence of sin, it is human work that Gutiérrez thinks has the power to overcome sin and bring creation to its fulfillment. "When we assert that humanity fulfills itself by continuing the work of creation by means of its labor, we are saying that it places itself . . . within an all-embracing salvific process. To work, to transform this world, is to become a man and to build the human community; it is also to save" (TL 91). Human work to build a just society and to overcome the broken and sinful relations which bring misery and oppression is already "a part of the saving, which is moving towards . . . complete fulfillment" (TL 91). Autonomous human work in building a just society is caught up in the process of salvation which God has initiated in human history. While Gutiérrez rejects anything that resembles an abstract pure nature, he wants to recognize a legitimate sphere of human autonomy. This secular sphere is not under the direct influence of grace but rather the workings of grace within it are hidden and mediated. Grace does not operate by taking over for nature but rather grace influences nature in hidden ways without disrupting nature. Human work and agency provide a site for the deepest strivings of the human spirit to interact with and participate in the saving work of God by bringing to completion the creative activity of God.

It is human activity, according to Gutiérrez, that mediates between creation and salvation, nature and grace, secular society and the Kingdom of God. But how does this mediation occur? Here Gutiérrez has recourse to a notion of utopia in order to provide a structure that can mediate between the values aimed at by concrete human activity in the social and historical world and the ultimate ideal of the Kingdom of God. Gutiérrez identifies a utopia as a product of the creative political imagination which presents a vision for a radically different ordering of the social order that can be effected by *praxis*, human activity. The construction of a utopia involves both the denunciation of the disvalues of the present social order and the annunciation that things could be otherwise, that positive values could replace negative disvalues. "Utopia is also an annunciation, an annunciation of what is not yet, but will be; it is the forecast of a different order of things, a new society" (TL 136). Gutiérrez understands the construction of a utopia as an eminently rational activity that invokes the creative political imagination. This constitutes the use of reason as emancipative rather than instrumental.

The use of emancipative reason indicates that the secular sphere can be the source of human aspirations and desires that are congruent with the Gospel message. The construction of a utopia embodies these aspirations. "The historical plan, the utopia of liberation as the creation of a new social consciousness . . . is the proper arena of the cultural revolution. That is to say, it is the arena of the permanent creation of a new humanity in a different society characterized by solidarity" (TL 139). While these aspirations can never be equivalent to the Kingdom of God because they are products of the finite human imagination, they can be on the same trajectory as the Kingdom of God. "The Gospel does not provide a utopia for us; this is a human work. The Word is a free gift of the Lord. But the Gospel is not alien to the historical plan; on the contrary, the human plan and the gift of God imply each other" (TL 139). Thus while the Kingdom of God will always exceed any finite construction of a utopia, the deepest aspirations of the human spirit expressed in these desires are in line and congruent with the Kingdom. The construction of a utopia weaves the spiritual and human elements of the process of liberation into an overall unity. Human activity in striving for justice participates in the salvific plan of God without losing its authentic autonomy and independence. On the one hand, the deepest desires of humanity for a just society might concretize in a specific historical plan. But this historical plan is always subject to the "eschatological proviso." It is always revealed as finite and never quite expresses the absolute alterity of what is promised by God. A robust eschatology prevents a utopia from becoming an absolute end, but rather it is a way of mediating between the final end of the Kingdom of God whose positive nature is yet to be revealed and the concrete praxis of historical humans who must act now to realize this just society in some way.

For Gutiérrez there is never an opposition between human and divine agency, but rather while maintaining the value of autonomous human agency, he does not see human autonomy in conflict with ultimate dependence on God. Rather, he understands human autonomy as the fulfillment of God's plan for salvation. Ultimately theonomy, the divine rule of the world, is not in conflict with human autonomy, but reinforces it. Autonomous human activity is lifted from its concrete historical setting and taken up into the Kingdom of God without destroying its autonomy. God folds human agency into God's plan in a seamless fashion without doing violence to it. Human actions are able to take on multiple meanings without becoming completely detached from the human actor. This agency, however, is not completely absolute and self-identical. Human identity is never completely under the power of the subject who possesses this identity. Rather, individual identity is also constituted by a variety of other factors which imbue it with meanings that a particular subject may not intend or even be aware of. Thus, divine agency may interrupt human agency without destroying it. The secular social world may be the locus for the unfolding of the divine plan for liberation and freedom.

One can already see how the critique of liberation theology by Radical Orthodoxy theologians misses the mark. Radial Orthodoxy conceives of human autonomy and divine theonomy as radically incompatible. As a consequence of this, these RO theologians tend to embrace the critiques of human agency offered by many postmodern thinkers. However, liberation theologians, while embracing some portion of the Enlightenment project, do not conceive of the human person as an absolutely autonomous self-identical agent. RO theologians fail to recognize, as liberationists do, that grace can supervene in the secular world of autonomous human agency without destroying human agency. Christian faith does not have to be the norm for all social relations but rather the deepest aspirations of any human heart can reach toward the Kingdom of God.

There are, however, even deeper issues at stake in this debate between Liberation Theology and Radical Orthodoxy. Gutiérrez presents the construction of a utopia as mediating between legitimate human autonomy and total dependency of the world on the grace of God, while Radical Orthodoxy presents the direct realization of the City of God in the social realm as the only Christian response to politics, the only way to overcome the ontology of violence which founds the secular political sphere and replace it with the ontology of harmony that will bring peace. Gutiérrez would argue that this position consigns the whole of creation in its natural state to an ontology of violence with no hope of redemption. Creation and salvation are no longer intimately connected. According to Gutiérrez, the position of Radical Orthodoxy amounts to saying that the world is not worth saving and cannot be transformed in any way; this is a "dangerous politico-religious messianism which does not sufficiently respect either the autonomy of the political arena or that which belongs to an authentic faith, liberated from religious baggage" (TL 138). Gutiérrez thinks that grace is always already present within the world, not just where the City of God is manifest, but anywhere where people strive for justice. Salvation, liberation, grace and peace are not the exclusive property of those explicit citizens of the City of God, but rather are at work in all of creation. The task of the Christian is to discover where these are hidden, uncover them, and make them effective for the transformation of the world.

Milbank finds a naturalizing tendency in liberation theology. He makes a distinction between theological methodologies which "naturalize the supernatural" and those which "supernaturalize the natural," placing liberation theology in the former category. Liberation theology must reject this distinction. These operations—naturalizing and supernaturalizing—are not mutually exclusive interpretations of reality, but are two aspects of one process. An adequate approach to the problem of nature and grace requires both directions of this one process. First, one needs to begin in human experience and understand the limits of that experience where consciousness seems to open up to something beyond this world. This is the philosophical direction. However, this openness of the human spirit to a beyond is met and answered by the God of Revelation who communicates himself precisely at these limits of experience. This is the properly theological direction. A theology that respects the integral relationship between nature and grace, human experience and revelation, will balance both of these directions without inordinately favoring one or the other. This is the project of liberation theology which seeks to mediate between political action, human experience, and the Kingdom of God. It seeks to understand this mediation as a part of the single process of liberation that has multiple aspects interwoven into one process where divine and human elements interact through the mediating factor of a utopia. The methodology of Radical Orthodoxy devalues any examination of human experience in favor of the absolute value of the revelation of God. This approach does violence to the legitimate strivings of human nature that can participate in the process of liberation. For RO, freedom and peace can only come from God and are never to be found in creation.

Finally, liberation theology is able to provide an overarching goal which can guide human *praxis*. Political action for liberation theology is not simply limited to strategies for resistance, but enables an imaginative thinking otherwise that can envision a better society without necessarily fixing the concrete form of this society. Gutiérrez employs the concept of utopia in just this way. A utopia is not simply a vision of an absolutely just society because it is the product of finite human reason. Rather, a utopia is where human reason reaches its limits and is open to the Revelation of a God who can bring about a perfect human society. A utopia, according to Gutiérrez, would specify concrete historical steps which might move in the direction of the ideal society, but would still fall short of this ideal. Only God can bring this society into being. But this does not happen without human praxis. God's plan supervenes upon limited human efforts expressed in a utopia to move humankind closer to its realization.

Gutiérrez would be critical of an RO solution, like that of Bell, which conceives of political activity only in terms of strategies of resistance (Bell 144). Bell seems to think that working toward a just society will only ever buttress the existing power structures rather than transform them for the better. He abandons all concrete activities to build a just society and suggests that forgiveness and continued acceptance of suffering are resistive strategies for those who await the coming of the Kingdom. Political activity can achieve no higher goals on its own, but can only continue to resist and await the Kingdom. Gutiérrez argues that the construction of utopia allows human communities to a catch a vision of a just society that can be achieved and provides concrete historical recommendations for action beyond resistance strategies.

RO theologians might reply that there is no need for a mediating structure like a utopia to intervene between the Church and the world because the Church can witness directly to the presence of God in creation.[6] It is the Church herself that provides the site where the deepest desires of the human heart for justice can be expressed. However, this is problematic because not everyone can have access to this witness or speak the language of the Church. A mediating structure is required to interface with other language games and discourses operative within a pluralistic and global society. A utopia can help the Church translate between its own limited theological discourse and the plurivocal discourses of the public square. Unmediated contact between the Church and the world of culture risks violence.

One might also argue that I have mischaracterized Radical Orthodoxy as denigrating creation by claiming that these theologians think that the world is not worth saving. And it is true that RO posits a certain kind of theological materialism that recognizes the value of creation as created.[7] However, my main worry is that here the material world is again best understood as having no autonomy of its own to be explored through a process of rational discovery and as a site for the common activity of all the human race in solidarity but is always to be understood through its direct relation to God. Liberationist understand the natural and social world as something in need of healing and transformation. Human work is the site where divine providence interacts with human freedom to bring about a better world modeled on the Kingdom.

In conclusion, I believe liberation theology can provide a response to the objection of Radical Orthodoxy. Liberationists will insist that divine and human agency are not incompatible; divine agency can supervene on the secular realm of autonomous human agency through the mediation of a utopia—a historical and rational construction that expresses the deepest strivings of the human spirit toward justice. Creation and salvation are never independent but are intimately related through human work for justice—temporal human labor participates in the divine plan of salvation. It is through such participation that liberationists can escape the complaints that their theories of subjectivity are excessively modern without abandoning the notion of secular politics altogether.

Villanova University

Notes

1. Gustovo Gutiérrez, *A Theology of Liberation* (Maryknoll, N.Y.: Orbis Books, 1988). Abbreviated in the text as TL.

2. See John Milbank, *Theology and Social Theory: Beyond Secular Reason* (Oxford: Basil Blackwell Ltd., 1990). Abbreviated in the text as TST.

3. See James C. Livingston and Francis Schussler Fiorenza, *Modern Christian Thought Volume II: The Twentieth Century* (Upper Saddle River, N.J.: Prentice Hall, 2000), 198–199.

4. See Livingston and Fiorenza, *Modern Christian Thought*, 202–204.

5. See Daniel M. Bell, *Liberation Theology After the End of History: The Refusal to Cease Suffering* (London: Routledge, 2001).

6. Thanks to Joel Garver for his comments which develop the objections in this paragraph and the next one.

7. Especially in more recent works. TST is not as sensitive to this issue.

American Catholic Philosophical Association
Seventy-ninth Annual Meeting

Minutes of the 2005 Executive Council Meeting

University of Notre Dame, Notre Dame, IN
October 28, 2005

The meeting was called to order by ACPA President James Marsh at 10:05 a.m., and commenced with a prayer. Those in attendance were: James Marsh (President), Anthony Lisska (Vice-President/President-Elect), Michael Baur (Secretary), William Jaworski (Treasurer), Gavin Colvert, Jonathan Jacobs, Siobhan Nash-Marshall (3rd-year Executive Council members), Howard Kainz, Gyula Klima, Thomas Michaud, Katherin Rogers (2nd-year Executive Council members), Patrick Byrne, David Foster, Michael Gorman, John P. O'Callaghan, Mary Catherine Sommers (1st-year Executive Council members), John Deely, Timothy Noone (non-voting observers whose Council terms will commence at the conclusion of the 2005 Annual Meeting), and Lance Simmons (*ACPQ* Associate Editor, standing in for *ACPQ* Editor Robert Wood as ex officio, non-voting member of the Executive Council).

As the first item of business, the ACPA Secretary's Report was presented and accepted by the Council. Next, the ACPA Treasurer's Report was presented and accepted by the Council. Third, the *ACPQ* Editor's Report was presented and accepted by the Council.

Next, the Council voted (in accordance with the ACPA's Constitution at III. D.) to elect to ACPA membership all those who had been proposed for membership and who paid membership dues in 2004.

The Council then turned to the issue of awarding the next Aquinas Medal. After some discussion, the Council voted to award the Aquinas Medal in the year 2006 to Sir Anthony Kenny.

Next, the Council turned to the topic of future annual meetings of the Association. Anthony Lisska (Vice-President/President-Elect) reminded Council members that the theme of the 2006 annual meeting will be "Intelligence and the Philosophy of Mind," and that the meeting will take place October 27–29, 2006 in Granville, Ohio (hosted by Denison University in Granville). Professor Lisska also announced that the Program Committee for the 2006 annual meeting will include: Joan Franks, Michael Gorman, Douglas Rasmussen, and James South. Timothy Noone (Vice-President-Elect) then proposed the following theme for the 2007 annual meeting: "Freedom, Will, and Nature." The Council then voted to approve this theme as proposed.

Next, the Council elected the following two members of the Executive Council to membership in the Executive Committee (for terms commencing at the end of the 2005 Annual Meeting): Gyula Klima and Katherin Rogers.

Finally, the Council took up the matter of replacing one of its own members, Terry Tekippe, who sadly passed away since the time of the last ACPA annual meeting. Following past practice, the Council voted to appoint Bernardo Cantens to fill out the remainder of Terry Tekippe's Executive Council term (which ends at the conclusion of the 2006 annual meeting), since Bernardo Cantens was the next-highest vote-getter in the 2003-04 ACPA election (the election in which Terry Tekippe was elected to the Council).

The meeting was adjourned at approximately 12:15 p.m.

Respectfully submitted,

Michael Baur, ACPA Secretary

American Catholic Philosophical Association

Secretary's Report (2004)

I. NEWS FROM THE NATIONAL OFFICE

A. The ACPA's New World Wide Web Page (www.acpaweb.org)

The migration of content from the ACPA's old web-page (www.acpa-main.org) to its new web-page (www.acpaweb.org) is complete, and the old site now points directly to the new site. In the coming months, the old site will be entirely phased out. Members are encouraged to make note of the new web-address, and to visit the new site for announcements and updates.

B. Electronic Conversion of Back Issues of the ACPA's Publications

Dr. George Leaman, Director of the Philosophy Documentation Center (PDC), has recently written to report on the PDC's conversion of back issues of the *American Catholic Philosophical Quarterly* and the *Proceedings of the ACPA* to electronic format. Dr. Leaman writes:

"I'm pleased to report that we've made excellent progress this year and I hope the membership can help us locate the remaining print copies of *The New Scholasticism* and the *Proceedings* that we need to complete the conversion work.

ACPQ/ The New Scholasticism: This year we completed work on all issues from 1975 (vol. 49) to the present. All of these issues except one (77:4) have been integrated into *POIESIS: Philosophy Online Serials* and are now available. Work on issue 77:4 is complete and it will be added by the end of the year. Tables of contents to these issues are freely available and every word in the entire content of the collection is searchable. We now need print copies of *The New Scholasticism* volumes 1-48 (1927–1974) to proceed further and I'm hopeful that one of the ACPA's individual or institutional members would be willing to donate these volumes to us for the conversion work.

ACPA Proceedings: We've now completed work on thirty-three of these volumes and another twenty-two volumes are currently in production. Tables of contents to these thirty-three volumes are freely available and every word in the entire content of the collection is searchable in *POIESIS: Philosophy Online Serials*. We expect to complete work on twenty-two volumes within the next six months and they will be added as soon as possible. We have yet to locate print copies of volumes 1–15, 21–24, 26, 30, and 37 and as with *ACPQ* we're hopeful that one of the ACPA's individual or institutional members would be willing to donate these volumes to us for this work."

Members who have any of the needed issues—and who would be willing to part with them—are encouraged to contact George Leaman at the Philosophy Documentation Center by phone (434-220-3300 or 800-444-2419) or by e-mail (leaman@pdcnet.org).

C. Future Annual Meetings of the ACPA

The ACPA continues to encourage inquiries and offers from individuals who think that their institutions may be willing and able to sponsor a future Annual Meeting of the ACPA. As previously announced, the Executive Committee of the ACPA, in response to a very generous offer from Denison University, determined that the Association's 2006 Annual Meeting will take place in Granville, Ohio (October 27–29, 2006), and will be hosted by Denison University.

D. Details Regarding the 2006 Annual Meeting in Granville, Ohio

President-Elect Anthony Lisska announced (and the Executive Committee of the Association approved) the following theme for the Association's upcoming Annual Meeting, to be held October 27–29, 2006, in Granville, OH: "Intelligence and the Philosophy of Mind." An announcement of this theme, along with the submission guidelines, was mailed to all members in the May 2005 mailing. The call for papers for the 2006 Annual Meeting is also posted on the ACPA's web-site. The invited plenary speakers for the 2006 Annual Meeting are:

John Haldane (University of St. Andrews)
Anthony Kenny (Oxford University)
Kurt Pritzl (The Catholic University of America)

D. Deceased Members

ACPA members reported as deceased since the 2004 Annual Meeting include the following:

Marc F Griesbach
Dominick Iorio
Terry Tekippe
John Yardan

II. ACPA MEMBERSHIP

In 2004, the ACPA roster included 1208 *active* members. The number of *total* members from 1996 to 1998, and *active* members in 1999 through 2004 (all segregated according to membership category) is as follows:

Membership Category	2004	2003	2002	2001	2000	1999	1998	1997
Professor	209	198	185	198	198	209	213	208
Associate Professor	131	137	124	153	160	161	172	168
Assistant Professor	142	147	125	152	142	143	165	162
Instructor	73	68	53	64	63	50	37	32
Lecturer	39	41	37	43	41	44	35	35
Student	181	152	132	173	154	158	162	134
Emeritus/Emerita	132	129	122	139	134	133	122	120
Associate	97	91	80	100	99	102	147	141
Institutional	21	13	11	14	13	14	17	17
Library	66	60	58	63	62	60	55	55
Life	83	88	86	96	90	93	96	97
Exchanges	34	35	36	35	35			
Totals	1208	1159	1049	1230	1191	1167	1221	1169

Please note that the membership figures for 1998 and earlier represent the "unpurged" *total* number of members in the ACPA database. The membership figures for 1999 and later represent only those members listed as *active* in the ACPA database; starting in 1999 the Philosophy Documentation Center (the ACPA's database manager) instituted the practice of purging non-active members from the ACPA database, in order to present a more accurate picture of the ACPA's actual membership. Please note also that the total membership figures for 1999 and earlier include "Exchange" memberships, but not as a separate category. "Exchange" memberships have been listed as a separate category only since 2000.

III. ACPA PUBLICATIONS

A. ACPQ

In 2004, four issues of the *American Catholic Philosophical Quarterly* (volume 78) were published. The journal is edited by Dr. Robert E. Wood, assisted by Drs. Philipp Rosemann and Lance Simmons.

The 1996–1998 distribution of the *ACPQ* to *all* ACPA members, etc., and the 1999–2004 distribution to *active* members, etc., are as follows:

Distribution Type	2004	2003	2002	2001	2000	1999	1998	1997	1996
ACPA Members	1174	1124	1013	1195	1156	934	1221	1169	1117
Subscribers	469	516	501	508	493	517	484	504	503
Exchanges	34	35	36	35	35	38	37	33	34
Totals	1677	1675	1550	1738	1684	1489	1742	1706	1654

B. Proceedings

Dr. Michael Baur edited volume 78 of the *Proceedings of the ACPA*, entitled *Reckoning with the Tradition*, which will appear in November of 2005.

The 1996–1998 distribution of the *Proceedings* to *all* ACPA members, etc., and the 1999–2004 distribution to *active* members, etc. are as follows:

Distribution Type	2004	2003	2002	2001	2000	1999	1998	1997	1996
ACPA Members	1174	1124	1013	1195	1156	934	1221	1169	1117
Subscribers	129	132	147	143	150	132	92	107	95
Exchanges	47	66	75	39	35	38	37	33	34
Totals	1350	1322	1235	1377	1341	1104	1350	1309	1246

C. Acknowledgments

On behalf of the ACPA, the Secretary would like to thank Dr. Robert E. Wood, Dr. Lance Simmons, and Dr. Philipp Rosemann, all at the University of Dallas, for their work in producing the *American Catholic Philosophical Quarterly*. The Secretary would also like to thank the University of Dallas for its ongoing institutional support of the *American Catholic Philosophical Quarterly*.

IV. ACPA ANNUAL MEETINGS

A. Seventy-eighth Annual Meeting (2004)

The Seventy-eighth Annual Meeting of the ACPA was held November 5-7, 2004, at the Wyndham Miami Beach Resort, in Miami, FL. The conference theme, selected by ACPA President Nicholas Rescher, was: "Reckoning with the Tradition." The Program Committee included: Drs. David H. Carey, James Madden, and Katherin Rogers. Papers read at the meeting and reports of the official business of the Association will be published in volume 78 of the *Proceedings of the ACPA*, edited by Michael Baur. The winner of the 2004 Young Scholar's Award was Max J. Latona of Saint Anselm College, for his paper, "New Technologies, Old Distinctions: What's Wrong with Cloning." Barry University in Miami provided financial support to help cover the costs of coffee breaks, refreshments, receptions, and travel for invited plenary speakers. On behalf of the Association, the Secretary would like to thank Barry University as well as the Local Organizing Committee (chaired by Bernardo Cantens of Barry University).

B. Seventy-ninth Annual Meeting (2005)

The Seventy-ninth Annual Meeting of the ACPA will be held October 28–30, 2005, at the University of Notre Dame, in South Bend, IN. The conference theme, selected by ACPA President James Marsh, will be: "Social Justice: Its Theory and Practice." The winner of the 2005 Young Scholar's Award is Bernard G. Prusak, of Villanova University, for his paper, "The Ancients, the Moderns, and the Court."

On behalf of the Association, the Secretary would like to thank the 2005 Program Committee: Drs. Thomas Jeannot, David Kaplan, and Anne Pomeroy. The Secretary would also like to thank the Local Organizing Committee, chaired by Paul Weithman of the University of Notre Dame. Finally, the Secretary would like to thank the host institution, the University of Notre Dame, for its very generous financial and organizational support.

V. ACPA ELECTIONS

The results of the most recent ACPA election (concluded on April 1, 2005) are as follows:

Vice-President/President-Elect:
　　Timothy B. Noone (The Catholic University of America)
New Executive Council Members:
　　John Deely (University of St. Thomas, Houston, TX)
　　Marie I. George (St. John's University)
　　Patrick Lee (Franciscan University of Steubenville)
　　Kurt Pritzl (The Catholic University of America)
　　Alice Ramos (St. John's University)

On behalf of the Association, the Secretary would like to congratulate these newly-elected individuals, and to thank all who were willing to stand for election. Without the participation and enthusiasm of such people, the Association could not continue to thrive.

VI. THANKS AND ACKNOWLEDGMENTS

On behalf of the ACPA, the Secretary would first like to thank Eleanor Helms for her excellent work as the Fordham-sponsored graduate student assistant to the ACPA during the 2004–2005 and 2005–2006 academic years. Secondly, the Secretary would like to thank the newly appointed ACPA Treasurer, Bill Jaworski, for his hard work, boundless energy, warm encouragement, and unconditional willingness to help out with various tasks at the National Office. Thirdly, the Secretary would like to thank Fordham University for its very generous financial and institutional support, without which the Association would not be in the healthy condition that it is today. Finally and most importantly, the Secretary would like to thank his dear wife, Dr. Christine Baur, for everything that she has done and continues to do for her husband and for the Association.

Respectfully submitted,

Michael Baur, ACPA Secretary

American Catholic Philopsophical Association

Treasurer's Report (2004)

I. Financial Statement

The Financial Statement shows that 2004 was a very positive year for the ACPA. In 2004, the ACPA's total excess of revenues over expenses was $30,896 (as compared to $4,954 in 2003). The Financial Statement shows that at the end of 2004, the Association's total liabilities and net assets were $269,395 (as compared to $285,400 in 2003). Of this $269,395, $267,584 represents net (unrestricted) assets (as compared to $236,688 in unrestricted assets in 2003). Thus the ACPA's net assets grew by $30,896 in 2004.

II. Annual Revenues and Expenses

Between 2003 and 2004, total annual revenues increased by $15,842 (total revenues in 2004 were $78,166, while they were $62,324 in 2003), and total annual expenses decreased by $10,100 (total expenses in 2004 were $47,270, while they were $57,370 in 2003). The increase in gross revenues and decrease in gross expenses are attributable to the fact that the year 2004 was the first year during which the publication agreement between the ACPA and the PDC (authorized by the ACPA Executive Council in 2001) was in effect for a full year (the agreement took effect in May of 2003). According to this agreement, the PDC incurs all expenses and retains all revenues for producing the ACPA's publications, and—in turn—makes regular royalty payments to the ACPA. Under the publication agreement, the PDC becomes the ACPA's publisher and assumes the responsibilities and costs for producing the ACPA's publications; as a result, the direct expenses to the ACPA began to decrease, and its revenues began to increase, as of May 2003.

III. Annual Meeting

A summary of revenues and expenses in connection with the 2004 Annual Meeting is attached.

The Association is very grateful to the local host institution—Barry University in Miami—for its very generous financial support (totaling $11,572) in connection with the meeting. On behalf of the Association, the Treasurer would also like to thank the host institution of the National Office—Fordham University—for contributing $4,938 towards this meeting.

The attached financial statements show that the 2004 Annual Meeting resulted in an $8,020 excess of revenues over expenses.

IV. Assets and Investments—Total: $269,395

The Statement of Financial Position lists our assets on December 31, 2004, as follows:

A. Cash and Cash Equivalents: $109,620

On December 31, 2004, the Association held $109,620 in a Chase Manhattan checking and savings account.

B. Inventory and Supplies: $912

C. Non-cash Investments: $140,733

On December 31, 2004, the Association's non-cash investment holdings with Portfolio Strategies, Inc., were valued at $140,733.

D. Accounts Receivable: $18,130

On December 31, 2004, the Association's assets included $5,553 in accounts receivable from the PDC, and $12,577 in accounts receivable from other sources.

V. Liabilities—Total: $1,811

Account Payable: $1,811

The amount of $1,811 represents expenses incurred by the ACPA in 2004 (e.g., service fees attributable to work performed in 2004, etc.), but not yet paid-for until after December 31, 2004, i.e., after the closing date for 2004 statements from the ACPA's bank and investment manager. Accordingly, the ACPA carries these 'not-yet-paid-for' expenses as a liability.

VI. Reminder

The Association depends heavily for revenue on membership dues and subscription payments. Therefore, the National Office reminds members to be prompt in paying their dues and/or subscription charges.

VII. Donations

As always, the Association welcomes donations. Since the ACPA is a tax-exempt organization under section 501(c)(3) of the Internal Revenue Code, all donations to Association are tax-deductible to the full extent allowed by law.

VIII. Acknowledgements

On the behalf of the Association, the Treasurer would like to thank Fordham University for its generous financial support of the Association. In 2004, the Association received over $26,019 in cash donations from Fordham University. In addition to this direct financial support, Fordham also continues to provide a substantial amount of non-cash, or "in-kind," institutional support, including office space, tuition remission for the graduate student assistant, and a course reduction for the Fordham faculty member in the office of Secretary. The Association is deeply grateful to Fordham for this generous financial and institutional support. Finally, the Treasurer would like to thank the Association's Secretary, Dr. Michael Baur, for his hard work, sage advice, and ongoing dedication to the Association.

Respectfully submitted,

William Jaworski, ACPA Treasurer

American Catholic Philosophical Association
Financial Statements

Years Ended December 31, 2004 and 2003

American Catholic Philosophical Association
Accountants' Compilation Report

Years Ended December 31, 2004 and 2003

TABLE OF CONTENTS

American Catholic Philosophical Association
Accountants' Compilation Report

Years Ended December 31, 2004 and 2003

To the Executive Council
American Catholic Philosophical Association
Bronx, New York

We have compiled the accompanying statements of financial position of American Catholic Philosophical Association (the Association) as of December 31, 2004 and 2003, and the related statements of activities and changes in net assets and cash flows for the years then ended and the accompanying supplementary information contained in Schedule I, in accordance with Statements on Standards for Accounting and Review Services issued by the American Institute of Certified Public Accountants.

A compilation is limited to presenting in the form of financial statements information that is the representation of management. We have not audited or reviewed the accompanying financial statements and, accordingly, do not express an opinion or any other form of assurance on them.

Management has elected to omit substantially all of the disclosures required by accounting principles generally accepted in the United States of America. If the omitted disclosures were included in the financial statements, they might influence the user's conclusions about the Association's financial position, results of operations, and cash flows. Accordingly, these financial statements are not designed for those who are not informed about such matters.

Hutchinson and Bloodgood LLP

Glendale, California
October 25, 2005

American Catholic Philosophical Association
Statements of Financial Position

Years Ended December 31, 2004 and 2003

ASSETS	2004	2003
Current assets		
Cash-checking and savings	$ 109,620	$ 112,984
Accounts receivable—Fordham	—	8,142
Accounts receivable—PDC Royalty	5,553	13,760
Accounts receivable—Others	12,577	11,828
Inventory and supplies	912	950
Investments, at market value	140,733	137,736
Total assets	$ 269,395	$ 285,400
LIABILITIES AND NET ASSETS		
Current liabilities		
Accounts payable and accrued expenses	$ 1,811	$ 2,825
Deferred income—dues and subscriptions	—	45,887
Total liabilities	1,811	48,712
Unrestricted net assets	267,584	236,688
Total liabilities and net assets	$ 269,395	$ 285,400

American Catholic Philosophical Association
Statements of Activities and Changes in Net Assets

Years Ended December 31, 2004 and 2003

SUPPORT AND REVENUES	2004	2003
Annual meeting	29,087	22,706
Subscriptions	—	28,469
Royalties	24,652	13,760
Donations from Fordham University	26,019	15,613
Miscellaneous income	1,107	106
Interest and dividends	1,092	4,339
Net realized and unrealized loss in investments	(3,791)	(22,669)
Total support and revenues	78,166	62,324
EXPENSES		
Salaries and wages	15,492	5,526
Annual meeting	21,067	21,352
Publications	—	20,018
Postage	589	1,384
Telephone/communication	303	289
Office supplies and expenses	1,852	66
Insurance	818	765
Investment expenses	3,682	4,088
Accounting services	2,900	2,700
Bank service charges	158	119
Web service charges	363	1,063
Duplicating expenses	46	—
Total expenses	47,270	57,370
Increase in unrestricted net assets	30,896	4,954
NET ASSETS, BEGINNING OF YEAR	**236,688**	231,734
NET ASSETS, END OF YEAR	**$ 267,584**	**$ 236,688**

American Catholic Philosophical Association
Statements of Cash Flow

Years Ended December 31, 2004 and 2003

CASH FLOWS FROM OPERATING ACTIVITIES	2004	2003
Increase in unrestricted net assets	$ 30,896	$ 4,954
Adjustments to reconcile increase in unrestricted net assets to net cash provided by (used in) operating activities		
Net realized and unrealized losses in investments	3,791	22,693
Net change in:		
Accounts receivable	15,600	(23,374)
Inventory and supplies	38	37
Accounts payable and accrued expenses	(1,014)	(16,817)
Deferred income	(45,887)	8,088
Net cash provided by (used in) operating activities	3,424	(4,419)
CASH FLOWS FROM INVESTING ACTIVITIES		
Net change in investments and money market accounts	(6,788)	14,436
Net cash provided by investing activities	(6,788)	14,436
Net increase in cash and cash equivalents	(3,364)	10,017
CASH AND CASH EQUIVALENTS AT BEGINNING OF YEAR	112,984	102,967
CASH AND CASH EQUIVALENTS AT END OF YEAR	$ 109,620	$ 112,984

American Catholic Philosophical Association
Schedule I: Revenues and Expenses of Annual Meeting

Years Ended December 31, 2004 and 2003

REVENUES	2004	2003
Registration and banquet	$ 10,455	$ 9,416
Book exchange, exhibits and advertising	2,122	2,411
Donations:		
Local institutions	11,572	6,800
Fordham University	4,938	4,079
	29,087	22,706
EXPENSES		
Program, travel and other	589	4,326
Banquet expenses	11,572	11,112
Invited speakers costs	3,638	2,775
Young scholar's award	250	250
Aquinas medal and engraving	80	87
Meeting registration services	2,866	2,802
Duplicating expenses	964	—
Postage expenses	1,108	—
	21,067	21,352
Excess of revenues over expenses	$ 8,020	$ 1,354

Available Back Issues of the Proceedings

Volumes

No.	Year	
29	1955	*Knowledge and Expression*
33	1959	*Contemporary American Philosophy*
35	1961	*Philosophy and Psychiatry*
36	1962	*Justice*
38	1964	*History and Philosophy of Science*
39	1965	*Philosophy of the Arts*
41	1967	*The Nature of Philosophical Inquiry*
44	1970	*Philosophy and Christian Theology*
45	1971	*Myth and Philosophy*
46	1972	*The Existence of God*
48	1974	*Thomas and Bonaventure*
50	1976	*Freedom*
51	1977	*Ethical Wisdom East and/or West*
52	1978	*Immateriality*
53	1979	*The Human Person*
55	1981	*Infinity*
56	1982	*The Role and Responsibility of the Moral Philosopher*
57	1983	*The ACPA in Today's Intellectual World*
58	1984	*Practical Reasoning*
61	1987	*The Metaphysics of Substance*
63	1989	*The Ethics of Having Children*
64	1990	*Ways to World Meaning*
65	1991	*Religions and the Virtue of Religion*
66	1992	*Relations: From Having to Being*
67	1993	*The Importance of Truth*
68	1994	*Reason in History*
69	1995	*The Recovery of Form*
70	1996	*Philosophy of Technology*
71	1997	*Virtues and Virtue Theories*

72	1998	*Texts and Their Interpretation*
73	1999	*Insight and Inference*
74	2000	*Philosophical Theology*
75	2001	*Person, Soul, and Immortality*
76	2002	*Philosophy at the Boundary of Reason*
77	2003	*Philosophy and Intercultural Understanding*
78	2004	*Reckoning with the Tradition*
79	2005	*Social Justice: Its Theory and Practice*

Please send orders to:
Philosophy Documentation Center
P.O. Box 7147
Charlottesville, VA 22906-7147
800-444-2419 (U.S. & Canada), or 434-220-3300
Fax: 434-220-3301
E-mail: order@pdcnet.org
Web: www.pdcnet.org

All back issues of the *Proceedings* are $30 each, plus shipping (see rates below). Make checks payable to the Philosophy Documentation Center. Please send checks in U.S. dollars only. Visa, MasterCard, and Discover are accepted for your convenience.

Shipping and handling charges for book orders are as follows:

Total Price	Delivery within U.S.	Delivery outside U.S.
$ .01–$ 50.00	$ 5.00	$ 8.00
$ 50.01–$ 100.00	$ 7.50	$ 12.00
$ 100.01–$ 200.00	$ 10.00	$ 16.00
$ 200.01–$ 300.00	$ 13.00	$ 19.00
$ 301.00–$ 400.00	$ 16.00	$ 22.00
$ 400.01–$ 500.00	$ 19.00	$ 25.00
$ 500.01–$ 1000.00	$ 22.00	$ 28.00
Over $ 1000.00	$ 25.00	$ 31.00

For international airmail rates, please contact the PDC.